Christmas, 1993 From Mum + Dad

To

RARE AMBITION

Michael Harris is an award-winning author, journalist and film-maker whose work has been recognized in both Canada and the United States. Harris's last work, *Unholy Orders*, was a national bestseller and his film version of the book captured a silver medal at the 1991 New York Festival. His first book, *Justice Denied*, has become a non-fiction classic and a motion picture. Harris appears regularly on CTV's *Sunday Edition*, and is co-host of the PBS series *Literatti* in New York. The author now lives in Lunenburg, Nova Scotia, with his wife Lynda and daughters Peyton and Emily. He is currently at work on a new book.

RARE AMBITION

The Crosbies of Newfoundland

MICHAEL HARRIS

Penguin Books

PENGUIN BOOKS
Published by the Penguin Group
Penguin Books Canada Ltd, 10 Alcorn Avenue, Toronto, Ontario, Canada M4V 3B2
Penguin Books Ltd, 27 Wrights Lane, London W8 5TZ, England
Penguin Books USA Inc., 375 Hudson Street, New York, New York 10014, U.S.A.
Penguin Books Australia Ltd, Ringwood, Victoria, Australia
Penguin Books (NZ) Ltd, 182-190 Wairau Road, Auckland 10, New Zealand

Penguin Books Ltd, Registered Offices:
Harmondsworth, Middlesex, England

First published in Viking by Penguin Books Canada Limited, 1992

Published in Penguin Books, 1993

10 9 8 7 6 5 4 3 2 1

Manufactured in Canada

Canadian Cataloguing in Publication Data

Harris, Michael, 1948–
Rare ambition: the Crosbies of Newfoundland

ISBN 0-14-023184-6

1. Crosbie family. 2. Crosbie, John, 1931–
3. Newfoundland – Politics and government.
4. Newfoundland – Biography. I. Title.

FC2176.1.A1H37 1989 971.8'009'92 C88-093024 – 1
F1121.8.H37 1989

This book is for Emily and Peyton,
children of Newfoundland,
children of my heart.

Front Cover: Photo Circa 1928

(left to right)

Top Row: Percy Manuel Crosbie (1913-1975)
John Chalker Crosbie (1908-1960)
Chesley Arthur Crosbie (1905-1962)

Second Row: Margaret Crosbie (1910-)
Olga Rogers (Crosbie) Ayre (1916-)
Lady Edith (Crosbie) Panckridge (1911-1983)
George Graham Crosbie (1907-1984)

Third Row: Ella Maud (Crosbie) Carleton (1904-)
Vera Elizabeth (Crosbie) Perlin (1902-1974)
Nina Louise (Crosbie) Bennett (1901-1980)

Seated: Alexander Harris Crosbie (1919-1981)
Sir John Chalker Crosbie (1876-1932)
June Louis Bennett (1924-1991)
Lady Mitchie Anne Crosbie (1876-1953)

Acknowledgments

The author is indebted to all of the many people who assisted in the preparation of this book, but the following individuals were especially helpful: John Crosbie gave generously of his time and also permitted access to his private papers lodged at the Centre for Newfoundland Studies Archives in St. John's. Andrew Crosbie, since deceased, spent hundreds of hours with the author and shared intimate recollections and family records that allowed much of the Crosbie saga to be told for the first time. John Jenkins Sr. and Gene Shinkle, as well as their children, spoke candidly about painful personal matters that made it possible to tell the tragic story of Andrew and John's sister, Joan Crosbie. John Crosbie Perlin and Edward Roberts were good enough to read portions of the manuscript and save a grateful author from a variety of stumbles, large and small. In addition, Mr. Perlin kindly made available his private collection of Sir John Crosbie's letters, as well as the family portrait that serves as the cover for *Rare Ambition.* Basil Dobbin shared his knowledge of the modern Crosbie era in Newfoundland and showed many kindnesses to the author over the years this book was researched and written. The author's deep appreciation goes out to Gwen and Bill Smith who have been unstinting supporters of his career over many years, never so generously as in the last few. As for the brilliant Lynda Harris, where words miss, they shouldn't be aimed, except to say that without her superb research skills and editorial insights there would be no history of the Crosbies.

The author would also like to acknowledge the staffs of both the Centre for Newfoundland Studies Library and Archives for their tireless assistance, in particular, archivist Bert Riggs. The staff at the Provincial Archives of Newfoundland and Labrador, including Helen Miller, was equally invaluable. The author is also grateful to the many people at Penguin Books — and some who have since moved on — who patiently and professionally saw this project through: editor-in-chief Cynthia Good, editors Meg Masters and Catherine Marjoribanks, and former Penguin executives Morty Mint and Iris Skeoch. The author is particularly indebted to three fine works that were constantly useful during the writing of *Rare Ambition* — S. J. R. Noel's *Politics in Newfoundland*; Richard Gwyn's *Smallwood: The Unlikely Revolutionary*; and Paul O'Neill's *The Oldest City: The Story of St. John's, Newfoundland.* Finally, a word of thanks to Paul Stevens, the professor who taught the author that the heartbeat of history is as real as the one that beats in all our breasts; the past, properly understood, is always contemporary.

Author's Note

WRITING IS A winding road full of surprises and so it was with *Rare Ambition*. The year was 1985, and I had just finished writing *Justice Denied*, a book that told the story of Donald Marshall, a young Micmac Indian who served eleven years in prison for a murder he didn't commit. The book was favourably noticed by David Kilgour of Penguin Books, who called my then-agent, Nancy Colbert, with a proposal for a new project. The three of us met in the bar of the Royal York Hotel in Toronto and, over cold beer and peanuts, discussed what he had in mind.

Kilgour was interested in an unauthorized biography of John Crosbie, the political dynamo from Newfoundland who had become a national figure during his career in federal politics, which included a serious run at the Conservative leadership in 1983. For a man who had played a central role in the events of the country since his arrival in Ottawa in 1976, precious little was known about John Carnell Crosbie, beyond his reputation as the best stand-up comic in Canadian politics, who, unfortunately, had literally brought down the House in his one serious moment in 1979 when he presented the Clark government's first and only federal "bodjit."

There were several reasons to bc interested in the project and a few to shun it. I had roots in Newfoundland, where my mother was born and where I had worked for extended periods of time. Coincidentally, I had been considering a return to St. John's to become publisher and editor-in-chief of *The Sunday Express*, a weekly newspaper being launched by Newfoundland businessman Harry Steele. And although I had never got to know John Crosbie, our paths had crossed professionally from time to time, sometimes in quite bizarre ways.

Just before the 1980 federal election, I was asked by the late Grit godfather, Don Jamieson, to run against Crosbie in St. John's West, which, next to the family jewels, was Crosbie's safest possession. A television journalist at the time, I had the same interest in politicians that a student of the racetrack has in horses; I enjoyed watching them run, but I didn't want to be a horse. Shortly after I declined Jamieson's offer, a front-page story appeared in the local newspaper naming me as a possible candidate in St. John's West. No doubt that information was noted and the appropriate conclusions reached by John Crosbie.

Our next encounter came in Ottawa, where I was then working as a parliamentary correspondent for *The Globe and Mail*. In 1985 I published a story about how Justice Minister Crosbie had quietly named his lawyer sons legal agents of the federal government — an appointment somewhere between a raisin and a plum, depending on the amount of government work the young men actually performed. With the mammoth Hibernia offshore oil development and all its related legal work just over the horizon, the betting was that the conflict of interest could turn out to be considerable. That is certainly how the political opposition saw it. After acrimonious attacks on the Justice minister in the House of Commons, the firms employing Ches and Michael Crosbie were forced to hand back their federal appointments.

Timing, as the saying goes, is all. My very next assignment was to cover John Crosbie at a Planning and Priorities meeting of cabinet at Harrington Lake. Although he dutifully answered my questions, he never once took his eyes off the horizon. Somehow the prospect of interviewing this man for a book at his rural home in Newfoundland as he gazed out over Hogan's Pond, imagining me at the bottom, was not my idea of how to spend the next few years.

But I had a much more serious reservation about taking on a book about John Crosbie. I had come to the conclusion that the world of Canadian letters featured all too many instant books about the country's public affairs and politicians, and I didn't really want to add to the cultural clutter. So I made a counter proposal: what about a history of the entire Crosbie family, a project that would not only tell readers where John Crosbie had come from, but make a permanent contribution to the history of the country as well? Kilgour agreed; if he understood, as he probably did, the naïvety of what I had so blithely suggested, he was too kind to tell me at the time.

Six years later, any intellectual pretensions I might have had were more than humbled. The job of following the Crosbie family through the mists of time was daunting. There would be a visit to the family seat in Dumfries, Scotland, and the dust of half a dozen archives would be disturbed to trace their ghostly footsteps through the ages, all the way back to a shadowy connection to the Norwegian royal court.

Life with the living was no less difficult. Relatives and friends were very reluctant to say much about the members — some living, others deceased — of a very powerful Canadian family, particularly when the person doing the writing was seen as an investigative gunslinger out to put another notch on his pistol. Although he would prove most helpful, John Crosbie himself complained early in the project, "It's not enough to assassinate me; now you've come back for the whole goddamn family!"

My goal was neither assassination nor glorification, but faithfulness to the facts. I quickly learned that even a popular historian presides over a tyranny of choice, selecting some events, ignoring others, developing this character and affording that one the briefest of mentions. But I always worked towards a composite that would transform the stark pronouncements of the record into the story of a father's smile or a mother's tears, a son's resolve or a daughter's dreams. If what follows is history of a sort, then I have tried to give it a human face.

Before this book was finished, another, *Unholy Orders*, intervened. It tells the story of homeless children at the

Mount Cashel Orphanage who were savagely abused by the religious order that was supposed to be taking care of them. If that sad chronicle showed what can happen to people without families, the saga of the Crosbies is testament to what can be accomplished when the family is strong. Theirs is a marvellous story of coming up from nothing, an immigrant's triumph of sweat and dreams. In a way, it is the quintessential Canadian success story, where those arch masqueraders, fame and fortune, obscure the tragedies and heartbreak that all families have in common. Finally, it is a way of understanding that strange and wonderful place, Newfoundland, that has knocked down and nurtured them through five generations, a river of life that flows on and on.

Michael Harris
Lunenburg, Nova Scotia
June 1992

CONTENTS

CHAPTER 1

Funeral Rites

"LITTLE BIG MAN" was buried on a day that would make you believe that God was a Liberal from Bonavista. The sun rose brilliantly out of a calm sea, and for once in the city of gales, the columns of wood-smoke from the frame houses in the old quarter of St. John's climbed poker-straight into the chill, blue sky.

From the Basilica of St. John the Baptist, where the last phase of Joey Smallwood's secular apotheosis would soon be taking place, the steel-blue Atlantic widened peacefully towards Ireland. A radiant, white mist hung over the mouth of the Narrows, and the motionless ships in St. John's Harbour, their flags lowered to half-mast, seemed to have been painted there overnight by some industrious giant. But it was cold, as cold as Death, who was, after all, the social convener of the morning's activities on this, the twenty-first day of December 1991.

Inside the Basilica was a scene as incongruous as the thought that Joey Smallwood was gone. Two rows of enormous television lights, pitiless and unblinking, hung beneath the dazzling stained-glass windows that ringed the congregation and main altar. High on the frescoed walls above the congregation, Matthew, Mark, Luke and John bent their saintly gaze to the raised wooden platforms built for the cameras of the CBC. It was as if the holy images were offering forgiveness to the headphoned technicians who were dollying their cameras to and fro across the rough planks, oblivious to sanctities any deeper than those of a well-framed shot. Other than the occasional grave nod to someone in the congregation, they worked with the jaunty detachment of a crew covering the Santa Claus Parade, except now the sleigh was empty.

By 10:00 a.m., the intrusion of the lights and cameras began to be overshadowed by the sheer size of the congregation, a crowd that was now a thousand strong, all of them waiting for Joey. It was no longer the shrivelled and pathetic stroke victim who had lost his golden gift of speech seven years ago that they awaited, nor the strutting megalomaniac who was finally undone by the absolute power that he had wielded for so long. In the subtle transformations that had begun four days earlier with the news that Joey had died peacefully in his sleep a week before his ninety-first birthday, there was no thought now of his hated policy of resettlement, the disastrous Upper Churchill hydro deal, the industrial fiascos of Come by Chance and Stephenville, the politics of intimidation and the cult of personality run amok. Death had been working quickly to touch up the official portrait, just as the earthly morticians had laboured over the ninety-pound corpse so that it could lie respectably on public view in the House of Assembly until this day had come and gone.

It was now the transubstantiated Joey, Joey the folk hero, that stirred their imaginations and adorned their hastily printed programs. It was the pig farmer from Gambo who had aspired to nation-building and heroically found the mark, the spellbinding conversationalist who could silence a Rothschild around the dinner table with an anecdote that ran longer than the main course, Newfoundland's "blind patriot" who covered and conjured away every blemish of his native province's immense inferiority complex with the hyperbolic blandishments of a moonstruck lover.

As the clock nudged closer to 11:00 a.m., the appointed hour for the service, all eyes turned to the slowly filling pews at the front of the church reserved for dignitaries and members of the Smallwood family. Official mourning made for strange bedfellows.

The venerable Jack Pickersgill, sharing a pew with Frank Moores, Brian Peckford and James McGrath, had never been so close to so many high-ranking Tories in his long political life. Some mischievous minion of protocol had also placed federal Liberal leader Jean Chrétien beside provincial Conservative boss Len Simms, the common denominator being that both patrolled the political wilderness of the Opposition. There was the Supreme Court judge who was once punched in the face by one of Joey's sons in the provincial legislature; legions of senators and former cabinet ministers who owed their former public glories — and their pensions — to Smallwood; frail former contractors who had made their fortunes through Liberal connections in the heady days of Newfoundland's government-financed cost-plus construction boom; true believers like Steve Neary, an old cabinet colleague, who stood by Joey's side both in and out of power.

Among the congregation were grateful seniors who once believed that their pension cheques came directly from Mr. Smallwood and who would often ask to have his portrait buried with them when they died. There was a surprising number of curious youths who knew little of the man who had come from a country they had never known, and crossed oceans they would never sail, but who, for all that, sensed that this was somehow a historic day. The Japanese lanterns of nostalgia and pomp and circumstance were bathing him in their kindly light, and Joey Smallwood the flesh-and-blood politician had all but disappeared in their flattering glow.

At precisely 10:24 a.m., a tall man wearing a brightly decorated blue parka, its hood trimmed in grey fur, walked slowly up the centre aisle of the Basilica accompanied by his more conservatively dressed wife. They stopped at pew number three, just to the left of the altar. Jane Crosbie took her seat and immediately bowed her head against the back of the pew in front of her. Her husband, John, sat bolt upright, staring straight ahead, considering, with more justification than most people in the church, the high irony of the moment and history's capricious eddies and whorls.

It had been John's father, Ches Crosbie, who fought Joey Smallwood every step of the way towards a confederation with Canada that he and his merchant class did not want. As leader of the Economic Union Party, Ches had advocated a return to full sovereignty for Newfoundland, followed by economic union with the United States. But the rugged entrepreneur — a kind of Hemingway without the novels — was no match for the messianic demagogue, either on the hustings or in the back-rooms. Joey carried the day in 1949, leaving Ches no choice but to accommodate himself to the new reality of Canada and to get on with the business of making his fortune.

Ches's wife, Jessie, proved a more stubborn devotee of her class. After Smallwood's first visit to the Crosbie home following the victory of the Confederates, she had the piece of furniture the premier sat on removed and fumigated. In Newfoundland, as John Crosbie knew better than most, people thought with their blood.

But Canada's Fisheries minister didn't have to rely on stories told by his father or mother this day to recall Joey Smallwood. In 1966, four years after his dying father had advised him to steer clear of Smallwood, John Crosbie had joined the provincial cabinet as minister of Municipal Affairs. His involvement in the Mad Hatter's tea party of Newfoundland provincial politics, however, was as bitter as it was brief. Criticizing Smallwood's industrial policies, many of which were modelled along the lines of a hastily planned Brinks hold-up, Crosbie and the man who would shortly be sitting in the pew in front of him, Clyde Wells, resigned from cabinet on May 14, 1968.

Feudal lord that he was, Smallwood's rebuke of his young critics was public and brutal. Although they had merely left cabinet, he had the desks of the two dissenters removed from the government side of the legislature and shifted across the floor to their new location beside the Opposition. A year later, Smallwood vanquished Crosbie in a leadership convention that could as easily have been held at Nuremberg as Memorial Stadium in St. John's, a convention that proved to be the Götterdämmerung of the Liberal Party in Newfoundland.

A murmur went round the church as the prime minister of Canada walked up the centre aisle of the Basilica towards pew number three. There were a few stops along the way to shake hands with old friends and colleagues, including Frank Duff Moores, who had engineered Brian Mulroney's forced march to the leadership of the Conservative Party in 1984 over a field of candidates that had included fellow Newfoundlander John Crosbie. Few people in the country knew about the intimate friendship between Moores and Mulroney that dated back to their drinking days, when Moores was premier of Newfoundland and the young Montreal lawyer was the president of the Iron Ore Company of Canada. Even fewer knew of the bond between Moores and Crosbie, which went back to private school at St. Andrew's College in Ontario. Moores, in fact, had been the one who lured Crosbie out of the provincial Liberal fold into the Progressive Conservative camp. Between the two of them, the pair of Newfoundlanders had had an enormous influence on both provincial and national politics for most of their adult lives.

Frank Moores knew a thing or two about Joey Smallwood. Although John Crosbie had belled the cat, it was the master politician from Harbour Grace who had finally robbed Joey of his ninth political life. Now both Crosbie and Moores were there to honour a man they had both spent much of their youth trying to bury.

At 10:50 a.m., moments after assuming his place in the pew, where he sat with his hands folded in his lap, Brian Mulroney leaned over House of Commons Speaker John Fraser and whispered to John Crosbie. Just two weeks earlier, the prime minister had made his first trip to Newfoundland since the failure of the Meech Lake Accord. The occasion had been the anniversary of Crosbie's twenty-fifth year in politics, and the prime minister had been the guest of honour that night at a five-hundred-dollar-a-plate dinner. Mulroney's praise had been so effusive that Crosbie would later quip that it had been more like listening to his obituary than a speech at a political fund-raiser.

Now, two weeks later, Brian Mulroney was back in Newfoundland to deliver a real eulogy to a man who in life had been one of John Crosbie's bitterest enemies. In fact, in the printed program of his twenty-fifth-anniversary dinner, Crosbie published this 1970 quote about Joey Smallwood: "The premier is the biggest dictator that ever skirted the island . . . he's like the dictator of a banana republic." Savouring these and other ironies, Crosbie allowed a thin smile to pass across his lips as Clyde Kirby Wells stopped at pew number three and shook hands with the prime minister, whose grandest design he had helped to derail just a year before. Musing on the gentlemanly hypocrisies of public life, Crosbie then shook hands with Wells, keenly aware that everyone in the Basilica was thinking of the days when they had both denounced the man they were here to honour and one of them to publicly lionize.

With Premier Wells and his family in pew number two, and Newfoundland's lieutenant-governor ensconced in the official lead position, tiny Clara Smallwood made the long trek to the front of the church supported by her two sons, Ramsay and Bill, and her daughter, Clara. The prime minister nodded as the old woman crept by, unaware of his silent commiserations. Looking more mystified than grief-stricken, Clara's elfin form all but disappeared behind the back of the pew when she finally took her front-row seat for her husband's last command performance.

At 11:04, the casket of Joseph Roberts Smallwood, draped in the flag of Newfoundland, the creation of artist Christopher Pratt, entered the Basilica of St. John the Baptist carried by eight strong men — four wearing the sky blue uniform of the Royal Newfoundland Constabulary and four the traditional red tunic of the Royal Canadian Mounted Police. Behind them, a member from each force carried the hats of the pallbearers — white helmets for the RNC and the famous brown Stetsons of the RCMP. The casket was set down in front of the altar with Joey's Companion of the Order of Canada on top. After a brief organ processional, the congregation sang "O Canada." Given the nature of the gathering, someone had scored a protocol bull's-eye.

Proceedings were now turned over to the gorgeously attired leaders of the seven religious denominations who had organized the ecumenical service. There was nothing surprising in this, at least not for anyone who had seen Joey's tiny bedroom in the house on Portugal Cove Road, where the only adornment besides a narrow cot, a chest of drawers and an exercise machine were the eight portraits of religious leaders that hung on the wall above his pillow. There were six Christians (three evangelical, three liturgical), a Jew and a Buddhist — Joey's self-styled "messengers." In the private shrine of Joey Smallwood, the religion was always politics, as the delicate balance of the list betrayed. Only the Buddhist would go unrepresented this day. Given former Archbishop Roche's fanatical opposition to Confederation, Joey would have found it greatly amusing that he was being laid to rest in a Roman Catholic church.

Along with the others, Brian Mulroney sang Joey's favourite hymn, "How Great Thou Art," and answered The Most Reverend James H. MacDonald, the Roman Catholic Archbishop of St. John's, in the Confession of Sin and the Assurance of Pardon. Then the prime minister slowly made his way past the casket to the podium, where he would deliver the eulogy.

For the next eight minutes he delivered an elegant and ingenious speech that both glorified Joey Smallwood and advanced the cause dearest to the prime minister's heart, national unity and constitutional renewal: "None would deny that this child of Newfoundland rose to confront that greatest of challenges — nation-building — and was not found wanting." The words applied to Smallwood, but they were also designed to resonate in the mind of Clyde Wells, who would speak next. Had he been such a man during the Meech Lake debate? Had he risen to the occasion? Directing a final oblique jibe at Newfoundland's unbending premier, the prime minister said, "Canada's history was a lesson in generous compromise. Canada's unity was a gift to be cherished. . . ." Joey Smallwood had given "an enhanced degree of national unity" to the country. The unspoken question was this: when the chips were down, would Clyde Kirby Wells do the same?

Sitting quietly in his pew, John Crosbie listened approvingly to the prime minister's words. He had been disgusted with the premier's role during Meech Lake and openly warned Clyde Wells that there would be economic repercussions for the province if the federal government's plans to bring Quebec into the constitution were scuttled by Newfoundland. Scuttled they were, but instead of facing reprisals, the province had been given the $5.2-billion Hibernia development, largely because of John Crosbie's personal crusading inside the federal cabinet. Instead of engaging in the time-honoured quid pro quo of politics, which Crosbie lived by, Premier Wells had refused to change his position in the second attempt at constitutional reform, expressing doubt that the federal government's latest plan could save the country. It was not fair, but, as John Crosbie liked to remind people, Clyde Wells had not made a career out of admitting he was wrong. Another way of saying the same thing was that Newfoundland's premier was a man of principle.

On the way back to his seat, the prime minister paused by the flag-draped casket and gracefully bowed his head — a last goodbye to Joey Smallwood that touched off a flurry of camera shutters. In his two terms as prime minister of Canada, Mulroney had developed an uncanny sense of where the press contingent would be positioned at state functions. But there was something completely natural about this final gesture, which would dignify the front pages of Sunday newspapers all across the country the next morning.

It was now the turn of Clyde Wells, the first Liberal premier of Newfoundland since Joey Smallwood, to pay tribute to Newfoundland's greatest political leader — and to answer the prime minister's artful innuendos. Wells called Smallwood *the* giant of Newfoundland history, a man whose contributions to public life would never be equalled in the future of the province. He praised him for the miracle of Confederation, the ensuing social and economic development of the province, and his great encyclopedia of Newfoundland and Labrador, begun after he left politics but never finished. The single thread uniting these disparate careers was their selflessness, the premier said, pointing out that Smallwood had used his considerable talents for the public good rather than his own enrichment.

There was no mention of the politician whose ethics had driven a young Clyde Wells from public life, or the electorate's bitter memories of his dark days of decline that kept the Liberal Party out of power for nearly twenty years after Smallwood's political demise. The omission was appropriate. Joey Smallwood no longer existed in the normal sense of the word, but had risen into the sunny zones of pure legend; the premier was merely adding flourishes of his own to the official portrait. "All of us who live here will also be aware of his [Smallwood's] unseen monument — our status as *equal* citizens of the most favoured nation on earth."

In just six minutes, Clyde Wells had both praised Caesar and buried him. He had also deftly served notice on the prime minister that a Canada where some citizens were more equal than others was just as unacceptable now as it had been when he and Elijah Harper sent a flaming arrow into the Meech Lake Accord.

After the remaining prayers, and with the four candles at the corners of the altar guttering down, the congregation realized Joey Smallwood's last request by ending the service with the "Ode to Newfoundland," his province's stirring anthem. Then, with the organ playing the recessional with so much bass that it resonated in the bellies of the mourners (was the organist trying to make up for the fact that the Basilica's bells were embarrassingly out of commission for renovations?), the pallbearers lifted their burden for the long walk to the waiting hearse and the motorcade to nearby Mount Pleasant Cemetery, where Joey Smallwood would be lowered into the ground at exactly twenty-five minutes past one.

John Crosbie would not be at graveside when the greatest Newfoundlander of them all disappeared under the eye of a small band of loyalists who braved the subzero weather while the Salvation Army Band played a final salute. Perhaps the memories of burying his own brother, Andrew, almost exactly a year before, were still too painful for that. Or maybe there were intimations of his own mortality to be dealt with.

Leaving the last act of Joey's apotheosis to others, he retreated to his rural home just outside the city, where the ghosts of events long gone rose up once more and danced and howled on the keening wind that blew in that night from the frigid Atlantic. As he looked out over the frozen expanse of Hogan's Pond, knowing that he was now the greatest living politician in the province, he might have been thinking of the words of the "Ode to Newfoundland" echoing from the morning's service.

As loved our fathers, so we love,
Where once they stood we stand;
Their prayer we raise to Heaven above,
God guard thee, Newfoundland.

For four generations, John Crosbie's family had been raising that prayer in the teeth of storms and on days that passed like heaven on earth. What a distance they had come, and into what a strange, turbulent and elemental land.

CHAPTER 2

Newfoundland

THE SOUL OF the island is cloaked in forbidding isolation. Awesome and aloof, Newfoundland commands the Gulf of St. Lawrence, with its back to the North American continent and its most settled shore, the Avalon Peninsula, looking across the Atlantic to the island's European roots. Through four centuries, the brute forces of geography and climate have nurtured Newfoundland's singular personality and, until comparatively recently, muffled the cultural din from mainland North America. The world's tenth largest island was in its beginnings, and remains, a place apart.

Three hundred and twenty miles wide and again as deep, Newfoundland's huge, triangular land mass is sparsely populated to this day; boulder-strewn and denuded of soil during the last ice age, its forty-three thousand square miles is a wilderness of rugged mountain ranges, desolate barrens, scrub forests, stunning fiords, tremendous rivers, unnamed ponds, impassable bogs and six thousand miles of coastline that rear up out of the Atlantic like the ramparts of a giant's castle.

To the north, across the narrow Strait of Belle Isle, is Labrador, a windfall of the 1927 ruling by the Judicial Committee of the Privy Council in London that awarded the disputed area to the Dominion of Newfoundland rather than to Canada. Part of mainland North America, it is roughly three times the size of the island, and its spectacular coastal regions are the geological cousins of what Newfoundland's first premier under Confederation, Joey Smallwood, called his "poor, bald rock." Further inland, the rocky headlands give way to virgin forests and wild waterways, a last frontier that white men saw for the first time in 1838, and then only at their peril. It was a truly daunting place, chilled year-round by the ice-infested Labrador current and blasted by some of the harshest winters on earth; yet, in summer, the land blossoms — a brief Eden on the continent's North Atlantic frontier.

For thousands of years, the inhabitants here were a mixture of nomadic Native peoples, migrant Indians from the east coast of the continent: first, Dorset Eskimos; later, Inuit from Alaska; and then the descendants of the Maritime Archaic people, the Naskapi–Montagnais tribe, who still inhabit the interior of Labrador. They built distinctive cultures around fishing, hunting and foraging, according to the territory they had staked out and the seasonal food supplies at hand — fish, fowl, seal and caribou. But when the first marauding Europeans landed their boats on Newfoundland's northern shores, the clock began running for the island's Native population. For some, like the Beothuk Indians, discovery led directly, and barbarously, to extinction. With the death in 1829 of Shananditit, the last Beothuk, the heart of an entire people was stilled. Her scalp and skull were presented to the Royal College of Physicians in London by a Newfoundland politician who understood, it would seem, the enormity of what had happened.

The initial contact came around 1000 A.D. with the landing of the Norsemen at a site believed to be L'Anse aux Meadows at Epaves Bay on the Great Northern Peninsula. The fragments of their colony, including a Norse spindle-whorl, suggesting that women were present in the ancient camp, were discovered in 1960. Like most early pioneering efforts in Newfoundland, Thorfinn Karlsefni's attempt to colonize "Vinland" was abandoned after three dreary winters — grinding seasons of snow, ice and incessant gales whose wretchedness was not improved by the arrows and harpoons of the hostile Native population.

In spite of this reprieve from the jarring impact of European civilization, the island was ultimately doomed: five hundred years after the failure of the Norse settlement, the Old and New Worlds met again on the voyage of a Venetian adventurer out to extend the empires of his patron, Henry VII of England. The year was 1497 and Newfoundland was about to experience the first wave of outsiders who would set out to exploit commercially "the silver mine of the Atlantic," a fishery that was nothing short of fabulous.

Although John Cabot received the royal tithe as the man who discovered the new island for King Henry, it was the French, Spanish and Portuguese who first sent their fishing fleets on the heels of explorers like Gaspar Corte-Real and Jacques Cartier to prosecute the new western fishery. The Basques travelled even farther afield, establishing a whaling station at Red Bay on the southern coast of Labrador. The traditional fishing efforts of these European countries would play an enormous part in the island's history, forming the basis of future claims to fishing rights in and around the waters of Newfoundland that are unresolved to this day.

On land, foreign claims to Newfoundland soil would still be made fifty years after the colony was granted responsible government. It was not until the Anglo-French *entente cordiale* of 1904 that the colony's territorial integrity was secured, when France renounced its historic rights to the "French Shore," an enormous area accounting for approximately a third of the island's coastline. In return, French control of the islands St. Pierre and Miquelon off Newfoundland's south coast, first granted under the 1763 Treaty of Paris, was confirmed. Despite their size, they were of great importance to France's fishing effort in the New World.

Towards the end of the sixteenth century, with the advent of a new "dry" method of curing fish, the English fishing fleet followed its continental rivals into Newfoundland waters. But there was a crucial difference in how the competing European powers prosecuted the fishery, a difference that would have a profound effect on the future development of Newfoundland. Countries like Spain and Portugal, with easy access to cheap supplies of salt, preserved their catch at sea and then shipped it back home for further processing. Without the principal raw material needed for this "green fishery" — cheap salt — the English had to cure their catch before taking it back to Britain. The curing process required land bases — wharves, flakes and fishing rooms where cod could be split, gutted, dried and stored. This original commercial use of the land shaped settlement patterns in St. John's and around the great bays of Newfoundland.

On August 5, 1583, Sir Humphrey Gilbert claimed the "New Found Land" for Queen Elizabeth, establishing three laws: public worship was to be according to the Church of England; attempts to undermine Elizabeth's possession of the territory were high treason punishable by hanging, drawing and quartering; and anyone uttering "words of dishonour" against the Queen would lose his goods, his ships and his ears. But Sir Humphrey was never to know Her Majesty's gratitude. The hapless navigator with the jaunty motto — "Why Not?" — was lost at sea on the return trip to England.

Over the next fifty years, a succession of settlers, or "planters," beginning with John Guy in 1610, tried to establish English colonies on the Avalon Peninsula. But they found neither the furs nor the minerals that English investors had been led to believe could be readily obtained in Newfoundland; worse, they discovered that the soil was too thin to support the cultivation of grain.

Englishmen with a yen to colonize tended to follow the example of George Calvert, later Lord Baltimore, who, after bringing his family to the island in 1627, was mortified by the experience of his one and only Newfoundland winter. He decided that there were better places to begin a brave new world. Although he held a royal patent ceding Newfoundland to him, he abandoned the island after the winter of 1628 and moved to Maryland. He wouldn't be the last sojourner in Newfoundland to pull up stakes; to "pack west" was to live out one of the island's archetypal stories.

Faced with the dismal record of these early settlements, England gave up trying to make Newfoundland a colony and turned the island into little more than a fishing station for the powerful West Country merchants who sailed from ports like Plymouth, Exeter, Poole and Southampton and who built enormous fortunes on Newfoundland cod. Every spring, as many as three hundred fishing vessels would leave England for the fishing grounds off Newfoundland, returning in the fall with enough cured fish to add £20,000 in customs revenues to the coffers of the English Crown.

The British government reaped an even more valuable dividend from the Newfoundland ship-fishery — a ready supply of trained seamen who could be pressed into duty in the Royal Navy whenever England was threatened with war, a not uncommon state of affairs in the turbulent decades of the seventeenth and eighteenth centuries. As for the West Country merchants themselves, the advantages conferred by the Newfoundland fishery were substantial and varied — mansions like Widdecombe House near Dartmouth, Devon, and enough political clout at Westminster to keep meaningful settlement out of Newfoundland for 150 years.

Under the Western Charter of 1634, which was modified but ultimately reconfirmed by the King William's Act in 1699, Newfoundland was ruled, harbour by harbour, by the first ship's captain who arrived from England each spring. These "admirals of the harbour" were charged with settling disputes between the few permanent settlers on the island and the people directly involved in the West Country ship-fishery. Although they had no formal mandate, their seasonal authority was the only civil government Newfoundland then enjoyed.

As for the few year-round settlers in Newfoundland, they were forbidden to establish plantations or to cut wood within six miles of the sea; these were measures designed to preserve valuable coastal land and building materials for the fishing premises of the migrant fishermen. The merchants of the West Country knew a good thing when they saw it: by discouraging settlement, they hoped to avoid local regulation and, in particular, taxation of a fishery that had made so many of them wealthy and powerful in England and lords of the bays in which they fished.

The only practical check on the power of an admiral of the harbour was the commander of the naval convoy, who was responsible for protecting the fishing fleet on its annual voyages to and from Newfoundland. If local inhabitants or other ships' captains took issue with a ruling by an admiral of the harbour, they could appeal to the commander of the naval convoy. This informal role was institutionalized in 1729 when the naval commander became governor and commander-in-chief in Newfoundland, dropping anchor in the spring and departing again well before the gales of November began to blow. For nearly a century, Newfoundland would be ruled by this fair-weather naval ascendancy.

Despite the harsh climate and England's official attempts to preserve the Newfoundland fishery for the merchants of the West Country, the island's residential population slowly grew. By the end of the eighteenth century, Newfoundland had about 20,000 people, most of them of English and Irish descent.

If this ethnic mix was the strength of the nascent colony, it also contained the seeds of one of Newfoundland's most serious domestic problems, sectarian bigotry that led to bitterness and bloodshed in the early days of responsible and representative government and which existed well into the twentieth century, though in somewhat subtler forms. Whether it was Orangemen murdered during the annual parade celebrating the Battle of the Boyne or a newspaper editor whose ears were cut off after he publicly attacked the Roman Catholic Church's meddling in politics, there was a time in the mid-nineteenth century when Newfoundland lived up to its billing as "John Bull's other Ireland."

Newfoundland's resident English population was made up of West Country sailors and servants (fishermen-labourers) associated with the ship-fishery who chose to settle on the island rather than return to England when times, and fishing customs, changed. They were staunch Protestants who formed a natural elite, participating in the new island-based fishery and often going into business for themselves.

The island's Irish population, which was solidly Catholic, had very different roots, coming out from southern Irish ports like Waterford and Cork as servants of the West Countrymen on their annual fishing voyages to Newfoundland. Since they were untrained and uneducated, their prospects were, if anything, even dimmer in Newfoundland than they were at home, given the religious discrimination of the day. Most of them were indentured to planters and fishermen in Newfoundland, usually for two summers and a winter, before returning to Ireland, hence the pejorative term "winter Irish."

The Irish were consigned to the bottom of the social ladder, and discriminated against as lazy, thieving and alcoholic. Irish women were actually sold in the colony as servants or wives. Their bad reputation wasn't enhanced by England's practice of sending shiploads of Irish convicts to North America. When one convict ship put 102 of these penniless wretches off in Bay Bulls, south of St. John's, the local inhabitants were incensed. The miserable convicts were promptly herded into a concentration camp and summarily deported, though by the time the authorities caught up with them, twenty-nine had escaped to enrich the local stock!

Relations between the English establishment and Newfoundland's resident Irish were further strained by a few spectacular crimes of the period, particularly the murder of Magistrate William Keene, who was also a member of the St. John's merchant establishment. The mastermind of the crime was Mistress Eleanor Power, Keene's former servant, who recruited ten Irishmen to help her steal the gold she knew the wealthy merchant kept in his house.

Things ran amok, with dire consequences for everyone. After making off with what they thought was the magistrate's money chest, the thieves discovered that they had instead stolen his private supply of fine brandies. Led by the brazen Mistress Power, they returned to the house to try again. The doomed Keene awakened as Eleanor was dragging his money chest from under his bed; he was promptly dispatched with a scythe blade and a musket butt. Unfortunately for the larcenous lady, the magistrate lived long enough to identify her as one of his attackers. Eleanor Power, along with her husband, went to the gallows on Keene's Wharf on October 11, 1754 — the first female in British North America to meet her maker at the end of a rope.

The Irish in Newfoundland faced a repressive Anglo-Protestant establishment that stifled them at every turn. Roman Catholic priests were banned in the colony; property used for religious purposes was destroyed; Catholic children were forcibly baptized in the Anglican Church; Catholics were forbidden to operate public houses; and quarterdeck justice was meted out to Catholics by surrogate judges who were often members of the Protestant clergy when they weren't officers of that other much-loved institution in Ireland, the British navy.

By the mid-eighteenth century, there was a concerted effort to reduce their numbers through the rigid enforcement of the colony's anti-papist laws. This unenlightened persecution got the response it deserved. When the naval governor of the day asked the three hundred Irish residents of St. John's to take the oath of allegiance to the Crown in 1749, only six complied. And when the French subsequently took St. John's during the Seven Years' War, there were reports that the Irish went over to the enemy and manned a vessel patrolling St. John's harbour. Underlying discrimination against the Newfoundland Irish was the fear that, in any hostilities between England and France, they would take the side of their fellow Roman Catholics.

Yet despite religious discrimination, which officially ended in 1784, the colony continued to grow. One of the principal reasons was England's preoccupation with war — namely, the American Revolution, which was swiftly followed by the epic struggle with Napoleon in Europe. It was impossible to conduct the traditional ship-fishery under such unstable conditions, and gradually the annual spring flotilla of English fishing vessels was supplanted by a Newfoundland-based fishery controlled by merchants who lived on the island.

With the demise of the ship-fishery, the merchants of St. John's expanded their ocean harvesting to include a vigorous offshore seal hunt in Labrador based in outports like Harbour Grace and Brigus. Fortunes were made on the pelts, fat and meat of the huge herds that gave birth to their young on the ice fields as they drifted southward every spring. The princes of Water Street traded vigorously with the New England states and moved into lumbering, shipbuilding and provisioning. There was also a thriving trade with privateers who plied the waters off Newfoundland and who offered their contraband to enterprising island businessmen at bargain rates. Rum-running on the south coast between Grand Bank and the French islands of St. Pierre and Miquelon became a virtual cottage industry.

In fact, rum arm-wrestled with religion for most of Newfoundland's early history with grog, not God, enjoying the upper hand for more than two hundred years. In 1726, of the 450 families living in Newfoundland, 65 kept public houses. St. John's, with only 42 permanent houses, had 16 taverns. In the early nineteenth century, the island was importing nearly half a million gallons of rum to slake the thirst of a population of only a few thousand people. The daily ration of rum was ingrained in the island's seafaring tradition, and Newfoundlanders not only drank astonishing quantities of alcohol themselves, they also gave it to their children, according to the practice of the times. At twenty-five cents a gallon, it was one of the only recreations available to those first brave souls who settled the island. Given the length and severity of the Newfoundland winter, it would be difficult to decide which arrival was most welcome in the early days of the island — spring or the sack ship from England.

With a few important local wrinkles, it was the old story of colonization in North America; with permanent residency came economic development, which in turn created a social elite that pressed for political autonomy. By the early nineteenth century, Newfoundland started down the road that would lead to political independence, along with England's other territories.

There was great scope for the reforming zeal of the Scottish doctor who became the William Lyon Mackenzie of Newfoundland politics. When William Carson arrived in St. John's in 1808, there was much to offend his Whiggish sensibilities, including abject poverty, sectarian tension, an unprofessional judiciary, and most objectionable of all, the autocratic ascendancy of absentee naval governors.

Both Carson and his Irish associate, Patrick Morris, were imbued with the reforming spirit of the age, which, fortunately for them, was making a no less vigorous appearance in England. Although their criticisms of colonial conditions in Newfoundland were deemed "poisonous and vicious" by local officials, the British government was more liberally inclined. To deflect the charge that Newfoundland was essentially administered in absentia, the naval governor was ordered to winter over in St. John's in 1817. It was the first time such an order had ever been issued, and as far as the unfortunate office-holder of the day was concerned it was to be the last. Admiral Pickmore perished in spartan official quarters at Fort Townshend in 1818 during the harshest winter on record in Newfoundland history.

Luckily for Carson and Morris, the will to reform proved hardier than the unfortunate admiral. Newfoundland was granted representative government in 1832 — 75 years later than neighbouring Nova Scotia — and by the time Carson died in 1843, most of the things he had fought against had been reformed. The surrogate courts, run by the clergy and the military, were dismantled and replaced by a circuit-court system. Valuable harbour land previously frozen for the exclusive use of the West Countrymen was granted to local merchants for commercial use, enabling places like St. John's to develop. Churches, schools, newspapers, hospitals, libraries, a police force and local farms sunk delicate roots as the island began to shake off the controls of the mother country and to take on an existence of its own.

Organized religion played a special role in the developing society, ministering first to the spiritual needs of Newfoundlanders and then to those secular requirements that governments were slow to address. Beginning with the Anglicans and Roman Catholics, and eventually including the various evangelical churches, religious leaders pioneered the beginnings of a social welfare system. They also played a key role in the education system, which was plagued by a lack of teachers and funds. Newfoundland's rural communities were poor, tiny and far flung and it required true missionary zeal to bring the rudiments of formal education to the outports. The immense influence of the church on the schooling of Newfoundlanders evolved into a formal denominational education system by 1874. It endures to this day, much to the chagrin of critics who believe it to be an unaffordable anachronism in a secular world.

Beneath this advancing tide of economic and political maturation, which led to responsible government for the colony in 1855, powerful undertows tugged at the emerging society. Although St. John's was growing rapidly, the economic power of the town was only as strong as the fishery, which was concentrated in the hands of a few local merchants. To the poor, whose hovels overlooked the impressive business establishments of the St. John's merchants on the south side of Water Street, the situation could hardly have been much of an improvement over the old days of the English ascendancy. Exacerbated by religious differences, Newfoundland's obvious class system would be an easily lit political powder keg for the next fifty years.

The influence of the St. John's merchants extended beyond the town to the outports, which, by the late nineteenth century, grew increasingly isolated from the rest of the world and more and more dependent on Newfoundland's biggest town. The Water Street merchants advanced credit to outport fishermen against their fishing season and then settled accounts when the boats tied up for the year. Although this system had many practical benefits in a place where ready cash was scarce, it stacked the deck in favour of the St. John's merchants, who set the price of the goods they advanced and the price of the fish they accepted as payment.

The result was an isolated and dependent outport population that in good times was controlled by the merchants of Water Street and in bad times relied on government to stave off disaster — a never too distant possibility in a rural economy based on the vagaries of the inshore fishery and the thin harvests of subsistence agriculture. The colony's fragile existence, hitched as it was to the inevitable cycle of boom and bust in the fishery, would test the resourcefulness of more than one government in the coming decades.

In its salad days, responsible government looked as if it would supply just one more jousting ground for Newfoundland's English Protestant establishment and its Irish

Catholic majority. The Liberal Party formed the first elected government in 1855 featuring two Catholics, Philip Little and John Kent, as premier and colonial secretary. Behind these two reformers was John Thomas Mullock, the powerful Roman Catholic Bishop of St. John's.

Things ran smoothly enough for Premier Little, but his successor, Kent, was not so lucky. The 1859 election that brought him to power was marred by sectarian violence and charges of vote rigging by the official Opposition. Kent then suffered the wrath of Bishop Mullock, who withdrew his support over the government's failure to provide a steamer service to outport Newfoundland in 1860. The bishop's punitive response might have had more to do with an affront to him than to coastal Newfoundland. During a trip to New York, he had hired a steamship for the coastal service without troubling to consult with the government of the day. When they refused to honour his unilateral commitment on their behalf, the bishop abandoned them in a political sulk.

The flashpoint for Kent's administration came when he withdrew his government's currency bill, which would have seen the governor, the Opposition, and certain judges paid in Newfoundland rather than British currency for the first time. Premier Kent charged that the governor and a few cronies had conspired to sink the bill, prompting Governor Sir Alexander Bannerman, who was personally prejudiced against the Catholics, to insist that Kent prove his allegations or resign. When he refused, Kent was dismissed from office and the leader of the Protestant Opposition, Hugh Hoyles, became premier.

Sectarian violence erupted in the subsequent 1861 election, won by Hoyles. Rioting broke out in St. John's when two disputed members of the House of Assembly tried to take their seats. With three dead and twenty injured, it looked like Newfoundland was heading down the road to a bloody, religious war. But Bishop Mullock intervened and Protestant-Catholic relations steadily improved, as a result of what two Newfoundland scholars, Peter Neary and Patrick O'Flaherty, have called "an elaborate denominational truce, based on the judicious distribution of patronage at every level."

In the middle of the nineteenth century, Newfoundland went about its turbulent business only temporarily distracted by the great political event going on in British North America — the union of several independent colonies into the new country of Canada. Although attracted by the political romancing of John A. Macdonald, who had designs on Newfoundland to consolidate Canada's Atlantic defences, Newfoundlanders were not seduced as their maritime neighbours were soon to be. But they did some flirting. Ambrose Shea, the Leader of the Opposition, and Frederick Carter, the Speaker of the House of Assembly, were sent to the Quebec Conference in 1864 to observe the political groundwork that would lead to the creation of Canada three years later. The Newfoundland legislature subsequently passed a resolution promising to put the issue of Confederation to the electorate before it took a position on the momentous resolutions adopted at Quebec.

Although Confederation was an issue in the election of 1865, Premier-elect Carter had no mandate to pursue the matter actively, and the legislative session of 1866 passed without a decision either way. (Since 1855, Newfoundland had been internally self-governing, on an equal constitutional footing with other British North American colonies.) A year later, Canada came into being — without Newfoundland. In 1869, Premier Carter, a pro-Confederate, successfully negotiated terms of union with Ottawa. But before he could have the deal ratified by the Newfoundland House of Assembly, his government was defeated in the great anti-Confederate provincial election of that year, a campaign that clearly showed the strength of Newfoundland nationalism. As one member of a British royal commission looking into Newfoundland's political future would write sixty years later, "The people of Newfoundland would much prefer to be masters in their own home, however poor, than to play the part of Cinderella in the Canadian mansion."

It would take another eighty years, a cruel depression and the messianic wiles of Joe Smallwood to overcome that deep-seated preference.

CHAPTER 3

The Patriarch

THE CROSBIE NAME, so closely associated with Scotland, has its real beginnings in Viking lore. The family was Scandinavian, with connections to the Royal House of Norway. By 980 A.D. the Crosbies were the governors of the Isle of Man, where they built "Crosbie Castle." The villages that sprang up around the castle are still called Great Crosby and Little Crosby. When Eric Bloodaxe, the son of Norse King Harold Haarfager, was driven out of his father's kingdom, he sought and was granted refuge with the Crosbies.

Like other Vikings, the Crosbies made raids along the Mersey and Lancashire coast, where they eventually settled, as well as on the Cumberland shore. In 1092, Richard Crosbie was granted land by King William II on the banks of the river Eden, which flowed from the north of England into the Solway Firth. He built a castle by the Eden called "Corby." Several villages exist there to this day bearing the Crosbie name: High Crosby, Low Crosby, Crosby-on-Eden, Crosby-Garrett and Crosby Ravensworth. (Genealogists note that the family name has been variously spelt Crosbj, Crossebei, Crossebi, Crosby and Crosbie as the centuries passed and the family moved from Norway to Britain and then on to North America.)

Another branch of the ancient family settled in Annandale and married into the De Brus, or Bruce family, long before

Robert Bruce became King of Scotland. Colonel Robert Crosbie was an ardent supporter of Bruce, and brought five of his seven sons to Bruce's camp when he was raising an army to fight the English. The Crosbies fought with Bruce at Bannockburn where he defeated the English on June 24, 1314. All five of Colonel Crosbie's sons — Adam, David, John, William and Richard — died at Bannockburn.

The famous battle spawned a Crosbie legend. As he left the battlefield after the Scottish victory, the story goes, Robert Crosbie noticed a crowd of people tending to a fallen English officer. Riding over to investigate, he discovered that it was his own son, who had been sent to England to be educated by a priest and who had ended up fighting on the English side. The enraged patriarch rode his mount over his own son's body, crushing the young man's upturned face under his horse's hooves and killing him.

Back at Corby Castle, the battle-hardened campaigner told his pregnant wife what had happened. Meanwhile, when the English priest learned that his student had been brutally murdered by his own father, he cursed the family forever, warning that "all they acquired would bring them no permanent good, and would ultimately pass to others. They would never be able to hold permanently any titles or wealth; these would always pass from them in the course of time. The results of their toil, their cleverness, their kindness or their loyalty would always benefit others, not themselves." According to legend, when Robert Crosbie's son was born, there was a horseshoe birthmark on the infant's forehead.

But romance proved more dangerous to the Crosbies than curses. Robert Crosbie's lands and Corby Castle passed from the family when the heiress, Janet Crosbie, married the first Earl of Carlisle in 1437. The Earl retained the Crosbie arms — a red cross on a gold ground — merely reversing the colours to mark the passage of the Crosbie lands into his own family.

The Crosbies fell into relative obscurity after Bannockburn, becoming poorer and poorer until they eventually lost their property in Annandale. But by 1650, with the birth of John Crosbie in Dumfries, the lowland capital of southern Scotland, the irrepressible clan was on the rise again. Clever and ambitious, Crosbie married Margaret Herries, the daughter of Lord Herries of Herries around 1670. He went on to become Provost of Dumfries and a successful merchant. As he grew more prosperous, he bought the estate of Holm in 1708, a beautiful mansion with famous gardens just south of the town.

On the way up the social ladder, John Crosbie showed that he wasn't afraid to do his civic duty, whatever that might be. On May 18, 1671, Crosbie and one Thomas Anderson were paid for erecting a gibbet. An unfortunate citizen of Dumfries, Elspeth Thomsone, was told that she had "shaken off all fear of God and reverence, she had betaken herself to the service of Satan, that she had taken his marks upon her body, had practised diverse and sundrie devilish charms, witchcraft, sorcerie, that she had carnal dealings with the devil, and has hereby hurt and damnified his majesty's subjects in their goods and persons." John Crosbie was one of the witnesses against the alleged witch. He testified that Elspeth had had a heated argument with his wife, Margaret, because the Crosbies hadn't invited her to their child's christening. When Margaret later became ill, Crosbie went to Elspeth's house and brought three pulls of thatch from above her door. He took them home, and burnt them in front of Margaret — a ritual he hoped would revive his bewitched wife. Margaret recovered, but shortly afterwards, their first baby died.

Other neighbours backed up Crosbie's accusation that Elspeth was a witch, and the wretched woman was found guilty and sentenced to death under a law passed in 1563 that made witchcraft in Scotland a capital offence. On a sunny day in May, dressed in hair shirts soaked in vinegar, she and another unfortunate woman, Janet McMuldroche, were strangled at the stake. While the good citizens of Dumfries, including a vindicated John Crosbie, looked on, the bodies of the two women were burned and their ashes scattered to the four winds between the hours of two and four o'clock in the afternoon. This was to be the fate of the mortal remains of a thousand people, mostly poor, middle-aged or elderly women until the law was repealed in 1735.

(John Crosbie's pious bones were destined for more congenial repose when he died in 1720. Of all the gravestones in the crowded St. Michael's Churchyard in Dumfries, his is one of the most imposing, boasting furls of marble curtains and stone books hinting that Robbie Burns, a resident of Dumfries who died there in 1797 and was also buried in St. Michael's, was not the only literary man in town.)

John and Margaret Crosbie produced five children. The eldest, Andrew, went on to become provost of Dumfries by 1732. Like his father, who had been involved in military campaigns against the Stuarts and their Jacobite supporters in their bid to claim the throne, Andrew opposed Prince Charles Edward Stuart when he marched into Dumfries with his troops in 1745 looking for taxes and booty.

The rebels were also looking for a little revenge. Not only had the town council of Dumfries ignored the Pretender's demand for taxes, but a small raiding party of Dumfries men had even ambushed the Prince's men on their way south to Carlisle, relieving them of their baggage and supplies. Bonnie Prince Charlie and his four thousand soldiers got even by fining the town £2,000, 1,000 pairs of shoes and all of its weapons. Dumfries was given twenty-four hours to come up with the loot. According to the diary of a local minister, the Reverend Mr. Duncan, "They were most rude in the town — pillaged some shops and pulled shoes off gentlemen's feet in the streets."

With the town overrun with tartaned Highlanders, few people ventured outside. Carruthers and Graham, two local officials, knocked on every door but with just a few hours to go on the deadline, they had collected only £1,195 and 255 pairs of shoes. Luckily, news came in the nick of time that the Duke of Cumberland had captured nearby Carlisle and was on his way to meet the Prince and his rebels. On a chilly Monday morning two days before Christmas, the Scottish prince and his army began their retreat along the road to Glasgow, taking Andrew Crosbie, the sixty-one-year-old former provost of Dumfries as a hostage. He was released in Glasgow when the balance of the levy was paid in full.

That spring, on April 16, 1746, Prince Charles Edward Stuart was defeated by the English at Culloden. The people of Dumfries were less concerned about the Prince's escape to France than they were about recovering the taxes he had illegally levied. This was accomplished in part by an assessment to all citizens of the town and a £3,000 payment from the forfeited estates of Lord Elcho, who had made the fatal mistake of fighting for the Prince on the wrong side of history.

As for Andrew Crosbie, there seem to have been no lingering effects from his brief kidnapping. He died at Holm in 1762 at the age of eighty-eight (some sources claim "the great age of ninety-five") after a long illness. His eldest son, Andrew, would become the first genuinely tragic figure of the ambitious but star-crossed clan.

Andrew Crosbie of Holm became Dean of the Faculty of Advocates in 1765. Considered a genius by his law professors and fellow students, Andrew was a daring and eloquent advocate who, according to the custom of the day, conducted most of his business in the taverns and coffee houses of High Street in Edinburgh. His favourite haunt was The Crown Tavern, but he could also be found at The Star and Garter or Clerihugh's, a tavern in Writer's Court. The flamboyant advocate was the model for the character High Jinks Pleydell in Sir Walter Scott's novel *Guy Mannering*. When Dr. Samuel Johnson visited Scotland in 1783, Andrew was considered to be the only local who held his own in conversation with the great English wit. Two years after Johnson's sojourn, Crosbie paid him a visit in London where the two men discussed a mutual interest — alchemy.

Andrew had an extensive library (the motto "Resurgam," or "I shall rise again" — graced all his book plates) and he believed that "a lawyer without history or literature is a mechanic, a mere working mason." Warmed by liquor, "nothing could be more joyous and interesting than his discourse, there being a happy mixture of wit and humour and information." In addition to literature and the law, he was also fond of "dogs, horses and cocks," on which he regularly wagered.

At the height of Andrew's reputation, the Crosbie curse struck again. Reduced to comparative poverty by the Douglas, Heron and Company bank failure, he lost his Holm estate, which eventually ended up in the hands of Walter

Riddell. Riddell changed its name to Woodley Park after the maiden name of his beautiful and accomplished wife, Maria Woodley, the "Maria" in the poetry of "Caledonia's Bard," Robbie Burns. In the wake of his financial reversals, Andrew sought refuge in the bottle, "which indeed had long possessed for him a dangerous fascination." He would not be the last Crosbie to be so afflicted.

Andrew died on February 25, 1785, at the age of forty-nine. The Faculty of Advocates granted his widow an annuity of forty pounds. An oil painting of Crosbie, decked out in his barrister's wig and gown, still hangs in Parliament House, Edinburgh.

Roughly coinciding with Andrew's death came the beginnings of the great Scottish diaspora and with it the genesis of the Crosbie family outside of Scotland. Thomas Crosbie, who moved his family to North America, was born in the county of Dumfries in 1796, the year that Robbie Burns died. At that time, Dumfries was a place where the citizens were considerably more cosmopolitan than their more homespun neighbours. Even though it was close to the marshes of the Solway, which gave the place a perpetual dampness and humidity, Dumfries was a lively town of 5,600 inhabitants — neat, well built and boasting a new theatre and orderly, paved streets. Officers of the local regiments stationed in the town gave Dumfries a certain glamour, which was reinforced during the annual festival week by nobles, squires and ladies, who took part in the hunt and ball. A contemporary historian, Robert Heron, described Dumfries during festivities week as "a place of higher gaiety and elegance than any other town in Scotland of the same size."

Thomas Crosbie shows up in the 1841 census living in Georgetown, a suburb of Dumfries. He was a stonecutter by trade, particularly adept at working with the Dumfries Basin red sandstone from which so much of the town was built. By 1832, the population of Dumfries had ballooned to 12,000, partially as a result of the infamous Highland Clearances. After the battle of Culloden, the highland chieftains abandoned their traditional obligations to their clansmen who worked the land. The chieftains found that it was more profitable to lease their glens as pasture to English or Scottish sheep farmers. Police and soldiers were used to clear the land by force, resulting in widespread poverty, illness and starvation. Economic conditions were so desperate that the government was forced to set up the Board of Destitution, a relief agency that put displaced farmers to work on "meal roads" to keep them from starving to death. As one writer of the day described the heartless agricultural policy that displaced thousands of crofters, driving many of them to seek berths on the emigrant ships bound for the New World, "They want fine fields, what care they for men?"

Towards the middle of the nineteenth century, two distinct elements of Scottish society were coming out to the colonies, each for reasons of its own. While Highland Scots were fleeing the horrors of the "Clearances," their Lowland brethren, people like Thomas Crosbie, were leaving the homeland to seek their fortunes in North America, relying on a formidable combination of the Protestant work ethic and a flair for commerce to make their way.

By 1812, advertisements began to appear in Dumfries's two newspapers, *The Courier* and *The Journal*, for berths on emigrant ships. A bustling trade developed: Scots were delivered to the New World and timber was brought back from the Miramichi region of New Brunswick, which Dumfries shipwrights used to build more vessels. In 1851 alone, more than ten thousand people sailed to North America from Dumfries. It would not be until near the end of the nineteenth century that the emigrant trade moved from Dumfries to the larger ports of Glasgow and Liverpool.

Motivated by population pressure in Dumfries caused by the Highland Clearances, or perhaps by the terrible cholera epidemic of 1832 that wiped out 6 percent of the population, Thomas and his wife Margaret decided to leave their native town and strike out for Napan, which straddled Northumberland and Glenelg counties in Miramichi, New Brunswick. In 1840, forty-nine-year-old Margaret Crosbie left Scotland with her three sons — James, thirteen, John, eleven, and George Graham Crosbie, just five years old.

It is not known whether Margaret and her sons were alone

for their first three years in North America. In 1837, a William Crosbie shows up in the area, but no record exists to link him to Thomas and Margaret. What is known is that Thomas was thirty-one and Margaret was thirty-six when their son James was born. Could William have been their eldest son who had preceded the family to Miramichi? Was it to join him that Margaret and her other children left Scotland in 1840? Time has closed over the facts, but the Crosbie name was rare in Miramichi, and it seems strange that a woman of Margaret's age with three young sons would strike out for the wilds of New Brunswick alone. Whatever the reason for her separation from her husband, it ended in 1843 when Thomas finally joined his wife and children in Chatham, having left Dumfries on the heels of its last recorded food riot.

By 1851, the census for the parish of Chatham listed Thomas as a farmer and property owner. Since there are no records of a land grant to the family, it is conceivable that Thomas chose to send his wife ahead so that he could stay behind in Scotland plying his trade until he'd saved up enough money to buy a farm in New Brunswick. One son, James, was also listed as a farmer in the Crosbie household, while another, John, was described as a plasterer. He was employed by a fellow Scot, James Patterson, with whom he lived for a time. Sixteen-year-old George was listed as a labourer training in the plastering trade like his brother John. Seven years later, at the age of twenty-three, he would carry the banner of the Dumfries Crosbies to Newfoundland.

Although there is nothing left to document why George Crosbie left New Brunswick, history offers some clues. New Brunswick's abundant supply of timber fed a vigorous shipbuilding industry in the ports of Pictou and Miramichi, where George Crosbie worked. Until the age of steam, New Brunswick timber was an important source of masts for the Royal Navy. The Scots, who controlled these two ports, also built extensively for the Newfoundland fishery, so that any interesting news of the island would be readily available to Scottish artisans working in either port. In April, 1858 — shortly before George Crosbie embarked for the island — there was a disastrous fire in Harbour Grace, one of

Newfoundland's busiest sealing ports. For an enterprising young tradesman, the clouds of smoke might have promised a silver lining. There was certain to be a building boom in the wake of the fire, and the wealthy sealing captains and merchants of the town would need specialized tradesmen to put the final touches to their new homes.

There might also have been another inducement to leave Miramichi. A year earlier, in 1857, steam propulsion was applied for the first time to the sealing and whaling industry by Scottish interests in the Greenland hunt. The canny young tradesman might have foreseen that Miramichi was bound to go into decline as the age of sail came to a close. Whatever his motives, this much is clear: by 1858 George Graham Crosbie had abandoned the Miramichi and was living and working in Newfoundland.

If the young plasterer had indeed come in expectation of boom times, he must have been sorely disappointed. The recession of the 1860s in Newfoundland was so severe that it raised doubts about the island's ability to go it alone with a growing population relying almost totally on the fishery. The grinding poverty of the period began with a succession of poor cod fisheries — still, and dangerously, the mainstay of Newfoundland's outport economy. The Labrador seal fishery also failed. Not even the first steamships that appeared in Newfoundland in 1862 could penetrate the terrible ice conditions that prevailed that year in coastal Labrador and eastern Newfoundland. The American Civil War added to Newfoundland's problems by interrupting the traditional herring fishery with the United States. On land, there was an island-wide potato blight that must have brought back terrifying memories to Newfoundlanders of Irish descent, some of whom had fled famine in their own country only to face it again in their adoptive home.

By 1869, one-third of the government's revenues was being used to provide relief to needy Newfoundlanders, a state of affairs that alarmed the colony's political and economic establishment. Authorities worried that too many people were looking for dole rather than jobs, and a conscious effort was made to make public assistance modest in scope and painful to receive. Relief took the form of Indian meal and molasses and had to be worked off on government road projects — a chilling reminder of Scotland's Board of Destitution. And there were new and humiliating wrinkles: if a Newfoundlander was on relief in the one-year period before or after an election, he was disenfranchised.

Judging from George Crosbie's steady business progress through the 1860s, he neither lost his vote nor supped on Indian meal and molasses. On the contrary, he appears to have navigated well enough through the hard times that greeted him in his new home — first in Harbour Grace and later in Brigus. On Saturday, July 30, 1862, he married Martha Ellen Chalker, whose father, Thomas Chalker, was a cooper in Brigus, practising a well-respected trade that was vitally important to the salt fish industry. The ceremony was conducted by the Methodist Missionary at Harbour Grace, Rev. E. Brettle, and was duly recorded in the Harbour Grace *Standard.*

Martha's mother was a Parker, who had married Thomas in 1832. Although the couple had tied the knot in Brigus, their daughter was born in Dartmouth, England, suggesting that Thomas must have been a prosperous tradesman; only Newfoundland women of means wintered in England or returned there to have their children. Apparently, George Crosbie had married well: making felicitous commercial alliances while pursuing matters of the heart would become something of a family trait.

George and Martha set up house in Brigus, which, thanks to the sealing and salt fish industries, was one of the most prosperous outports in Conception Bay. In winter, more than a hundred fishing vessels anchored there, packing the harbour so tightly that it was possible to cross it by jumping from deck to deck. In its heyday, between 1830 and 1860, there were more jobs in Brigus than there were people to fill them; it was a vacuum that attracted an influx of carpenters, shipwrights, sailmakers and apprentices from England, Ireland and the North American colonies. With seal pelts valued at eight dollars per quintal (a measure equal to 112 pounds), and plentiful cod in both Newfoundland and Labrador waters, fortunes could accumulate rapidly if the voyages were good.

The town featured large, comfortable houses that were built at odd angles to take advantage of the marvellous scenery that set off one of the finest natural harbours on the island. Sheep and goats grazed on the high barrens that surrounded the village, and wild berries grew in profusion on the rocky hillsides above the sea. With its picket fences and winding lanes, the place was built on the model of the English West Country villages that so many of its oldest families — the Percys, Spracklins, Leamons, Mundens, Pikes, Roberts and Bartletts — had left behind to come to Newfoundland. As the town prospered, several of the leading families imported "British ladies" for their wives, prompting one old salt to observe, "Visitors from nearby settlements said that the Brigus women have changed and are now high-minded like the goats."

The Crosbies shared a duplex called "Lakeside" with William and Mary Bartlett, members of one of Newfoundland's most famous seafaring families. Their son, Robert Bartlett, would later become the greatest Arctic navigator of the century, piloting Robert Peary and Vilhyalmur Stefansson on their historic expedition to the North Pole. In a book he wrote in 1928, the renowned skipper remembered his father's friend, George Crosbie, as "a well-to-do merchant with schooners and wharves and all that." One of Bob Bartlett's best friends was George's son, "Jack" Crosbie, later to become Sir John, the founder of the Crosbie business empire and grandfather of a future Canadian Finance minister.

The Crosbie–Bartlett duplex was anything but ostentatious. In fact, it had been converted from an unused granary — the perfect base from which a proper and ambitious Methodist family could climb the rungs of commercial success. And climb them George did. Soon after arriving in Brigus, Crosbie expanded his business activities well beyond the plastering trade. The *Newfoundland Directory* of 1871 listed his name in capital letters as a general dealer in dry goods, groceries, provisions, crockery, boots and shoes. He also operated a sawmill behind his Brigus home, using the power from a small river that ran through town; it was one of 900 such mills built around Newfoundland by 1900 to furnish lumber for local use. In 1875, a ship, the *Kersage*, was built by the Manuel shipyard in Exploits for George Crosbie, by this time described in commercial documents as "a merchant of Brigus." Crosbie used the *Kersage* to supply the Brigus-based fishermen who went to the Labrador each spring and summer in search of seals and northern cod. It was a fickle business, as George Crosbie told a friend who was writing a pamphlet on "the Supplying Trade."

"To illustrate the precarious nature of our fisheries," he said, "I can give you an instance of what happened to myself. One fall, during the time I supplied for the fisheries, a man came upon my wharf whom I had supplied for the Labrador. He said, 'Why, you must have had a big lot of men here this morning,' alluding to the fact that so much fish and oil were about the premises.' 'No,' I replied, 'this was all put in by one crew. They gave me 1,500 quintals of fish and a corresponding quantity of oil.' This made him open his eyes, and he said, 'I'd like to know where they got it, then!' All the voyage that he had was about 20 quintals of fish and as much oil as one cask, partly filled, could hold. Next year 'twas that man had the big voyage — and the others had nothing."

As Crosbie's business interests grew, so too did his family. He and Martha Ellen produced eight children: Margaret, Thomas, Martha Ellen, Jennie, Walter, George Lamont, John Chalker and Robert. The last child was born in 1879. Martha Ellen, or "Ellie," as she was known, was the natural leader amongst the children, partly because of her age but mostly on account of her imperious temperament. If anyone picked on the Crosbie brood, it was Ellie they had to deal with. Six foot two in heels, with a ramrod straight carriage and a fiercely determined spirit, she was nicknamed "Nelson" after the indomitable British admiral.

With their father's prosperity and the formidable Ellie to stand up for them, the children enjoyed all the advantages of belonging to one of the most influential families in Brigus. By 1874, George Crosbie was a member of the Brigus Methodist Board of Education and, along with Abraham Bartlett, one of the most generous contributors to the Brigus Methodist Church. When the new church opened in 1875, George Crosbie was listed as one of its fourteen trustees, a position reserved for only the most respected citizens. By 1878, the rising businessman had added "Esquire" to his name. A year later, he served on a Grand Jury of Inquiry into destitution, a subject of perennial relevance in Newfoundland.

But as settled as the family was in Brigus, George Crosbie was a man quick to feel the winds of change and just as quick to take a new tack if the times demanded. As steamships replaced wooden vessels, the economy of Brigus and other outports began to decline. Steam-powered vessels like the *Retriever*, the first Conception Bay-owned steamer out of Harbour Grace to be rigged for the seal hunt, required fewer men to sail them, and wages for their crews dropped from half to a third of the catch. The steamers were able to make two trips to the ice fields instead of the single voyage of the sailing vessels, an advantage that seriously reduced the size of the herd, since older breeding seals were often taken on the second trip. As the herd diminished, so did the demand for seal oil, a commodity that was eventually replaced by mineral and vegetable products.

In the years between 1884 and 1891, the population of Brigus dropped by a third. But the decline in the seal fishery wasn't the only factor. According to Captain Harold Bartlett, the demise of the town was hastened by rampant drunkenness that "unfitted the sons of the old Captains of industry to take their fathers' places." One local clergyman complained in his circuit book that "some of our young men who met with us fell through the snare of strong drink and its collateral vices," the latter observation referring to the rising number of illegitimate births in his flock.

By the end of the century, the outport seal fishery was virtually over as a large-scale commercial enterprise, and the best captains had signed on with steamers owned by merchants in Harbour Grace and St. John's. The only signs of the tiny outport's former importance were the elaborate grave markers of the village's famous sea captains, "that for value and sculpture cannot be equalled in any part of Newfoundland."

As local entrepreneurs began to go bankrupt, George

Crosbie realized he would either have to leave Brigus or suffer the same fate. Several prominent Brigus families headed for New York, Boston or Canada, but Crosbie chose to remain in Newfoundland. With that decision, there was really only one place for an ambitious entrepreneur to go — St. John's. In 1884, the forty-six-year-old merchant pulled up stakes and moved his family to the city that was frequently referred to as the "emporium" of Newfoundland. A bustling trading hub, St. John's was now the undisputed centre of the fishery, partly because the St. John's merchants were the only ones who had access to the larger amounts of capital needed to invest in the new steam-powered fishing vessels.

According to a diarist of the day, quoted in Joey Smallwood's *Book of Newfoundland*, the commercial scene that greeted George Crosbie in his new city of 25,000 looked something like this:

> You will see one shop ornamented with the sign of a white polar-bear, another with a big black seal, here a dog over a door, there a golden codfish. One noticeable thing is the startling frequency of drinking-shops. Every second store seems to be 'Licensed to sell Ale, Wine, and Spiritous Liquors.'
>
> Through the streets drive little fish carts drawn by diminutive, shaggy horses. Burly, red-whiskered men in blue guernseys walk along trailing heavy cod in their hands. A knot of bulky, black dogs are snarling over some fish refuse. There are scores of dogs. You see them prowling the streets, roaming with the children, or sunning themselves in doorways. No matter where you go, you are always knocking against some bass-voiced dog or other. Everybody owns one.

A congenial enough place, but one that could use a little refinement. George Crosbie, eager to put his hand to a new undertaking, decided to supply some. Very shortly after landing in St. John's, he bought a hotel. "Knight's Home" had been built twenty years earlier by Samuel Knight. The premises were in bad repair, and Crosbie spent months personally renovating and redecorating the dining rooms and the ballroom and installing modern washrooms. In the process, he taught his three eldest sons, Thomas, Walter and George, the plastering trade. When the newly christened Central Hotel reopened on May 1, 1886, a well-ventilated smoking room had been added, as well as a billiards room. The new enterprise boasted all the latest comforts, including the use of the first telephone service in Newfoundland, which was installed by the Anglo-American Telegraph Company next door to the hotel, above John Lindberg's jewellery store.

Five years after the family moved to St. John's, Martha Ellen Crosbie, George and Martha's third child, reached back to her Brigus roots for a husband. On January 9, 1889, the intrepid "Nelson" married Captain Henry Bellamy Bartlett, the youngest son of Abraham and Elizabeth Bartlett. "Harry" Bartlett had grown up on the sea, fishing every summer from the family establishment in Turnavick in Labrador and making the annual spring sealing expedition on his father's ship, the S.S. *Panther*. At twenty-one, in his first voyage as master of a ship, he took the family schooner, the *General Grant*, to St. John's to take on gear and supplies. In 1889, at the age of twenty-six, he became skipper of the sealing vessel *Nimrod*, which he took to the hunt for the next three years. In 1893 and 1894, he commanded the sealer *Algerine* and between voyages kept up the family tradition of piloting explorers through the northern ice fields. Although Bartlett was often away, he and Ellie had a happy, if doomed, union.

For the next six years, the Central Hotel prospered, in part because of the increase in travel caused by the new Newfoundland railway. It soon became one of the most popular dining establishments in St. John's. Looking for a way to get a further competitive advantage, George Crosbie purchased Clovelly Farm on Logy Bay Road to supply the hotel with fresh meat and produce. The elimination of a middleman enabled Crosbie to keep his rates lower than the competition — a modest $1.50 a day. Yet another service offered by the enterprising businessman was an in-house sewing machine franchise. Crosbie became the Newfoundland agent for White sewing machines. (In the decades ahead, Newfoundland businessmen would compete fiercely to become the manufacturer's agent for a popular product, eager for the steady flow of commissions that were independent of the fickle fishery.)

While their father was busy making his mark in St. John's, his three sons followed the time-honoured tradition of leaving Newfoundland to find their fortunes. Equipped with the skills of the plastering trade, the three young Crosbies headed for New York. Thomas, the eldest, soon returned to St. John's, where he worked as an articling clerk in the law office of Morrison, Morine, and Gibbs, applying to the Newfoundland bar in 1895. Thereafter, he mysteriously sank from sight. He never appeared at family functions and his name is even stricken from subsequent family death notices, including his mother's in 1924.

After a lengthy period in the United States, his brother, George Lamont Crosbie, eventually made his way to Nova Scotia, where he bought an apple orchard in the Annapolis Valley. George had four children, three sons and a daughter, all of whom grew up in Nova Scotia. One son, Alexander George Crosbie, returned to Newfoundland in the 1940s and became a salesman for one of Newfoundland's leading dry-goods stores, Bowring Brothers of St. John's.

Walter, who left home at seventeen, kept the closest ties with the family of any of the expatriate Crosbie sons. He regularly returned home for visits and married a Newfoundlander, Mary Rebecca Pursell, a talented musician from Bay Roberts. The couple had five children, the first two in New York and the remaining three in Bay Roberts. In his wandering years, Walter's prowess as a master plasterer and masonry contractor had won him work as far away as Bermuda. On his return to Newfoundland, he put his talents to work on some of St. John's finest buildings, including the Nickel, Star and Majestic Theatres and the Cochrane Street United Church.

The boys weren't the only ones to leave home. In February 1892, another of the Crosbie daughters took a husband. Margaret, George and Martha's first child, married Charles Rogers, the second son of the Honourable Benjamin Rogers of Alberton, Prince Edward Island. The wedding took place just after Valentine's Day in her father's St. John's residence.

It was the beginning of an enduring Crosbie connection with Canada's smallest province.

The newlyweds moved to Summerside, where their two children, Olga and Graham, were born. While visiting her sister in P.E.I., Jennie Crosbie, George and Martha's youngest daughter, met her future husband, Thomas Woodman. Ironically, the transplanted Crosbie sisters feuded for years for reasons that no one remembers. But they retained close ties with their relatives in Newfoundland. A parade of Crosbie nieces and nephews went to school in P.E.I., and honeymooning Newfoundland Crosbies made a point of visiting Margaret and Jennie on their way to more exotic destinations.

George Crosbie continued to consolidate the family business until a dark day in July wiped out the fruits of his labours and two-thirds of St. John's in the same disastrous stroke. The summer of 1892 was hot, dry and windy, a sultry season of smoke and fire. On July 8 of that year, the two o'clock temperature in the city climbed to a sweltering 87 degrees Fahrenheit and a strong wind from the northwest whipped the normally tranquil harbour into whitecaps. A haze from distant forest fires around Conception Bay hung over the city, suffusing the air with the faint smell of wood-smoke.

At four-thirty that afternoon, Tommy Fitzpatrick, a drayman, was smoking a pipe as he went about his chores in the stable of his employer, Timothy O'Brien. He stumbled and dropped his pipe, igniting some hay. Fitzpatrick wasn't overly concerned. He didn't know that the water supply to the city had been turned off that morning to lay new mains. Although it had been turned back on at three o'clock, the flow had not yet reached the junction of Freshwater and Pennywell Roads, the location of O'Brien's stable.

When Fitzpatrick went to get water to douse the flames, the pump was dry. He then discovered that a nearby reservoir tank had been emptied during a practice fire drill and no one had bothered to refill it. By five o'clock the stable was ablaze. Without water to fight the fire, which was being fanned by high winds, the flames quickly spread. The tinderbox of St. John's was about to be destroyed by fire for the third time in its history; this time, the destruction was to be truly catastrophic.

The inferno continued throughout the night. Everyone, including the Archbishop of St. John's, fought desperately to get it under control. The next day, with smoke rising from the charred ruins in the dawn light, the enormity of what had happened was laid bare for all to see. Most of the city had been burned to the ground, including two thousand homes, the major churches, all six newspaper printing plants, the entire business district and five hotels. All that was left of George Crosbie's Central Hotel was part of one stone wall and the chimney. Miraculously, no one had been killed, but eleven thousand people were homeless and $20 million worth of property had been destroyed. To make matters worse, only a quarter of the city's buildings were insured.

Almost immediately, Timothy O'Brien paid a price for the bad luck of having the fire that engulfed St. John's start on his premises: the horses previously stabled in the ill-fated building had their tongues cut out. Tommy Fitzpatrick, whose pipe had started the inferno, and who had been fired by O'Brien for his carelessness, was quickly arrested. No record survives to say whether the unfortunate man was ever convicted of committing the atrocity on O'Brien's horses.

George Crosbie had every reason to be crushed by the disaster, but he took the misfortune in stride. Now in his mid-fifties, the tireless merchant immediately set to work rebuilding his shattered business. Within days of the fire, he found temporary quarters in a large store on a nearby city street that, miraculously, had been spared by the flames. He worked day and night renovating the interior of the building and, on September 1, just before the cold weather set in, he moved his guests into the new premises. His clients remained loyal, as a newspaper account of the day made clear: "Nothing showed more plainly the esteem and respect in which both he [Crosbie] and his kind lady were held, than that, though better accommodation could at that time have been obtained elsewhere, nearly all his friends from Canada, the States or other parts of the island, remained true to him, preferring rather the temporary discomfort than sever congenial relations."

Since most of the city's lodging places had been destroyed, including the Atlantic Hotel, which had been his main competition before the fire, Crosbie sensed that the time was right to build a bigger and more ambitious establishment. He bought property on Duckworth Street, where the old *Courier* newspaper offices had been, and went to work clearing the site of his second hotel, engaging W. T. Whiteway as architect and Messieurs E. & G. Darcy as builders.

The plans called for a four-storey hotel that could accommodate eighty guests, with a dining room large enough to feed them all at one sitting. The hotel had eighty feet of frontage on Duckworth Street and boasted electricity, hot-water heating, bathrooms on every floor and a telephone with a number that showed the extent of the service in those days — 107!

Just before the new hotel was officially opened, tragedy struck again. In 1893, Ellie's husband, Captain Harry Bartlett, piloted Peary's expedition to northern Greenland, returning aboard the S.S. *Falcon* the following year to take the explorer back to Philadelphia. His wife Ellie accompanied him on the trip. After loading the *Falcon* with coal for the return voyage to Newfoundland, Captain Bartlett, who feared a rough crossing, decided to send his wife home aboard a different ship.

The precaution saved Ellie's life. The *Falcon* went down with all hands in a hurricane off New York on October 9, 1894, the crew disappearing without a trace beneath the grey and unforgiving Atlantic. A few months later, Ellie gave birth to the couple's second daughter, Elizabeth. In the years to come, Ellie would more than live up to her reputation for toughness, running a business, raising her two daughters and then a second family when she remarried four years later.

Two months after the loss of his son-in-law, George Crosbie opened the second Central Hotel, the largest and best-appointed establishment in St. John's. Already clouded by personal tragedy, the opening on December 10, 1894, was inauspicious for another reason. While Crosbie's guests were lounging in their hot baths or sampling the fare in the new hotel's dining room, the Union and Commercial Banks collapsed. Their demise was the result of a British bank calling loans the Commercial Bank couldn't repay. The Commercial Bank, in turn, began calling in loans from its clients, loans the merchants couldn't honour because the money had already been advanced to fishermen for the spring fishing season. Without the money to pay the British bank, the Commercial Bank was forced to lock its doors. This prompted a run on Newfoundland's other commercial bank, the Union, which was also forced to cease operations.

"Black Monday" ushered in a period of financial chaos that threatened to lead to the political disintegration of the colony. Paper money was suddenly worthless, and employers were forced to lay off large numbers of workers to keep afloat. In a desperate attempt to keep commerce alive, several of the merchant princes of Water Street issued their own scrip to meet their payrolls. It was thumb-in-the-dike economics that couldn't hold back the deluge for long. Bread riots soon broke out and a hungry population took to feeding itself by looting local stores. St. John's was one short step away from anarchy and the authorities knew it.

The government petitioned London for sailors to keep the peace and an immediate million dollar loan to restore financial order. It got the sailors. Embarrassed by his failure to secure the necessary emergency funds, Liberal Premier A. F. Goodridge resigned from office. Daniel Greene was sworn in as his replacement on December 13, 1894, only to step down fifty days later after he, too, was unable to get financing to see the colony through the crisis. Sir William Whiteway then jumped into the breach, becoming premier on February 8, 1895.

Desperate to find a way out of the financial crisis, the governor of Newfoundland, Sir Terence O'Brien, sent an urgent message to the Governor-General of Canada suggesting that Canada and Newfoundland resume negotiations for union — the classic Newfoundland reaction during times of financial panic. The discussions were unsuccessful and, because of the remarkable intervention of another Whiteway minister, Sir Robert Bond, ultimately unnecessary. By pledging his personal fortune of $100,000, Bond was able to secure a $3-million loan in London. The economy rebounded, the crisis passed, and with it, Newfoundland's interest in joining Canada.

But George Crosbie didn't live to enjoy the burst of prosperity that followed Newfoundland's brush with financial disaster. Three months after the opening of his new hotel and the chaos of "Black Monday," the worn-out merchant "exchanged mortality for the larger life," the victim of a sudden, unspecified illness. Like his father, Thomas, he was fifty-nine when he died. As the record of successive generations would prove, it was a dangerous age for Crosbie men.

George Crosbie had only lived in St. John's for ten years, but the cream of the city's business establishment turned out for his funeral, including the Masonic Lodge which held an emergency meeting the day before he was buried and mourned him in full regalia. George Herder crafted the casket that carried him through the city streets to the General Protestant Cemetery, but its gleaming wood was barely visible through the mounds of wreaths and flowers that adorned it — a mark of the respect in which this industrious Scotsman, who had chosen Newfoundland as his home, was held.

James Murray, an old friend of the deceased's, recorded an incident that took place just days before George Crosbie died. It was typical of the eulogies that marked the businessman's passing: "It was only one day last week that I met Mr. Crosbie on Water Street when collecting for the Athenaeum Library, and with the goodness of heart for which he was proverbial, and which made him so popular with all classes, he subscribed five pounds, saying pleasantly, 'It will go hard with me if I can't help you to that extent.' "

After a mere thirty-five years on the island, George Crosbie had risen from a tradesman in outport Newfoundland to one of the city's most enterprising businessmen, rebounding from a variety of harsh blows along the way. But his contribution to the development of St. John's and of Newfoundland went much deeper than the impressive facade of the Central Hotel, whose paint, in time, would crack and fade in the salt air. George Crosbie's real legacy was the remarkable children he left behind. In the generation to come they would build on their father's ambition, establishing not so much a dynasty, in the normal sense of the word, as a rough-and-tumble tradition of involvement that would put Crosbies at the heart of Newfoundland's affairs from that day forward.

Up or down, they were a force to be reckoned with.

CHAPTER 4

The Crosbie Hotel

ON THE DEATH of her husband in 1895, the family business passed into the hands of Martha Ellen Crosbie, who was then fifty-six. Suffering as she did from chronic asthma, it was too much for the aging matriarch to run the hotel on her own. With her older sons living either outside St. John's or off the island altogether, "Grannie" Crosbie turned to her second-youngest boy, John, for help. Just nineteen, the remarkable teenager was already inured to a life of responsibility well beyond his years. He readily became his mother's strong right hand, though running the family business was not exactly the sort of life he had had in mind.

John Chalker Crosbie had graduated at sixteen from the Methodist College in St. John's in 1892, intending to become a doctor. But the great fire of that summer put his academic plans on hold, pressing him into the family effort to rebuild the Central Hotel. At the same time, he learned what he could from his father and older brother Walter about the plastering trade. (The most important thing he learned was that he didn't like it.) Then, shortly after the new premises opened, his father died, and with him, young John's dream of studying medicine.

As an economy measure, Grannie Crosbie took up residence in the hotel after her husband's death. The first thing she and John did was change the name from the Central to the Crosbie Hotel, a tribute to the dogged industry of the man who had built it and the family's emerging self-awareness. But young John was too ambitious to be satisfied with the lot of a hotelier, however successful the enterprise might prove to be. As soon as the business was on a solid footing — the Crosbies were catering to three thousand customers a year by the turn of the century — he turned to other ventures. His place at the Crosbie Hotel was taken by his sister, Ellie, who purchased the business from her mother in 1901.

Ellie, or "Aunt Ellie," as she was known in the family, had used the years since her first husband's tragic death to rebuild a life for herself and her two daughters, Sybil and Elizabeth. In 1898 she married Sam Bell, a forty-five-year-old widower from Grand Bank whose first wife had been Sarah Lake, daughter of James Lake of Fortune, a very prominent Newfoundland fish merchant. Her second husband was a talented shipwright who helped the Simpson Construction Company build the first St. John's dry dock in 1885. He handled major repair contracts and did such a good job on the S.S. *Rotterdam* that its owners exhibited the vessel at its home port of Newcastle-on-Tyne. Bell was regarded as the leading expert in his field in Newfoundland. Although he would be appointed to Newfoundland's Upper House by two premiers, the unassuming Mason and Methodist remained neutral in politics and studiously low-key in private life — a far cry from the robustly partisan and public family into which he had married.

Being the wife of an accomplished shipwright brought its little rewards. Delighted with a yacht Bell had built for him, a wealthy Scottish railway baron invited Sam and Ellie on a lengthy tour of the British Isles aboard the new vessel. But except for that romantic junket, the marriage seemed to be an alliance against loneliness, or as Sam Bell's grandson put it, "I think grandfather went his own way. He lived at home, but he did his own thing. He and my grandmother, I guess, both having second marriages, married for companionship."

Aunt Ellie remained a domineering and, to some extent, pioneering force throughout her second marriage. She was one of the first women in Newfoundland to bob her hair, twenty years before the flappers created a vogue for shorter styles. She also hired a woman to act as her office manager at the hotel, a position usually reserved for men. As Randy Bell recalled his grandmother, "She wasn't interested in whether men or women should do it; if it had to be done, she just wanted to get on with it."

Ironically, Ellie was also a traditionalist. She regularly attended the Gower Street United Church, where she and the minister of the day played out a weekly ritual. Every Sunday, Ellie would arrive a few minutes late for the service, and the accommodating cleric would stand in the pulpit, coughing and shuffling, until she made her way down the aisle and took her place in her pew. An understanding smile passed between them, and only then would the service begin.

Ellie was less indulgent on her own turf than the good minister was on his. In the fine weather, the hotel staff was lined up outside so that their mistress could inspect their uniforms, bows and aprons — a habit she continued with her household servants when she moved into her private residence at 18 Rennies Mill Road.

As the chatelaine of a fine house, Ellie watched her money with the same eagle eye she cast over her staff. It was the custom at the time to go to the estate auctions of acquaintances to buy a remembrance. At one of these auctions, Ellie bought a cut-glass perfume bottle to remind her of a particular friend. But when she brought it home, a relative pointed out a small chip in the neck of the bottle. The keepsake went back and a refund was promptly demanded and received: one did not waste one's money on inferior goods, or allow slick auctioneers to pull the wool over one's eyes — not if one knew the value of a dollar — or, in the case of Ellie's chipped perfume bottle, fifty cents!

Ellie's frugality took many forms, including a certain reluctance to render unto Caesar what was Caesar's, as John Crosbie learned. Returning from a trip abroad, she was met at dockside by her brother, who was by that time Newfoundland's minister of Customs and Excise. "He went down to the pier to meet her and he went on board and said, 'If you've got everything declared, you can come ashore with me, you don't have to wait for the customs officer.' She said,

'I've got nothing to declare, Jack.' With that she started down the gangway and there was a loud plunk as a large bottle of French perfume fell out of her bloomers which, of course, were the old elastic-legged kind," one of her relatives, John Perlin, remembered.

This would have been embarrassment enough for any minister of Customs and Excise, but it was the more so for John Crosbie; he had just hired an official whose specific task it was to stamp out the plague of smuggling that was depriving Newfoundland's treasury of its rightful due!

In keeping with her childhood nickname, Ellie appears to have prevailed in most important decisions affecting the family. Although she and her husband both had children from their previous marriages, only Ellie's became part of the new family unit. Bell's six children from his marriage to Sarah Lake — four girls and two boys — were farmed out to relatives by mutual agreement. To cement the new relationship, Ellie quickly had two more children with Sam Bell — Robert in 1900 and Charles in 1901. She doted on her second family with the same devotion she showed her girls from the Bartlett marriage. A great deal of emphasis was placed on education, which sometimes put strains on the relationship with her rural relatives. One summer, she sent young Charlie to her brother Walter's house "around the Bay." Later, back at his own dinner table in St. John's, Charlie said, "Pass I da butter, mudder." It would be a long time before he made another trip to Bay Roberts.

Both boys were eventually sent off to boarding school in Nova Scotia to get the best education Sam and Ellie could afford to give them — a decision that would deal the couple the hardest blow of their marriage. Robert Bell died of a burst appendix at Kings College in Windsor, Nova Scotia, at the age of eleven. Travelling was always difficult to arrange from Newfoundland and it took Ellie a week to reach her dead son and his ten-year-old brother, Charlie, who was attending the same Annapolis Valley private school. Both boys were brought back to Newfoundland, one to be buried, the other to be doted on with all the care his grief-stricken mother could muster.

With the help of her husband, Ellie ran a tight ship at the

Crosbie Hotel. But there was more to her than spiritual flint. To her father's business sense she added a natural grace, which gave her establishment a warmth that had been lacking in George Crosbie's earlier operations. Relaxing her Methodist upbringing in the interests of commerce, she added a smoking room, just as her father had in the original Central Hotel. It quickly became a favourite haunt for the young bankers and businessmen of St. John's. Many of them spent the long winter evenings in front of a roaring fire discussing the burning issues of the day — the new railroad, reciprocity with the United States and union with Canada.

By far the hottest topic was Confederation. With the colony drifting perilously close to bankruptcy, the greatest potential benefit of joining Canada was financial. Knowing that, Ottawa had put together a seductive economic package it hoped the storm-tossed colony couldn't refuse. The Dominion of Canada would assume $8.3 million of Newfoundland's $16-million debt, throw in $6,000 per mile towards the unfinished portion of the ruinously expensive Newfoundland railway and grant the colony a subsidy equal to $50 per head for each citizen in the colony. That, according to a letter written to the pro-Confederate *Evening Herald*, worked out to an annual subsidy of roughly $400,000 per year, less than half of what it actually cost to run the colony. Still, the paper staunchly supported joining Canada, as this 1895 editorial makes clear:

"The tide is rising fast and will soon sweep away the old rotten barriers that have been obstructions in the past. The ancient superstitions, born of ignorance, and nursed by deceitful cliques, which have brooded so long over the public mind, and blinded our people to their true interests, are vanishing like shadows at the morn; and in union with the great Dominion they are getting to see that their future strength and advance must lie."

On the other side of the debate, the anti-Confederate *Evening Telegram* eulogized the premier of the day when he announced in the House of Assembly that, thanks to a loan from the United States that ended the colony's financial crisis, Newfoundland would be able to meet all its financial obligations in 1895:

"Sir William Whiteway, in moving the adjournment of the House till Monday, (Saturday being the date fixed by proclamation to celebrate the Queen's birthday), stated that Terra Nova [Newfoundland] had so far triumphed over her financial difficulties as to be able to respond to all the demands that would be made upon the Government on the 30th of June next. This practically places the colony once more on the highroad to prosperity. We appealed to the Mother Country and how did Mrs. Britannia treat us? Why she refused a paltry guarantee of twenty thousand pounds. . . . Then we approached Canada, her oldest daughter, but with no better result. Now, as a *dernier ressort*, we have applied to the American people, and THE HELPING HAND HAS BEEN EXTENDED TO US."

Confederation failed, and the lyrics to a popular anti-Confederate song from 1869 captured the mood as the clock ticked down to the turn of the century.

Hurrah for our own native isle, Newfoundland,
Not a stranger shall hold one inch of its strand,
Her face turns to Britain, her back to the Gulf,
Come near at your peril, Canadian Wolf.

Arguments surrounding Confederation and other public issues often erupted around the fireplace of the Crosbie Hotel, but things never got out of hand as long as the formidable Ellie Bell patrolled the halls of the popular establishment.

Though consecrated to business, the hotel was also available for the pleasure of the Crosbies. Ellie kept a special drawing room, number six, for their exclusive use. The Crosbie children who attended nearby schools went there for lunch, and John Crosbie often took his meals around the gleaming Chippendale table with his favourite sister whose business advice he respected. Throughout their lives, neither Ellie nor John took major business decisions without consulting each other first.

During school breaks, Crosbie children who lived outside the city came to the hotel for holidays as the guests of their grandmother. Although she appeared severe in her rimless eyeglasses, high-necked black dress and dainty white cap, the impression was softened by her gentle disposition. When Walter's children visited from Bay Roberts, Grannie Crosbie handed out fruit and other delicacies they didn't often see at home, including special biscuits that she kept in a tin under her bed. She even took the drive belt off of her treadle sewing machine so the children could make the wheels spin around without hurting themselves.

When the children of her youngest brother, Robert, came to the hotel, they would invade Grannie's private sitting room and make a tent out of her long black underskirts by draping them over a chair and pinning the hem to the wall. Only after Grannie retired for her afternoon nap would Janet and Robert Jr. creep into their makeshift casino and play cards — a forbidden pastime in Grannie's Methodist domain. Their homage to religion was stealth; the cards were always returned to their hiding place beneath a piece of furniture long before their grandmother awakened.

Aunt Ellie provided a strict but fair counterpoint to her mother's gentle indulgence. One day, when Janet Crosbie was lunching with her aunt, an incident occurred that demonstrated both traits. The maid had finished serving the soup and main course when Aunt Ellie herself brought in a special pudding, which she liked to cut with a flourish at the table. There was a ledge bordering the high, moulded ceiling on which Ellie's handsome collection of Wedgwood plates was displayed. As the statuesque Ellie cut away at the pudding, a touch too vigorously perhaps, an enormous meat platter slipped off the ledge and crashed on the floor behind her, sending shards of china skittering across the wooden floor in every direction.

Ellie started violently and let out such a screech that her luncheon guest started laughing and couldn't stop. Ellie was not amused and exiled her niece to her room. Moments later, a maid appeared with the message that her aunt wanted to see her. Trembling at what might lie in store for her, Janet was astonished to get her freedom — and an apology — from a repentant Aunt Ellie. This was no small thing coming from a woman whose reputation in the family was not built on rescinding her own orders or expressing contrition on those rare occasions when she did.

The Crosbie Hotel benefited from Ellie's reputation as a prodigious collector almost as much as it did from her managerial skills. It was loaded with little treasures she'd accumulated over the years. A shameless pack-rat, she scoured hundreds of auctions, where she was quick to spot a good buy and ruthless in making sure she prevailed over other bidders. Even family members weren't safe from her acquisitive marauding. Walter Crosbie's wife, Mary, hooked rugs to help pass the long, hard winters, but the best of them had a habit of making their way back to St. John's in Ellie's valise after a visit. "Roll up the rugs" was the way of announcing that Aunt Ellie was on her way to Bay Roberts. (Years later when relatives were cleaning out Ellie's attic after her death in 1941, they found three dining-room sets, a large trunk of silver, bolts of damask silk brought back from her trip to England and a complete place setting for forty-eight!)

Dominant though she was, Ellie wasn't the only Crosbie who built on her father's dream. Robert Crosbie, George and Martha Ellen's youngest child, helped out at the hotel and ran the farm that his father had so prudently acquired to supply the business with fresh meat and vegetables. For Robert, who was something of a Byronic character, settling down had not been easy. He had run away to New York in his teens, only to be rescued by his sister Jennie, who found him there by accident and brought him back to live with her in Prince Edward Island.

After returning to Newfoundland, the restless Robert took a job at the hotel. On a bitterly cold night in January 1903, the guests at the Crosbie Hotel were awakened by a fire alarm. Robert was the first to respond, dashing to the ground-floor flat to find that the furnace room was ablaze. The furnace had been stoked up higher than usual to counter the frosty weather; soot in the pipes had been ignited by the terrific heat, quickly spreading the fire through the joisting and inner ceiling to the upper floors. Robert single-handedly fought the flames with a chemical fire-retardant until a guest rang the alarm at the foot of nearby Prescott Street and the fire department arrived.

When his brother-in-law, Sam Bell, retold the story years later, he always expressed the opinion that without Robert's quick action, the Crosbie Hotel would have burned to the ground. *The Evening Telegram* of that day recorded Robert's act of bravery, calling him one of "the lions of the hour."

In 1915 Robert married Ethel Myra Keeping. Ethel was a great beauty, but in some quarters of the family the match was greeted with tacit disapproval, most noticeably in the chilly zones of John Crosbie's household. Although no one came right out and said it, there was a sense of disappointment that the dashing Robert had married the daughter of an Anglo-American Telegraph Company worker, instead of one of the daughters of the St. John's establishment.

But if the love-match was a disappointment to others, Robert and Ethel didn't seem to notice. The couple had five children and lived happily in Clovelly's large farmhouse bordered by lilacs and spring flowers. The house itself had a stone pantry for processing the dairy products that were used at the hotel and an ice-house to keep the milk cold. The heart of the living quarters was a huge dining room with a slate fireplace. After dinner, Robert and his children would move to the living room where he would sit in his favourite chair while they combed his luxuriant black hair with an ebony-backed brush. There were five bedrooms upstairs, one of which was always reserved for Grannie Crosbie, who doted on Robert and spent the summers at Clovelly. If any of the children were sick, they bedded in with Grannie, who would spend hours rocking their cradle with her foot. Surrounded by his adoring wife and children and his two collie dogs, Kipp and Pearl, Robert was much happier running Clovelly than he had ever been helping out around the hotel.

As *The Evening Telegram* had been there to report his heroism, it was also there on August 25, 1924 to record Robert's untimely death. He was forty-five. The obituary noted that he had passed away after an illness of ten days, leaving a wife, five children, a mother and six brothers and sisters to mourn him. The cause of death was in fact kidney failure brought on by severe alcoholism, or "the family failing" as it would come to be known. For several years, Robert had periodically "gone on a bat," succumbing for weeks at a time, despite Ethel's heroic efforts to help him battle his drinking. The day he died, his beloved collie, Pearl, took to the field in front of the farmhouse at Clovelly and whined for hours — a story Ethel never tired of telling her dazed and heartbroken children.

After Robert's wake, which was held at John Crosbie's Devon Place residence, a family decision was made to relieve some of the pressure on Ethel, who was then three months pregnant, by helping her raise her large family. Robert's son, Robert Jr., was sent to school in St. John's and lived with Aunt Ellie, while his brother, Graham, was raised by Aunt Margaret in Prince Edward Island. Their mother took over the running of Clovelly with the help of a hired man. If there was a problem, Ethel knew she could rely on "Uncle Jack," as John Crosbie was known in the family. When the child was born, she called her Roberta. Ethel put away the ebony-backed brush forever, but not her husband's memory. She remained a widow for the rest of her life.

The loss of her precious Robert was more than his elderly mother could bear. Three months after the family buried him in the General Protestant Cemetery — inexplicably without a grave-marker — they were laying Grannie Crosbie in the family plot beside George Graham, the man she had married sixty-two years earlier.

The Crosbies had been in the hotel business for nearly fifty years, but it was a chapter of the family's economic history that was drawing to an end. In 1926, Mrs. Bell's son Charlie returned from McGill to manage the hotel, but like John Crosbie before him, Charlie saw it as no more than a temporary measure. He was soon off to New York, where he lived for several years, before returning to Newfoundland in 1932 to start his own highly successful wholesale business. (When he finally married Ruth Hickman at thirty-nine, Ellie was so concerned that he would not be looked after properly that she provided him with a cook who knew how to prepare the food he liked!)

One of the last hurrahs for the hotel came on September 12, 1932, when VOGY, Newfoundland's first full-time commercial radio station, made its maiden broadcast from a studio in the Crosbie Hotel. Less that two years later, the radio station would move to the mammoth new Newfoundland Hotel. Built at a cost of $1,300,000, it was an enormous project that could only have been undertaken with government loan guarantees. Unable to compete with the new establishment, and lacking a family member interested in running the Crosbie Hotel, Ellie and Sam sold out in 1933. The hotel would operate under several different owners for the next fifty years until the city of St. John's had it torn down as a fire hazard in 1981.

Even the indomitable Ellie wore down in the years following the sale of the hotel, the iron in her spirit eventually weakened by the sad harvests of old age. There was little solace in her children and much to mourn. Her daughter Sybil married Hugh Anderson, brother of the dashing John Murray Anderson, or "Uncle Broadway," as he was quickly dubbed in the family. The two brothers got their start buying furniture in outport Newfoundland and reselling it in their New York antique store. Sybil supplemented the family income by running a children's specialty shop called "Christopher Robin's."

The brothers then branched out into show business, rivalling Florenz Siegfeld as theatrical producers. They discovered Bette Davis, among others, and after Ziegfeld's death, ran the famous Follies for several years. Then, suddenly, Sybil divorced her husband and Hugh Anderson was a forbidden subject in Ellie's home. Sybil eventually remarried and moved to the Caribbean island of Tobago where her second husband, a Montrealer named Hamilton Harrower, was chief of police.

Ellie's other daughter, Beth, ran an Elizabeth Arden shop in Washington, D.C., and remained single until her mid-forties. Although she lived in the United States, she met her husband at the officers' mess in St. John's while home on a visit. After a whirlwind romance, the couple was married in Bermuda. Aunt Ellie was not only in attendance, she insisted on giving the bride away, since Elizabeth's father, Captain Bartlett, was long since dead, as was her stepfather, Sam Bell, who died in 1930.

But once more tragedy darkened Ellie's long-awaited moment of happiness. A few months after the Bermuda wedding, Elizabeth died of a bowel blockage. She was the third child Ellie had buried during her long and difficult life, and the old woman lost the will to live. She died a few months after Beth on September 26, 1941 at the age of seventy-seven.

If she had experienced more than her share of grief, Ellie had at least lived long enough to see the Crosbies climb to the very pinnacle of commercial and political life in Newfoundland. George Graham Crosbie had wanted to establish a business, and Ellie had seen the dream through; her brother John went on to build an empire, and became a knight of the realm in the bargain.

CHAPTER 5

Sir John

ON A PERFECT autumn day in 1899, John Chalker Crosbie swaggered across the bridge connecting the East and West Harbours of Exploits Island with his new bride, striding towards a business empire, a tumultuous political career, and a new century. The twenty-three-year-old's lifelong partner in all of these pursuits was the dark-haired and determined Mitchie Anne Manuel, daughter of Josiah and Elizabeth Manuel. The Manuels were the leading merchant and shipbuilding family in the rugged outport community on Notre Dame Bay. Such was the influence of the Manuels, who owned much of Exploits, that the official opening of the bridge was delayed so that the newlyweds could be the first to walk across it — the bride in a grey silk wedding gown and the groom in a black jacket and something that had never been seen before by the 517 residents of Exploits — dazzling white flannels.

Both families were sufficiently prominent that *The Daily Review* in St. John's carried a notice of the marriage. The Methodist minister of Exploits performed the ceremony, and a "Miss Davis" of New York and Mitchie Anne's older sister, Jennie, were bridesmaids. The best man was Chesley Arthur Manuel, the brother of the bride and namesake of the couple's first son, who would be born six years later. The wedding party left Exploits that night to catch the train at

Norris's Arm for the first leg of a five-week honeymoon through the United States, with a stop in Prince Edward Island to visit John's sisters, Margaret and Jennie, who by then had lived on the island for several years. The newlyweds were accompanied on the trip by John's sister, Ellie, and her second husband, Sam Bell.

There is not much doubt that the union was a love-match. John had first noticed Mitchie Anne in St. John's where she'd been sent to school by her education-conscious family. They met at the Cochrane Street Wesleyan Church, where she sat in her pew perfectly poised "with a nice lift to her head." Judging from family lore, her posture wasn't the only thing that attracted her future husband. But Mitchie Anne, or "Mippy," as John called her, was a stickler about good carriage; she once admonished her first granddaughter, June Bennett, to "stand up straight or I'm going to put a board down your back!" From young John's point of view, it was love at first sight, and he vowed to marry the pretty stranger who gave him a better reason to go to church regularly than his mother's dour insistence, or so the story goes.

It was an advantageous match for the ambitious young Crosbie who had balked at making a career out of running the Crosbie Hotel or following in his brother Walter's footsteps as a plasterer. The Crosbies had certainly been associated with Exploits through business and family ties since their early days in Brigus. The Manuels had built the *Kersage* for John's father, George Graham, and Martha Ellen, John's mother, had Exploits connections through the Chalker side of the family. The Manuels had been a force in Newfoundland since the 1750s and their pursuits might have inspired lustier ambitions in the young man, steeped as they were in the island's seafaring lore.

Mitchie Anne's father, Josiah, was one of thirteen children of Joseph and Elizabeth Manuel. Of their seven sons, all of whom became sea captains, Josiah had the keenest business mind. The Manuel men worked in the woods in winter, using the timber they cut to supply the family shipbuilding operation. In 1884, seven schooners and thirteen fishing vessels were built in Exploits, many of them by Josiah Manuel. Between the Labrador and inshore fishery, the tiny island outport landed more than a quarter of a million pounds of fish a year — a fact that hatched more than one mercantile plan in John Crosbie's busy head.

Josiah's wife, Elizabeth Butt, exemplified Captain Abraham Bartlett's comment on Newfoundland's apparently patriarchal society. "I command the ship," he said, "but my wife commands when I come off the ship." The mother of twelve children, only five of whom reached the age of majority, Elizabeth was always first up in the morning, making sure that the men, maids and gardener were at their chores. Mitchie Anne would later subject the Crosbie household to the same spartan regimen, prompting her daughter Olga to recall, "I would say my mother was the stronger character of my parents, in her own quiet way."

No one in the family ever recalled Mitchie Anne losing her temper or even raising her voice, possibly because her husband did enough bawling for any two adults. A very close family friend extended Olga Crosbie's remembrance of her mother, crediting Mitchie Anne with "being the power behind the throne," and "making Sir John": "The Crosbies were addicted to drink — I don't mean that in any nasty way — but she was a very strict woman. There's no doubt about it. Sir John would have gone on the rocks without her because of his drinking. You know, the trait has followed right through the Crosbie family. The women were predominant."

At the turn of the century, Newfoundland's economy was booming, based on high prices for salt fish. At that time, a small group of powerful merchants led by the Jobs, the Harveys and the Bowrings controlled fish-marketing in Newfoundland. They either owned outright the ships that took the fish to market or managed vessels owned by individual captains. They formed a tight and powerful convoy of privilege, and anyone trying to break into their charmed circle had to navigate some very rough water.

Shortly after returning from his honeymoon, John Crosbie decided to buck the odds and get into Newfoundland's most important business. He formed a partnership with the Manuel brothers to export fish to Spain and Portugal through a new firm, Crosbie and Company. The Manuel connection was important, bringing with it a reliable supply of fish and a potential source of vessels to take them to market. Crosbie began as a managing partner, but three years later he bought out his associates and became the sole proprietor of the firm.

The eyes of the princes of Water Street followed the young upstart as he set up shop in the old Duder premises in St. John's. The Duders had been one of the biggest fish merchants in Newfoundland, boasting more than two hundred vessels in their fleet before the company was wiped out in the bank crash of 1894. The former proprietor, Edward Duder, had been unable to repay a loan of $668,676 — an enormous sum at a time when a dollar a day was considered to be a good working wage.

If John Crosbie had had reservations about nailing on laths and mixing materials when he was learning the plastering trade from brother Walter, he stoically pursued his odoriferous apprenticeship in the fish business, working elbow to elbow with his employees on the dock, even though the salt used in the curing process caused his hands to break out in painful attacks of eczema. His impatience to get ahead made him oblivious to such minor annoyances. In jig time, he became an expert on the seven grades of fish — Choice, Merchantable, Madeira, West-India, Labrador #1, Labrador #2 and Cullage — each with its own characteristics and price.

To Crosbie, no knowledge was merely theoretical. When his company later got into a dispute over the purchase price of a shipload of fish from south coast fish brokers A. S. Rendell & Company, he was quick to put his expertise to work. Crosbie and Company agreed to pay $13,833 for Rendell's fish, subject to cull; once the cargo had been inspected, they reduced the price to $11,348. Rendell's agent, Robert Webb, objected to the strictness of the cull, but Crosbie was unmoved: "I do not interfere with my cullers. If Webb does not like that, let him take it away." Rendell paid the lesser amount into court and sued Crosbie, arguing that he had been cheated on the cull. The court saw it otherwise. Crosbie and Company got the fish at the lower rate, and Rendell was stuck with the court costs.

Having mastered the grading and handling of fish, Crosbie's next task was to learn the markets — a job he undertook with typical bravura. Although he had a sales agent in London, Crosbie decided to pay a personal visit to the places where his fish was being sold. In the spring of 1902, he boarded the *Dictator*, the first vessel to fly the red Crosbie "C" on its white pennant, and sailed for Spain. Of the many lessons he learned, not the least important was that this mercantile Sinbad was no sailor; the miserable landlubber became so violently seasick that at one point in the voyage he called Captain Cyril Horwood into his cabin and made out his will!

Fortunately for its tormented proprietor, the *Dictator*, a small, two-masted vessel, was exceptionally fast and made the port of Gibraltar in eleven days, when fifteen would have been considered a swift crossing. Once on land, Crosbie quickly recovered from his illness and visited the markets he had come to inspect. His business done, he sacrificed his berth on the *Dictator* and made alternate arrangements for the return trip to Newfoundland — on an ocean liner with a comfortable stateroom.

As a businessman, John Crosbie was quick to spot talent and just as swift to reward it, inspiring a fierce loyalty in the men who sailed under the Crosbie flag. Cyril Horwood, for example, remained a senior captain with Crosbie and Company for forty-six years. The *Dictator* was dubbed "Crosbie's Training Home" because it was always the first command for new Crosbie captains.

Charlie Moore was bosun on the *Dictator* when John Crosbie made his marketing voyage to Spain. Crosbie was impressed with the young man and promised that, when he was ready to assume a command of his own, a vessel would be found for him. The second time Moore signed articles with the Crosbies, it was as captain of the *Dictator*. The distinguished sailor would command thirteen ships under the Crosbie flag and when, in the last winter of Josiah Manuel's life, he built the *Nina L.*, named for Crosbie's daughter, Captain Moore was put in command.

In the days before radio communications, the shipping business was no place for the faint-hearted. From the moment a vessel's sails disappeared over the horizon, there was no contact until the captain sent a telegram notifying the owner that he had made port. John Crosbie was temperamentally well suited to the nerve-wracking enterprise, as an incident remembered by his daughter, Dolly, makes clear. After one of his ships had embarked for Spain, he turned to the always apprehensive Mitchie Anne and said, "Well now, Mitchie, we don't need to worry because we can't hear anything until they make port." Lady Luck rewarded his fatalistic attitude to the business. Although he would lose ships to both fire and storm during his many years in the shipping business, he never lost a crew.

Despite the connection with the Manuels, most of Crosbie's sailing fleet came from Nova Scotia, including the *Jessie L. Smith*, the *Ich Dien* (from the motto on the crest of the Prince of Wales meaning, "I serve"), the *Jean*, the *Lucille*, the *Lady Napier* and the *Cluthra*. It was simple economics. With the dawn of the steam age, the market for wooden vessels collapsed overnight. Magnificent Lunenburg schooners like the *Jean* could be purchased for a fraction of their real value, and Crosbie was quick to take advantage of these floating bargains.

The Newfoundland Quarterly for July 1909 described John Crosbie as "one of the younger of our merchants, an aggressive and enterprising businessman" with "five splendid foreign-going vessels" that freighted his fish to a variety of international destinations. The *Quarterly* noted that the young merchant had won his place in the commercial world of St. John's "by sheer ability and perseverance." He was chief stockholder and managing director of Crosbie and Company, which became the Newfoundland Produce Company as his fish business grew. Struck, perhaps, by the business opportunities afforded by shipping's calamities, he branched out into marine and fire insurance, ultimately forming an association with Lloyd's of London.

Since his mid-twenties, John Crosbie had been eyeing politics, partly to vary his preoccupation with commercial pursuits, partly to augment them. The up-and-coming merchant made his first appearance in the bullring of Newfoundland public life as a Conservative in 1904, running for the House of Assembly in the rural seat of Bay-de-Verde. If, as some people observed, "he probably thought the people should elect him because he was [a] Crosbie," the young candidate soon learned that cocky self-assuredness wasn't enough to make him an instant political success. He lost by a handful of votes, but immediately determined to run again at the next election.

The political manoeuvrings leading up to the 1908 election were elaborate, to say the least. The popular Edward Morris suddenly resigned from the Liberal administration of Sir Robert Bond along with Michael Cashin, another young and ambitious politician whose path would cross Crosbie's more than once in their tumultuous careers. J. R. Bennett, the future father-in-law of John Crosbie's daughter Nina, followed them across the floor. They sat as Independent Liberals and formed a close alliance with the Conservative Opposition. Since the weak Conservatives did not have a capable leader, it wasn't long before the dynamic Morris was tacitly accepted as the de facto Leader of the Opposition.

On March 5, 1908 Morris issued a thirty-point manifesto announcing the creation of a new political creature called the People's Party (a misnomer of absurd proportions in the party's more mature years, when it became the shameless champion of big business). Several thousand outport men were in St. John's to sign on for the annual seal fishery when the manifesto was unveiled. After attending the huge public rally that launched it, the sealers eagerly carried news of the new party back home.

The manifesto was a populist document, holding out something for fishermen, farmers, the poor, trade unionists and the business community. Much was offered to win the support of this last group. Railway contractors were courted by the promise of more branch lines for the Newfoundland Railway and fish exporters were guaranteed subsidized steamship service to the West Indies — an important market for Newfoundland salt-cod. Deeply involved in the fish business, John Crosbie cast his political fate with the People's Party, knowing better than most how dramatically his shipping costs would go down if Morris formed the government and followed through on his promise.

Sir Robert Bond was not unduly concerned by these political upstarts and their unrealistic, if ringing, manifesto. Having presided over the settlement of the French Shore problem that finally ended French territorial rights on the island of Newfoundland after centuries of conflict, he was the greatest statesman the colony had so far produced. He was also the man who had personally saved the colony from financial collapse in the 1890s and who had negotiated the Bond–Blaine and Bond–Hay free-trade agreements with the United States — only to see them quickly scuttled by Britain at Canada's insistence. Canada's governor-general of the day, Lord Minto, feared that a Newfoundland–American reciprocity agreement would "encourage sympathies with our neighbours [the Americans], and if the sympathies of the island, as years go on, agree with the teachings of an advanced Monroe doctrine, we shall lose Newfoundland and with it, the command of the St. Lawrence." Furthermore, in the budget of 1907, there had even been a $125,000 surplus, a rarity in a place where the financial picture is usually expressed in more colourful ink.

But unfortunately for Premier Bond, fate was advancing in the streetcars of day-to-day desires rather than the carriages of statesmanship. Past accomplishments paled beside more topical — and scandalous — matters. A grand jury had been investigating conditions in the penitentiary, the lunatic asylum and the poorhouse in St. John's, and their report was released during the campaign of 1908, with unfelicitous results for the Liberals. It showed that children under the age of sixteen were imprisoned in the same cells as hardened criminals, some of whom were serving lengthy sentences for sex offences. The asylum was shamefully overcrowded, and the poorhouse was no more than an abattoir of hope where the old and the sick waited to die. The Bond administration quickly announced that land had been purchased for a new asylum, but the intended defence quickly became a new point of attack for the Opposition when it was revealed that the property in question had been purchased from a prominent Liberal supporter at an inflated price.

In the autumn of 1908, amid the swirl of these and other controversies, John Crosbie chose to run in the seat he had lost by a mere twelve votes four years earlier, Bay-de-Verde on the north shore of Conception Bay. Denominational rivalry was strong in the constituency and the electorate could swing either way. Morris opened his campaign with a whistle-stop tour of the seat, playing the anti-sectarian card to perfection. Donald Morison, a prominent Orangeman and future Justice minister, joined Morris on every platform and helped the Catholic politician condemn the Liberals as "fomentors of sectarian strife."

While the Liberal Party tried desperately to counter Morris's effective campaign, money poured into the coffers of the People's Party from Bond's enemies — Lord Grey in the Colonial Office (who knew Bond opposed Confederation and erroneously believed Morris favoured it), Canadian financial institutions and executives of the Reid railway interests. Many years later, Sir W. D. Reid, who became president of the Reid Newfoundland Company on the death of his tycoon father in 1908, claimed that he had personally contributed enough money to Morris to finance his entire campaign! It was chequebook politics at its most vindictive. After having concluded an extremely lucrative contract with the Conservative government in 1898, which gave them a virtual monopoly over Newfoundland's transportation and communications systems, the Reids were forced by Bond to renegotiate their sweetheart deal just two years later on far less favourable terms. They never forgave or forgot.

Another key factor that worked against the reelection of the Bond government was the disastrous drop in the price of fish, which still accounted for 70 percent of Newfoundland's exports at that time. In 1905, the government had been happy to take credit for the highest fish prices in nearly a hundred years, and when they dropped by half in the fall of 1908, Sir Robert could hardly avoid accepting the blame.

Newfoundlanders went to the polls on November 2, 1908, but it was a full nine days before the results were known. When the counting was finally done, the colony found itself in a constitutional crisis. Bond's Liberals and Morris's People's Party had each elected eighteen members. One of Morris's successful candidates was John Crosbie. In the crucial Conception Bay North constituencies, the Liberals won only two of seven seats — Harbour Grace by a single vote and Carbonear by fourteen. Overall, Bond's popular vote dropped from 60.4 percent in 1904 to 49.8 percent in 1908. The political bottom-line was clear: Catholics had deserted the Liberal Party, which depended on them, and voted in a block for Morris.

The constitutional deadlock was finally settled by a second election in which Morris won a convincing victory. It was a mini-revolution in Newfoundland politics. Morris's People's Party consisted of self-made men, distinct from the old merchant Tories who had grown corrupt and enervated. These were outport merchants on the way up, men who had made a good pass on a buoyant fishery and the railway boom and who were hungrily seeking more grist for their mill. "They were characteristically tough-minded, able, and more than a little ruthless. They were also ambitious, and as always in Newfoundland, where business alone provided none of the outlets for talent that it did in the United States or Canada, 'ambition' turned easily into 'political ambition'," wrote S. J. R. Noel. It is little wonder that John Crosbie felt comfortable in such company.

Crosbie's part in the election of 1909 was noteworthy for two reasons: he retained the seat he'd won in the 1908 election, and he nearly drowned the premier of Newfoundland in the process. While he and Sir Robert were campaigning in the outports, the hefty Mr. Crosbie, who in later life came to resemble a hogshead turned on end, managed to upset Mr. Bond as he was climbing up from a mailboat to the wharf at Western Bay.

Exactly what happened is unclear. According to one account, the incident was straightforward enough: someone gave the premier "a brutal kick in the chest, knocking him into the sea." Members of the Crosbie family maintain that the "someone" was John himself, although they say he merely stepped on Sir Robert's fingers as he was mounting the wharf rather than giving him a swift kick. Their wan smiles leave it to the imagination of their listener to decide whether this was done as an item of clumsiness or policy. For Bond, it was all the same: a non-swimmer, he was caught in a powerful undertow and would have drowned except for the heroics of the mailboat's crew. In a vitriolic attack on Crosbie nearly ten years later, the Liberal newspaper, *The Morning Post*, noted the episode and referred to Crosbie as "the same fellow who it is said was the man who engineered the dastardly attempt on Sir Robert Bond's life at Western Bay."

Just thirty-three, Crosbie entered the executive council of the Morris administration as minister without portfolio. Not surprisingly, Premier Morris supported new branch lines for the railway, just as he had promised to in both the 1908 and 1909 political campaigns. Although the settlement of the French Shore issue in 1904 had doubtless raised the spirits of Newfoundlanders, the railway was probably the chief reason for the heady optimism of the period. It had given Newfoundlanders cash purchasing power, in contrast to the credit system that had dominated commercial transactions for so long, and foreign capital was increasingly attracted to the colony as the railway opened up the interior. The railway also gave Newfoundlanders easier access to the outside world and to each other. By 1898, they could take the train from St. John's to Port aux Basques on the west coast of the island and connect with the S. S. *Bruce* for the trip across the Gulf of St. Lawrence to North Sydney, Nova Scotia.

The proprietors of the London *Daily Mail* formed the Anglo-Newfoundland Development Company in 1905 to construct a huge paper mill at Grand Falls, which was the first community in Newfoundland to be established out of sight and sound of the sea. In October 1909, when newsprint production began, it triggered a speculation boom in timber leases that Newfoundland's new entrepreneurs found irresistible. The railway provided contracts and legal fees and, as was the case in both Canada and the United States, a virtual honey-pot of political patronage.

Premier Morris swiftly rewarded the Reids for their financial support during the election with contracts to build 250 miles of branch lines into Bonavista, Grates Cove, Trepassey, Fortune and Bonne Bay — popular but financially ruinous projects that were announced in the Throne Speech of 1909. The Reids would get $15,000 per mile, which worked out to $3,750,000 all told — a princely sum that was paid out in gold rather than government debentures. To sweeten the deal, the company also received an operating bonus of four thousand acres of land for every mile of railway constructed. The million acres that went to the Reids under this arrangement were nothing to sneeze at, given that the grant included all mineral and timber rights. Work began on the Bonavista Branch without tenders being called and even before a contract had been approved by the legislature!

Despite the colony's national debt of nearly $23 million, John Crosbie endorsed his government's policy of railway expansion, largely because the extension would bring train service to his own riding. "The people demanded branch lines and the people will have them. The voice of the people is the voice of God," the member for Bay-de-Verde has often been credited with saying.

The words were quotable enough, but, contrary to what otherwise accurate historians have maintained, they were not John Crosbie's. They were, in fact, spoken by Crosbie's cabinet colleague without portfolio, C. H. Emerson, in the House of Assembly in 1910. They had, however, first been uttered considerably earlier than that — in 800 A.D. by Alcuin in a letter to the Emperor Charlemagne! Considering the role of the railway in Newfoundland's later financial disaster, politicians of the day would have been better advised to have mused on the entire quote instead of cannibalizing the part of it that justified their ill-considered largesse: "And the people should not be listened to who keep saying that the voice of the people is the voice of God, since the riotousness of the crowd is very close to madness."

Unlike other contemporary politicians, who quoted from Shakespeare, Byron or Browning to express their support for the railway, Crosbie made his arguments in "good plain Newfoundland style." He declared that his constituents were just as entitled to rail service as those who already enjoyed it — particularly since the ten thousand people in his district contributed $125,000 annually to the colony's revenues. Crosbie pointed out that, despite that sizeable tax burden, there wasn't a public wharf that could accommodate a thirty-ton schooner from Freshwater to Grates Cove.

Although his argument was made with all the hyperbole of a local politician out to get what he could for his district, there was more to his words than mere pork-barrelling. In the previous fishing season, not a single load of fish had been shipped out of Bay-de-Verde after November because the seas had been too rough to load any vessels. As a result, 10,000 quintals of fish (1,120,000 pounds) had remained unsold on the fishermen's stages, and they were unable to lay in their winter supplies. Disaster was only averted when a steamer managed to get to Lower Island Cove with badly needed foodstuffs the following January.

Crosbie's success in securing goodies for his riding brought him special attention from the Liberal Opposition, who referred to some of his constituents who had been given work on the railway as "able-bodied paupers," a sarcastic reference to government's practice of using railway work as a relief measure in hard times. The member for Bay-de-Verde made no apologies, claiming that the men in question gave "an honest day's labour for an honest day's pay." He then "went aboard" Sir Robert Bond, who hadn't hesitated to take his full $300 sessional pay even though he had spent a mere hour in the House during the previous sitting. (Fifteen years later, Crosbie himself would be accused of collecting his $1,000 for the 1922 session of the legislature without sitting in the House at all!) Crosbie delighted in reminding the venerable Liberal leader that it was "the good, honest, hard-working fisherman who pays the revenue of the colony and keeps the average so-called gentleman in luxuries."

During its first term, the People's Party claimed to be the inheritors of true liberalism in the country, espousing a policy of progress, development and opening up the country through the railway so that the "surplus population could engage in other industries than the fisheries." It was the old rallying cry of Newfoundland politics — economic diversification to break the island's crippling dependency on cod.

One of the population's favourite industries was one that the Morris government frowned on — drinking. In St. John's alone, there were fifty-nine public houses which were so popular that they were tearing apart the fabric of society.

John Crosbie supported a bill that prohibited taverns from selling liquor before 9:00 a.m. or on credit. Before the law was passed, working men would often get into their cups on the way to work, buying drinks on credit against their week's wages. By the time Saturday rolled around, they would owe the tavern-keeper the better part of their pay, and their families would go hungry.

Crosbie, himself a heavy drinker, was careful to state time and time again that he knew of no more sober or hardworking men than the labouring and fishing classes of Newfoundland. It might have been the Methodist in him that voted for liquor law reform, but it was the politician who took away the implied slight with the flattering qualification. Or perhaps Crosbie simply had problems with hypocrisy. In 1929, he and a close friend would be dispatched to Kellogg's Hospital in Battle Creek, Michigan, where they both received treatment for severe alcoholism. The son of Crosbie's friend remembered what his father told the therapists about his own drinking habits, supplying in the process a hint as to why he and Sir John had no choice but to make the trip.

"They wanted to know how much I drank. Well, I said, I get up in the morning at six o'clock, have a lookout for the weather, and I pour myself a noggin of rum with a spoonful of molasses in it and a drop of milk to make sure I get back to sleep again. I go back and snore for about another hour, get dressed, and before I had my breakfast I'd always have a drink. Afterwards, I'd go and see the jobs in the plastering business and if I was up in the West End I'd drop into Job Roberts's office and we'd have a couple of snorts there. Then I'd go in and see Sam Bell, Charlie's father, at the Crosbie Hotel and have a few more there and he'd get a cab and drive me home. I'd have a couple of drinks with my lunch and go out to work again. I told the doctor I didn't drink that much and he looked at me and said, 'What would you call drinking?' "

In Crosbie's own case, the more severe drinking bouts generated their own special quirks. "He used to come in to Clovelly farm. My wife tells me that she can see him sitting down in the big leather chair and he's brushing away flies that weren't there, you know," one relative recalled.

Crosbie and his government colleagues strayed from the straight and narrow in more than liquid ways. Land speculation was rampant after amendments were made to the 1903 Crown Lands Act, and at least one cabinet minister quietly took advantage. William Coaker, the crusading leader of the Fishermen's Protective Union, unearthed the fact that Donald Morison, Justice minister and attorney-general in the Morris government, was a quarter-owner of a Boston-based company — the Anglo-American Development Company — that had acquired 13,853 square miles of Labrador in 1910. Despite clear proof of Coaker's allegations, the British government, through its governor, supported Morris and his embattled minister and publicly absolved Morison "of all dishonour in respect to the charges made against you." If there was one thing the establishment liked less than corrupt public officials, it was dangerous agitators like Coaker who presumed to air the system's dirty laundry in public. If such vigilance were encouraged, politics could easily turn into a long and very unsightly clothesline running roughly parallel to the hundreds of miles of the Newfoundland railway.

Morison wasn't the only member of the cabinet who occasionally mingled his personal and public affairs. A governor's dispatch to the Colonial Office in 1911 noted that the Morris government's shipping business had been transferred from a relatively non-political firm to one "largely owned and controlled by one of the premier's ministers without portfolio, the Honorable John Crosbie." Like a lot of other fish merchants, Crosbie suffered when salt fish prices dropped in 1908, and he used his government influence to augment his profits from the boom years and ride out the difficult economic times. In the Newfoundland of the day, survival was the first priority. It was often said that a Newfoundland businessman needed three enterprises to stay afloat: one that was nearly bankrupt, one that was nearly solvent, and one from which he could make a living.

From 1899 to the outbreak of World War I, Portugal, Spain and Italy jostled for first place in consumption of Newfoundland salt fish, with Spain eventually emerging as the island's most important European market. In the meantime, Brazil had become Newfoundland's (and Crosbie's) single biggest market, accounting for 37 percent of salt fish sales by 1914. With the boom years between 1900 and 1907 behind it, the salt fish industry went into a general decline, largely because the people who ran it were slow to modernize their operations.

Coaker realized what was necessary to keep Newfoundland in the running with the colony's main competitors. Better than any other politician of his day, he knew that the fishery had not kept up with technological changes. Poor-quality fish coupled with a chaotic marketing system allowed forward-looking fishing nations like Norway and Iceland to successfully infiltrate Newfoundland's markets.

To reverse these trends, Coaker came up with the Bonavista Platform in 1912, a series of recommendations to bring the Newfoundland fishery into the modern era. Under Coaker's plan, trade agents would be appointed abroad, and there would be a system of standardized grading that would keep poor-quality fish off the market. The plan also called for the use of government cash to introduce gasoline engines to the fishery, and to build cold-storage bait depots. To accommodate these and other changes, Coaker called for the wholesale reorganization of Newfoundland's Fisheries Department.

Coaker's Union Party and the Liberals had formed a united Opposition with Sir Robert Bond as leader. Bond had in turn adopted fifteen of the thirty-one articles of the Bonavista Platform. But Coaker's plan was considered to be dangerously revolutionary and was violently opposed by the merchant class, including John Crosbie. Twenty years later, when a panel of royal commissioners was looking into the reasons behind the collapse of the Newfoundland economy, the merchants were singled out for their venal shortsightedness:

"Intent only on outdoing their local rivals in a scramble for immediate profits, they have failed to realize that time does not stand still. While the industry in Newfoundland, with its haphazard, hand-to-mouth methods and an entire lack of organization, has stagnated, if indeed it has not declined, the industries of Norway and Iceland, Newfoundland's chief competitors in the salt fish markets, have been modernized on a national and scientific basis."

Despite the enlightened policies of the united Opposition, and the timber-lease scandal involving Morris's Justice minister, the People's Party was returned in the 1913 election, though with a reduced majority. The only real change was that Coaker's Union Party won more seats than Bond's Liberals, capturing eight of the nine districts in which it ran candidates. John Crosbie was the only candidate the Union Party could not defeat; he won his Bay-de-Verde seat by a slim ten votes, a margin that nicely expressed the fact that although Crosbie was a successful politician, he was not an overwhelmingly popular one.

It looked like a new age was about to dawn in Newfoundland politics. In January 1914, an ill and dejected Sir Robert Bond resigned his Twillingate seat and the leadership of the Liberal party. It appeared that Coaker and his new political movement were on the verge of great things, fuelled by the same combination of cooperativism and working-class solidarity that would drive the Progressive party in Canada and the British Labour Party.

Single-handedly, Coaker revolutionized the lives of Newfoundland's outport fishermen. He gave them their first union, forty of their own cash stores, a newspaper, a shipbuilding company and, most important of all, the Union Exporting Company, which was the colony's largest exporter of salt-cod by 1924. Newfoundlanders were now a quarter of a million strong, and thousands of them marched to the anthem of the Fishermen's Protective Union, a stirring ode to their new sense of independence and their old resentment of the politicians and merchants who had so completely controlled their destinies for centuries.

We are coming, Mr. Coaker, from the East, West, North and South,
You have called us and we're coming for to put our foes to rout.
By merchants and by governments too long we've been misruled,
We're determined now in future and no longer we'll be fooled.
We'll be brothers all and free men and we'll rightify each wrong,
We are coming, Mr. Coaker, and we're forty thousand strong.

But Newfoundland's experiment with cooperativism never got off the ground. By August 1914, Britain was at war with Germany and, as part of the empire, Newfoundland followed her onto the bloody battlefields of Europe.

The only real military presence in Newfoundland was the Royal Naval Reserve, a force of six hundred men. All but seventy of the reservists were away at the fishery when war broke out. Extravagant in her support of the mother country, Newfoundland promised Whitehall that it would increase the strength of the Naval Reserve to one thousand and provide another five hundred infantry troops. Press censorship was quickly imposed, and by the time parliament reconvened there was a separate Newfoundland Regiment in training, including John Crosbie's nephew, George Graham, the son of his brother Walter. The namesake of the Crosbie clan's patriarch would be one of hundreds of Newfoundlanders slaughtered at Beaumont Hamel in the bloody Battle of the Somme.

By 1916, casualties were so heavy in the Newfoundland Regiment that getting reinforcements became almost impossible, despite the passionate propaganda of both church and state. In April 1917, Edward Morris was forced to return from the Imperial War Conference in London to deal with the crisis. The situation awaiting him was extremely delicate. The very people the government needed to press into the war effort — the fishermen — were the natural constituency of Coaker's Union Party. Already angered by the Legislative Council's refusal to pass Coaker's Sealing Bill, which would have reformed an industry in which 251 men had been lost in two recent disasters, the fishermen would almost certainly use a conscription election to defeat the government, or so Morris's advisers told him. He could not afford to take the electoral risk.

Instead, he began intensive negotiations aimed at co-opting the political opposition by forming an all-party National Government. A month later, on July 16, 1917, he succeeded. Morris left for London to rejoin the Imperial War Conference and on December 31 resigned as premier. In the New Year's Honours List, he became Baron Morris of Waterford. The new Liberal leader, W. F. Lloyd, became acting premier of Newfoundland, and the National Government took office on January 5, 1918. It was under this new administration that John Crosbie would make his greatest contribution to the Empire, Newfoundland and — as several of his critics would soon charge — to himself.

As minister of Shipping under the National Government, Crosbie was responsible for keeping Newfoundland's economy going despite the war. He put together a special committee that included A. E. Hickman and William Coaker to come up with ways to keep goods and supplies moving in and out of the island. Since so many fishermen had volunteered for the armed forces, his first priority was to attract men to the merchant marine. Crosbie jumped into his new job with hobnailed boots. He offered pensions and benefits to merchant mariners equal to those given to naval recruits and made up for the shortage of available tonnage by using sailing vessels in addition to steamships to get Newfoundland's goods to market.

The disruption of the Newfoundland fishery had the beneficial effect of increasing demand for fish and driving up prices. The salt fish trade put on a late bloom. In 1917, high prices and record production were the order of the day. A cold-storage plant was built in St. John's by interests of Sir Robert Reid, and over one hundred new sailing vessels were built in Newfoundland to carry fish to Europe. Crosbie and his committee managed to keep open key markets in Spain, Portugal, Italy and Greece for most of the war, despite the deadly marauding of German warships and submarines. Keeping the sea lanes open to shipping was dangerous work, as John Crosbie knew from bitter personal experience. Just before Christmas 1916, one of his own ships, the *Jean*, sailed for Brazil with a cargo of salt fish. January and February passed without word from the vessel. There were whispers that she had been lost, but confidence ran high in the Royal Navy's ability to protect Newfoundland shipping.

Then Crosbie received word that Captain Edgar Burke and his crew had been taken prisoner near the equator by the German raider *Moewe*. After sinking the *Jean*, the Germans had engaged a British merchantman modified for war in a swift and deadly battle, with the Newfoundland prisoners nervously awaiting the outcome below decks, fully aware that a victory for their ally would also be their death sentence. The British vessel was sunk and no prisoners were taken. Burke and his crew were offered their release if they promised to serve in the German army or navy. They refused. Their next two years were spent in various German prison camps, awaiting the end of the war.

For the minister of Shipping, it was a season of tragedy and sudden death. Some of the grief was crushingly personal. On a cold January night in 1918, as Crosbie sat sipping his beloved Scotch whisky and reading war dispatches in the living room of his Forest Road home, he received a call informing him that his eldest daughter, Jean, who had been sent to a tuberculosis sanatorium in the United States at Saranac Lake, needed an emergency operation for an attack of appendicitis. The family doctor advised Crosbie that signing the permission form for the operation was probably equal to signing Jean's death warrant, given the weakened condition of her lungs. But there was no choice in the matter; without the operation, the seventeen-year-old would certainly die. The doctor was right. Jean never regained consciousness after the operation. Her body was brought home in a private railway car, and she was buried in a white dress with a blue ribbon in her hair, "looking like a princess."

Less than a month after his daughter's death, public calamity crowded in on private grief. On the night of February 23, 1918, the S.S. *Florizel*, a luxury passenger liner on her way to New York, struck rocks in a storm at Horn Head Point near Cappahayden on the southern shore. At 5:15 a.m. on Sunday, February 24, he was awakened by a call informing him that an SOS had been received from the *Florizel* with the message, "Going to pieces near Cape Race." His first thought was that the ship had been torpedoed. Her sister-ship, the *Stephano*, had been sunk by the Germans en route to St. John's from New York in 1916 — luckily, without loss of life.

Intimately familiar with the *Florizel* from its days as a sealing ship and a troop carrier, Crosbie personally organized the rescue operation. He immediately dispatched a train carrying medical supplies, a special device to fire a line on board the wreck and what might have been the most difficult item to get considering that prohibition had come into force the year before — a gallon of rum and a small stock of whisky for the survivors. He scrambled naval reservists to man the rescue vessels and worked around the clock until the plan was in motion. When the operation was over, Crosbie received the grim news: of 138 souls aboard the *Florizel*, 94 had perished in the frigid North Atlantic. Among the dead was the young goddaughter of Sir Edgar Bowring, the owner of the *Florizel*.

Against the backdrop of this emotional battering, the politics of the day whirled on with a life of its own. Although Morris had dealt with the immediate crisis of a manpower shortage, the political coalition he put together was ultimately left to deal with the unpopular issue of recruiting more men for the war effort. In the opening days of 1918, the British Army Council was demanding more troops — three hundred right away and sixty per month — to shore up Newfoundland's badly mauled regiment.

The unpalatable but inevitable moment had arrived. On April 23, 1918, Lloyd committed his government to the Military Service Act which would see all single, able-bodied men between the ages of nineteen and thirty-nine sent to Europe. Not surprisingly, the legislation was violently opposed, but the authorities were brooking no public debate. The police raided the offices of a St. John's weekly newspaper, *The Plaindealer*, and confiscated an anti-conscription issue.

Faced with the real possibility of armed resistance in the outports, Coaker reluctantly agreed to support the Military Service Act as a member of the National Government. It was a compromise he need not have made. Even though the first draftees were sent to England, hostilities were over before reinforcements were ever needed at the front. The war had ended and with it William Coaker's unique influence on Newfoundland politics. Although he would continue in public life, still believing he could work his fishery reforms through the system, he had fallen in the estimation of his followers. The one-time god had been relegated by the vagaries of history to being a mere politician.

On June 3, 1919, King George V celebrated his fifty-fourth birthday and three thousand miles away the son of an emigrant plasterer became a knight of the realm for his service during the war. On the Canadian mainland, the lustre had gone off such honours, mainly because of rising nationalism in the wake of the war effort. In 1917, J. Ross Robertson, owner of *The Evening Telegram* in Toronto, declined a knighthood and a Senate seat on the same day. George Brown, Edward Blake and Alexander Mackenzie also turned down the K-B-E. Commenting on Robertson's refusal, *The Sydney Record* in Nova Scotia editorialized that Robertson "had the good sense to decline one of these wooden-sword and tin-helmet knighthoods which are getting so cheap and common."

But Newfoundland's long-standing connection to Great Britain meant that knighthood was still a high honour, even if you had to pay for it, as one of Sir John's former employees, Greg Power, remembers being told: "He used to say, 'I paid on the barrelhead for it.' "

Whether bought or bestowed, John Chalker Crosbie received the Knight Commander of the Order of the British Empire in a solemn ceremony at Government House. Few could begrudge him the recognition. Thanks in no small part to his energy and imagination, Newfoundland's economy had not only survived but actually prospered during the war years. The National Government had revenues of $7 million (twice that of Nova Scotia, which had double the population) and a surplus of $1,170,000. Everyone was impressed, including one of his most ardent political detractors, William Coaker:

"During the war period, he utilized his outstanding abilities and energy to overcome numerous obstacles on behalf of the trade, and I am quite sure his greatest public services were rendered during the period he served the country as Minister of Shipping. No other member of the administration of 1917 and 1918 would have been as equal to the performance of the duties of that office as Sir John. He loved power and under the War Measures Act, as Minister of Shipping, he possessed all the power he wished to avail of and as an associate of his on the Tonnage Committee of the

Executive Council I concede to him the distinction of one knowing his job well and performing it with marked ability."

Crosbie's political enemies were quick to point out that the hardworking minister wasn't above using his position to fatten his own purse, as he was alleged to have done in the famous "spars incident." A close family friend of the period recalled the scandal, in which Crosbie acquired two spars (rounded pieces of wood used for masts or booms to support a vessel's rigging) from a wrecked schooner and sold them at a profit:

"There is a thing that Crosbie had bought up spars cheap for war purposes, he'd bought a lot of these cheap and there was a great complaint, did he use his position to get these things cheap? And there was a great hoo-ha. . . . He bought them cheap and sold them dear, but that was basic business. . . . And he went to the place where they were talking about it the most [Western Bay], and he jumps up on the platform and he says, 'I'se the buck that sold the spars.' Then he talked about it. His thing was, you seize the opportunity when people are against you, you jump up and get right in there."

Out of the spars affair, a rhyme was born:

Oh the awful price I paid for those two old soggy spars,
The spars will kill Crosbie in the North Shar.

The incident also found its way onto the floor of the House of Assembly in 1926, where Sir John tried to pillory Sir Michael Cashin for selling him two hundred cases of bad whisky for $3,000. "My heavens, that is not Rye Whiskey," Sir John told the House, "it is worse even than moonshine; it's not fit for human consumption."

In defending himself, Sir Michael reminded the House of Sir John's famous peccadillo: "I am rum and the Minister of Finance is spars. This is the man who sold the spars to the Government at an exorbitant figure. The spars were already paid for so to speak. They were salvaged out of a vessel in St. Mary's Bay and the Minister of Finance had received the insurance in full and then he sold them to the Government for a thousand dollars."

The incident faded but its impact did not. For the rest of

his political career, Sir John was known by his detractors as "Spars" Crosbie, and the issue did eventually come back to haunt him in his political wars on the North Shore. Reflecting on the affair sixty years later, one of Sir John's daughters opined, "I've always said, God help me, I've always said there's never an honest politician. You go in honest, you mean to be, but you're not."

Another relative, Gert Crosbie, interpreted the event against the mores of the times. "You have to judge that everybody lived by bits in those days, you had to do a bit of this, a bit of that to survive. You had to buy salt cheap and sell it for more. You had to do what you could. He was a quick-thinking man who could jump on an opportunity and use it."

It was a good trait to possess in postwar Newfoundland. The island had become a place of great expectations. People had cash money for the first time in their lives and they would not soon go back to the isolated and poverty-stricken ways of the prewar years. Stripped of its dictatorial powers and anxious to please the electorate, government borrowed to satisfy their desires, conveniently forgetting that the war effort had cost Newfoundland a crushing $35 million to finance. While political parties jockeyed for position in the pending election, a terrible financial reckoning was on the way for the new Dominion.

WITH THE COLLAPSE of the National Government in May 1919, electoral politics returned to Newfoundland for the first time in nearly six years. Public life was as shabby as it had ever been, a state of affairs that wasn't helped by the potential for corruption brought on by prohibition. The People's Party had grown decadent, the bloated puppet of merchants, manufacturers and railway and shipping interests. Anxious to make a comeback, the Liberals turned to Sir Robert Bond. But the aging statesman was so appalled by the state of politics that he spurned his former colleagues in no uncertain terms: "I have had a surfeit of Newfoundland politics lately, and I turn from the dirty business with contempt and loathing."

It was the moment of destiny for Richard Anderson Squires, a crafty Harbour Grace lawyer who sensed an opportunity to seize power. Just as Morris deserted the Liberals in 1908 to set up the People's Party, Squires quit the People's Party and organized a massive rally to announce the formation of the new Liberal Reform Party. Weakened by Coaker's stand on conscription, the Union Party had little choice but to align itself with Squires against the party of privilege, the former People's Party, which now became the Liberal–Progressives with Michael Cashin as its leader.

The election that followed set new lows in a jurisdiction not known for conducting its political contests in white gloves. It was, in fact, a pier six brawl in which at least one of the objectives was to rig as many nominations as possible. Sir John was front and centre in the scramble for the electoral marbles. On Saturday, October 11, 1919, he showed up at the Royal Stores in downtown St. John's accompanied by his wharf manager, Thomas Lockyer, and demanded that a clerk who worked there, Jethro Penny, nominate their chosen candidate, W. J. Higgins. Penny refused and Sir John went off like a rocket. According to the beleaguered clerk, Sir John "indulged in some of the most filthy abuse and indecent language that has ever been heard in St. John's."

Sir John's tirade was faithfully and fully recorded in the Friday, October 17 edition of *The Morning Post*, under the front-page banner headline, "John Crosbie Says 'The Pope and the Archbishop Can Kiss My ____,' " a phrase he was supposed to have shouted out in its unexpurgated form in the middle of the Royal Stores. The article went on to say that Sir John tried to "beat, bribe, bully, and blackmail" Penny into doing his bidding and in the process used "some very vile and offensive language concerning His Grace, Archbishop Roache, and generally behaved like a drunken hooligan." It also credited Sir John with boasting that he had made more money than any other man in Newfoundland during the war — so much, in fact, that he could bribe every elector in his chosen district of Port de Grave in Conception Bay.

The newspaper didn't bother to reserve its judgment on Crosbie's reported behaviour for the editorial page. In the same front-page story, *The Morning Post* called Sir John an "ill-mannered and purse proud upstart" who had "no more idea of manliness than a pig has feathers." His outburst about the pope and archbishop stamped him as "a dangerous character, a low bred scoundrel, and a person utterly devoid of the common instincts of man." It concluded: "Of late years, Newfoundland has been breeding millionaires of the Crosbie type, men out for the spoils of office and after the glory of power."

Crosbie sued the newspaper for libel, and its editor, Harris Mosdell, prepared to argue justification as his defence. The court ruled that the language in the articles was so gross that it was calculated to make a fair hearing of the libel action impossible. *The Morning Post* was found to be in contempt of court and fined two hundred dollars.

The Protestant voters of Port de Grave district were unmoved by this vilification of Crosbie, possibly because the newspaper's owner was one Richard Squires, leader of the Liberal Reform Party. Sir John won his district, but his party was consigned to His Majesty's Loyal Opposition as the coalition of Squires and Coaker formed Newfoundland's first elected postwar government.

Coaker became minister of Marine and Fisheries in the Squires government, and the aging reformer believed he would now have his chance to implement his long-held dream of a state-regulated fishery. Because of a slump in the European fish markets, a voluntary agreement among the largest Newfoundland fish exporters, including Sir John, to set prices and conditions of shipment collapsed. Coaker reacted with a proclamation requiring Newfoundland cod exporters to obtain export licences. The fish merchants, accustomed to having a free hand, were outraged, and when the minister brought in his comprehensive package to reform the fishery, they refused to support it.

In the meantime, the Squires government had more pressing problems to deal with. Interest payments on the public debt were rising dramatically, and more and more Newfoundlanders were on relief as the postwar recession set in. Unemployed workers staged street demonstrations, and the House of Assembly was twice suspended because of disturbances in the public gallery.

Squires, who had come to power on the slogan "the Grafters must go," soon presided over an administration more corrupt than the one he had supplanted. But the smooth-talking premier won the 1923 election with exactly the same number of seats he had captured in 1919, largely on the strength of his promise to build a $20-million paper mill on the Humber River in western Newfoundland.

One of the casualties of the 1923 election was John Crosbie, partly because his Opposition status prevented him from handing out the patronage plums his constituents had come to expect. The election was close, and Crosbie tried everything to sway the voters in his Conception Bay district, including the threat that he wouldn't sell another quintal of fish for anyone who supported the Liberal Reform Party. But Harry Roberts remembered that his father, Joby Roberts, who was also in the fish business, neutralized Sir John's threat. "Father went over and said, 'Don't mind what Crosbie told you, I can look after selling all your fish and Mr. Barr [a Roberts associate] will buy all the fish you produce.' "

The Liberal–Labour–Progressive ticket of John Crosbie and John Puddester was defeated by the Liberal Reform ticket of William Cave and Richard Cramm. To rub salt in the wound, Cramm became minister of Finance and Customs. Sir John took the defeat badly. He never spoke to Joby Roberts again because of his support of the Liberal Reform Party. Even though Sir John continued to do business with Roberts, he used his son, Ches, as an interlocutor — even when the three men were strolling down the wharf in St. John's cutting a deal.

AFTER FIFTEEN YEARS of public life, Sir John had consolidated the gains of his early years in business. The hotelier who had once studied to become a plasterer was now the largest fish merchant in the country, and his flamboyant personal style had won him friends in strange places. Even his political rival, Coaker, couldn't totally resist Sir John's rough charms. "I liked him as a businessman. He wanted his ounce of flesh, but he would sooner do one more good than harm."

By the age of forty-seven he had fathered twelve children, dominated the cabinet in the governments of Morris and Lloyd and added a knighthood to his list of accomplishments. As his business grew, the family moved to a succession of bigger and better houses until they took up residence in Devon Place, a huge duplex on Kingsbridge Road that was one of the city's most illustrious residences. At various times, it had been home to the cream of Newfoundland's social elite: James Murray, a wealthy merchant; Robert Pinsent, a Supreme Court judge; Robert Thorburn, premier of Newfoundland in 1885; and Sir Ambrose Shea, a Father of Confederation.

Crosbie bought Devon Place from the widow of John Shannon Munn. The famous merchant and his three-year-old daughter, Betty, had perished in the *Florizel* disaster while on their way to visit Mrs. Munn, who was in New York for medical treatment. Sir John's new neighbour was the railway magnate H. D. Reid, who, in 1903, along with his brother R. G. Reid, were the first people in Newfoundland to own automobiles. The Crosbies weren't far behind; they travelled to Europe with their daughter Vera to buy a magnificent, dark-green twelve-cylinder Fiat touring car in Milan.

Mitchie Anne, or Lady Crosbie as she was known after her husband's KBE, brought up her large, energetic family with the help of relatives and a household staff. The children were all delivered at home by a midwife and raised in the nursery. If tonsils needed to be removed, the operation was performed by Dr. Cowperthwaite, the family doctor, on a table in the nursery. Only after reaching the age of sixteen were the children permitted to participate in the "big debates" that took place in the huge dining room before a roaring fire. Olga, Sir John and Lady Crosbie's youngest daughter, loved every minute of growing up at Devon Place: "Whenever I think of my home and my parents I get a very happy glow. I just loved it all. I could live it all over again without any problem."

Mitchie Anne's children had arrived on an average of one every eighteen months since her wedding day in 1899. She was forty-eight when her last child, Thomas, died in infancy in 1924 — the same year her first grandchild, June Bennett, the daughter of Nina Crosbie and Frank Bennett, was born. Commenting on the size of Sir John's family, a close friend quipped, "there was a lot of heat in that man's body." Or as one of Sir John's daughters put it, "In Newfoundland there's either blueberry picking or those long winter nights, one or the other."

As a mother, Mitchie Anne instilled the ethic of charitable work in all of her children, as the future accomplishments of Vera Crosbie Perlin would so dramatically show. Rita Tobin, a former maid at Devon Place, remembered Mitchie Anne as a "wonderful lady" who treated household staff like people rather than servants. Although she didn't try to put on airs, Mitchie Anne wasn't averse to indulging in some of the finer things that money could buy. A smart dresser, her clothes were custom-made for her in Montreal and her silk undergarments were handsewn by seamstresses in St. John's.

During their childhood, the Crosbies had the best of both worlds — a comfortable upbringing in a happy household where education was valued and summers "around the Bay" at the Manuel home in Exploits, where they learned to fish and sail. And there was always Clovelly. Part of the family's strength was that it never forgot its roots in rural Newfoundland, although, as the family businesses grew, there was less and less time for recreation.

But if the Crosbie home was happy, it was also strict and a little on the formal side. According to the mores of the time, the boys said "yes, sir" and "no, sir" to a father who was often away on business or preoccupied with politics as they were growing up. The older boys were expected to be up at 6:00 a.m. to deliver milk from the family dairy or pack fish on the wharf. If they didn't perform their duties to Sir John's satisfaction, they could expect to be on the receiving end of humiliating tirades in front of the help, a dubious tradition that was carried on by Ches Crosbie when he took over the family business.

Sir John ruled with a firm hand — or boot, as the circumstances required. He once hired his son Percy and a friend, Jim Chalker, to pick dandelions off the front lawn of the family home. The boys were supposed to put the dandelions in a box, and Sir John would pay them a cent apiece for each of the weeds. The arrangement was going along well enough until the boys got the idea of slinking back to the dandelion box and filling their pockets with the weeds in order to get paid twice. Sir John caught them and gave them a kick in the pants for their dark enterprise — no doubt taking note that they were bound to go on to great careers in the fish business.

In addition to his sense of opportunism, Sir John's sons inherited his astonishing stamina. When they slipped away to burn the candle at both ends, their sister Dolly quietly let them in through the dining room's French doors so they wouldn't be caught by their mother. Swearing was strictly forbidden (a prohibition honoured more in the breach than the observance as far as Sir John was concerned; in addition to cursing, and smoking Brazilian cigars, he also liked to spit). The older girls had to be home by midnight, and the entire family was expected to attend the Cochrane Street United Church on Sundays. When Lady Crosbie entered the room, the children would rise.

Despite the pressures of his official schedule, Sir John was close to his children and included them in what privileges of office he could. He took his daughter Dolly (christened Ella Maud, she was given this nickname as a baby based on her tininess) on an official trip to England when she was a teenager. Sir John, who was also accompanied by his personal secretary, Cahill, knew that a luncheon had been arranged in his honour by the British House of Lords and warned Dolly that if they served oysters, "you're going to have to eat them." Horrified, she informed him that under no circumstances could she comply with his oyster edict. The oysters in fact appeared at the luncheon, but so, luckily, did an English gentleman. Noticing the look of panic on the face of his young guest, he asked, "Miss Crosbie, I'm having a grapefruit, would you like one?"

Sir John then left Dolly in London while he made a quick business trip to Paris. She attended a ball at the Albert Hall and later shopped her way into what she was sure would be trouble when her father added up the bills. She listened apprehensively through the door while the English doctor who had been attending her for a sudden tuberculosis attack during the trip told her father of the damage she had done to the family treasury. Sir John merely laughed. Even when overwhelmed with official duties, one of his personal pleasures was shopping for his girls. Before returning to Newfoundland, Sir John bought five pairs of high-cut Russian boots, which were all the rage that season in London.

If Sir John was generous, he was also fun-loving. Much of the spark in life at Devon Place came from his penchant for practical jokes. An avowed flower-lover, he once planted the artificial variety in the garden at Devon Place and then rushed Mitchie Anne outdoors to witness the "miracle." On another occasion he arranged to have a nasty note sent to his stern sister, Ellie, alleging that the Crosbie Hotel hadn't paid its bill from the Newfoundland Butter Company, which he owned. The formidable "Nelson" turned up at Devon Place in full sail. "Jack, they're dunning me for my bill, and you know I'm never behind in my bills," she complained. Laughter was the only collection agency she faced.

With the exception of Robert, Sir John remained close to his brothers and sisters. While in politics, he would frequently drop in at Walter's house in Bay Roberts on the way through his riding of Bay-de-Verde. He would head for the kitchen and lift up the pot lids, hoping to find his favourite dishes on the boil — turnip-tops and corned beef. The portly guest would then pace around the house, puffing on a cigar, giving the family the political news of the day. When he left, there was usually a five-dollar bill for his nephew Bill, who remembered his uncle as a buzzing dynamo of a man: "I'd hardly see Uncle Jack sit down, only barely long enough to eat, when he came to visit."

On one occasion, Sir John decided to pay a surprise visit to Clovelly Farm and recapture a little of his youth in the process by riding out on horseback from St. John's. But the lithe fellow of his early youth had turned into the ample businessman of middle age — too ample, in fact, for his horse. The barrel-chested rider was forced to lead his exhausted charge the last few hundred yards to Clovelly and opted to drive back to St. John's in his car while Chipman, his unfortunate chauffeur, was left to deal with the horse.

There was no active connection with relatives in Dumfries and little said about them until a Scottish Crosbie, Charles Edward Crosbie of Kipp, made a most unusual overture. Charles, who was "without issue," was looking for a twelve-year-old male heir, and he placed a newspaper advertisement offering to adopt a Newfoundland Crosbie for £1000. Sir John jokingly threatened his children that if they misbehaved they would be shipped off to the ancestral seat, but everyone knew how much he valued his family. After the birth of his youngest surviving son, Bill, in 1919, Sir John said that he wouldn't give a plugged nickel for another child, but he wouldn't part with any of the ones that he had for a million dollars.

In and out of politics, Sir John was a very familiar figure at his fish business on Water Street, prowling the alleyways in the morning and addressing his employees by their first names. The Crosbie premises had their own wharf where the firm's ships could tie up and barrels of salt fish would be stacked ready for loading. It was a good place to work. If you attended to your duties, you had a job for life, and Sir John was always there to help in an emergency.

As former Newfoundland archivist, Burnham Gill recalled of Sir John: "He was a good Christian gentleman whose main interest, of course, was business, but he never did forget the people. The Crosbie family was *famous* for their interest in and concern for the people who worked for them. That went right down through and it's come right down today that John Crosbie, young John, is of the same type as all of them. They never forgot their people."

Sir John's brief respite from public life ended in 1924 with the spectacular political demise of Richard Squires. The Liberal premier who had come to power on the promise to industrialize Newfoundland — a manifesto that captivated a young labour organizer named Joe Smallwood — soon found himself facing a revolt from within his own party. To the horror of his cabinet, Squires agreed with the Reid family to cancel their operating contract for the financially troubled Newfoundland railway and have his cash-strapped government take over the enterprise. To add insult to injury, he also agreed to pay the former operators $2 million and to allow them to retain their huge land grants. The cabinet revolt was led by Squires's justice minister, William Warren.

Before long, however, the railway issue was eclipsed by a much more serious crisis for Squires — the allegation of corruption at the very heart of his government. At the eye of the storm was Squires's minister of Agriculture, Dr. Alex Campbell. Armed with evidence of egregious election corruption garnered from the auditor-general's report, four of Campbell's own cabinet colleagues pressed Squires to fire the minister. The premier refused. Led by William Warren, all four ministers then resigned, and the former Justice minister asked the British government to investigate his allegations of corruption.

Hollis Walker, a prominent English lawyer, was appointed to lead the investigation. Vindicating Warren and his colleagues, Walker reported that Newfoundland's economy wasn't the only thing that Richard Squires was interested in diversifying. The investigator reported that Squires, known for his lavish personal lifestyle, had supplemented his own income with large cash payments from companies with whom the government of Newfoundland had been negotiating.

The Hollis Walker Commission went beyond Warren's original allegations to indict Newfoundland's political system of the day. The premier of Newfoundland was arrested and, just over a year into its second term, his beleaguered government was forced back to the polls. Squires was convicted of income tax evasion in 1925. Though he was charged with stealing $20,000 in public funds, a grand jury refused to indict him on the grounds of insufficient evidence. He never stood trial on any other criminal allegations arising out of Walker's findings of personal corruption.

With the party system in a shambles, the election of June 1924 turned into a political free-for-all. Walter Monroe, the leader of the Liberal Conservative Party, "a true merchant party of the nineteenth century type," won 25 seats, including St. John's West which was captured by Sir John Crosbie. The battered Liberal–Progressives under A. E. Hickman dropped to a mere ten seats, and William Warren, the man who had instigated the Hollis Walker Commission, was elected as an Independent from the district of Fortune.

If anyone held "the rosy merchant-conservative view of society," it was Walter Monroe. Quoted by historian S. J. R. Noel, he stated that he and the fishermen were in business together, "they to catch, I to export. If they prosper, I prosper. If their energies and rewards decrease, so will mine. We have a common interest and a common cause, and should work together for the common good. This is a fisherman's paradise and we should work together for the good of each other." But Monroe's stirring social compact didn't provide for much economic democracy when it came to the distribution of profits. Under his paternalistic regime, the rich stayed rich and the poor got poorer — the former group including the premier, his colonial secretary, J. R. Bennett, and his new minister of Finance and Customs, the ever-opportunistic Sir John Crosbie.

All showed a remarkable ability to equate the public good with their own prosperity. Monroe, for example, had pledged to reform the tax structure, which up until that time allowed for the collection of 90 percent of Newfoundland's revenues from customs duties and indirect taxation. In February 1925 he made good on his promise by raising tariffs on imported cigarettes, tobacco, rope, twine and fishing nets. Oddly enough, the premier had a financial interest in the Imperial Tobacco Company of St. John's and the Colonial Cordage Co., Newfoundland's only manufacturer of rope, twine and fishing nets.

The Monroe government also repealed prohibition in its first term, a move that met with universal support from a thirsty population. The minister responsible for bringing back the bottle was J. R. Bennett, who just happened to be co-owner of the largest brewery in St. John's — and the father-in-law of Crosbie's daughter, Nina.

Sir John himself founded the Newfoundland Butter Company, one of his most successful enterprises, just as the government brought in stiff new tariffs against foreign margarine. (In Newfoundland, "butter" means margarine, and "table butter" refers to the dairy product.) The preferential rate was six cents per pound in favour of Newfoundland-produced margarine — no small advantage in a market that consumed six million pounds of margarine a year!

In Crosbie's case, the tariff advantage was not in itself a guarantee that the Newfoundland Butter Company would be a success. One of Newfoundland's oldest firms, Harvey and Company, had been manufacturing margarine since 1883, using marine oil products in their production process. It was a very lucrative business because of the absence of a large-scale, commercial dairy industry in Newfoundland and a lack of refrigeration facilities, which prevented the storage of table butter. The business was so profitable that Robert A. Brehm took over the operation of a second margarine company in 1900, which also prospered.

In 1925, Sir John sensed that the time was ripe to make a move on the established companies. For years, he had been a major exporter of whale and seal oils to Europe, and now he imported European expertise in the person of George Ehlers, a Danish chemist who developed a product formula suited to Newfoundland conditions.

At the time, margarine was sold in "winter-keeping" and "summer-keeping" formulas, which were altered according to the climate. The Newfoundland Butter Company marketed brands called Silver Spread and Golden Spread in fifty-pound tubs. To induce consumers to switch to the new brands, Crosbie ordered that silver and gold coins be buried in random tubs. In June 1925, Sir John's daughter, Dolly, turned the sod at the Newfoundland Butter Company, and his favourite grandchild, June Bennett, pulled the switch to electrify the first neon sign in Newfoundland — a huge cow atop the modern, efficient factory.

The new firm boasted the first pension plan and full medical benefits for employees. It also allowed Sir John to unveil a new process that would have profound effects on public health in Newfoundland. Deeply concerned about the intestinal tuberculosis that ravaged Newfoundlanders because of impure dairy products, the owner of the Newfoundland Butter Company introduced pasteurization.

As forward-looking as the Newfoundland Butter Company was, at least one of Sir John's political opponents was more interested in another aspect of the enterprise — the conflict of interest in which it squarely placed the minister of Finance. "The present Minister of Finance and Customs sells butter to the public institutions and no other butter is allowed to be brought in because they are afraid to buy it because they are afraid they will lose their jobs. And then we are told Coaker was autocratic. He is a mild lad compared with the present Minister of Finance and Customs," Sir Michael Cashin charged in the House of Assembly.

Later, when travelling in Brazil, one of his biggest markets for salt fish, Sir John realized that the South American country was very similar to Newfoundland in at least two respects: it was poor and had very little refrigeration. He subsequently established a very successful margarine company there, only to have it nationalized by the Brazilian government several years later. Although the Crosbies were compensated for the takeover, getting their profits out of the country was another matter.

Sir John didn't have to look abroad to find new ways to add to the family fortune. In October 1925 an employee of the Finance and Customs Department accused the minister himself of customs fraud. Michael Foley complained to His Excellency William Lamond Allardyce, the governor of Newfoundland, that Sir John had ordered that certain goods, including one and a half million cigarettes, were to be sold at public auction after their owner failed to pay the customs duties on them. The deputy minister of Finance and Customs issued instructions that the cigarettes should not be sold for less than the outstanding duty. Mr. Foley explained what happened next:

"There were no bidders for the cigarettes at this price. The following day, upon the order of Sir John Crosbie, the cigarettes were sold to Mr. Thomas Smyth, an intimate friend of the said Mr. Crosbie for the sum of $400, which sum of money Sir John Crosbie took from his pocket and handed to Thomas Smyth to pay for the cigarettes. The duty on said cigarettes amounted to approximately $20,000. . . ."

Mr. Foley went on to explain that the minister's bargain-shopping somehow made it into the pages of *The Fishermen's Advocate*. After the published accounts appeared, Foley claimed he was called into Mr. Crosbie's office and asked to "stand by" the minister in his attempt to have the newspaper "muzzled" by the time-honoured expedient of launching a libel action. The civil servant refused, informing Sir John that if called to court he would have to tell the truth about the cigarettes. Foley, who wanted the minister suspended until an impartial tribunal could investigate his allegations, then says he was dismissed from the public service.

In a breezy letter to the governor, Sir John pointed out that since he had commenced a libel suit against *The Fishermen's Advocate* the whole matter was *sub judice* and ought to be dealt with by government only after it had been disposed of by the courts. He ended with a Parthian shot at his detractor, Michael Foley, whose civic-mindedness he invested with another motive: "I cannot, however, forbear pointing out that the charges emanate from a man who made no effort to bring them to Your Excellency's attention for many weeks after the events which he relates took place, and that he did not do so until he had been dismissed from the public service for drunkenness." His Excellency's obedient servant had managed to respond to Foley's accusations without denying them!

Looking after his own interests was one thing, but no amount of entrepreneurial brigandage in the energetic Sir John Crosbie could make much of a dent in the sorry state of Newfoundland's finances. Soon after assuming his duties as Finance minister, he realized that the whole department was in a state of chaos. He brought in accountants and auditors to put the department on a business-like footing, but the situation needed much more than administrative reform. The man who had entered politics in 1908 supporting railway branch lines simply because the people wanted them had become a fiscal conservative. He realized that taxes could no longer cover the expenditures of the government and embarked on an ambitious scheme to slash public spending. It was either balance the books or perish, as he strongly hinted in his budget speech of 1924: "If Newfoundlanders have the spirit I think they have, they will always be willing to pay their share if by so doing they will keep the old ship on an even keel and be able to weather the financial storms when they arise."

The old ship might have been about to be swamped, but Sir John did his best to keep her afloat a little longer. In the budget year 1925–26, he raised more than $200,000 from tax-evaders alone, including former premier Richard Squires. When Squires wasn't forthcoming with his taxes, Sir John ordered that his car be towed away. A distraught Squires made a swift and personal appeal to the minister of Finance: "My God, John, you can't do this, I've got no way to get about." According to Sir John's nephew, Crosbie replied, "Well, you'd better come up and make some arrangements then, Richard."

A man who could dun an ex-premier was bound to do wonders for the government's finances. Crosbie's vigorous methods of collecting tax arrears and unpaid duties led to a surplus in the current account for that year of $71,506.23 — quite an accomplishment in a jurisdiction that was on its way to bankruptcy.

Convinced that millions of dollars of government revenues had been lost by false invoices and the undervaluing of goods, Sir John put government agents into warehouses to ensure that importers were paying the proper duties on imported goods. He also reformed outport post offices, cutting back on the number of public employees. But cutting government expenditures and reducing the number of civil servants in the outports was not easy. As Sir John lamented in the House of Assembly, "to carry out retrenchment in this country you want a Mussolini around here who can control a government in absolute union." The avuncular Walter Monroe was no Il Duce.

But not all of Sir John's initiatives were geared to gathering precious revenues for the government or preventing abuses in the public administration. As Finance minister, he also removed the income tax and the business-profits tax, apparently believing that if the rich prospered, they would reinvest their profits in their businesses and the benefit would trickle down to the working class. It was the "rosy merchant view" of society writ large, the Reaganomics of the Roaring Twenties. When an Opposition member said that the minister of Finance "was like the father of a family who was trying to make two ends meet," Sir John was delighted. It conformed perfectly to his paternalistic view of society and his own privileged place in it — a standing he had worked long and hard to achieve.

September 11, 1926, was another big day in the history of the Crosbie family and not just because Sir John was celebrating his fiftieth birthday. On that day, his daughter Vera married Albert Perlin, the twenty-four-year-old who had been her constant suitor since 1922, when he was a reporter for *The Evening Telegram*. Perlin had joined the paper when a former school chum, Joe Smallwood, had left the *Telegram* to further his career in New York. Two years later, Albert joined his own family's dry-goods business in St. John's and became a frequent dinner guest at the Crosbie home.

From the very beginning, Albert believed that his dream of marrying Vera was doomed — the heartbreaking conclusion to the drama of a Jewish boy in love with a daughter of the WASP establishment. He recorded his feelings about the situation in his diary after a rapturous but frustrating evening at Devon Place on Friday, January 20, 1922: "It's rather sickening to think that I can never be anything more than a friend to Vera although it is a great thing to be her friend. If only there could be a common religion, what a difference it would make."

The courtship proceeded with touching tenderness. The young couple went on long walks, revelled in each other's conversation and took in plays and concerts at the Nickel and Star Theatres. Perlin played 45's with Sir John and bridge with Lady Crosbie and her sister, Jeanette Manuel, but the real attraction was Vera, and Sir John knew it. With the gramophone playing in the hall, he watched a little apprehensively as Vera and Albert danced happily beside the other young couples who were regular visitors in his house. He finally asked his daughter what her feelings were for the earnest young man, leaving the impression with her in his own indelicate way that he would not ultimately stand in the way of an alliance: he did not care about the religion of the man she married, he told her, provided "he was not a Roman Catholic."

Thanks to a rakish Joe Smallwood, Albert very nearly lost his chance to marry the woman he worshipped. In

May 1922, Smallwood had picked up some chorus girls who were performing at the Gaiety Theatre and asked them out to tea. The girl he was interested in would come only if he provided a date for her girlfriend. Smallwood turned to Albert. The foursome was walking past the Gower Street United Church when Sir John's car loomed ominously into sight down Long's Hill with Vera in the front seat. Albert took to his heels before his beloved caught sight of him, later recording in his diary his feelings about the man who had almost gotten him into a romantic pickle: "He had the nerve to ask them [the chorus girls] to tea and included me in the invite. I gave him what for afterwards."

A few months later, Albert made another, and far more pleasant, entry in his diary: "She allowed me to kiss her hand tonight but she wanted to kiss mine also. We had a few moments of unalloyed bliss when I had her in my arms. If only time would pass, so that she could be mine forever."

The wedding that granted him that wish took place in Asheville, North Carolina, a fashionable resort town that the Crosbies had been visiting since the early 1900s. Vera had also been a frequent visitor at Asheville's modern sanatorium during those times when she needed treatment for recurring bouts of tuberculosis. Whether the wedding was held outside Newfoundland to spare the feelings of Albert's parents, Israel and Adelle Perlin, who might have been upset at the prospect of their son marrying outside his faith, or because Sir John himself didn't want to draw attention to the union, is uncertain. What is known is that while Lady Crosbie and two of her daughters accompanied Vera to Asheville, where the ceremony would be held in the home of Mr. and Mrs. Wilbur Devendorf, friends of the family, Sir John did not. His daughter Dolly remembers sitting with him at Devon Place on the night Vera and Albert became man and wife: "Father was quite upset, and so was Mr. Perlin, because for an older Jewish son to marry was a big thing. I kept saying to Father, 'He must be more worried than you are, because that's a big thing to Mr. Perlin.' I said, 'Father, you may as well stop, because the good Lord isn't going to ask who the six girls are going to marry.' "

IF NEWFOUNDLAND HAD fared as well as the young couple that got their start in Asheville that late summer day in 1926, it would have been a very happy and prosperous place. But as the dominion spiralled lazily towards the financial crisis of the thirties, there was just enough good news around to lull Newfoundlanders into a false sense of well-being. During the Monroe administration, cod-liver-oil exports were sharply up, and the ownership of Labrador was awarded to Newfoundland over the claims of Quebec. Sir John was elated at the decision, recognizing the tremendous hydro potential of the Hamilton River, later to become Churchill Falls. In his budget speech for 1927, he said, "What this means to the people of Newfoundland it is difficult for the ordinary person to conceive, but that it is an asset which will increase in value year after year [is] without question."

Had he been able to peer into the future, and see the day when the development of Churchill Falls would enrich Quebec and deprive Newfoundland of both power and profits on a massive scale, he might not have seen the $250,000 the government invested in arguing its case as money well spent.

By 1928, the financial situation was desperate. As of June 30, 1928, the public debt of the dominion was nearly $75 million. More than 40 percent of Newfoundland's revenues were swallowed up servicing the debt. The stark reality of Newfoundland's economic position had already given John Crosbie more than a few moments of despondency. In late 1926, he wrote to Prime Minister Monroe to advise him that in his opinion the dominion was bankrupt:

"Ever since the 1919 election I have had no other thought but that final bankruptcy was before us, and my fears in this respect have been gradually borne out during my term as Member of the House of Assembly from 1919 to 1923. . . . The Auditor General says the deficit will be from $850,000 to $900,000 on the 30th of June next, but I have no hesitation in saying it will be over one million dollars. Adding this to the deficit on the Colony's current account will practically leave us $3,562,000 short on the 30th of June. . . . I feel like delivering this letter to you to-day, but remembering how near Christmas is, I have on second thought decided to let Christmas Day pass before sending it."

In one of his last budget speeches, the increasingly frustrated Finance minister summed up Newfoundland's financial situation in relation to his lengthy political career.

"Financing this country is not the sinecure it was when I had the honour to first sit in this Assembly. At that time the total expenditure for Newfoundland was no bigger than our interest charges of today, and while it is true that our Revenue collections were very small, yet they sufficed to cover all demands. We had no railway problem in the sense that we have it today. There were no Naval and Military Pensions to provide. The War Debt Interest did not exist and the Finance Minister had not to worry about Interest guarantees. Our fisheries were stable and the markets flourishing and the very thought of the 'dole' was repugnant to all men with a sense of independence."

By 1928, the political fortunes of the Monroe government paralleled the chaos in the economy. Weakened by defections that left the premier barely able to hold on to power, and shaken by the criticism that his government was an oligarchy serving the interests of the rich, Walter Monroe was forced to resign on July 21, 1928.

One of the ministers that refused to abandon the leader was John Crosbie. "When a Crosbie signs articles for four years with his captain, he does so in the darkest hour," he said. Although he was offered the leadership of the party, Sir John wisely declined. His four years as Finance minister had been difficult ones. Physically exhausted, the man who had acted as premier when Monroe was out of the province was rapidly losing interest in what was fast becoming an untenable situation. He followed his leader into private life, devoting his few remaining years to his family and his business.

In failing health, Sir John spent the summer of 1932, the last summer of his life, at "The Bungalow," his beloved retreat in Placentia. His constant companion was his youngest son Bill. The boy had been given the name Alexander Harris Crosbie, after Sir Charles Alexander Harris, Newfoundland's governor from 1917 to 1922. When asked why Sir John had chosen to bestow this honour on so official a personage, Alex quipped, "Well, probably Father was trying to get a good deal with him." But somehow, Alexander Harris simply didn't stick to the Crosbie who would grow up as the baby of the family at Devon Place. Sir John bought his boy a Buffalo Bill outfit for his birthday, and little Alex wore it so much that everyone started calling him "Bill." The moniker stuck.

Father and son had been made strangers by the demands of business and politics, but in those last few months of Sir John's life, they finally got to spend some time together. The thirteen-year-old boy never forgot the fishing trips down the cape shore near Branch where his father loved to fish for sea trout:

"I recall one conversation during that summer. He said, 'Undoubtedly you'll get a good education. You'll have an opportunity to go to school, possibly in Canada. . . . The only thing I would say to you is that you are not being educated to leave Newfoundland.'. . . He made this point very clearly, he said, 'The money came from Newfoundland [to put you through] and don't forget it.' I said, 'Father, there is no way that I would ever leave Newfoundland.' But that was before I had gone to Canada. And there did come a time when the war was over that I seriously considered not returning to Newfoundland, and had several offers of jobs in the Canadian mainland. But I remembered that conversation, so I did come home."

By 1932, the much-loved June Bennett had been joined by four more grandchildren for Sir John and Lady Crosbie — Joan Elise and John Carnell Crosbie, the children of their eldest son Ches and his wife Jessie; Ann Elizabeth Perlin, the daughter of Vera Crosbie Perlin and her husband Albert; and Mitchie Anne Carleton, the daughter of Ella Maud (Dolly) Crosbie Carleton and her husband Jack. The day Mitchie Anne was born, her grandfather hoisted the flag at the summer house in South East Placentia. The fact that the child was named for her grandmother delighted Sir John, as he made plain in a letter to the new mother:

Hello My Darling,

How are you and Mippy? Just got a message from Jack and was pleased to know you were doing fairly well. Funny, great minds think alike, I was writing you this afternoon when I got Jack's message this morning. I told Jack that I was writing and mailing a cheque for 300 "bucks" to you & young Mippy. Hurrah, another Mippy, two great women!

You must pardon this short note as I'm per usual very much rushed, but take care of your sweet old self and if you want anything else just let Big Jack know.

With fondest love to you,
sweet Mippy, and Jack,

Yours, Dad

During Sir John's final illness, he still managed to indulge June Bennett, the grandchild who had so lit up his life. In healthier days, he had delighted in the child's companionship on the long trips down the old Placentia Highway to The Bungalow. Sir John was always careful to bring a large supply of towels along because June got terribly car-sick. The doting grandfather would clean up the little girl and then hurl the towels out the window, all the while urging his chauffeur to drive faster along a road that was little more than an elevated cowpath.

Now, as her grandfather lay dying, June Bennett was summoned to Sir John's bedside. Looking at her gravely, he said, "I heard that you said you were my favourite grandchild. Did you say that?"

"Oh no, Grandfather," came the reply. "I said I was the oldest."

Sir John knew right away that the accusation had been true but was delighted with how quickly the young girl responded with a plausible reply. A grin spread across his face "about a mile wide." He told her that she mustn't be heard saying such a thing — even though they both knew it was true. As his granddaughter recalled more than fifty years later, Sir John and the child understood each other's hearts.

Another visitor at his bedside that autumn was his daughter-in-law, Evelyn Shaver Crosbie, who was married to his son John. She was three months pregnant with her first son. Sir John confided to her that he had always wanted to be a doctor, but his dream had gone up in the smoke of the great fire of 1892, which had pressed him into the family business. He told the young woman that he had the feeling that the child she was carrying would realize his boyhood ambition. He was more right than he thought. Two of Evelyn's sons became doctors, and the youngest of them, Douglas, ended up attending Joe Smallwood in his declining years.

Whether through diabetes, intestinal cancer or, as some family members believed, cirrhosis, Sir John grew progressively worse. Two days before he died, he spoke to his daughter Dolly, who had returned home to convalesce from a bout of tuberculosis. He told her he had no regrets, but wished that "his Mippy" could go with him. Just before midnight on the evening of October 5, after Sir John had been taken to hospital, the telephone rang at Devon Place. It was answered by a nurse, "Curtie," who was in the house taking care of Dolly. Thirteen-year-old Bill was standing by the phone in his plaid dressing gown. He suspected his father was dead when Curtie uttered the stark and single word, "When?" He was certain when she quickly asked, "How is Lady Crosbie?"

Fighting back the tears, he went downstairs and said to his sister, "Boys don't cry, do they, Doll?" Early the next morning, Mitchie Anne returned from the hospital, where she had been keeping a vigil, and climbed the wide staircase to the upstairs sitting room, ramrod-straight but with an uncharacteristic heaviness in her step. "He's gone," she said softly.

With those words, the surviving Crosbies were left to face the gloom of the thirties without the man who had elevated them from an enterprising outport family to one of Newfoundland's most powerful clans. In the cold light of the October morning, more than one person in St. John's wondered if the passing of Sir John marked the end of a dynasty or merely the dawn of a new patriarch.

It would be up to the iron lady from Exploits, and her remarkable, if as yet untried son, Ches, to provide the answer.

CHAPTER 6

The Torch

ON THE DAY her grandfather was buried, June Bennett wasn't allowed to ride her bicycle. The little girl watched in hushed amazement from an upstairs window as the funeral procession crept along the leaf-strewn street below, the black-suited men respectfully tipping their hats as they passed the Bennett household on the way to the General Protestant Cemetery in the city's west end.

The cortege had set out in the waxen, yellow light of early October from Devon Place, where Sir John's funeral was held. His casket, flanked by an honour guard from the Orange and Whiteway Masonic Lodges, was preceded by a flower-laden hearse. Lt. Col. Leonard C. Outerbridge represented the governor, and a large crowd lined the route to the cemetery (though detractors would later claim they had turned out for the funeral of an ordinary working man who was buried the same day as Sir John). As the sombre retinue filed by Ches Crosbie's Water Street West residence, four-year-old Joan Crosbie, yet to grasp death's dark mystery, expected her grandfather to be sitting up in his casket. Disappointed, she asked her parents where he was.

Sir John would be buried in the shadow of a curved, art nouveau headstone that Mitchie Anne feared might be too ostentatious. Whether or not that was true, it was certainly a far cry from his brother Robert's unmarked grave.

"Sir John was a sturdy political fighter," *The Daily News* wrote in his obituary, "a man of strong opinions and fearless in his expression of them. But it can be said of him that although at times he hit hard, it was not with malice. He was big-hearted and generous, and even his strongest opponents found him a good friend in time of need."

In 1930s Newfoundland, however, life was for the living. In the harsh world of the island's business community, the opportunities presented by even such a distinguished death could not be ignored for long. Within three hours of Sir John's passing, five rival fish merchants had sent telegrams to his customers soliciting their accounts. Many people, including the dead man's old business and political rival William Coaker, believed that there was no fish exporter of Sir John's experience to fill the gap, particularly since foreign markets had virtually collapsed in the first bleak days of the Great Depression. Although Coaker knew that Ches Crosbie had been trained by his father to take over the family business, he predicted that it would be many years before Sir John's son would be able to fill his shoes.

Along with most other businesses, Sir John's fishing enterprise had been shaken to its foundations by the first shock waves of the Depression. In Newfoundland, the value of the fisheries in 1929 was $10 million; by 1931, two years after the collapse of Wall Street, it had fallen to $3 million. Crosbie and Company had worked with the Newfoundland Exporters' Association to develop a policy of quality controls to protect the all-important Brazilian market, but there was little that could be done when exports of drum-fish, (dried and salted codfish packed in wooden cylindrical containers for shipment to the South American market) dropped by half in the early thirties. The situation was painfully clear: the Crosbie fish business would either have to be refinanced or go bankrupt.

It didn't help matters that Sir John had personally lost $250,000 in the stock market crash. But the wily merchant-politician, who had pulled his family through so many vagaries of the Newfoundland economy during his lifetime, saved the day once more — this time, from beyond the grave. Several months before his death, Sir John had travelled to Montreal for a thorough medical check-up, feeling, perhaps, vague premonitions of what was to come. Although his doctor gave him a clean bill of health, the exhausted patriarch knew better. In May 1932, he took out a $300,000 life insurance policy, the largest he could buy. Five months later he was dead.

Sir John directed his executors — his wife, Mitchie Anne, and their sons Ches, George and John — to pay all his "just and true debts" and bequeathed all his property and effects to Lady Crosbie in a will signed on March 5, 1932. When the document was probated two weeks after his death, the estate was valued at $122,325.31. Coupled with Sir John's life insurance, which went into a spousal trust for Mitchie Anne, the Crosbie fortune stood at approximately $420,000 — out of which would come the money to keep the family empire afloat until the economy, along with the guns of war, boomed once more.

In the meantime, however, the gloom inspired by Sir John's passing was matched by the pall that hung over Newfoundland's economy. The dominion was paying a terrible price for years of financial mismanagement and political corruption. In 1928, Richard Squires had risen from the political dead to become premier of Newfoundland once again. Within two years, the Depression had struck Newfoundland like an iceberg below the waterline and the Harbour Grace lawyer had become captain of the *Titanic*. The bottom dropped out of Newfoundland's fish markets and some of the lowest catches of the century were recorded at a time when unemployment was soaring. The national debt quickly hit the frightening level of $110 million and interest charges now accounted for a staggering 65 percent of government expenditures. Sir John's worst fears about the economy were coming to pass. With thousands of Newfoundlanders on relief and hundreds more suffering from malnutrition, Squires desperately sought credit to keep the dominion afloat. He even offered to sell Labrador, so recently awarded to Newfoundland, for the bargain price of $110 million! Ottawa, with huge economic problems of its own, passed on the real estate bargain of the century.

At the eleventh hour, the Canadian banks came through with a loan to meet Newfoundland's interest payments on its huge debt, largely in response to pressure from the Canadian government, which in turn had been lobbied by Britain. In return, the banks were left in complete control of the island's finances. Two of the measures the banks demanded and got were an increase in the tax on food and a cut in pensions to war veterans — hardly the kind of economizing calculated to win the support of a population that was going hungry and which had lost so many of its sons on the bloody battlefields of Europe. Newfoundland politicians were learning the bitter lesson that he who pays the piper calls the tune.

Just when Newfoundland needed leadership of the highest order from its politicians, the mercurial Richard Squires betrayed the public trust and disgraced himself for the second time in his career. In February 1932, Peter Cashin, Newfoundland's Finance minister, resigned from the Squires government and charged the premier with paying himself $5,000 a year from the War Reparation Commission, the equivalent of stealing from widows and orphans.

The public brooded over the scandal, bitterly reflecting on the premier's malfeasance of 1923, before exploding in a black and ugly rage. A mob of several hundred people attacked the court house where Squires had his office, intending to lay hands on the premier. Luckily, Squires was nowhere to be found. Then, on April 4, 1932, a delegation of concerned citizens tried to present a petition to the House of Assembly asking for a proper investigation into the charges against Squires. The exercise swiftly escalated into a full-scale riot, the principal aim of which seemed to be to lynch the premier. Squires was spirited out of the House, which the mob then tried to sack and burn. After smashing the windows of the legislature, the rioters turned on the city, looting and burning until their supercharged emotions were played out.

Incredibly, Squires did not resign; he called a June election instead. His once great Liberal Party won only two seats, and F. C. Alderdice came to power, or rather powerlessness. There was nothing Newfoundland could do about the financial morass into which it was disappearing other than to cut services, stint its own employees and default on the interest owed on its $110-million national debt.

For reasons of their own, Britain and Canada came to the rescue and paid the interest on Newfoundland's debt for the last six months of 1932. In return, Newfoundland agreed to a British Royal Commission that would look into the island's desperate financial situation and come up with ways it could be improved. Among the findings of the three commissioners, led by Lord Amulree, was the recommendation that representative government in Newfoundland be suspended until the country was self-supporting again. In November 1933, the House of Assembly adopted a measure asking the king to suspend Newfoundland's constitution. The Newfoundland Bill passed swiftly through the British House of Commons and on February 11, 1934, Premier Alderdice signed away Newfoundland's political sovereignty for what turned out to be fifteen years.

It could not have been lost on Newfoundlanders that the first chairman of the Commission of Government, Sir David Murray Anderson, was a retired admiral in the British Navy. There were three other British commissioners and three Newfoundlanders in the new regime, including former premier Alderdice. In one fell swoop, the island's political history had been set back a hundred years. For defaulting on its bills, Newfoundland had been sent to the constitutional poorhouse — the only western democracy to suffer such an ignominious fate. As one Newfoundlander, E. D. Elliott, would observe from the bitter perspective of the mid-1930s, Newfoundland was now worse off within the British Empire than "the Kaffirs of Africa."

Surrounded on all sides by unsettling political and economic change, Lady Crosbie tried to make the big white house on Kingsbridge Road a safe harbour for her large family, running the place just as she had when Sir John was alive. The children were encouraged to bring their friends home, and dinner at Devon Place typically featured ten people or more. Sir John's den was sometimes used by Vera's charming husband, Albert Perlin, who was fast becoming Newfoundland's leading journalist.

In 1932, shortly after her father's death, Edith Crosbie married Robert Panckridge, an officer in the Royal Navy. The two had met at the annual dance at Government House, just before the navy took Newfoundland's lieutenant governor on his summer tour of the island. At the time, Edith was engaged to an American, but when she met "the really gorgeous" Robert, she had a change of heart. She had only two problems; how to break her engagement, and how to meet Robert again.

The Crosbie girls were quick on their feet. The smitten young woman knew that her fiancé would shortly be coming to Montreal for a visit, so she called her sister, Dolly, who lived in Montreal, and asked her to send a cable to St. John's requesting that Edith come up to help her care for her baby, Mitchie Anne. Edith then arranged a rendezvous with Panckridge in Montreal. After meeting her fiancé's train and breaking their engagement, she was only a cab-ride away from the arms of her new love.

They were married in New York with sister Olga and sister-in-law Evelyn in attendance. The strikingly handsome British officer and the plain Edith, who looked out on the world from behind thick glasses, appeared to be a strange match. But like her older sister Margaret, Edith had a sparkling personality and a winningly spontaneous nature. Years later, after her husband was promoted to the rank of Admiral and knighted, the uppercrust British got a taste of "Lady Panckridge's" uninhibited personality. Lord and Lady Mountbatten were dining with the Panckridges, and Edith had had a bell installed under the table beside her foot to summon the maid when the time came to clear the table.

"This particular night they forgot to put the bell under her foot," her niece, Debbie Powers, recalled. "So when the table had to be cleared, she kept pushing her foot and nothing happened. Completely undaunted, up went the table cloth, 'Excuse me,' and under she went until she found it!"

Despite the growing number of her children who had married and left home, Lady Crosbie remained the centre of her energetic clan. Once a week, on Thursdays, she hosted her famous "Boys Day" luncheons. On these occasions, her sons and their business associates gathered in the dining room of Devon Place, much to the chagrin of the Crosbie wives, whose attendance was expressly forbidden. (It was at one of these luncheons, after the death of Sir John, that Lady Crosbie agreed to lend her son Ches $50,000 from the estate to keep the near-bankrupt Crosbie companies afloat.) The tradition would endure for nearly twenty years. There would be drinks for the men before lunch and, on rare occasions, Lady Crosbie would herself have a glass of sherry. The news of the day — Commission of Government, business prospects and the choicest gossip of a gossipy town were discussed over roast beef, pease pudding and Newfoundland berries from the family garden. Although local topics dominated the table talk, Mitchie Anne, like everyone else, worried about the war clouds gathering over Europe and the state of the Empire — a concern that was reinforced after she watched a special newsreel of the Coronation Parade at the governor's residence. She especially hoped that a solution could be found to "the King's Dilemma" over Mrs. Simpson — a dangerous liaison that she had learned about during a trip to England before the scandal became public. In America, the spectre of abdication was an intriguing titillation; in Newfoundland, where the British connection ran deep, it was the stuff of genuine tragedy.

Seven of Lady Crosbie's children — Nina, Vera, Dolly, Edith, Ches, George and Jack — were now married, but the ones who remained at home were treated to the same advantages, despite the hard times, that their older brothers and sisters had enjoyed. The Crosbie commitment to education was equally strong for daughters as for sons. Vera and Nina had been sent to Westminister Ladies School in Toronto; Dolly to Queen's Gate in South Kensington, London; Margaret and Edith to finishing school in Virginia; Ches, George and Percy to St. Andrew's College in Ontario.

Now Olga became the second Crosbie daughter to attend Queen's Gate. When her sister Dolly had first arrived there, her European classmates had expected the first Newfoundlander they had ever seen to be an "Esquimo"; they were sorely disappointed when she turned out to be someone who looked a lot like them. The year after his father's death,

Bill was sent to Appleby College in Oakville. The family felt that since Ches had excelled in football at St. Andrew's, where sports was an important part of the curriculum, it would simply be too much to ask of the sedentary Bill to follow in his robust brother's footsteps. Homesick and miserable, the young boy wrote the words "Newfoundland is Heaven" across the top of all of his examinations — the same words that would later be chiselled on his tombstone.

Wherever her children were, Lady Crosbie kept in touch with marvellous, newsy letters larded with information about the family and solid Victorian advice. She offered pointers on whether a gentleman should remove his glove to shake hands, extolled the virtues of a good tailor and the propriety of linen handkerchiefs. She even had words of wisdom on how to ride a horse: "Don't let the horse bounce you up and down when it canters or gallops. Lift yourself, it comes easily and naturally. You need to be absolutely fearless. A horse can always tell if one is afraid and that makes it harder to control."

She was equally at home in deeper waters. When sixteen-year-old Bill confided that he was experiencing a certain religious "unrest" as his educational horizons broadened, his mother nudged him back into the fold, calling his disquiet "God's happy spirit speaking to your spirit." She told him about her own conversion as a girl of seventeen during communion at the Cochrane Street Wesleyan Church, an event that sustained her through life's later trials. Compared to her brother Jabez's earthy advice to young Bill — "Keep your pecker up" — her words of wisdom were positively sublime. Later, when Bill began reading about communism and socialism, she tried to take the lustre off the alluring new politics of the thirties by referring to a family friend who had recently walked across Russia, observing that he was "not nearly so much communistic after the trip. I think Russia cured him of that."

Although there was money to send Bill to the University of Toronto (Lady Crosbie had had the young man's head measured by a phrenologist and was delighted when the results augured well for high intellectual achievement), there was none to waste. And as a letter she wrote to him made clear, he was expected to make the most of his educational opportunity. Lady Crosbie's words also revealed a duty-bound pragmatist anxious to instill the work ethic in her maturing children.

"Your duty to me and to yourself, your name and the family, to your father, whose work and money make it possible for you to go to University, is to work seriously at the course you have chosen — don't let yourself be side-tracked and take on too many other interests that will not leave you time for the important work, however good they may be in themselves. Keep an open mind, study from the view-point of the onlooker, judge people by their conduct, what they do more than what they say. Times are changing, men's thoughts are changing. By the time you get through University, you will be able to bring a trained mind to think about things as they are. One of the hardest things in life is to think. So many just leave the thinking out of things to others."

One of Mitchie Anne's formulas for self-improvement was the ability to speak other languages. She encouraged Bill to master French, remembering a trip she herself had made to South America to look into the family's margarine business in Sao Paulo, Brazil, shortly after Sir John's death: "We found Brazilians who could not speak a word of English could speak French well, so if we had known French, as we should have, we could have gotten along well together." The experience brought her to one of her favourite maxims. "All educated people speak more than one language." Had her grandson, little John Crosbie, been listening and taken her advice to heart, it might have carried him all the way to 24 Sussex Drive.

While Lady Crosbie toiled to keep her large and energetic family together, it fell to her sons to look after the business interests left to them by their father. Just as Sir John had come to the aid of his mother, Martha Ellen, in 1895 when George Graham died, Ches Crosbie now became Mitchie Anne's strong right arm. He was twenty-seven years old, rough as a pine plank, bull-strong and, as his Aunt Ellie Bell once remarked, the kind of person who made you feel good just by walking into a room — even when he had herring sticking to his boots!

Despite his youthfulness, Chesley Arthur Crosbie was the obvious choice to assume the presidency of Crosbie and Company. All his life he had worked for his father in the family's shipping and salt fish business on the North Shore. While away from home as a teenager, he'd lived with his Uncle Walter, who had to leave the front door open for his carousing boarder so he could creep to bed in the wee hours of the morning. Even when his father came up from St. John's to check on him, the roistering Ches would somehow manage to beat Sir John to the fish plant, no matter how late he'd been out the night before. On one occasion, the motorbike Ches and his younger brother George were riding ran out of gas on their way home from a particularly wild night. Working on the theory that the evening's activities had turned their bodies into fuel reservoirs, they urinated into the gas tank. The fortified fluid wouldn't burn, but their father's ears did when he heard about the escapade!

Like all the Crosbie children, Ches was sent away to boarding school. After finishing at St. Andrew's College, where he was better remembered for his football than his scholarship, Ches told Sir John that he wanted to become an electrical engineer. Hoping to harness his son's boundless energy and personal charisma for the family business, Sir John nixed the proposal. But his past had tempered his autocratic streak. Remembering his own derailed university plans of thirty years earlier, he offered his headstrong son a compromise. If Ches would agree to throw in his lot with his father, he would be given a year off to do whatever he wanted at Sir John's expense.

It may have been the most important deal Sir John ever made. Ches agreed to join the family firm and, at the age of eighteen, the swashbuckling heir to Crosbie and Company packed a sea trunk for Europe, where he sowed some wild oats. Like his parents, the stocky young man with the razor-thin moustache and glittering dark eyes had a strong practical side and lived by the informal Crosbie motto, work hard, play hard. Ches ended his European junket with a five-month accountancy course in England, which provided the basis for his later expertise in foreign exchange matters. On his way back home, he signed on with a steam trawler in

Hull, England, and learned firsthand about commercial fishing in Iceland and the White Sea. If he was going to one day run the family fish business, then he wanted to see how the competition operated. All his life, Ches Crosbie would be hungry for any new ideas that could be put to work in Newfoundland. Forgetting sometimes how innately conservative his island society was, particularly when it came to its ingrained fishing habits, he would occasionally pay a heavy price for being too far ahead of his time.

Like his father, Ches married young. He was just twenty-one when he wed the majestically beautiful Jessie Carnell. The two had been childhood sweethearts. St. John's was a closed society in those days and the prominent families — the Chalkers, the Crosbies, the Carnells, the Ayres, the Bowrings, the Murrays, the Bells and the Jobs — had a way of keeping to their peer group. An endless string of garden parties where the merchant aristocracy mingled had a way of leading to wedding parties in which their children were the principals. It had always been taken for granted that Ches and Jessie would end up together, and no one was particularly surprised when their first child, Joan, was born almost nine months to the day after their wedding. As one family acquaintance quipped, "Jessie was pregnant before the honeymoon ship got out of the harbour." Three years later, their first son, John, came along, and a year later, their last child, Andrew. Afterwards, their stormy history served as an illustration of the edict of Tennessee Williams, who said that when a relationship goes on the rocks, the rocks can be found in the marriage bed.

Despite the obvious physical attraction between them in the beginning, it would have been difficult to find a less compatible couple than Ches and Jessie Crosbie. Their next-door neighbour on Water Street West, Dr. Harry Roberts, echoed many people's thoughts when he observed, "I don't know how in the Christ he ever got her to marry him because Ches was a rough Crosbie and Jessie was a perfect lady." So perfect, in fact, that her nickname was "the Duchess." The blue-eyed beauty with the thick mane of hair that went prematurely — and strikingly — grey was Boston-educated, bought her clothes in New York and would one day be featured in *New Liberty* magazine as one of Canada's ten best-dressed women.

Her father, Andrew Carnell, was the colourful patriarch of one of the oldest business families in St. John's. Four generations before him, Gilbert Carnell had opened a carriage factory on Duckworth Street. From as early as 1780, Carnell's was building carriages and sleighs and had set up a special branch for funeral undertaking, including a coffin-making shop. By the time Andrew Carnell took over the family business with a first-class certificate from the United States School of Embalmery in Chicago, class of 1902, making him the first licensed embalmer in Newfoundland, the company had expanded to five separate departments: a wheelwright division, which made carriages, sleighs, carts, wheelbarrows, express wagons, coal carts, bread wagons and other horse-drawn vehicles; a forge division, which produced wagon springs and rubber tires for all sizes of wheels; an upholstering division, which made wagon seats, convertible tops and automobile interiors; a garage, which specialized in repairs, painting and body work; and, last but not least, a funeral home division which also specialized in body work and offered a full line of custom-made coffins!

The history of the Carnell business interests was the history of business in Newfoundland — constant adaptation to new circumstances in the always uncertain project of commercial survival. In his own efforts to secure and expand his father's company, Ches Crosbie learned many lessons from his wife's talented and gregarious father, who, after his first mayoralty election in 1933 was known as "the Mayor of Newfoundland." (There were no other elected mayors in Newfoundland in 1934.) As for Ches's eldest son, John, who was born in 1931, it was often remarked that he was more of a Carnell than a Crosbie, sharing with his maternal grandfather a love of politics and an acid wit that was the envy of his colleagues and the scourge of his opponents.

With Ches away so much on business — a bitter bone of contention between the couple throughout their thirty-five-year marriage — Jessie Crosbie was the undisputed matriarch of her young family. She brought all the Carnell virtues of strictness and stubbornness to the task of single-handedly rearing her energetic, inquisitive and at times rambunctious children. While Joan (described by one family member as "the most beautiful baby" she had ever seen) and Andrew were basically good-natured and easy to get along with, cranky John was his own baby at age two. Rejecting any food that was covered in skin, he once faced down his determined mother for two hours, refusing to chew on the mouthful of peas she had given him.

As a boy, John Crosbie was a member in good standing of the Sudbury Street Gang — a band of local desperadoes who hung out in Thompson's Field behind the Crosbie's Water Street West residence. In winter, there was sliding and skating; in summer, they played soccer and baseball and John's favourite pastime, cowboys and Indians. Even then, John could be a mean hombre. "I remember one time we took young Jim Chalker up about twelve rungs of a ladder and we stood him up on a box and we tied his arms to the rung of the ladder and [John] kicked the boxes away so Jim was left hanging by his arms about eight feet off the ground," brother Andrew recalled.

When housebound, there was the usual sibling rivalry between the two Crosbie boys. One day, John peeked through a keyhole to see what his brother was up to, and a mischievous Andrew blew dust into the spy's inquisitive eye. One-eyed John, the "enforcer" of the Sudbury Street Gang "split the door of the attic to get at him." At such times, Jessie would arrive on the scene and wade into the fray with "a big, long, white rubber belt, slashing and dashing like a lion-tamer."

Vexed by her husband's attendance at Lady Crosbie's exclusive "Boys Day" luncheons, Jessie Crosbie began a parallel tradition with her own children, except that the hosts of the weekly meetings were the Carnells. Every Thursday at lunch break, John and Andrew would dine with their grandmother, Mabel Carnell, and her husband, Andrew, who became such an influence on young John. At the end of every lunch both boys would be served their favourite desserts — chocolate pudding with sunshine sauce for John and gingerbread pudding with hard sauce for Andrew.

Routinely concealed, John's emotions ran deep. When his grandmother Carnell died, the teenager wrote a poem called "Grannie":

Down to earth, simple, homespun, . . .
Loved, adored by us, her grandchildren
Ever since we were able to understand feelings,
Grannie made the chocolate pudding with the sunshine sauce,
We went to Grannie's for afternoon tea,
She was the one who bounced us on her knee
Grannie lived the old life of the home . . .

The children's relationship with their father in the early years was distant. There was always a certain amount of tension in the air between the young husband and his aristocratic wife when Ches was at home, particularly if he had been drinking. As John Crosbie recalled, when his father was sober, he was "a prince of a man, and very charming. When he was drinking, he was the exact opposite." Afflicted with the family failing, which would in time turn into chronic alcoholism, Ches would alternate between periods of abstinence and great, bawdy benders that could go on for weeks at a time. When the children saw him raise that first, tell-tale glass of sherry, they knew he would be "on the booze" a few days later. At such times, they gave their father a wide berth and their mother their sympathy. Only later, when they better understood the forces at work in the deteriorating marriage, would their judgment be more even-handed.

In the early years of Ches Crosbie's stewardship of Crosbie and Company, the firm was primarily involved in salt codfish, shipping, margarine and insurance. The Crosbie interests were varied and far flung, so it was necessary to lean on other family members to run the various businesses smoothly. At first, Ches's principal help came from his brother George, who was a year younger. Where Ches liked to shock, and was so gruff by nature that his own relatives often thought he was angry with them, "Gentleman George" always stood when a lady entered the room, he opened doors and displayed impeccable manners.

Such sensibility in rough-and-ready St. John's was destined for caricature. It was normal for "Mr. George" to arrive at the Butter Company in the morning dressed immaculately, wearing a Homburg and dangling a cigarette-holder in his hand. It was his custom to say good morning to the staff — a little grandly — as he mounted the long staircase to his office. On one occasion, he took off his coat and hat and handed his cigarette-holder to an employee at the bottom of the stairs. George's daughter, Deborah Powers, recalled what happened next.

"He said, 'Myron, take that upstairs for me.' He could be typically Crosbie when he approached you that way. So Dick took it up, and when he got to the top of the stairs, unbeknownst to my father, Dick put on the hat, the coat and held the cigarette-holder between his index and middle fingers. He had the hat pulled right down to the eyes, the coat just dragged right across his heels because he was so much shorter, and Dick came down the stairs pretending to be Mr. George. 'Good morning, good morning,' he intoned. Of course, the place went up. And then there was suddenly this hush, and you-know-who was standing at the door, watching the whole performance. Well, he turned around and growled, 'Myron, get up those goddamned stairs.' There was a silence in which you could have heard a pin drop before Father added, 'And do it all over again!' By which time he was killing himself laughing!"

The dandyish exterior concealed a shrewd businessman who had learned at Sir John's knee how to run a business in Newfoundland. Although Sir John had wanted George to go to university, the young man had preferred instead to earn his spurs at the Butter Company, a decision he never regretted. In keeping with Sir John's view that his children should learn the business from the ground up, his initial job in 1925 was to paint the new factory's smoke-stack. Only after that was he given "inside" responsibilities. Finally, he travelled Newfoundland selling the company's product, an easy job for the man with the Clark Gable good looks who dressed and acted like a Hollywood movie star. Referring to his father, George once said, "He only lived seven years after I went to work for the company. From a business point of view, seven years of working with him was better than all the university I could get anywhere."

A case in point was the Butter Company's employee benefits package. When he first went to work for Sir John, George asked why the company spent so much on medical and pension plans for its workers: "He told me that, over the years, you appreciate your machinery and provide repairs and maintenance. So what about the human element? They wear out too, and it makes sense to provide medical and pension plans."

History provides an interesting footnote to the Crosbie approach to employee relations. By 1942, the employees of the Butter Company had unionized and George Crosbie, as managing director, had signed the contract. But within a year, the employees had asked for permission to tear up their own agreement. The generous medical and pension schemes that Sir John had set up in 1925 were superior to the regulated benefits under unionization. Many years later, George Crosbie would underscore the corporate benefits of his family's attitude towards its workforce: "We lose girls through marriage, we lose people through death, but that's about it. Every other employee becomes a goodwill ambassador for the company."

George was assisted at the Newfoundland Butter Company by his brother John Chalker Crosbie. Described by friends as a "solid, sincere individual" somewhere between the roughness of Ches and the refined good manners of George, "Jack" Crosbie had gone the university route, studying dairy technology at the University of Guelph, where he earned a Bachelor of Science degree in agriculture. During the Commission of Government era, Jack worked with Newfoundland's Director of Agriculture to improve the diet of Newfoundlanders.

At the time, beriberi (a condition brought on by thiamine deficiency) and even scurvy — particularly infantile scurvy (caused by an absence of Vitamin C) were widespread in Newfoundland. The effects of these deficiencies were tragically increased by the social stigma attached to eating brown or "dole" bread. No Newfoundlander would eat brown bread if he could afford white, even though it contained the crucially important Vitamin B. A family would often give white bread to a pregnant woman while they themselves ate the brown, believing they were making a beneficial sacrifice. Often, she would then be brought into a clinic unable to walk, suffering from paralysis brought on by beriberi.

Jack Crosbie tried to educate Newfoundlanders about good nutritional habits at the agricultural fairs that he helped the Commission of Government organize. He also inspected all of Newfoundland's sixty dairy farms, suggesting improvements in general operations and sanitary conditions. As a result of Crosbie's work, and a comprehensive medical survey requested by the Commission of Government in 1944, margarine was fortified with Vitamins A and B to improve the general health of the populace.

With "Gentleman George" and Jack taking care of the family's margarine business, Percy Crosbie helped his older brother Ches on the shipping and fishing side. Based on his study of a new fishing technology, the use of trawlers in the North Sea, Ches set up the Newfoundland Trawling Company in 1935. The company bought a British steam trawler, *The Imperialist*, to supply their modernized curing plant at Harbour Grace. It was the first trawler to fish out of Newfoundland. Nineteen-year-old Percy went on board to get a grounding in the business. It was Percy who managed the drying operation on the North Shore, where the Crosbies cured split fish in the sun on frames covered with wire mesh instead of the traditional bough-covered flakes. At its peak, the operation employed more than two hundred workers. Percy also oversaw the operation of *The Linda May*, captained by Les Winsor, as well as other Crosbie sealing ships. When the seal fishery eventually came crashing down in an atmosphere of international controversy, sparked by the activities of movie stars like Brigitte Bardot, it was Percy Crosbie who spoke for devastated Newfoundland sealers on the CBC.

Percy Manuel Crosbie was the perfect foil for his more visionary and volatile brother. He shared Ches's enthusiasm for new ideas, but he was more cautious about the practical implications of adopting them. As a personality in the company, he was, if anything, even more gregarious than Ches, and enjoyed the respect of his employees. His formal education was reinforced by the rigours of personal participation in the seal hunt and the Grand Banks cod fishery. A shrewd businessman, his near-fatal flaw was the family failing, a severe alcoholism that he survived only because he developed diabetes. Unable to drink, he turned his talents to business and his recreational time to blackjack in the casinos of Puerto Rico. Like most of the Crosbies, he had the touch with people. A close friend remembered, "He was a good horse-driver. He didn't tighten the reins, just gradually got them all in pace and they were all running the same. Percy lived to make money." For more than thirty years, he and Ches would do just that as they guided the companies into an era Sir John could not have imagined.

Assisted though he was by those of his brothers who were old enough to roll up their sleeves and pitch in, it was Ches Crosbie who put the family on the map during the first, dark days of the Depression. In the uncertain and archly conservative business atmosphere of 1933, Ches became a "national hero" in Newfoundland when his ship the *Ungava*, under Captain Peter Carter, brought in a record-breaking amount of seal fat. The sealers on board received $80.36 a man as their share of the catch — a fortune by Depression standards. The remarkable thing about the *Ungava*'s trip was that it was one of the first business decisions the young man had made since assuming control of Crosbie and Company. Newfoundland governor, Sir David Murray Anderson, flanked by Ches and George, met the *Ungava* when it docked in St. John's with its precious cargo destined for the margarine plant. In one stroke, Ches Crosbie's reputation as a risk-taker and rugged man of action was secured at a time when many of his rivals were hiding under the economic bed waiting for the storm to pass.

Nor was Ches reluctant to continue some of the grander traditions of his father, despite the hard economic times. One day in 1933, he was on his way to see Captain Olaf Olsen, an associate in the whaling industry, when his latest acquisition, a smart, two-toned blue Nash Eighty-Eight, equipped with every option including overdrive, chugged to a halt. Ches and his wharf boss, Tom Lockyear, were peering uncertainly under the hood when Tom Dormady happened along and quickly fixed the car's sticky choke cable. On the spot, Ches offered him a job as his chauffeur, only to find out that both Dormady's father and grandfather had worked for Sir John. Dormady signed on and never forgot the time he spent with Sir John's hard-driving successor. There were many trips around Conception Bay in the Nash with time out along the way for one of Ches's favourite pastimes — target practice in gravel pits using German Lugers that belonged to J. W. Morris of the Newfoundland Light and Power Company. As a matter of record, Tom Dormady's boss was a dead shot.

"A day spent with Ches Crosbie was a day well spent. The man was agreeable, pleasant to work for, a brilliant conversationalist, and, like his dad, Sir John, he had firsthand knowledge of ships and shipping in Newfoundland," Dormady would recall fifty years later.

But when his faithful chauffeur wasn't in the driver's seat, Ches Crosbie's car turned into hell on wheels, as an encounter he had with the local constabulary chillingly illustrates. At five o'clock in the afternoon on July 7, 1939, Sergeant William Case was motoring along Topsail Road when a car shot past him "at a very high rate of speed," even though the posted limit was just 25 miles per hour. Sergeant Case ordered the speeding vehicle to be chased, concluding that "the driver must be drunk or mad," apparently overlooking the possibility that he might be both.

For nine winding miles the policeman ate Ches Crosbie's dust, finally losing him when it was decided that a 70-mile-per-hour police chase was just too dangerous to the public. That opinion was shared by an unfortunate motorist who was fixing his truck at the side of the road when the speeding vehicles loomed menacingly into sight around a corner, forcing him to scramble for his life. When the policeman finally intercepted the suspect's car, Ches was charged with and later convicted of "furious driving" and "driving to the danger of the public." The penalty for his joy ride was sixty dollars; the lesson was to leave the driving to the chauffeur.

BY HOOK OR by crook, Ches guided the family fortunes through the lean years of the thirties. But the world was going through changes; the old ways of Sir John couldn't help the business now. The Commission of Government astutely recognized that Newfoundland's fishery — which by then was far behind the modernized fisheries of its competitors, Norway and Iceland — had to be overhauled and diversified. The commissioners decided to invest in fresh fish marketing because poor countries had become too poor to buy Newfoundland's salt fish. This was not good news for the Crosbies, who had built their entire business around salt fish and lacked the capital to make the expensive conversion to the new enterprise, which required trawlers and processing plants.

Then, in 1938, there was another major blow to Crosbie and Company, which at that time was the largest shipper of salt fish to Brazil. The Brazilian government levied a new tariff on their product that made it impossible to sell there at a profit. The ink was changing colour on the company's balance sheet and the message to the young businessman was clear: adjust or perish.

Ches realized that the family would have to ease out of the fish business, at least temporarily, and diversify its interests. Other Newfoundland businessmen were doing well as manufacturers' agents — wholesale distributors of foodstuffs and manufactured goods from outside the province which they had the exclusive right to sell at a commission. Ches set his sights on expanding his grandfather's success with the White sewing machine line, but in the meantime looked for new sources of capital. In late 1937, he formed a partnership with one of Newfoundland's richest men, Chesley A. Pippy.

Crosbie, who had already introduced the first trawler into the Newfoundland fishery, now built the province's first indoor arena with artificial ice. Under the management of Arthur Johnson, the rink flourished as one of the most popular entertainments in St. John's until it was destroyed by fire in 1941. The construction of the arena was typical of a pattern that Ches Crosbie would follow all his life; backed into an economic corner, he would come out fighting with a new venture or innovation, sometimes profitable, sometimes not. This new venture, of no great moment in itself, foreshadowed a dramatic shift by the Crosbies into the lucrative construction business that would make the firm so wealthy in the fifties and sixties.

In 1938, the Crosbie companies were in desperate need of new capital to stay afloat. The margarine factory in Sao Paulo was still profitable, but, as Ches found out when he travelled there in 1937, he couldn't take any of his profits out of the country. Although he was owed roughly $100,000, he would finally have to resort to the black market and a little gentlemanly smuggling to get even two-thirds of his assets back into Newfoundland. For the time being, it was Sir John's business acumen that once again saved the day.

The margarine factory that Sir John started in 1925 was doing so well that it attracted the attention of Unilever, the food giant from the United Kingdom. Unilever had already bought out Harvey–Brehm, the Newfoundland Butter Company's principal competition, and Lady Crosbie reasoned that it was better to sell than be overwhelmed by the powerful, multinational firm. The new owners kept the name of the company (in 1950, the Newfoundland Butter Company became the Newfoundland Margarine Company Limited) and retained George and Jack Crosbie to run it. Writing to her youngest son, Bill, who was away at school, the matriarch of the Crosbie clan explained: "If we had waited, we might have had to sell at their price. It was certainly a good idea of your father's starting that business. He has looked after us all."

(It is interesting to note that, prior to Newfoundland joining Confederation in 1949, the manufacture of margarine in Canada was illegal; this was a commercial restriction imposed largely through the influence of the country's powerful butter lobby. When Newfoundland was permitted to produce margarine under Term 46 of the Terms of Union, several mainland businesses pressed Ottawa for the same right as Canada's newest province. Although the federal government acceded to their demands, Canadian margarine was sold for years in an unappetizing white block with a package of artificial colouring that had to be added by the consumer. The butter lobby had been defeated but not yet routed.)

With the businesses on a steady keel thanks to Ches and his brothers, Lady Crosbie was able to preside over her family's interests like the dowager she was. Part of that meant raising the children who were still at home. On Friday night, January 18, 1935, she threw a party for her daughter Olga. It must have been a gay sight to anyone passing by on Kingsbridge Road as the young guests danced in the dining and drawing rooms of Devon Place and took a late supper in the upstairs sitting room overlooking the street. Percy was even persuaded to wear tails and a white vest and tie, and although he grumbled he was, in Lady Crosbie's opinion, secretly pleased with the figure he cut. The affair was a huge success and the band played "God Save the King" at 1:45 a.m.

Two years later, on Olga's twenty-first birthday, Lady Crosbie held another great party, this time with a pirate theme. Olga's young niece, June Bennett, dressed up as a cabin boy and was allowed to stay up until the late supper was served. June slept in the same bedroom as her aunt and was awakened early that morning by Olga, who had something to show her. "Look what Lewis gave me," she gasped. It was a travel alarm clock in a leather case. Every time Olga touched the face of the clock, she repolished the crystal with the edge of the bedsheet.

Lewis Ayre and Olga had been close since the age of twelve, and a year after the pirate party they would marry. Lady Crosbie must have been pleased with the match. The Ayres were an old and prosperous St. John's merchant family who had opened their first store on Water Street in 1859, while George Graham Crosbie was still trying to get used to the Newfoundland weather!

The wedding was set for March 1939 at the Cochrane Street United Church. Lady Crosbie, Olga and her sisters Dolly, Vera and the beautiful Margaret went to New York to buy the bride's trousseau. Olga's wedding dress came from Lord & Taylor. The women made merry in New York from their base in Suite 701 of the Weylin Hotel, shopping and taking in Broadway shows as they prepared for Olga's big day.

Back in Newfoundland, Olga had a "doe" dinner to complement her husband's stag party. Verses were written on shower presents, and eight of Olga's intimate friends gave the young bride a "riding" about what was in store for her. (More than fifty years later, Olga Ayre, now widowed, still takes part in biweekly poker parties with six of the women who attended her doe party.)

On the day of the wedding, the church was packed with friends and well-wishers. The Ayres closed the family store in honour of the occasion. The church doors were thrown open so that the young couple could march down the centre aisle to meet the crowds outside. Just as they were opened to the early spring air, they had to be quickly closed again. Eight-year-old John Crosbie, one of the pages, "wished to wash his hands" as it was delicately put at the time. It was quite a day for little John, who had also managed a ride on the bride's train as the procession made its way towards the altar.

After the wedding, Olga and Lewis took the train for their honeymoon in Montreal. What should have been an overnight journey turned into a nine-day ordeal as the train got stuck in one of central Newfoundland's formidable snowstorms. A mainland hockey team was on the same train, and every time Olga stepped out of her drawing room, the cry would go up from one end of their car to the other, "Here comes the Bridie!" Things didn't improve much when the train finally reached its destination. Their steamer proceeded to get icebound in the Gulf of St. Lawrence! As for the marriage itself, it was clear sailing for a lifetime.

LIKE THE NEWLYWEDS, Newfoundland society remained lodged in the ice of the Depression for most of the 1930s, despite the best efforts of the Commission of Government. Charged with a forbidding task during a worldwide depression — the economic, political, and moral rehabilitation of the former dominion — the governor and his six commissioners — three from Whitehall and three from Newfoundland — were gradually mired in the swamp they were trying to drain.

There was no question about who ran the Commission of Government. British career diplomats who had learned their skills in the Home Office of the greatest imperial power in the world were firmly in charge of the lost Dominion. At a time when Mussolini was taking Italian society by the neck and giving it a good shake, Newfoundland had Commissioner Thomas Lodge, a brilliant, bureaucratic snob who quickly became Newfoundland's king of condescension as he set out to save the local inhabitants, most of whom he regarded as cultural cave-dwellers. "With the possible exception of Russia and a couple of the Balkan States, I doubt whether there is any purely white community in the world on such a low cultural level or where complete ignorance of anything outside the daily task is so widespread," he observed in a memorandum to the Dominions Office.

In keeping with Lodge's elitist insensitivities, Commission of Government began with a series of public relations disasters and ended the decade in economic circumstances more desperate than the ones that brought it into being. For starters, the commissioners gutted the national legislature and turned it into office space. A people defeated on the battlefield couldn't have received a more resounding slap in the face than to see the former seat of its democratic institutions put to so mundane a use. Adding insult to injury, the national museum was closed, its priceless treasures left to decay in carelessly chosen sites around the city. Worst of all, the governor and his commissioners became the ultimate backroom boys of public administration. With the visible signs of their lost status all around them, Newfoundlanders were kept in the dark as to how their enlightened English masters intended to save them.

Given the foolhardiness of the government's plan, it is probably just as well. Despite Newfoundland's long-standing maritime tradition, and a workforce comprised almost exclusively of highly skilled fishermen, Lodge convinced his associates that unemployed Newfoundlanders should be turned into farmers! He based his conclusion on his view of Newfoundland as an overpopulated island that relied too heavily on the capriciousness of the fishery. He reasoned that if the unemployed couldn't make a living from the sea, or in the island's mines, the alternatives were clear: emigration or land settlement. Since the former course was politically unacceptable, he forcefully advocated land settlement. There was only one problem with the mandarin's elegantly logical solution: Newfoundland had no soil. The government's homesteading policy was a two-edged disaster; virtually no permanent farms were ever established, and funds desperately needed to finance the modernization of the Newfoundland fishery were wasted on Lodge's ill-conceived attempt to have fishermen trade their sou'westers for Stetsons.

But there was at least one bright spot on the record of the Commission of Government. To their credit, the English commissioners worked a minor miracle in the administrative reorganization of Newfoundland's government. Where once there had been chaos in the island's public service, order now reigned supreme. There was a downsizing in the number of government departments, with each new entity run by one of the commissioners; while Mussolini was making the trains run on time in Italy, British bureaucrats in Newfoundland were seeing to it that the mail got delivered and that customs and tariffs were collected in an efficient and systematic way. Public health and welfare services were put on a sound administrative footing, and even though sectarian intransigence made reform of the denominational education system extremely difficult, teachers were given a raise.

If the fishery didn't recuperate, it at least got a face-lift. There was widespread support for such measures as dropping the tax on fishermen's gasoline. But caulk and bail as they might, the ship the Commission of Government commanded continued to sink with all hands. As the spring snow of 1939 began to melt, 85,000 Newfoundlanders out of a total population of 290,000 were wards of His Majesty, receiving just forty-two cents a week to keep body and soul together.

Where the administrative genius of the British Empire had failed to work an economic miracle, Adolf Hitler was about to succeed. The Great Depression would be ended by the Great Dictator and unprecedented prosperity in Newfoundland was only a world war away.

CHAPTER 7

War

FOR NEWFOUNDLANDERS, THE modern era swept in behind the dust of Hitler's panzer divisions and Britain's martial response to the invasion of Poland. In the dog days of what would become the greatest armed conflict in history, the mother country's fight with Germany began as its dread predecessor had — with conscription at home and an appeal to the Empire to send what help it could. But for Newfoundland, World War II soon became a fundamentally different experience from "the war to end all wars." German U-boats brought hostilities to North America as they tried to strangle the convoy of war supplies flowing from Canada and the United States to a defiant but isolated Britain. In the crucially important Battle of the Atlantic, the outcome of which would determine whether or not Hitler conquered Britain and, perhaps, unleashed his forces on North America, Newfoundland was the most important piece of real estate in the hemisphere. It was from Newfoundland that Allied warships and planes hunted German submarines, from Newfoundland that Hudson bombers, so badly needed by the Royal Air Force, were ferried across the Atlantic, from Newfoundland that great merchant-marine convoys set out to relieve Britain. And it would be Fortress Newfoundland, carved out of the island's formidable rock and garrisoned by the armed forces of Canada and the

United States, that would be the first line of defence if North America were invaded by the Germans. (In 1943, German forces actually landed at Martin Bay in Labrador and established an unmanned instrument weather station.) Once more, the prince of war had kissed the sleeping colony, and Newfoundland was awake, alert and on the march.

In the initial stages of the war effort, the order of the day was sacrifice rather than profit. For the Commission of Government, that meant renouncing the annual grant from Britain needed to balance the colony's budget. To make up for the shortfall in 1939 — nearly $6 million — the commissioners reduced expenditures, levied imaginative taxes (including one on alcoholic beverages) and financed new borrowing with a bond issue. So great was the patriotic fervour to save Britain that budgetary surpluses generated by the boom of the war years were funnelled back to her. As in so many other areas of the island's life, war turned recent history on its ear; the bankrupt was now saving the benefactor with grants or interest-free loans that would total more than $38 million by war's end.

As their fathers had in the Great War, individual Newfoundlanders were quick to assume their traditional wartime roles as loyal subjects of the British Empire. In early 1939, the colony began to mobilize to fight the Nazis. Newfoundlanders made up two artillery regiments in the British Army: the 166th Newfoundland Field Regiment and the 59th Newfoundland Heavy Regiment. In February 1940, Governor Walwyn issued a proclamation asking for volunteers to serve in the Royal Artillery. Within a week, 400 Newfoundlanders had answered the call. The First Royal Artillery Contingent marched to the railway station in St. John's in April 1940. Another 3,500 Newfoundlanders enlisted in the Royal Navy, and 700 joined the Royal Canadian Navy. And in what was perhaps the most dangerous assignment of all, a full squadron of Newfoundlanders flew as night-fighters in the Royal Air Force, pitting their Spitfires and Hurricanes against the Messerschmitts of the German *Luftwaffe* in the Battle of Britain.

Beyond the opportunity for valour, the struggle with

Germany also brought deep irony, particularly for Newfoundlanders of Scottish descent who made their contribution to the war effort with axes and bucksaws. Among the 3,500 recruits who served in the Newfoundland Overseas Forestry Unit, they returned to the Scottish Highlands of their ancestors to harvest trees that would supply pitprops for trenches. By the time the Axis powers capitulated in 1945, more than 12,000 Newfoundlanders, including 524 women, had answered Britain's call to arms.

One of them was Sir John's youngest son, twenty-two-year-old Bill, who'd been studying philosophy and history at Trinity College, University of Toronto, when hostilities broke out. He promptly joined the Canadian Officers Training Corps attached to the university and exchanged Spinoza for technical manuals on radio signals.

The decision to join the Canadian armed forces was a deliberate one. Bill had seriously considered going overseas in 1940 with the First Royal Artillery Contingent, but he wanted to make his own mark without any assistance from his famous name: "If I went overseas and I achieved anything, people would say, 'Well why the hell wouldn't he, he was a Crosbie, he's bound to be commissioned or he's bound to be this or that.' I wanted to get away from the taint of my home association so if I did do anything in the war, I did it on my own, where the name Crosbie had no meaning whatsoever."

In May 1941 Bill donned the uniform of the Governor General's Horse Guards out of Toronto. His first stop was basic training at Brockville, Ontario, an experience that tested the young man to his physical limits, as he duly reported in a letter to his mother on August 5, 1941:

"I hardly dare discuss the last two weeks at Brockville for they were the bitterest endurance test I've ever [experienced]. We marched 200 miles in 10 days carrying full equipment and under the strictest discipline. For example, we were only allowed to take off our steel helmets during a rest period and I'm not exaggerating when I say that in the sun you could touch them and that was all. The last 4 days were the worst as we did 100 miles and slept out all the time. Six each morning they used to wake us up with gas bombs and we had to dress with respirators on. I enjoyed the whole affair immensely for it gave you some idea of how much you could stand and I certainly got an eye-opener of the calibre of Canadian Officers — they were magnificent."

From Brockville, the young second lieutenant was transferred to the army's Advanced Training Centre at Camp Borden. His new superior, a Sergeant Major Witherspoon, met him with an unpleasant surprise: he was to become his regiment's new signalling officer. Despite his protestations, including the sound argument that signalling was the only course he had failed at Brockville during basic training, the orders stood. The crestfallen young officer remained philosophical:

"At least when this war is over," he wrote his mother, "I'll be able to get a job as a radio technician! If I had only known that philosophy would lead to this. Quite frankly, I'm terrified of electricity but I console myself with this quotation.

'Sound, sound the clarion, strike the fife,
To all the sensual world proclaim
One crowded hour of glorious life
As worth an age without a name.'

"Now Spinoza and all his kin must lie dusty on the shelf — perhaps even be pushed off as books on Elements of Electricity, the Mystery of Radio and the Story of the Transformer become the very essence of all my thoughts."

Despite his sense of disappointment, Bill soon discovered that there was more to military life than blisters and bully beef, particularly for a recruit with the Crosbie connections. During his stay at Camp Borden, Bill took his weekend passes in Toronto, where he lodged at the King Edward Hotel, taking tea with people like future Ontario premier Mitch Hepburn and the owner of the *Globe and Mail*, George McCullagh. But despite these pleasant respites, Bill learned that the military could be a precarious calling long before the first German soldier would have a chance to get him in his sights at Lake Comacchio in Italy.

One of the first things Bill was given was a pair of regulation glasses from Imperial Optical of the type favoured by the military — round lenses with rugged steel rims. After picking them up in Toronto, Bill decided to take in a movie that was causing quite a sensation at the time, Walt Disney's *Fantasia*. He was seated in the upper gallery of a suffocatingly hot Royal Alexandra Theatre, which was packed to the rafters. Engrossed in the film, Bill suddenly heard what he thought were two pistol shots. When he put his hands to his now stinging face, the lenses were gone from his glasses and he could feel shards of glass lodged in his eyes.

"What had happened was, because of the steel frames, and the heat, the glass expanded far faster than the steel frames, so they exploded, and that was the pistol shots I heard. So that was the first early warning I had that things can go very wrong in the army." Luckily, his eyes were not permanently damaged.

In the fall of 1941, Bill and his brigade began their "European education," setting sail from Halifax bound for Wiltshire, England. Two of his sisters, Margaret and Edith, were already overseas, driving ambulances during the London blitz. The tranquillity of Bill's crossing belied the bellicose purpose of the voyage. Over sumptuous dinners, he and his fellow officers listened to the orchestra playing Beethoven and Bach, half forgetting about the dreaded German U-boats, which, luckily, never materialized. When he landed in London, Bill used his last leave for three months to visit old friends at the Newfoundland Trade Commissioner's office. Later that first week, he took in a play aptly called *No Time for Comedy* starring Rex Harrison. Bill met some sailors from home at the intermission and after the performance hustled his new companions off to a bar, where they drank to the health of St. John's.

When he finally reported for duty, Bill was faced with barracks that were both impressive and unnerving. The solid, all-brick buildings contained individual units complete with their own stoves to help keep out the legendary British dampness. But what struck the young officer was how permanent the barracks looked; for the first time, he confronted the possibility that the war might be a long one.

What the idealistic young man couldn't have guessed was that it would be almost five years before he would see Newfoundland again, and that when he did, he would be a major and a war hero. As he entered the darkened tunnel of World War II, the light ahead of him was always his beloved island. He left his watch on Newfoundland time, shaved with a kit his older brother Ches had given him the previous Christmas and carried around a small effigy of a seal given to him by his mother as a good-luck piece.

In his first month in Europe, he was showered with parcels from home — five from a doting Lady Crosbie, two more from sisters Vera and Olga and a third from sister-in-law Ella. Barracks life was the story of free men at war everywhere — the exhilaration of contributing to the downfall of a tyrant accompanied by patriotic indigestion. In Bill's case, that initially meant training recruits as wireless operators and choking down sausages that appeared to consist of sawdust with a little meat flavouring, a dietary staple the men called "breadcrumbs in battledress," or, more indelicately, "horse cock." Bill sought relief from Lord Woolton's Sausage (named for Britain's then Minister of Food) at a small hotel not far from the barracks where you could get an excellent meal and fine wine for five shillings. But these gastronomic sorties were mere diversionary tactics. His secret weapons in the continuing war with Lord Woolton's cuisine, which also included such enduring favourites as carrot fudge and whale meat soaked in vinegar, came from Newfoundland in the form of calcium tablets and cod-liver oil sent over by his mother. Despite the hardships, the young Newfoundlander thrived on military life. "Since landing here," he wrote home, ". . . I've never been happier or more contented because for the first time since I've joined the army, I can feel real progress in which I'm playing my part and that progress is creating a bond of comradeship throughout all ranks which is the essence of a first class fighting outfit."

Missing home, but buoyed by his service to king and country, Bill spent his first Christmas at war attending morning services at a six-hundred-year-old church presided over by an ancient minister, "who has a delightful habit of wandering around to see why you aren't singing the hymns and on occasion to see how the collection is coming . . . " Later, he joined his fellow officers waiting tables at a special holiday dinner for enlisted men. The son of privilege was deeply moved by their patriotism. "Never before have they been so consciously Canadian and upon the slightest excuse they'll burst into *The Maple Leaf Forever* or *Oh Canada.* I would have given my heart and soul to join in — yes, even in singing *Oh Canada.*" For a man brought up on the "Ode to Newfoundland," it was quite an admission.

WHILE BILL CROSBIE waited for the not-too-distant day when he would face the enemy in continental Europe at the head of a tank column, his island home was experiencing an invasion of its own that would alter its history and forever change the way Newfoundlanders saw themselves. The first agents of that remarkable change came from the mainland and arrived wearing the uniforms of the Canadian military.

On September 8, 1939, Prime Minister Mackenzie King announced in the House of Commons that Canada would undertake the defence of Newfoundland and Labrador as an essential element of his national security plan. Within a matter of months, two searchlights and two artillery guns were established for the defence of Bell Island, an important iron-ore source for the war effort located off Portugal Cove just a few miles from St. John's, and an early target of enemy U-boats. After a wrangle with imperial authorities in London, Canada's request to take over the Newfoundland Airport in the central part of the province was granted. The Canadians spent $1,370,000 expanding the facility, and by the summer of 1940 it had the new name under which it would become world famous in the early days of transatlantic aviation: Gander Airport.

At exactly 10:50 a.m. on June 17, 1940, five Digby aircraft of the RCAF's Number 10 (Bomber Reconnaissance) Squadron landed at Gander from their former base in Dartmouth, Nova Scotia. Fighter squadrons quickly followed, and finally a full infantry battalion. With Canadian naval headquarters in St. John's, as well as a new, Canadian-built airport in the capital city and another at Goose Bay, "Johnny Canuck" had made his presence felt everywhere. By war's end, more than a hundred million Canadian dollars had been poured into Newfoundland, Canada had supplanted the United Kingdom as the island's most important trading partner and Mackenzie King had a high commissioner firmly ensconced in St. John's. Ottawa had set the stage to woo one of Britain's oldest colonial daughters into a political marriage she had steadfastly refused for nearly a hundred years.

But there was a more dashing suitor on the scene who had caught the lady's eye. The real transformation of Newfoundland from an economically stagnant colony of Great Britain to a booming outpost of democracy ready to repel any German invasion of North America began in earnest on August 22, 1940, when Britain and the United States agreed to the Lend Lease Agreement. In exchange for fifty U.S. naval destroyers, fighter planes and war materials, Britain agreed to lease land to the American military in three of its territories — Bermuda, the West Indies and Newfoundland — for ninety-nine years.

The intention was to establish a series of bases to protect the western hemisphere from invasion, particularly once Germany and Italy declared war on the United States in December 1941, a week after the Japanese invasion of Pearl Harbour. German U-boats were operating virtually unopposed in the waters off eastern North America, turning the shipping lanes 200 kilometres southwest of Newfoundland into a zone nicknamed "Torpedo Alley." Four ships were torpedoed off Bell Island with the loss of 69 lives. In October 1942, the S.S. *Caribou*, operating between Port aux Basques on Newfoundland's west coast and Sydney, Nova Scotia, was also sunk by an enemy submarine, killing 137. At the height of their power, the German "wolf packs," ten to a group, were sinking four ships a day, racking up almost half a billion tons of Allied merchant shipping by mid-1941. If the Battle of the Atlantic were to be won, the Americans and their Canadian comrades in arms knew that those horrendous losses would have to be stopped.

Like Ernest Hemingway, who patrolled the north coast of Cuba in a converted fishing boat looking for German U-boats, Ches Crosbie did his part to limit the effectiveness of Hitler's invisible navy. As a commander in the Royal Canadian Volunteer Reserves stationed in Newfoundland, he hunted submarines in a forty-five-foot enclosed plywood speedboat. On two occasions while cruising the Gulf of St. Lawrence out of Corner Brook, Ches and his men spotted submarines but chose to report the sightings rather than open up with their bow-mounted fifty-calibre machine gun. As his son Andrew put it, "With a plywood speedboat against German steel, Dad said he preferred to call in the pros."

By 1942, the "pros" were everywhere. The American base building boom touched every part of the island, from Goose Bay in Labrador, to Harmon Air Field in Stephenville, to Fort McAndrew in Placentia Bay near Argentia. But in a way, the huge Argentia Naval Base best symbolized the enormity of the American influence on Newfoundland during the years of World War II and for a long time afterwards. When the U.S.S. *Bowditch* arrived in Little Placentia, a fishing community of five hundred souls on Newfoundland's Avalon Peninsula, none of the residents could imagine what was about to happen to their tiny home.

After the first wave of engineers had completed their work, a second ship, the U.S.S. *Richard Peck,* arrived with 1,500 American construction workers and more engineers. For two years, the ship became the permanent home of the Americans who built Argentia, with the help of 15,000 Newfoundland labourers. During the construction phase, many Newfoundlanders lived on schooners anchored in Placentia Bay. By the time the harbour was dredged, the runways were paved and the last building erected, Argentia Naval Base was the largest military facility in the world outside of the United States, carrying a hefty price-tag of $53 million! Part of that windfall went into the pockets of Newfoundlanders, who for the first time in their lives knew what it meant to have disposable income. The American presence brought security, excitement, the sights and sounds of the modern world (stars like Frank Sinatra and

Edgar Bergen entertained the troops at Argentia) and dizzying material wealth. For better or worse, there would be no turning back the clock to the old days of the fish merchant's paternalistic credit system and forced barter.

Like the Canadian military complex at Gander, Argentia's impact on the war effort in the North Atlantic was immediate and, in the long run, decisive. With a Fleet Air Wing flying anti-submarine missions from the naval base's world-class airfield, German U-boats no longer had a free hand in Torpedo Alley. U.S. naval destroyers now escorted the merchant ships across the Atlantic and, aided by a powerful new invention, sonar, waged effective war against the marauding wolf packs. The base also served as the support centre for a full U.S. naval task force and scores of ships from the Allied navies. The initial threat of a German invasion had been so effectively dealt with by the summer of 1941 that President Roosevelt and Prime Minister Churchill felt secure enough to hold their famous Atlantic Conference under the noses of the German U-boats aboard the *Prince of Wales*, anchored in Placentia Bay.

Newfoundland had become a formidable and prosperous armed camp playing a key role on the world stage. Unemployment had been virtually wiped out and the degrading poverty of the thirties was replaced by the beginnings of a cash economy and new optimism about the future. With each passing year of the war, the stream of Americans into Newfoundland became a torrent. Three-quarters of a million U.S. military personnel passed through the island's network of new military bases on their way to the European theatre, and the American government spent more than $300 million in Newfoundland during the war. At the peak of the war effort, 100,000 American troops were permanently stationed in Newfoundland.

Long after the barrels had rusted on the gun emplacements overlooking Bell Island and the quitch grass had pushed up through cracks in the tarmac at Harmon Field, the immense social impact on Newfoundland of the American war effort would still be felt. An astonishing 25,000 American servicemen married Newfoundland women. One of these casualties of the heart was Ches Crosbie's eldest child, the beautiful, headstrong and hopelessly spoiled Joan. The tragic princess was about to meet the boy next door, who turned out to be a piano player from Cincinnati.

MIDNIGHT AND THE enforced blackout enveloped the city like a shroud. For hours, as the American troopship awaited permission to enter St. John's Harbour, the tall, thin soldier had been pacing the deck. Gunnery Sergeant Gene Shinkle of the 24th Separate Coast Artillery Battalion had been dividing his time between worrying about German U-boats and wondering what his new home would look like. But as he passed through the Narrows under the huge, granite shoulder of Signal Hill, which had earned this strange island the nickname of the Gibraltar of the West, all was in darkness. Suddenly, as the ship eased toward the American docks in the Battery, voices shouted salutations out of the darkness to the startled troops on deck. The twenty-year-old could not see the shantytown clinging to the rocky outcropping on one side of the Narrows, nor the eager faces that poked out of windows to welcome the ship into port. So far, all he knew was that he had just come from America to a cold, new place he could not see. He would later learn that the voyage had been considerably more fantastic than that. He had set sail from contemporary America, November 1944, but it was Victorian England where his ship dropped anchor.

Despite his initial sense that the luckier members of his outfit had been stationed in Bermuda or Cuba (hence the word "Separate" in his outfit's name), the personable young American soon began to appreciate his exotic posting. Shortly after arriving, he transferred from the artillery battalion to become a classification officer in the Adjutant General's Branch. There, he tested and rated servicemen and officers to find out which jobs they were best suited to perform. In addition to his official duties, "Shink," as his friends called him, organized shows with local talent and played piano at the USO canteen in Fort Pepperrell, which was the headquarters for the Newfoundland Army

Command. Except for a damaged finger that prevented him from playing certain sharps with precision, he had the talent of a concert pianist. And on the dance floor, he led his partners through the waltzes as though they were floating on clouds.

By 1944, the worst of the military tragedies in Newfoundland had already happened — the torpedoing of the S.S. *Caribou*, the crash of the British bomber that claimed the life of Dr. Frederick Banting and the burning of a night club in St. John's (possibly the work of sabotage) that killed 99 people. Although naval convoys were constantly coming and going, leaving their wounded in St. John's for medical care, the heavy military presence now provided a romantic backdrop to the social life of a city and province that was no longer directly threatened by the enemy. Apprehension caused by rationing, blackouts and the sight of freighters in the harbour with their hulls ripped open by torpedoes was counterbalanced by dances at the USO and the Colony Club and an endless round of socializing between military personnel and the local population. As Dolly Crosbie put it, "There were some doings, my dear. It was a wild country in the war." With his good looks, talent and easy going manner, it was inevitable that Gene Shinkle would soon be in great demand at the best parties.

His meeting with his wife-to-be resulted from one of those vagaries of fate that rule human affairs. A fellow American serviceman from North Carolina, whose mother had met Vera (Crosbie) Perlin in Asheville when Vera was taking a TB rest cure, asked Gene if he would be interested in spending Christmas with a Newfoundland family. Missing his own family and anxious to get off the base, he readily accepted. Without knowing who they were, he found himself in the home of Ches and Jessie Crosbie.

It was a big, beautiful old house with an impressive front entrance and cozy front and back parlours. The fragrance of crackling birch logs filled the place, mingled with the smells of slowly roasting turkey and ham wafting in from the kitchen. Gene met Ches, Jessie and their three children, Joan, John and Andrew. Although his eye might have lingered a little longer on the lovely girl with the striking black hair, the young soldier had the idea that she was somehow older than he was, a mistaken impression created by her Branksome Hall education in Toronto and her cosmopolitan air. In fact, at seventeen, she was three years Shink's junior. There were drinks before dinner, and later thirteen-year-old John Crosbie proudly took out a projector he had been given for Christmas and they all watched home movies.

Just after dark, a knock came on the door. A servant appeared and informed Jessie that some neighbourhood children were at the door and wanted to come in and look at the Crosbie Christmas tree. Jessie said no, but Ches overruled her.

"And so, these five little kids came into the front hallway and the serving girl made them take their boots off, of course. And they came in with the holes in their socks and everything and had a look at the Christmas tree. And then Nan [Jessie] said, 'All right, you've seen the Christmas tree, good night.' And of course they were given some candies and this sort of stuff, almost like Hallowe'en, and off they went," Gene Shinkle recalled.

The young officer was taken aback. In Dickensian fashion, he had just been introduced to the two sides of Newfoundland's social structure — the haves and the have-nots — and realized with a start that there was absolutely nothing in between. And that, he thought, included him. When he said his goodbyes at the door that night, he figured the odds were slim to none that he would ever be returning to 18 Rennies Mill Road. But the war was a road with strange turns. A year later, he would be engaged to Ches and Jessie Crosbie's only daughter.

WITH THE ENTRY of America into the conflict in December 1941, World War II began to tilt in the Allies' favour. Hitler soon found himself on the defensive in Europe and it was only a matter of time before the Fatherland itself would be invaded. But the German army was still a formidable fighting force and stubbornly defended the territory it had won in the early days of bullying and *blitzkrieg*.

In the fall of 1943, Bill Crosbie's regiment left England on a troopship bound for Italy. Although it was against regulations to have liquor on board, Bill and his mates managed to get their hands on some contraband liquid comfort. After a few drinks, someone decided that "Daisy May," the paperweight seal that was Bill's good-luck piece, should not have to suffer the indignity of being taken to a hot country. She was unceremoniously snapped off the top of Bill's tank, where he had lovingly welded her, and thrown overboard "so she could go back to Newfoundland." It was the kind of incident that illustrated Bill's opinion that although the Governor General's Horse Guards were primarily a Toronto outfit, its eight or nine Newfoundland members "were the bit of yeast put in that regiment to make something of it." In the grim days ahead of them, in which they would see their company strength fall from a full complement of 160 men down to a mere 50 by the fall of 1944, morale would be a crucial factor in their fight to survive.

Their introduction to Italy began with disappointed expectations and queasy stomachs. Expecting certain new and exotic creature comforts in the fabled south, the regiment disembarked around Naples in a blinding rainstorm at two in the morning. They proceeded to march for eight miles until they found themselves mired in "the muddiest potato patch that ever existed." The men set up their pup tents and settled in for a brief and uncomfortable night.

Early the next morning, Bill could feel that their mood was as sodden as the blankets in which they were wrapped. He collected as much money as he could from his dispirited troops, commandeered a truck and ordered a most unhappy Salvation Army officer attached to their outfit to take the truck and "not come back until he'd got some vino" that the men could have with their supper that night. Morning dragged into afternoon, and afternoon faded into early evening with the men waiting patiently inside their canvas *palazzos* pitched in the middle of an enormous Italian mud puddle. Towards evening, with a light rain falling, a mighty cheer went up at the sight of the Salvation Army officer returning with what all hoped was a truckload of wine.

Given the Sally Ann's view of alcohol, Bill was a little surprised that this particular mission had apparently been accomplished as assigned.

Regrettably, Crosbie had underestimated the possibilities for sabotage. The reluctant sommelier explained that while he had been able to buy the wine, the only thing he could get to carry it in were forty-five gallon drums last used to transport petrol. Those brave enough to imbibe the tainted vintage immediately fell violently ill. Faced with the unwanted battlefield miracle of wine turned into gasoline, Bill dumped the remaining cargo and tipped his hat to the wiles of the Salvation Army.

The Italian campaign turned into the acid test of Bill Crosbie's military career. He started out as a lieutenant, but before he entered the battle of Cassino he had made captain and was second-in-command of his squadron. They were a tightly knit group; each man knew the virtues and the faults of his comrades and accepted them. No one was more understanding of the foibles of his men than Bill:

"We had a chap who was with us through the war, who was a regimental champion boxer and an outstanding athlete. Then we went into action. And when we came under constant shell-fire this was beyond his capacity to accept. And I've had him trembling, begging me not to go back up to the front line as we approach and clear the foxholes. We did go back, and we, as a family if you like, we took him back and we carried him on."

When squadron commander Major Allen Burton, the future chairman of Simpsons in Toronto and husband of Betty Kennedy, was hospitalized, Bill was promoted to major and led his outfit in a series of actions for which he was eventually awarded a Distinguished Service Order, which, next to the Victoria Cross, was the highest battlefield decoration in the Empire. His finest hour came at Lake Comacchio in Italy during the battle of the Reno River.

Crosbie's men were working their way around Lake Comacchio when they encountered stiff German resistance on the Reno River. Their orders were to secure their side of the Reno for the Allied advance. Knowing that the river flowed into the Adriatic Sea, Major Crosbie made a reconnaissance, hoping to devise a plan that would take the

Germans by surprise. "I said surely being a Newfoundlander, the sea can be a help," he later reminisced. He waterproofed his tanks and discovered that the seabed was strong enough to support an armoured advance towards the enemy with only the turrets of his tanks visible above the water. Ordering a frontal assault on the German position, he slipped two tanks through the Adriatic, which simultaneously attacked from the rear. In the fierce battle that followed, sixty Germans were killed and seventy captured. There were no casualties in Bill's squadron.

The official army communiqué announcing Bill's DSO referred to his "brilliant operation" on the Reno River, as well as a "skilful and determined" engagement with German forces at Otterloo in Holland in the spring of 1945. The college boy's dream had been fulfilled. With no help from the family name, the kid who couldn't play football had starred on his generation's most glorious playing field.

Bill's regiment left Italy in January 1945 and made its way through southern France into Belgium and finally Holland. Then, like a black fog lifting from the world, it was spring and the war was over. Although he was overcome with "the maddest, wildest desire" to get back to Newfoundland, Bill could not be discharged until his regiment came home. He was appointed regimental education officer and given the task of setting up polling booths so that servicemen could vote in the federal election of 1945. The men had little affection for Prime Minister Mackenzie King, whom they had booed during a troop inspection in England. An astonishing 98 percent of Bill's regiment turned out to vote. "The election took place and the SOB got back again," Bill bitterly recalled. Like a lot of other veterans, he was angry over the "Zombie" scandal that saw some recruits in Canada drafted only to serve in Canada at a time when their countrymen were crying out for reinforcements — and dying — in Europe.

The British, too, went to the polls in 1945 and Bill heard Winston Churchill deliver the opening salvo of the campaign. Churchill warned that if the people elected a socialist government, they would also get a Gestapo-like police to enforce the rules and regulations Labour would bring in to govern society. Bill's close association with British troops during the war left him convinced that Churchill had struck the wrong note. “I was always dumbfounded at how completely Bolshie the British troops were. There was an utter determination that they were not going back to what they left.” The major put his political intuition to work and won £300 betting on the outcome of the election that left Britain’s cigar-smoking bulldog of the war years looking for a new occupation.

While in Holland, Bill got another lesson in human nature and returned it with one on integrity. Walking down the street, he overheard the champion boxer from his outfit, comfortable again in his role as a “big shot,” lambasting his former comrades. Bill lost his temper and broke the cardinal rule in the military which absolutely forbade you to touch another man. “I grabbed him by his jacket and I said ‘You son of a bitch. If I ever hear you say something again against one of these men, I’ll call the squadron together and I’ll tell them about you crying and begging that you never be taken up to the front line again.’ ”

After V-E Day, word circulated that Canada was looking for volunteers for an armoured brigade being formed to accompany the Americans on the final attack on Japan. Believing that the war in the Pacific was almost over, Bill “took the gamble” and, along with a few comrades from his regiment, volunteered for duty in the Pacific theatre.

Major Crosbie was ordered to return to North America, where he was to link up with his new outfit. Before sailing from England, he was put in charge of repatriating 385 Cape Breton Highlanders who were being discharged. But during the crossing, the world changed terribly; flying at 31,060 feet, Colonel Paul Tibbets gave the order to drop “Little Boy,” the world’s first combat atomic bomb, from his B-29 Superfortress on Hiroshima. Three days later “Fat Man” annihilated Nagasaki. The 509th Composite Group of the United States Air Force had become death, and Bill Crosbie’s tanks were no longer needed to humble the Japanese. The young warrior docked in Quebec City on V-J Day. He had been ready to face the Japanese; instead, the uncharted path of his own future lay ahead of him in a world that had taken up residence under the gates of hell.

After a brief detour through Toronto, it was time to get back to heaven.

Twenty-three-year-old John Chalker Crosbie and his wife Mitchie Anne Manuel on their wedding day in 1899. The couple would have thirteen children and go on to found a business and political dynasty in Newfoundland.

CROSBIE FAMILY COLLECTION

Robert Crosbie, wife Ethel and son Robert at Clovelly Farm circa 1916. The collie dog with them was called "Kipp," possibly after the Crosbie family estate in Dumfries.

PUBLIC ARCHIVES OF NEWFOUNDLAND AND LABRADOR, ST. JOHN'S

The Crosbie Hotel in St. John's, built by George Graham Crosbie after th great fire of 1892. In this 1919 photo, the hotel is festooned with flags t celebrate the royal visit of the Prince of Wales, the future Edward VIII.

CROSBIE FAMILY COLLECTION

Ellie (Crosbie) Bell, the formidable daughter of George Graham who ran the Crosbie Hotel with her brother John after her father's death in 1895. By 1901 she had become the hotel's sole proprietor.

CROSBIE FAMILY COLLECTION

Sir John Crosbie at his belove Bungalow at South East Placenti just before his death in 1932.

CROSBIE FAMILY COLLECTION

A young Ches Crosbie with his wife Jessie (Carnell) Crosbie and their daughter Joan Elise in 1929. Three years later, he would find himself in charge of the Crosbie business empire.

CROSBIE FAMILY COLLECTION

John, Andrew, and Joan circa 1938. Throughout his life, John would relax from the rigours of politics by watching cowboy movies.

CROSBIE FAMILY COLLECTION

The "Crosbie Boys," Andrew and John, circa 1942.

CROSBIE FAMILY COLLECTION

"Three beauties": John Crosbie (left), his cousin, John Crosbie Perlin and Andrew Crosbie, having a little fun in borrowed robes circa 1942.

CROSBIE FAMILY COLLECTION

CROSBIE FAMILY COLLECTION

Like father, like son. Ches Crosbie (left) circa 1923 and his son, John Crosbie circa 1948, decked out in the highland kilt of St. Andrew's College, in Ontario.

Hamming it up for the camera: the vivacious Joan Crosbie and Gene Shinkle, the American serviceman she would marry in 1947, having some fun in the sun.

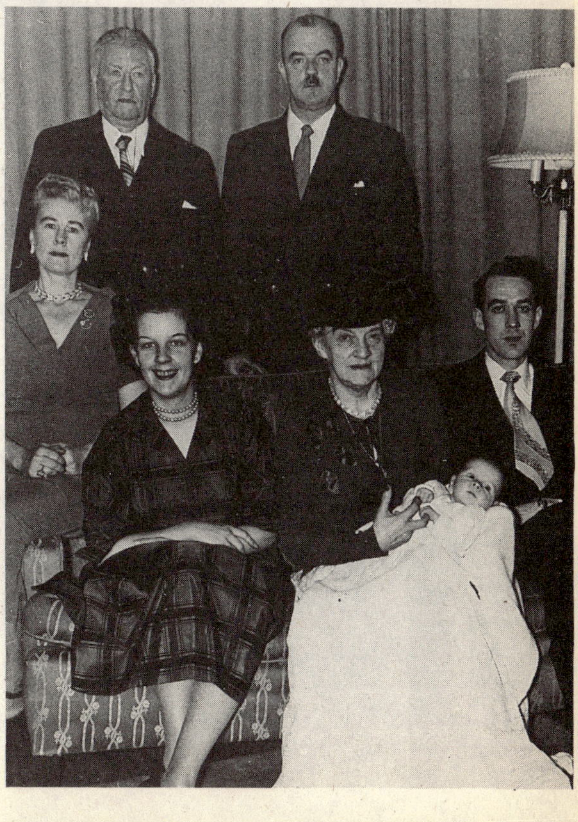

CROSBIE FAMILY COLLECTION

Four generations (1951): Lady Mitchie Anne Crosbie proudly holds Lee Shinkle, the son of her grand-daughter Joan. Beside her on the sofa are Joan and Gene Shinkle. Jessie Crosbie is seated to the left of her daughter, and her father, Andrew Carnell (left) and Ches Crosbie are standing behind.

CROSBIE FAMILY COLLECTION

Putting on the Ritz: Ches and Jessie Crosbie enjoy a formal moment. The "Duchess as Jessie was known, was one of Canada's ten best-dressed women, a striking figur with her prematurely silver hair.

CROSBIE FAMILY COLLECTION

Anchors away: Ches Crosbie (dark glasses), brother Percy, Clara Smallwood an Joe Smallwood pose for the camera at the launching of the Sir John Crosbie at th Port Weller Drydock in July 1962.

The prodigal daughter: Joan Crosbie circa 1981, shortly before her tragic death. After leaving Newfoundland in 1959, the woman who lived for "romance" returned in 1975 to spend the last six years of her life caring for her mother in the house where she'd grown up.

The Grand-dad Express: John Crosbie pushes around the family future in a wheelbarrow at Hogan's Pond. Getting the ride of their lives are granddaughters Megan, Charlotte, and Jane.

CROSBIE FAMILY COLLECTION

John and Jane Crosbie and the future of the family.

CHAPTER 8

Unfinished Business

ENERGIZED BY WORLD War II, Newfoundland faced the postwar years with high hopes and some historic unfinished business. Ever since the humiliation of 1933, when bankruptcy had led to the loss of responsible government, everyone knew that the day would come when Newfoundland would have to come to grips with the question of how the island and Labrador would eventually be governed. The countdown to destiny began on December 11, 1945, when British Prime Minister Clement Attlee announced the election of a National Assembly in Newfoundland. During the next two years, from 1946 to 1948, its job would be to examine alternate forms of government for the former dominion and to present its options to the people of Newfoundland, who would then express their preference in a referendum.

Newfoundland's first trip to the polls since the loss of responsible government was hardly a ringing endorsement of democracy: on June 21, 1946, a mere 50 percent of those eligible to vote returned forty-five members to the National Convention. One of those delegates was Ches Crosbie, who won his place with the largest majority of any candidate, representing St. John's West. And that included the enigmatic socialist from Gambo, Joseph R. Smallwood, now forty-five years old, who would soon be locked in a historic battle to bring Newfoundland into Confederation.

When the convention began sitting in September 1946, two-thirds of the delegates were opposed to Confederation with Canada. Ches Crosbie wasn't one of them. Although he had no particular objection to joining Canada, he did feel very strongly about one thing: before choosing any foreign political or economic partner, Newfoundland should begin by replacing the Commission of Government with responsible government. That way she would be free to negotiate the best possible deal for a renewed Newfoundland, drawing from the widest possible range of options. His conviction that responsible government was a necessary first step down the road to political renewal hardened as he became convinced that Newfoundland's future was being cynically engineered in the corridors of power in Ottawa and London.

From the moment the first, chaotic session of the National Convention was gavelled into existence, luck was on the side of Joe Smallwood and the supporters of Confederation. Early in the convention's tenure, its first chairman, Judge Cyril Fox, died. His replacement was Gordon Bradley, who, despite being a closet Confederate, received a unanimous endorsement from his fellow delegates based on his imagined impartiality. In fact, Smallwood and Bradley had quietly agreed in the first few days of the Convention's life that if they could bring Newfoundland into Confederation, they would divide the spoils of their coup; Bradley would represent Newfoundland in the federal government in Ottawa and Smallwood would become the new province's first premier. As they shook hands that day at Bradley's Bonavista home, neither man knew how broadly fate was smiling on their clandestine pact.

But Smallwood had an even bigger advantage than friends at court in the National Convention. The Dominions Office decided to rebroadcast each day's proceedings of the convention across Newfoundland on radio station VONF. With his background as a broadcaster and his brilliance as an impromptu political orator, Smallwood had every right to be delighted. By comparison, Ches Crosbie behind a microphone was a man whose talents lay in other directions. He was as awkward as Smallwood was eloquent, as wooden as Joey was almost supernaturally animated.

During the two years of those nightly broadcasts, outport Newfoundland huddled around the radio dutifully listening to "Skipper Ches" but utterly captivated by the spellbinding enchanter who was so fanatically dedicated to winning their hearts, minds and, ultimately, their votes. When one of his own supporters asked Smallwood why he insisted on saying everything over and over again *ad nauseam*, the canny politician replied, "I know it sounds laboured and repetitious to you, but it's not you I have to convince — it's the voters out in Scratch-Arse Tickle, where it will only sink in if I say it ten times over in slightly different words. I'm talking to the Huskies and the Jakitars and the swile [seal] hunters, even if I have to address my remarks to Johnnie McEvoy." (McEvoy was the last chairman of the National Convention.)

Unlike Smallwood, for whom politics was a single-minded obsession, Ches Crosbie was a man with many irons in the fire. He was, after all, in charge of the Crosbie family's expanding business empire. Although the war may have been Newfoundland's biggest industry from 1939 to 1945, Ches knew that the fishery was its long-term future. Ever anxious to diversify his business interests, he was quick to see the commercial possibilities of a new idea developed by his friend and future business partner, Captain Olaf Olsen.

Olsen had gone to the Newfoundland Fisheries Board in November 1936 with a proposal to set up a plant to manufacture fish oil and fish meal, a protein-rich product that Ches believed would be suitable for livestock and poultry feed. He planned to produce these commodities by processing herring caught by purse-seiners, large vessels that dragged huge nets behind them in a deadly semicircle that gradually tightened around its tightly packed catch. At that time, purse-seining was banned in Newfoundland because fishermen feared that corporate operators would use the technology to monopolize the herring industry and wipe out fish stocks.

In the nineteenth century, herring had been used primarily as bait in the Newfoundland fishery. But in the early years of the new century an important new industry sprang up on Newfoundland's west coast in the Bay of Islands. Using a new processing method called "Scotch Packing," herring was pickled and sold by the barrel on the world market. It was to protect these herring fishermen, who could afford only smaller nets and vessels, that the Newfoundland government had outlawed purse-seining.

After taking the chairman of Newfoundland's Fisheries Board on a trip to Norway in December 1936, to see first-hand how the industry there worked, Captain Olsen persuaded the government to lift the ban on purse-seiners. He argued that his new business would be able to pay fishermen more for their herring than they could get from food-processors — a claim that proved untrue. The coast was now clear to develop a new industry and, typically, Ches Crosbie jumped in with both boots.

In 1941, Ches paid $700 and bought two and a half acres of land from Alfred Quigley in the Bay of Islands to erect his plant. The new company, the Newfoundland Dehydrating Process Company Ltd., was 50 percent financed by Crosbie and Olsen and 50 percent by Boston interests Ches knew from the fish business. The company operated on capital of $350,000 and the plant, which was exempted from the War Revenues Tax, and for which all construction materials and machinery entered Newfoundland duty-free, cost another $150,000 to build. When it was finished, it was one of the most modern facilities of its kind in the world.

Ches set up Herring-Un Ltd. as a subsidiary company to catch herring for his reduction plant. Appropriate herring vessels were his most pressing need, and he applied to government for financial assistance. But Ches wanted something else that showed how far ahead of his time his thinking often was. "After a great deal of consideration, I do not feel it is fair that a private company, burdened with heavy taxation, should be expected to pay all the costs of research and development of practical methods of fishing which would entail the purchase of considerable equipment. Without this research and development, the growth of the industry will be retarded for many years while our competitors in other countries are forging ahead," he wrote in his request for government funding.

It was an insightful and defensible proposition. Iceland, for example, had already spent $800,000 over six years to complete a survey on the habits of herring and the most efficient way of catching them. That competitive edge had allowed Icelandic fishermen to create an industry with an annual export value of $16 million. But Ches's request for research and development money was quietly ignored. Instead, the Commission of Government agreed to give Crosbie a $100,000 loan at 3.5 percent interest to build herring vessels. In granting the loan, the governor of Newfoundland sent a telegram to the secretary of state for Dominion Affairs on November 27, 1943, saying that he attached "great importance to this business which is [the] first real step in [the] proper development of [the] herring industry in [the] Bay of Islands."

Although fish oil and fish meal were to be the mainstays of Ches's Bay of Islands plant, the humble herring also contributed to another exotic if ersatz product. Thanks to Coco Chanel, the founder of the Paris fashion empire, there was a vogue in the 1940s for imitation pearls. In 1943, the village of Deer Lake, New Brunswick, population 1,200, had sold $77,000 worth of herring scales to the fashion industry to supply the glitter in pearls, sequins, buttons and iridescent paints. Ches, whom the government referred to as Newfoundland's "herring king," got in on the action thanks to a contact from L. J. Harnum of the Commission of Government's Industrial Development Board, who put him in touch with an interested American buyer.

The process was as straightforward as it was lucrative. The herring would be sucked up from smaller boats through a hose and spilled into three coffin-shaped boxes with a special wire mesh in the bottom that allowed water to pass through. As the fish passed towards the narrow end of the boxes and spilled into the collecting boat, the herring scales were removed by the mesh and gathered in baskets to drain and dry. They were then sent to Malden, Massachusetts, for the final stage of a process that would, unbeknownst to their wearers, see the necks of American fashion plates beautified with Newfoundland herring scales!

By 1942, the new plant was in production, operating its

own seiners as well as a collection ship that picked up the catches of local fishermen, who nevertheless remained sceptical of the enterprise. With its modern equipment, the Bay of Islands plant could process 300 tons of herring a day. Ches's mother, Lady Crosbie, was pessimistic about the new enterprise and told him so during the weekly Boys Day luncheons she continued to host throughout the 1940s at Devon Place. She knew from bitter personal experience that the herring business was notoriously capricious; fishermen might get three dollars a barrel at the beginning of the fishing season and then be forced to dump unwanted catches before it closed. Her own brother, a shrewd fish merchant, had gone bankrupt in the herring trade. Although she advised caution, Ches proceeded full-speed ahead. The aging Cassandra turned out to be right; disaster plagued the enterprise from the very beginning. With the company's managing director, Ches, away in Canada buying a new seiner, the two-year-old plant at Quigley's Cove burned to the ground on the night of September 8, 1944, along with $250,000 worth of inventory. It would take tough negotiations with the Commission of Government before financial assistance could be obtained to build a new and even larger plant and wharf in the Bay of Islands at a cost of $640,000. The question was, who would run it?

For both business and personal reasons, Ches realized that it couldn't be him. By 1945, when the new plant was nearly finished, Ches's partner, Captain Olaf Olsen, had died and Crosbie and Company had taken over Olsen Whaling and Sealing. It was a lucrative business, with the company's ships picking up whale oil at Williamsport in White Bay or Hawke's Harbour in Labrador for shipment around the world. At that time, Olsen's could produce whale oil for 14 cents a pound and sell it at 24 cents. But Ches knew he would have to modernize the aging facility if it were to be profitable in the future — a task that would take a great deal of both his time and energy.

The pressures created by new business responsibilities and very soon by politics paled beside the gathering storm clouds in his marriage. As the years passed, the real differences in temperament, values and personality between Ches and his wife Jessie had begun to show like cracks in the foundation of a once-sound building. The aristocratic Jessie would not give up the comforts of life in St. John's to accompany her rough-and-ready husband to the west coast during the years he was establishing the herring business. She resented his long absences from St. John's, which deprived her of a husband and their three children of a father. For his part, Ches used the freedoms of his imposed bachelorhood in Corner Brook to indulge himself in his two great loves outside business — drinking and women.

His great drinking companion on the west coast was Henry Montague Spencer Lewin. "Monty," as he was known by his friends, was the vice-president and general manager of the huge Bowater Paper Mill, the industry that was synonymous with the creation of Newfoundland's second city, Corner Brook. He wielded extraordinary power in the west coast community and his personal status was closer to that of a head of state than a businessman. When he returned from business trips to head office in England, for example, company employees would actually wash down the roads along his route to the company mansion in Corner Brook. Like Ches, he loved wine, women and song. They had one other thing in common: neither man could resist an opportunity to play a practical joke.

One evening, after putting on a glow, Ches and Monty decided to go to a circus that had come to town. Both men were delighted by a performing bear that was walking straighter lines that night than they were. When the act was finished, they kidnapped the animal and walked him on a leash back to the Glynmill Inn where they proceeded to try to check him in. Scandalized by the spectacle of a bear in her establishment, the hotel manager drove the unwanted customers out of the lobby with a broom. Ches and Monty then headed for the mill manager's house. After knocking on the door, they jumped into the bushes, leaving the bear standing on the threshold. When the manager opened the door, Ches gruffly said, "Gimme a drink."

Besides his drinking binges, which often lasted for weeks and ended with Jessie retrieving him from far-off watering holes in Montreal or New York, Ches, like his brothers, had a fine appreciation for a well-turned ankle. On most occasions, the boys did their womanizing in Montreal, where the only place hotter than The Normandy Roof of the old Mount Royal Hotel was Suite 4099–4100, the rooms the Crosbies kept for their frequent business trips to the mainland. But in the early years of the herring business, Ches brought his philandering closer to home when he took a mistress in Newfoundland, the editor of the Corner Brook newspaper, *The Western Star*. To Ches's sister, Dolly, it was no more than Ches following his natural instincts and Jessie following hers. "You know, they worked hard and they played hard. . . . Actually my brothers are very sexy boys . . . maybe . . . [Jessie] was just not that type. A lot of us are not. I mean the Crosbies are noted for it, all sorts of weird things in that way of life."

Ches had more obligations than he could handle, and in the interests of discharging them and keeping his marriage together, he decided to find someone in the family to help him out with the company's west coast operations. Given what was about to happen in the herring business, he couldn't have made a better choice than a man whose courage had been annealed in the deadly struggles of the recently concluded war — his youngest brother, Bill.

THE FUTURE THAT Bill Crosbie had been so unsure about on V-J Day began to unfold on a warm September afternoon in 1945 during his first ten-day visit home after five long years at war. On that day he drove his twenty-one-year-old niece, June Bennett, to Torbay Airport. Accompanying her on a two-week trip to New York City was Gertrude Murray, the only daughter of one of Newfoundland's oldest and most prosperous merchant families. Bill had first met "Gert" nearly ten years earlier on Gooseberry Beach, where he had playfully buried the adolescent girl and a friend, Patricia Hutchings, in the sand. Over the years, they'd met at parties and dances, and one summer Bill was invited to the Murray family's summer home on the Salmonier line (now the residence of artists Christopher and Mary Pratt).

Instead of participating in the obligatory tennis game organized by Gert's mother, the redoubtable matriarch of the Murray family, Bill stretched out on a bed and read André Malraux's *Ariel.* The young girl was astonished. "Imagine being brave enough to defy my mother," she thought.

At the airport that day, Bill kissed his niece goodbye and then teasingly said to her companion, "You'll have to wait until you get to New York." Gert, who was already dating someone else, gave it no more thought. In fact, she was intimidated by this self-assured son of the Crosbies: "I'd always been frightened of him, always rather shy of him. He was glamorous at university and lumpy-dumpy me. . . . you could never hope that he'd ever ask you out or look at you."

Three days later, who showed up in New York but Buffalo Bill himself. With June Bennett and her American army beau, Bill and Gert made a foursome, and the group decided to see the sights of the big city. The girls had been to the Elizabeth Arden salon that afternoon and paid $35 for a rum-and-egg shampoo, cut and permanent. They told their taxi driver to take them to the hottest spot in Greenwich Village and he dropped them at a gay club. After a few awkward moments, the Newfoundlanders were back on the street looking for another place. "I felt something on my head," Gert recalled. New York's pigeons had mounted a deadly sneak attack. Moments later the girls were laughing uncontrollably as Gert washed out her Elizabeth Arden perm in the ladies' washroom of The Brass Rail. The next day Bill accompanied the girls to Saks Fifth Avenue, posing as their sugar daddy so that they could try on the most expensive clothes. Gert was smitten. What she didn't realize was that Bill was too; two years later, in September 1947, they would marry.

After his brief trip to St. John's and the New York holiday, a restless Bill Crosbie went to Toronto in the fall of 1945 to attend law school. Although he stayed until Christmas break, academic life at Osgoode Hall was impossible. The war had left his nerves smouldering and created a taste for more robust pursuits than gathering the dessicated harvests of case law. Bill also turned down a job teaching at his old private school, Appleby College, remembering, perhaps, Sir John's admonition that he was not being educated to leave Newfoundland. Friends from his regiment tried to draw him into their orbit in Central Canada but it was Newfoundland that finally called him home. He packed up his kit bag and arrived back in St. John's on December 24 in time to share a rollicking Crosbie Christmas.

The rebuilding of the Crosbie herring operation in the Bay of Islands was now complete, and Ches offered Bill the job of running it. Bill liked the idea and it was agreed that he should move to Corner Brook and get to know the local fishermen. Ches had already arranged for him to stay with Robert McCarthy and his family on Wood's Island for a couple of months until he understood the attitudes of the people he would be working with.

It was much more than a public relations gesture. There was a great deal of local prejudice against the plant among herring fishermen who fished with small gill nets and who believed that the Crosbie technology was ruining their fishery. They were especially suspicious of the way Crosbie ships located schools of herring with sonar, a device they believed was frightening the fish from the bay. That suspicion played into the hands of the established fish-packers at Curling, whose food-processing operations directly competed with the Crosbies for the fishermen's herring. They encouraged the prejudiced belief in local fishermen that the reduction plant was ruining their livelihood, a propaganda campaign carried out with deadly effect. Some fishermen dropped rocks, iron bolts and horseshoes into a barge of fish offal the reduction plant had planned to process into animal feed. When the load was dumped into the processor, the machinery was promptly ruined.

Despite local resistance, the Crosbies pressed on. With an ultramodern plant, their constant requirement was to get enough herring to make the operation viable. To feed the plant, they assembled a modest fleet of vessels, including the *Western Star*, which was outfitted as a purse-seiner but which also served as a collector boat. She was anchored at Wood's Island and smaller vessels called trap boats would come alongside and off-load their herring catches. Fearing that the larger vessels would ruin their business, some local fishermen decided that enough was enough and took matters into their own hands.

Early one Saturday morning, after working around the clock, Bill was just nodding off in his berth on the *Western Star* when Robert McCarthy came aboard and wakened him. "Get up, Skipper, get up," he whispered. "They're out taking our seine." Bill bolted out of bed and the two men rowed the ship's dory across the harbour and climbed a hill from which they could look out over the bay. McCarthy was right. A crowd of local fishermen was taking the Crosbie bar seine and letting the herring go. Bill quickly returned to the *Western Star* to ponder his next move. But before he had worked out a strategy, several more boats had entered the harbour and headed to the wharf where the Crosbies stored their seines.

Tampering with other people's nets in Newfoundland was like stealing someone's horse in the Wild West — a very hostile act. Robert McCarthy jumped up on top of the Crosbie nets and confronted "Black John" from Lark Harbour, who was the first man to approach him. "Is yours the first hand to touch these seines?" he asked the menacing fisherman. Black John stopped in his tracks. By this time Bill had rowed to shore and joined McCarthy on the wharf.

"There's enough of you here to take these things, but that's only the beginning," Bill said. "It's not the end. We'll sue, we'll take to court anyone who steals our property."

The intruders retreated to consider their position and Bill and his men resumed the work of loading the *Western Star*. But at eleven o'clock that morning a flotilla put into the harbour from all the local coves in the area — fifteen to twenty vessels, each carrying six to eight men. With only seven crew members aboard the *Western Star*, Bill knew there was no protecting the company's seines. After they had been taken, the fishermen turned their attention to the *Western Star* itself, which they decided to seize.

Bill stood his ground. He ordered the ship's captain to run the Union Jack up the mast and told the first mate, "a great gorilla of a man," to take up a high-pressure hose, which was to be turned on the fishermen only if they attempted to come aboard. Bill then went to the prow of the boat carrying a wooden club and a piece of paper. As the small boats of the raiding party circled the *Western Star*, Jim McCarthy, Robert's son, called out the names of the men on board and Bill wrote them down. The men sullenly retreated and the ugly confrontation was over. Bill finished loading the herring and then went to confer with Ches, who was staying at the Glynmill Inn in Corner Brook, about what to do.

It was decided that Bill should go to Magistrate Timothy Wade and swear out summonses against the fishermen on his list. Early Sunday morning, Magistrate Wade, the head of the Fishermen's Union, and two police officers set out in the fisheries inspector's boat to serve summonses on the men. Their first stop was McIver's, where they were greeted with a volley of rocks from the shore. The union representative beseeched the men to show respect for the magistrate and the boat was finally allowed to land. Unnerved by the experience, Magistrate Wade told the fishermen he was there to hear their grievances. They in turn told him that they hadn't stolen the seines but had simply removed them until the herring season was over, at which time they would be returned in good order to their rightful owners. The magistrate came and went without breathing a word about the summonses. He repeated his performance at a number of settlements along the coast, including Wood's Island, where Robert McCarthy lived.

At seven-thirty on Monday morning, McCarthy and his gang arrived at the Glynmill Inn and told the Crosbies what the magistrate, who lived at the hotel, had been up to. Ches was furious, but he really began to fume when his men told him that the magistrate had begged the McCarthys to join in the protest against the Crosbies. Afraid of what Ches might do, Bill personally visited Magistrate Wade's office to discuss the situation. Wade defended his actions, claiming that his discretion had avoided a riot. Not satisfied, Bill pressed the magistrate to call Albert Walsh, Newfoundland's Commissioner for Justice and attorney-general, and he laid his complaint over the telephone. He insisted that the government immediately dispatch the police to reclaim the stolen Crosbie property.

After forcing the issue, Bill returned to the Glynmill Inn, intending to brief Ches over dinner about his meeting with Magistrate Wade. But when he reached his brother's room later that night, it was obvious that Ches was holding a meeting of his own with their timorous Solomon. Ches had Wade by the throat, pinned against his mattress. The magistrate was trying to tell Ches that he didn't know what he, Wade, had done that day. "You son of a bitch. I'll tell you something else you did this day you don't think I know about," he shouted. Try as he might, Bill couldn't pull his furious brother off the magistrate and ran to get a friend, Gordon Higgins, who was staying on the same floor. "Jesus, Gordon, come on! Ches is killing the magistrate!" The two men overpowered the raging bull of the Glynmill and took him back to his room to cool off.

Meanwhile, official wheels were turning back in St. John's. Magistrate Wade tried to get the Newfoundland Fisheries Board to close the herring season, thereby forcing the fishermen to return the Crosbie nets as they had promised. Chairman Raymond Gushue refused because there were still five weeks left in the season. Instead, a public meeting was called where the parties to the dispute could work out their differences in front of a member of the board, Harold Bradley. Bearing in mind that there were only seven policemen in Corner Brook, authorities decided to close all of the taverns on the day of the meeting. More than a thousand fishermen crowded into the meeting, which was held in the local theatre. The air was electric with the feeling that the leash of civility would snap at the first provocative exchange.

Both Ches and Bill addressed the fishermen, guaranteeing to take whatever herring they produced but arguing strenuously for their right to supplement those acquisitions with catches of their own in order to keep the plant running. The arguments went on all day and the fishermen finally agreed to give back the stolen gear to the Crosbies immediately in return for a meeting after the season was over to decide which areas of the Bay of Islands would be open to purse-seining.

It seemed like a reasonable solution until six o'clock the next morning, when Bill landed at Wood's Island aboard the

Western Star only to be told by Robert McCarthy that the fishermen had changed their minds overnight and would now be keeping the Crosbie seines until the last day of the season after all. Now it was Bill's turn to be furious. He set sail for Cox's Cove where he rowed ashore in a dory because the *Western Star* was too big to bring into the settlement. "I want yes or no," he demanded of a few fishermen who came to meet him. "Are you living up to your agreement or are you not living up to your agreement?" There was no reply.

Further up the harbour, at McIver's, all the men in the settlement met Bill as he rowed ashore and climbed onto their wharf. The size of the welcoming committee convinced him that the stolen equipment was in a two-storey loft behind the fishermen. Bill spoke to three or four men he knew by name, but they answered him with stony silence. He felt the hair bristle on the back of his neck. It was time to fish or cut bait. With Bill standing at the end of the wharf with a lead pipe in his hand and the sweat dripping off the tip of his nose, he nodded to Robert McCarthy, who boldly entered the loft, located the stolen gear and began throwing the seines down into the ship's dory. The fishermen turned their backs and there was a great murmuring as they tried to decide whether or not to throw Bill Crosbie and his man off the wharf. "This was worse than fighting the Germans," Bill would later say. "I looked upon us being in the Bay of Islands as the greatest thing that ever happened to me, and here I was in a horrifying battle with these fishermen. Standing on the wharf at McIver's was as frightening as anything I went through in the war years."

In the end, the fishermen let the two men go, largely because they were impressed with their courage in standing up for their rights. A week later, some men from McIver's showed up at the Crosbie plant with fish. Bill saw the opportunity to mend some nets with his neighbours and hurried out on the wharf to meet them. "You know, sir," they told him, "that gang you sent out in the fisheries boat, that gang was a little gang of mice come after us!"

After the fishing season of 1946, the promised meeting was held and it was decided that seines could not be used inside the headlands of the Bay of Islands. Since that was where the fish were, the decision was a farce as far as the Crosbies were concerned, a sellout by "that spineless wonder," the Commission of Government. The fishermen were delighted. Newfoundland Dehydrating was still left with crippling herring shortages and a strained working relationship with local fishermen.

Through the Fishermen's Union, the Crosbies arranged to have a delegation of Newfoundland fishermen from the Bay of Islands visit New Brunswick to see for themselves that seines and the trap fishery could work side by side. The most successful part of the mission, though, took place in Saint John, where colleagues of the Crosbies, the Connors brothers from Black Harbour, New Brunswick, arranged for the Newfoundlanders to have the run of the huge, local brewery. Although their opposition to purse-seines (and everything else) might have softened that day, it would be years before they would accept the Crosbies catching their own herring to keep the reduction plant going. By then, it would be too late.

LIKE BILL CROSBIE on the wharf at McIver's, young Gene Shinkle had a baptism of fire in Newfoundland that equalled anything he had faced during the war. The occasion was Christmas dinner, 1945, and the event was the announcement to the Crosbies that he was going to marry their only daughter. All that previous year, his affair with Joan had ridden the roller coaster of youthful romance — the dizzying heights, the heart-stopping dives and the surprising curves that left them both hanging on for dear life. After nursing Joan through a two-month bout with peritonitis, Gene ran into her at the movies on the arm of "an old navy friend." Meanwhile, Joan was just as astonished when Gene's name turned up in a gossip column in *The Daily News* linked with another local beauty, Marnie Lodge. The Crosbie family was not amused. Shink received a merciless tongue-lashing from Lady Crosbie. "I was called up by Skipper Ches and said they wanted me for dinner. . . . And I was taken down and had the boots put to me by Lady Mitch. 'This is not the sort of thing we do,' " she informed the startled young American. " 'And we don't get our name in that terrible newspaper.' " Shink bridled under what he considered to be a Victorian abuse of his freedom of action, but the relationship with Joan proceeded with a magical force all its own.

One night in late summer, the couple were sitting on the chesterfield in the back parlour of 18 Rennies Mill Road, the air delicately scented with the Fabergé perfume Joan liked to borrow from her mother, when she suddenly stretched out her arm and let her wrist go limp.

"Here," she said, "Take this off."

"What?" Shink asked her. It was the identification bracelet belonging to her navy friend. After removing it, they sat quietly for a moment, each expecting the other to say something.

"Fine," Joan said, "I'm going to give it back to him."

"Well," Shink offered, "that means you're not going out with Chuck anymore."

"No," Joan agreed, "I'm going out with you."

At the end of the summer, Joan returned to Branksome Hall. In late September, she wrote Shink a letter telling him that she had seen "this beautiful ring" in Birks. Shink sent her the money to buy it and then began to worry about how to break the news to the Crosbies.

"What do we tell your parents?" he asked. "Do they know?"

"No, they don't."

"Well, are you allowed to have it?"

"No, I'm not."

"Well, what are we going to do?"

"Well," Joan pertly replied, "I'm going to wear it when I come home at Christmas."

For weeks, Shink fretted over how the Crosbies would react. Not realizing the extent to which Joan could manipulate her parents to get just about anything she wanted, he worried that they might think he was unsuitable for their daughter. And they weren't the only ones. He himself had deep misgivings about whether or not such a marriage could work. There was a lot of cultural territory between Cincinnati and the back parlour of 18 Rennies Mill Road:

"I was scared to death. Here is a very, very middle-class American serviceman becoming involved in high society in a totally different social structure and in an area that was totally foreign to him. This is quite traumatic. You are aware of the fact that your parents are not wealthy. You are aware of the fact that they are not of a comparable social standing, and you think of the consequences and they are considerably frightening. Yet, you're deeply in love, very deeply in love with this woman. How do you bridge that gap? The answer that eventually resulted was a total loss of my own identity."

The reaction to Joan's surprise announcement was decidedly low-key. There were no questions from Ches or Jessie, who probably saw the whole thing as just another of their mercurial daughter's infatuations. Joan headed back to school in Ontario without the subject being brought up again. Shink had to return to the United States to be discharged from the army and got a job with the Southwestern Ohio Insurance Company in the cashiers and investment department.

The love affair continued by mail. During Easter break, Shink drove Joan from Toronto to Cincinnati to meet his parents. They were captivated by this exotic bird from the north, and the visit was a great success. During the long, lonely ride back from Toronto, Shink turned his thoughts to the future. He knew that he would have to go to university if he wanted to make a good living, and he was still anxious to pursue a career as a conductor. (An operation to shave an oversized bone in one finger was neutralized when the deformity grew back, ending any chance he had of becoming a concert pianist.) In his heart, he knew that he wasn't sure about this marriage. He wrote Joan and told her that it would be years before he finished school and that, because of the social differences between them, he believed their relationship could never work. To make his point, Shink returned Ches Crosbie's school ring from St. Andrew's, which she had given him at the time of their engagement. There were tearful phone calls and finally, in the spring of 1946, the surprising request from the Crosbies to meet Ches, Jessie and Joan at Parker House in Boston.

The meeting was cordial and to the point, probably because Ches was running it. "Look, Gene, Joan wants to marry you," Skipper Ches began. "She is very much in love with you. She's pretty hard to refuse. If nothing else, come to Newfoundland this summer and work for me. If at the end of the summer you and Joan determine it can't work and that you want to break it up, then go back and go to school."

And that is how a piano-playing gunnery sergeant from Cincinnati ended up in a third-floor bedroom at 18 Rennies Mill Road. Shink arrived back in St. John's wearing his one suit and carrying all his worldly goods in a single bag. After a few days, he was having dinner with the Crosbies when Ches suddenly said, "The *Olaf Olsen* is leaving for Williamsport day after tomorrow. Be aboard."

"Where am I going?" Shink asked.

"You're going to Williamsport to work on the slip," came Ches's gruff reply.

Shink soon learned that "the slip" as Ches called it was the place where whales were drawn up on land and butchered before being processed. It was odd work for a would-be conductor, but Shink was getting fifty dollars a week and had the companionship of Ches's youngest son, Andrew, who also spent part of the summer at Williamsport. It was almost his last. One of the furnaces blew up, burning the flesh from the fifteen-year-old's arm down to the bone, searing off his hair and eyebrows and moving a fifty-ton drying machine six feet down the shed. "I went to the manager's office and he was cutting dead skin that was falling off my arm with a pair of scissors," Andrew recalled. A vessel was called in from the whaling grounds to get Andrew back to civilization. Six days after the accident, he was finally checked into the burn unit of the Montreal General Hospital, where he spent the rest of his summer.

After paying his dues in Williamsport, Gene was given a task more in keeping with his training — bookkeeping for Marine Ironworks, another of Olaf Olsen's companies that Ches was now operating. While he was fixing up the books, the Crosbies were fixing a date for his marriage to their daughter, an event Joan informed him would be taking place in February 1947. Afterwards, the newlyweds would be going on an extended honeymoon in the United States. He was not to worry about his precarious financial situation.

The wedding, the honeymoon, spending money, an apartment, furniture and a job at the end of it all — everything was being taken care of by Ches: "That was the way they looked after me. I never felt worthy, I mean I never contributed. I got to believe that I didn't merit any of this stuff. I was totally dependent."

According to Joan's wishes, the wedding took place on February 5, 1947 at the Cochrane Street United Church. After the ceremony, there was a reception for 350 at the fashionable Colony Club. Sir John's daughter, Nina Bennett, secretly lent the couple her apartment in the west end of the city for their wedding night. The next morning, Harry Bugden of Bugden's Taxi Company personally drove the newlyweds to the airport. They climbed aboard the waiting DC-4 and had just settled into their seats when all hell broke loose. "I'm going to get on that goddamn plane and nobody is going to stop me." There was no mistaking that gruff voice of authority; it was Ches Crosbie, dishevelled and wildly cantankerous from an all-night drinking bout. He ran his eyes up and down the rows until he came to Joan and Gene. "Oh, there you are," he cried, a big smile breaking over his face. "I'm going with you to New York."

The threesome ended up at the Weylin Hotel in New York at 54th Street and Madison Avenue and partied indefatigably until Ches collapsed from the effects of his superhuman binge. Joan called Newfoundland and Jessie duly arrived to dry Ches out and take him home. The honeymoon was over, but for Gene Shinkle, a ten-year party was just beginning.

A FEW MONTHS after his trip to New York as a honeymoon helper, Ches Crosbie boarded a plane at Gander Airport and set out on one of the most sobering journeys of his life. As a Newfoundlander who had always been proud of being a British subject, he had high hopes for the vital meetings he was about to attend with the British government over Newfoundland's political future. Ches's mission, along with a handful of colleagues from the National Convention, was to assess the benefits of continued affiliation with Britain if

Newfoundland decided to stick with Commission of Government for another five years. The Newfoundland delegation also wanted to know what Britain's role would be if the colony opted for the return of responsible government. Finally, there was the vitally important question of exactly what political options the National Convention was empowered to put in front of the people of Newfoundland. But if the colony that Ches Crosbie described as the Cinderella of the British Empire expected to be fitted with a glass slipper at Whitehall, it was to be sorely disappointed; its representatives would leave as barefooted as they arrived.

From the very beginning, the British were rude, perfunctory and ruthlessly condescending to a group of men they clearly saw as a pack of semiliterate colonial boys out to stuff their pockets with candies paid for by His Majesty's Chancellor of the Exchequer. "The way we were received over there is of course now a famous story," Bert Butt, a member of the delegation, later remembered. "I'm not sure whether it was three, four, [or] five hours *outside* the hotel before we were invited in to get out of the cold. . . . I'd never met it before nor since, I didn't think it was possible for a group of people . . . to be so cold, and the word is cold, *freezing*."

The Newfoundlanders were kept waiting for two or three days for their first meeting with Viscount Addison, Britain's secretary of state for Dominion Affairs. There was no attempt to entertain them while they cooled their heels. The insult was obvious and calculated. In all, there were four meetings between the two groups. The British resented what they took to be the grousing attitude of the Newfoundlanders, who complained about the colony's large debt and the fact that Britain had entered into the U.S. military base agreement for her own benefit without making any restitution to Newfoundland for the use of her territory. Once raised, the hackles stayed up on the British side. They viewed the entire exercise as a kind of low-grade blackmail attempt by crude extortionists who had overvalued what they had to trade. As one British official smugly summed up Whitehall's strategy in his official report of the meetings, "No prizes were dangled in their eyes."

Ches was especially bitter about Britain's refusal to help

Newfoundland develop the fishery or work out more favourable trade and tariff arrangements with the United States. At one point during the heated discussions, Governor Gordon MacDonald's son, Kenneth, who was serving as his father's secretary, unwisely stood and whispered in Ches's ear what he ought to say. He promptly sat down again when he found one of Ches's well muscled arms swinging in his direction. The British recorded only a few scant references to Ches arising out of the meetings. "Crosbie, though a wealthy merchant, does not speak English very well."

An interesting sidelight of the London meetings was the surreptitious visit paid by Gordon Bradley, the pro-confederate Chairman of the National Convention, to the Dominions Office at Whitehall. Whatever his purpose in attending such a meeting, Bradley never mentioned it to his colleagues. But the rest of the delegation found out where he had been when a message was left at the hotel by the Dominions Office for someone to pick up Mr. Bradley's rubbers, which he had left behind. Ches Crosbie later claimed that Bradley, who would be lavishly fêted along with the rest of the Newfoundland delegation when they visited Ottawa a few weeks later, had in fact met with the British prime minister.

When the Newfoundland delegation set out from London on May 9 for the long trip home, they had little to show for their two-week humiliation at the hands of the Dominions Office. They now knew that if they chose responsible government, Britain was not prepared to pay any more of Newfoundland's bills. More importantly, Viscount Addison had also made it quite clear that the National Convention had the power to consider other future forms of government for Newfoundland in addition to a continuation of Commission of Government or a return to responsible government — a clear indication that Britain was open to, if not actively promoting, Confederation with Canada.

Many times during the long flight back, the Scotch whisky warming in his glass, Ches looked down at the gunmetal waters of the North Atlantic and pondered the riddle of Gordon Bradley's rubbers standing empty outside the secret doors of Whitehall.

CHAPTER 9

In the Belly of the Wolf

WHEN THE ST. John's readers of *The Daily News* and *The Sunday Herald* opened their newspapers on December 7, 1947, they were greeted by an advertisement announcing the creation of a new political party that called for economic union between Newfoundland and the United States. The response to the ads far exceeded the wildest dreams of James Halley, the young city lawyer who had placed them. Within a month, organizers claimed that more than ten thousand people had signed membership cards in the Economic Union Party (EUP) and hundreds more had besieged party headquarters to volunteer their help.

Halley shouldn't have been so surprised. The American war effort in Newfoundland, characterized by prosperity and an extraordinary public-relations triumph, had rekindled an old flame in the island's political life. Since the Bond–Blaine free-trade agreement of 1894 (technically disqualified by Britain but actually sabotaged by Canada), Newfoundlanders had understood the value of an economic deal with the United States. What could be more advantageous to a maritime country than an arrangement that would see Newfoundland fish entering the United States duty-free and American manufactured goods coming into the island without tariffs? Or having American capital underwrite the development of a fresh fish industry when the salt fish business was quickly going the way of wooden sailing ships? Making such a deal even more attractive was the fact that Newfoundland could retain her status as an independent country in the bargain, something the champions of Confederation could not offer.

The concept of customs unions was an idea whose time had already come in western Europe. The Benelux Treaty — a customs union between Belgium, the Netherlands and Luxembourg — had deeply impressed Bill Crosbie when he was stationed in Holland at the end of the war. Early in 1948, *Life* magazine published an article proposing such a customs union between Canada and the United States. "Canadians are the closest friends we have," the article read, "and they are in serious economic trouble. From the U.S. they need, and deserve, considerably less apathy about their plight. More than that, they need complete and permanent economic union with the U.S. The U.S. needs this too, and so does the future of a healthy world." The article stressed that Canada's political integrity was not an issue, since her ties with Britain were of the heart, not the pocketbook. Economic reality was forcing Britain into closer ties with Europe, so it was only reasonable that Canada should align herself with the United States on the continent the two countries so amicably shared.

Shortly after the ads appeared, Don Jamieson, a young salesman at the Bavarian Brewery, which was 25 percent owned by Ches Crosbie, was summoned to a meeting at Bill Crosbie's house. There, the leading proponents of economic union considered how to stop Joe Smallwood from making Newfoundland the tenth province of Canada. Twenty-six-year-old Jamieson and the dozen or so activists of the American option knew that they were the only thing between Newfoundland and the loss of her sovereignty. The ranks of the Responsible Government League, ultraconservative businessmen and shopworn politicians, were no match for Smallwood's zealous campaign on behalf of Canada. Their only answer to Smallwood's promise of universal baby bonuses and pensions was the cold edict of the London meeting with delegates of the National Convention: if Newfoundlanders voted for responsible government, they would have to go it alone financially. To stop Confederation, there would have to be a fresh option that offered tangible economic benefits and long-term security. Free trade with the United States, with its promise of prosperity based on American capital and full employment rather than Canada's social welfare programs, was the silver bullet the EUP hoped would lay low the approaching Canadian wolf.

They were a youthful, naïve, talented and ferociously nationalistic group. Don Jamieson was an up-and-coming gadfly who came by his preference for economic union honestly; as a young bell-hop at the Hotel Newfoundland, where his mother managed the restaurant, he learned that the biggest tippers were the American gangsters who ran rum out of St. Pierre and Miquelon into the United States during prohibition. Twenty-six-year-old Geoff Stirling was an American-educated visionary who as a teenager had quickly given up waiting tables at his father's Water Street restaurant to pursue a successful business career in the publishing industry. Bill Perlin was a member of one of the city's most respected merchant families and ran a thriving dry goods operation. Together with Lewis Ayre, Geoff Carnell, Gert and Bill Crosbie and a handful of others, their single passion was to stop Joe Smallwood. They had everything necessary for the task at hand but a leader, a plan and a place on the ballot in the upcoming referendum.

For a while it looked like that might not matter. On January 29, 1948, the National Convention decided by a vote of twenty-nine to sixteen that Confederation with Canada would not be one of the options considered in the June 3 vote to decide Newfoundland's political fate. Instead, there were to be only two choices: responsible government as it existed prior to 1934 and a continuation of Commission of Government. Joe Smallwood, who believed he was winning the battle to bring Newfoundland into Canada, exploded when the results of the vote were released. With characteristic vigour, he inveighed against the "twenty-nine dictators" who had tried to deal his cause a death-blow. Under Smallwood's rhetorical whip, the Confederates broke into a political gallop, collecting fifty thousand names on a petition aimed at reversing the decision of the National Convention.

The Dominion Affairs Office at Whitehall had always reserved the right to determine Newfoundland's political options, and on March 2, 1948, they exercised it. In an autocratic and stunning reversal of Newfoundland's elected National Convention, they allowed Confederation to be placed on the ballot, placating Smallwood and throwing the forces of responsible government into disarray in the same stroke. The ground rules for the June 3 referendum were adjusted accordingly: if no option won a clear majority on the first ballot, the least popular choice would be dropped and a second referendum held. Many Newfoundlanders were outraged, including Ches Crosbie, who was now more convinced than ever that Whitehall had turned the referendum process into a puppet show in which Britain and Canada were pulling the strings.

By the late 1940s, Ches Crosbie was easily the best known and most popular man in Newfoundland. He had entered the National Convention uncommitted, and even the Confederates had courted him as their leader. Although he was careful not to tip his hand too early, he did carry out his own assessment of the various options open to his country, rejecting Responsible Government because he believed it would pauperize Newfoundland in the long run, and deciding against Confederation because it was being promoted behind closed doors in other countries without regard for what Newfoundlanders themselves really wanted. Faced with the almost certain triumph of the Smallwood faction now that Confederation was on the ballot, Ches gave in to the persistent lobbying of brother Bill and young Don Jamieson (the same duo that had convinced him to run for the National Convention), but not before he made discreet inquiries in the United States to satisfy himself that the Americans were at least open to the idea of a free-trade agreement with Newfoundland. The most unlikely politician Newfoundland had ever seen was finally ready to throw his hat into the ring, where the world's tiniest lion-tamer was waiting for him.

Ches Crosbie's decision to accept the leadership of the Economic Union Party was hot news all over Newfoundland. Party organizers followed a splashy newspaper announcement with a special radio broadcast on the evening of Saturday, March 20, 1948. From the outset, there was a big problem. Ches did to the spoken word what his fish-digester at Quigley's Cove did to herring. To conceal this weakness, Don Jamieson had Ches pre-record a small segment of the address; then Jamieson himself read the balance of the party manifesto that night on VOCM. "Ches was deeply conscious of his inadequacy as a speechmaker. It embarrassed and humiliated him when it was necessary, as he knew it was, for me to follow him on the air and repeat his main arguments. This was the best method we could devise to get his message across. Because of it, the Confederates quickly dubbed me 'His Master's Voice,' 'Donald Duck' and 'The Circus Barker,' " Jamieson wrote.

Ches was mortified by these electronic deceptions but acknowledged their necessity; with help from wife Jessie and campaign manager Jamieson, he managed to produce a three-minute tape that was used to announce his plunge into the Confederation debates: "The history of Newfoundland has always been one of having to take half a loaf rather than no bread. Newfoundlanders have been kicked and tossed about for generations. We have never yet had a fair chance. I am convinced that the chance of a lifetime lies in economic union with the United States. . . ."

It was a stirring call on the radio, but when the venue shifted to the podium, Ches's mumbling and mispronouncing smothered rather than promoted the EUP's message. In the words of his own handlers, he had a voice that simply wouldn't go through a microphone. Astonished family members, who knew how charming Ches was one-on-one at a cocktail party or on the end of a wharf, wanted first-hand proof of his alleged fatal flaw.

One evening, Dolly Crosbie quietly slipped into the Star Hall in St. John's to hear her brother speak at a rally for economic union. After his first few grunts and growls, she accepted the view that he would never be a successful politician in Newfoundland. To test her conclusion, the always gregarious Dolly struck up a conversation with the elderly gentleman sitting next to her, telling him she lived in Montreal before soliciting his opinion of Ches's performance.

"He can't speak much," he offered.

"No, I don't think he can," she replied.

"Is this the first time you've heard him?" the man asked.

"No," Dolly answered, "I've known him for quite a long time."

"But you said you were from Montreal."

Giving up the ruse, Dolly replied, "I am. But I'm his sister."

"Glory be to God," the man cried, "wait a minute, mum." As gracefully as possible, he took his teeth out of his coat pocket and put them in. "I looks better now, don't I?" he said with a grin. It was one thing for a St. John's man to criticize a Crosbie, but when apprising another Crosbie of that fact it was *de rigueur* to convey the information with a complete set of teeth!

There may not have been music in Ches's voice, but there was magic in his presence and in the Crosbie name. The day after his carefully staged radio address, a thousand people showed up at the party's Henry Street headquarters in St. John's, and telegrams of encouragement poured in by the bagful. Several delegates to the National Convention, including J. P. Fowler and P. J. Lewis, rallied to Crosbie's side. Even the leaders of the Responsible Government League offered Ches their cautious support, based on the self-serving insight that any votes he attracted would ultimately have to come from the Confederation faction.

Supporters weren't the only people who had taken notice. Britain, Canada and the United States had all danced a careful diplomatic minuet as Newfoundland's hour of destiny approached. Britain had the most power to affect the outcome but worked hard at concealing its preference for Confederation for its former colony. The group of young nationalists around Prime Minister Mackenzie King definitely saw Newfoundland and Labrador as a prize, and feared that this missing piece of Canada's national mosaic would somehow fall under American influence if they failed to seize the day. And with the self-satisfied arrogance of the most important player in the world, the United States felt that if it showed the slightest interest in closer ties with Newfoundland, the EUP would easily win the referendum, an outcome that could offend old and important allies like Canada and Britain. The political correctness of their public statements to one side, it was the diplomatic pouch and not the press release that more closely mirrored the true positions of each of these impartial "spectators."

On March 22, 1948, just two days after Ches formally announced his leading role with the EUP, Paul Bridle, the acting Canadian high commisioner in St. John's, confirmed that he was a serious contender. Bridle wrote in his despatch: "Mr. Crosbie is aggressive, ambitious, a man of means, willing to spend it in the pursuit of political power. In spite of the flimsy basis upon which Mr. Crosbie has launched his campaign, his words will almost certainly possess a powerful appeal for uninformed fishermen who constitute the bulk of the electorate."

The American consul in St. John's was also quick to send his assessment to Washington: "The Newfoundlander is outwardly phlegmatic, but politically he appears to be immature and easily swayed. The response to Crosbie's announcement was instantaneous. Mr. Joseph R. Smallwood, the leader of the Confederationists, stated privately that Crosbie had come out with his party too soon and that before the referendum the Confederationists would demolish his party; but Smallwood appeared to be more worried than he was willing to concede."

Washington was fascinated. American Vice Consul L. O. Sanderhoff was instructed to meet informally with Ches to learn more about the EUP. On March 23, 1948, he filed a detailed despatch about his conversation with the party's new leader:

"I opened the conversation by mentioning that although the Consulate General's role was solely that of an interested spectator, we had to see to it that we reported on this matter intelligently. . . . Following these preliminaries, I asked Crosbie to clarify two matters: first, what did he mean, exactly, by economic union. Crosbie replied that by economic union he meant the lowering of trade barriers only. He was not concerned with immigration, postal, educational matters, et cetera. He did not espouse 'everything but the flag.' The second matter I asked him to clarify was the reason behind his statements that he believed the United States would be receptive to the idea of economic union. He answered that he could not disclose all names concerned, but stated that in part he was relying on Gushue's opinions [Ches's friend who was chairman of the Newfoundland Fisheries Board], based on the latter's conversations in Washington, D.C., particularly in December 1947. He stated also that a fish oil importer in New York who had occasion frequently to talk with State Department officials had given him his opinion that the United States would welcome approaches to unite economically provided Newfoundland first obtained its own government."

Once the first blush of enthusiasm for Ches Crosbie's leadership had faded, the EUP stood face to face with a string of all but insurmountable problems. The biggest one was not being on the referendum ballot as a separate choice. In order to get a chance to negotiate a customs union with the United States, Ches would first have to ally himself with the Responsible Government League, a group led by Major Peter Cashin and which stood for a return to Newfoundland's pre-1934 political situation — a kind of self-administered chaos in its dying days. But since responsible government was a necessary intermediate step along the longer road to economic union with the United States, Ches had no choice. He had to ask voters to support something he himself didn't want for the chance to get what the United States might later be willing to offer. It was an intrinsically flawed position. By comparison, what Joe Smallwood brought to the table you could put in the bank; by 1947, the National Convention had already received Canada's detailed proposals for Newfoundland entering Confederation. Compared to the EUP's promise to negotiate with the Americans, Smallwood's bird in the hand was worth two of Crosbie's in the political bush.

There was also the patriotic problem. Newfoundland had gone through two world wars in the twentieth century as part of the British Empire. Her history in North America had always been British, and when her political system fell apart in the Depression, it was Britain that supplied the steadying hand to get her colonial child back on its feet again. The Confederation option could be presented as an extension of that heritage. Canada, like Newfoundland, was part of the British Empire and shared many of the institutions and cultural values of the mother country. The EUP was asking Newfoundlanders to travel a much greater cultural distance to embrace a formal relationship with the United States, however pleasant the jitterbug of the war had been with their American dancing partners.

Ches's opposite number in the Confederation camp was keenly aware of these weaknesses in the EUP's position. Smallwood also believed that the whole concept was contrary to American international trade policy as expressed at a recent Geneva Conference of the International Trade Organization. But he also knew that there was political capital in the Crosbie name and a certain romantic lustre attached to America's wartime presence in Newfoundland. Most dangerous of all, Crosbie could, and shortly would, accuse Smallwood of selling his country out to get Canada's social programs, a charge that couldn't be flung back at his accuser. Unchecked, these factors in combination might have been able to derail Smallwood's master plan to make Newfoundland a part of Canada.

With characteristic political acumen, Smallwood probed for the Achilles' heel in Crosbie's political position and decided it was the American attitude towards economic union. If he could show that the United States was against the idea, or that for some other reason it was not a viable option, the EUP would be dead in the water.

For antagonists, the two men about to do battle for the soul of Newfoundland were remarkably fond of each other. Ches Crosbie was a member of Newfoundland's business elite and the inheritor of Sir John's social influence as the head of the Crosbie family. Joe Smallwood was a quirky, intellectual dynamo looking for a cause that always seemed to elude him. From his earliest years, the politics of the left had fascinated him. In 1925, young Smallwood walked the railroad tracks of Newfoundland to organize section men against company-planned pay cuts. Whether it was giving socialist speeches on a soap box in New York, working as an organizer in the Fishermen's Cooperative Union in

Newfoundland, or running an iconoclastic newspaper in St. John's, Smallwood was always championing the cause of the working man — often to the displeasure of the establishment.

"Smallwood is a mysterious man, getting along so to say solely on his wits. Actually I cannot say anything about him by way of a criminal nature, but he is what we usually term a 'shady character,' " a February 4, 1937 undercover police report to the Justice Department read. Not much had changed by 1946, when the U.S. consulate in St. John's described him in an official despatch as "a much hated man" whom Consul General George K. Donald had heard others refer to as "that dirty swine."

If Joe Smallwood was the *bête noir* of the St. John's business establishment, then Ches Crosbie was the club's odd man out. In fact, during the campaign for the National Convention, Ches and Smallwood met in a Gander apartment and argued all night about the best possible solution to Newfoundland's political dilemma. Ches, who told friends that "you couldn't help liking the little bugger," begged Smallwood to fight for responsible government first, whatever political alliance Newfoundland might later decide was in her best interests.

"Look Joe," he said, "we can have Confederation, we can perhaps do something with the States, or else if we want to we can join the bloody Russians! But let's get our own government first of all, and then let's decide what our future is to be."

"Ches, when this ragged arsed humanity knows I got baby bonuses and old age pensions, there's nothing in this world can stop me from having political power," Joey replied. It was 4:30 in the morning and the battle lines had been drawn.

Despite their political differences, Smallwood had long been the beneficiary of one of Crosbie's most attractive traits; Ches was always intrigued by the underdog and unselfishly lent his support to anyone trying to pull themselves up by their bootstraps. So at a time when Smallwood couldn't get past the mail clerk in most business establishments in St. John's, he was a welcome figure at Crosbie and

Company, where, with his arms flailing wildly, he would lay siege to Ches for hours with his unorthodox schemes for making money.

By 1936, the arrangement that saw the Smallwood family living off group contributions of vegetables and firewood in rural Newfoundland in exchange for his services as a union organizer came to an end when the fishermen no longer had any surplus to contribute. For the next several years Joe made a dollar where he could, and Ches Crosbie was always there to smooth the way, whether the project was pigs or encyclopaedias. When Smallwood wanted to buy three thousand woollen blankets from the War Assets Disposal Corporation at the end of the war for a dollar apiece, Ches called the bank manager in Gander on his behalf to secure the loan. The profit Smallwood made by reselling the blankets to the Bowater's mill in Corner Brook would later be used to finance the early stages of the Confederation campaign.

Casting around for a way to make larger amounts of money, Smallwood came across *The Book of Puerto Rico*, an informal history of the island, while reading in Newfoundland's first public library. He decided on the spot to write a parallel work, *The Book of Newfoundland*. Smallwood calculated that there were forty thousand libraries around the world, which he blithely assumed would all stock his new work, making him a fortune. He then contacted Richard Clay and Sons of Bungay, North Suffolk, England, to get an estimate of the printing costs. It really didn't matter what the printers said since he didn't have any money, but Smallwood always dreamt first and left it to others to worry about the details later.

An ardent lover of Newfoundland, Ches Crosbie was intrigued by Smallwood's project and invited him to Rennies Mill Road to discuss it further. It was an expensive breakfast. Ches invested a total of $25,000 in *The Book of Newfoundland* and gave Smallwood the use of the second floor of the Crosbie business headquarters on Water Street. Wisely, Ches arranged to have Smallwood limit the size of the edition to ten thousand two-volume sets. The prudent businessman also insisted as a condition of financing that his brother-in-law, A. B. Perlin, be named chairman of the board of editors. When the books came out in 1937, the first four thousand were sold door to door at five dollars a set. For two long years, the project languished in the doldrums of a stagnant economy. But then the war caused a boom in book sales. The last six thousand copies were snapped up by Canadian and American servicemen as souvenirs of their time in far-off Newfoundland.

Smallwood continued to scratch out an existence as best he could and by the 1940s, his best was getting better. Although he made no profit from the first *Book of Newfoundland*, he continued his writing and now supplemented his income by hosting a popular radio program called the "Barrelman Broadcasts." (A ship's barrelman was the seaman who kept watch from a small barrel on the masthead.) Every evening at 6:45, from Monday to Saturday, a ship's bell would ring six times and Joe's familiar voice would crackle out of the radio with another tall tale about Newfoundland. But his principal income came from raising hogs, chinchillas, rabbits and chickens on the forty-acre farm he had purchased just outside St. John's in 1939. Curiously, pigs were to pave his way into politics, and Ches was to foot the bill.

The commanding officer of the Royal Air Force Transport Command station at Gander was exactly the kind of dashing figure Joe Smallwood would be drawn to all his life. At the time, there was no highway into Gander so it was difficult for RAF Group Captain David Anderson to get a reliable supply of fresh meat for his men. To remedy the problem, he established a modest piggery at the base designed to produce twenty-five to thirty animals for the mess, which in turn provided the swill for the herd. When he heard about Smallwood's piggery in St. John's, Captain Anderson paid him a visit. It was agreed that Smallwood should visit Gander and assess the British operation.

Brimming with enthusiasm, the little man who was always ready to lose himself in the castle of a large thought saw the chance to establish a piggery of a thousand animals to take care of the needs of the base. He and Group Captain Anderson set up a joint company to be owned by Smallwood and the RAF Welfare Fund. There was only one problem;

Smallwood didn't have the money for his end of the deal. Once again he approached Ches Crosbie for financing. Ches gave him a $10,000 loan at 6 percent annual interest to cover Smallwood's share of the venture, and a promise of 40 percent of the profits. A 300-foot-by-40-foot piggery was built a few hundred feet from the main hangar on the British side of Gander airport. (Joe's establishment provided a measure of the charms possessed by World War II Gander as a tourist destination; the piggery became an obligatory stop for visiting dignitaries like Sir Anthony Eden, Field Marshall Jan Smuts and a delegation of Chinese diplomats who must have wondered if it was a Newfoundland custom to take visitors to the local hog farm!)

All went well until Smallwood was bitten by a new enthusiasm — the National Convention. It is one of the enduring ironies of Newfoundland politics that Joey was elected to the National Convention as a delegate from Bonavista Centre, thanks to Ches Crosbie's timely investment in his piggery. Had Smallwood been living in St. John's, which was staunchly anti-Confederate, getting elected would have been difficult if not impossible for the man who had a reputation in the city as a wild-eyed extremist.

Unaware that his mercurial partner had found a new way to bring home the bacon, Ches flew into Gander from a business trip and decided to fill in the time waiting for the train to St. John's with a visit to Joe's piggery. He was amazed to discover that there was a grand total of just twenty-five animals on the premises. When he got back to St. John's, Ches called Ross Young, his director of accounts, and asked how many pigs there were supposed to be in the Gander operation.

"Well, Mr. Ches, I suppose 200 or something — " He was cut off in mid-sentence.

"Where's Joe?"

To his surprise, Ches discovered that Joe's brother Reg was now in charge of the piggery. Joe explained that Reg had called him the previous week and asked him to hurry back to Gander to deal with an emergency. It seemed that the pig swill from the mess had somehow been laced with lye, poisoning the animals to varying degrees, depending on how much they had eaten. For days and nights on end, Joey and Reg prowled the herd, watching their pigs for any sign of distress. When one of them began its death throes, it was quickly butchered and delivered to the British mess. And that, explained Smallwood, was why Ches's investment had dwindled to twenty-five pigs!

Half an hour after his meeting with Smallwood, Ches got a call from Ross Young advising him that Joey had been asking questions about the piggery's insurance arrangements. Ches immediately got Smallwood on the phone.

"Listen, Joe, the last thing you're going to have out in Gander is a fire," he roared.

As Bill Crosbie would later recall, Smallwood "laughed like hell" and replied, "Ah, Ches, I was only thinking of ways and means. . . ."

THE HISTORY OF the critical six weeks leading up to the June 3 vote was the story of how Smallwood continued to find "ways and means" to defeat his opponents. A brilliant propagandist, likened by his adversaries to the infamous Dr. Goebbels, Smallwood assembled a youthful and talented team around him. Although Gordon Bradley, a smooth-talking lawyer and respected member of the establishment, was the party figurehead, the real power belonged to Smallwood and three of his cohorts, who were collectively known as "the four Bolsheviks." Greg Power was a talented poet and champion athlete who was married to Robert Crosbie's daughter, Mary. Power helped run and eventually bought Clovelly Farm. Harold Horwood was a fiery labour leader, intellectual and admirer of W. Irving Fogwill, the famous Newfoundland poet and trade unionist. Philip Forsey was a St. John's teacher and political activist who personally guaranteed the loan that paid for the first issue of *The Confederate*, the party's brilliantly satirical newspaper.

The paper itself would cost $50,000 to produce during the run-up to the referendum and Smallwood spared no expense to make it a first-class propaganda tool. Filled with the devastating satire of Power and Horwood, who unmercifully lampooned "Comic Union" with the United States, its eighty thousand copies also featured some professional help from Canada. Understanding the importance of powerful editorial cartoons that made his foes look ridiculous, Smallwood hired Jack Booth of *The Globe and Mail*. At the time, Booth was reputed to be the best political cartoonist in Canada, and Smallwood paid him $500 for each cartoon he contributed to *The Confederate*. By comparison, the attempts at satire by *The Independent*, the newspaper of the responsible government forces, were feeble and lifeless. As Bill Crosbie put it, "In today's language, they were a bunch of squares up against a pro when they got up against Smallwood."

But as usual, "Joseph and his motley gang," as they were dubbed by the pro-responsible government newspaper, *The Daily News*, had a bank account that wasn't up to the many ways they found to spend money. Despite literally selling Canadian senatorships on the instalment plan to local financial supporters like maverick businessman Alexander "Sandy" Baird (the going rate was $25,000), the cash-strapped Confederates ultimately turned to the one source that had a vested interest in the outcome of the political drama unfolding in Newfoundland — the Liberal Party of Canada.

Once more, the man at the centre of the machinations was Smallwood himself. Through New Brunswick Senator Neil McLean, the treasurer of the provincial Liberal Party, he was introduced to Canada's minister of National Revenue, Dr. James McCann. According to Smallwood, in an interview with Charles Granger, a clandestine meeting was arranged between Smallwood and the most powerful backroom player in the Liberal Party, the venerable C. D. Howe. "Howe was to come and see me at my room. Now this was shrewd, because where else could I go where I wouldn't attract attention, because what he did was get in the elevator and go up in the elevator to the floor above my floor and he walked right back to the rear end of the corridor on the fourth floor . . . and walked down the stairs. I was waiting. He didn't even need to tap on the door, I had it half open. He slipped in and if [he] . . . when he emerged into the third floor corridor had seen anyone, he would have walked past. But no one saw him and he came in and we talked. He said, 'All right, you've got a campaign and we've got to help you.' "

Despite his careful insistence that Canadian money never entered his faction's coffers until after Confederation, Smallwood never explained the reason for all the secrecy with C. D. Howe. After all, what would be so unusual about the president of the Liberal Party of Canada being seen in the Chateau Laurier with a would-be Liberal premier of a Canadian province, unless that would-be premier had not yet won the referendum that brought Newfoundland into Canada?

Smallwood's right-hand man, Greg Power, sheds some light on the controversial issue of whether or not official sources in Canada arranged the financing for a political campaign in a foreign territory. Power remembers sending Ray Petten, Smallwood's bagman, to see Prime Minister Mackenzie King to ask for money for the newspaper, *The Confederate*. When the talks appeared to be going nowhere, Power advised an exercise in political brinkmanship.

"Look," Power told Smallwood, "we should bring it to a head. Tell him the people who are fighting for Confederation have no money and they have to give it up." According to Power, the scare tactic worked. After waiting another forty-eight hours, Prime Minister Mackenzie King himself appeared at the Chateau Laurier and secretly met with Petten: "He knocked on the door and he handed Petten a page with a typewritten list of names. It was signed by Mackenzie King. Anyway, Petten went out the next morning and he struck oil everywhere he went. And he came home with the money. Now Joe shovelled it out to every fellow who came up."

Greg Power would later claim that the Confederates got access to $100,000 through their Liberal friends in Canada primarily from the liquor industry, without which the party's newspaper could never have been published. For Smallwood supporters who wanted to believe their hero when he said he got no financial support from Canada until after Confederation, there was another stubborn fact to deal with. On June 21, 1948, just about a month before the second referendum that decided Newfoundland's political destiny, Smallwood and Bradley wrote their friend and patron C. D. Howe with a request that is difficult to misinterpret: "We need money desperately. Taking into account what we will raise locally, we must have at least another $20,000. . . . We need it quickly."

Additional evidence that Canada helped finance the campaign that brought the country its tenth province came from a confidential memo sent to the U.S. State Department by Terry B. Sanders, Jr., the second secretary of the American Embassy in Ottawa, after a conversation he'd had with economic union activist, Geoff Stirling. Stirling was in Ottawa to counter the alleged lobbying of Kenneth MacDonald (the son of Newfoundland's governor), who wanted the Canadian government to pressure the Americans into a public statement that they weren't interested in economic union with Newfoundland. In the course of his conversations on March 31, 1948, Stirling raised the issue of Canadian funding for the Confederate cause:

"Stirling asserted it is a well known fact that Smallwood last year was promised by Secretary of State for External Affairs St. Laurent the premiership of Newfoundland province if the pro-confederation party wins the referendum and that Smallwood is receiving money from Canadian sources. (Both of these charges have been confirmed to the Embassy by Ottawa sources.)"

The Confederates put their Canadian dollars to good use. Emphasizing that joining Canada as a province would allow Newfoundlanders to continue their allegiance to the Union Jack and the Crown, Smallwood had fifty thousand posters printed bearing the words "British Union" against a full-colour Union Jack. On a second line, the single word "Confederation" was printed in larger letters. The implication was as clear as it was incorrect; a vote for economic union was a pledge to the American flag and a vote against the mother country — a mother country so overwhelmed with the task of reconstruction after the war that she had been working very hard since 1946 to deal Newfoundland off to Canada.

Despite his well-financed, brilliantly conducted political campaign, Smallwood knew that the Crosbie-led forces of economic union were gathering support. Smallwood's ingenuity as a campaign manager was counterbalanced by the youthful enthusiasm of Crosbie's workers. Don Jamieson was an excellent political propagandist in his own right, and could often be seen circling St. John's in an aeroplane, dropping leaflets to the curious citizens below. Geoff Stirling, who paid visits to the United States, where he had his faction's buttons and posters printed, also organized expatriate Newfoundlanders to urge their relatives living in Newfoundland to vote for economic union. Copies of his pro-economic union *Sunday Herald,* wrapped in pink paper, were even dropped by aeroplanes to Newfoundland sealers on the ice floes.

Fearful that the referendum might be slipping away from him, Smallwood made a remarkable offer to Ches during the Confederation debates. The two leaders met in Joe's basement apartment in a house that belonged to Ches's cousin, Dick Chalker.

" 'Look Ches, you back me and I'll make you premier. I can do it, I can make you premier. And if you want to have me as your right hand man, you can have me.' He was tempted, he was tempted, he was tempted," Joey told Charles Granger. Ches Crosbie turned down the Svengali of Newfoundland politics — something that neither of his sons, despite their father's sage advice, would be able to do.

Smallwood's feeling that his campaign might be in trouble sprang from more than Ches Crosbie's obvious popularity and the marketability of his party. Frightened by the social impact of what Smallwood was proposing, the powerful Roman Catholic Church had come out foursquare against Confederation. It exercised enormous influence over the 33 percent of the population whose Irish forefathers had borne the brunt of British Protestant oppression. Led by the iron-willed and acerbic Archbishop of St. John's, seventy-two-year-old Edward Patrick Roche, the church preached its anti-Confederate message from the pulpit and published it in its newspaper, *The Monitor.* The strident tone of the newspaper's editorials made very clear what Mother Church expected of the faithful: "The fate of Newfoundland will be irrevocably determined by weal or woe in the very near future. It would surely be the supreme tragedy of our history, if by apathy, indifference, lack of enlightened leadership, or the influence of sinister propaganda we were to alienate irretrievably the inheritance which was won for us by our patriotic forebears."

The campaign was aggressive and grassroots. Greg Power, himself a Catholic, would later tell the story of an encounter between his mother's maid, Mary Ann Collins, whom he had convinced to vote Confederate, and the parish priest.

"Father said, 'What are you voting, Mary Ann?'

" 'Voting for Greg, sir,' she replied.

" 'Oh my, oh my, what are you doing that for?'

" 'Going to get myself and Pa a pension, $40 a month!' she happily answered.

" 'Don't you believe a word of it,' the priest told her."

For the first time in Newfoundland's history, nuns and brothers would make their way to the polls. And when the votes were finally counted, it would be impossible to deny that the church had played a central role in getting out the anti-Confederate vote and inspiring an anti-Catholic backlash.

In the final stretch of the first referendum race, the Confederates hit the EUP with a political broadside they believed would send their cause to the bottom. J. B. McEvoy, the last chairman of the National Convention and a closet Confederate, secretly went to Washington in April 1948 and met with Dr. Manley O. Hudson, a professor of international and constitutional law at Harvard University. The eminent jurist supplied a written opinion that economic union between the United States and Newfoundland was not possible because any American concessions granted to Newfoundland would violate existing U.S. trade agreements with more senior and important trading partners. Relations between the United States, Britain and Canada would also prevent any trade agreement that was unacceptable to Canada or the U.K.:

"These relations are so intimate, and they are so important to the United States, that nothing is likely to be done in Washington to which either the United Kingdom or the Dominion of Canada offered objections. It is difficult to foresee a trade agreement which would give to Newfoundland advantages greater than those presented in the trade agreement with the U. K. of 17 November 1938. . . . I can see no prospect in the immediate future of establishing any enduring liens which would be of advantage to Newfoundland. The possibility of any political or economic union with the United States is remote and its achievement fraught with hazards."

Dr. Hudson's deadly words were duly reported in the May 8, 1948 edition of *The Evening Telegram*, whose publisher favoured Confederation. The effect of the so-called Hudson memo can be gauged from a despatch sent by Canada's high commissioner in St. John's to the minister for External Affairs, Louis St. Laurent. It reported that the professor's opinion would "practically sweep the ground from under Mr. Chesley A. Crosbie's movement to stampede the electorate with the promise of free trade with the United States and demonstrate, as conclusively as anything short of a statement from the United States government itself could do, that the promise was a vain and empty one. Seldom if ever in the political history of Newfoundland has an irresponsible promise boomeranged with such effect on the fortunes of the party that put it forward."

The American consul general, Wainwright Abbott, was not quite as sanguine as his Canadian counterpart but shared the opinion that Dr. Hudson's memo might tip the scales in favour of the Confederates. In a confidential telegram to the American Secretary of State, he wrote:

"Evening Telegram May 8 published a letter and lengthy memorandum addressed chairman national convention McEvoy by Manley Hudson of Harvard Law School in reply to McEvoy's oral inquiries in Cambridge as to possibility of, and U.S. receptivity to, economic union. . . . Hudson stated that after conferring in Washington with 'well informed friends' he does not believe such union feasible. McEvoy's inquiry was effort to make political capital against Crosbie

Party and Hudson's opinion may perhaps prove decisive in favour confederate cause."

Suddenly blood was in the political air. Like a fighter who knows his opponent is on the ropes, Joe Smallwood waded in and battered economic union as "a farce, a sham, a complete impossibility." The EUP reeled under Smallwood's relentless body blows. As Don Jamieson remembered, "We listened in depressed silence as an exuberant Smallwood took to the air to herald the news that Economic Union was finished. . . . For most of us, it was the low point of the campaign."

Ches Crosbie was the notable exception. Furious that Smallwood had made him look like a fool or a fraud, he summoned a team of legal and constitutional experts to Rennies Mill Road to prepare a counterattack. His own inquiries in Boston and Washington had confirmed that the Americans were open to discussing economic union, but Crosbie knew that that intelligence was useless unless he could make the electorate believe it. It was now the turn of a determined Geoff Stirling to replace Dr. Hudson's death certificate for the EUP with a birth certificate signed by the most influential American politicians he could find.

Working feverishly as the clock ticked down towards the June 3 referendum, Stirling interviewed sixty of America's ninety-six senators looking for a statement that they would indeed meet with a delegation from Newfoundland to discuss economic union. With the help of Ohio Senator Robert Taft, the young Newfoundlander was introduced to Senator Wayland "Curly" Brooks of Illinois, who agreed to make a recording confirming that economic union was open to discussion. Stirling had every reason to be ecstatic; the taped message from a U.S. senator would surely carry more weight with voters back in Newfoundland than the negative legal opinion of an Ivy League egghead. Stirling filed his bombshell story from Washington, and the May 23, 1948 edition of *The Sunday Herald* published the names of fifty-one U.S. senators who agreed to meet with a delegation from a sovereign Newfoundland to discuss free trade. "This is PROOF," the newspaper trumpeted, "that Economic Union is possible."

But Stirling's American mission was not yet complete. On May 24, 1948, he paid an unannounced visit to the State Department to see if he could get an official repudiation of the Hudson memo on the grounds that the professor had merely been stating his personal opinion and not the policy of the U.S. government. The officials at State, knowing that Hudson had, in fact, met with the chief of the European desk, refused to make a comment except to say that Professor Hudson was not an employee of the U.S. government. Armed with the recording by Senator Brooks, Stirling left Washington on May 27, 1948, confident that he could supply his "great hero" Ches Crosbie with a deadly rebuttal to the Hudson memo. For a party that was supposed to be dead in the water, the EUP was showing remarkable vital signs.

Delighted with the success of Stirling's mission, the EUP made plans to broadcast the Senator Brooks tape on Friday, May 28, at 10:30 p.m. *The Daily News* of the same day ran a banner headline reading, "VERY IMPORTANT BROADCAST TONIGHT." Thousands of curious Newfoundlanders huddled around their radios only to hear an announcer explain that the broadcast had been prohibited by order of Newfoundland's governor. Five days later, a more detailed picture of what had happened emerged in an American diplomatic despatch from St. John's to the American secretary of state in Washington.

"I have the honour to refer to my telegram No. 49 of May 29 regarding the last minute refusal of the Newfoundland Broadcasting Corporation to permit the broadcasting of the recording of Senator C. Wayland Brooks' statement relative to Economic Union between the United States and Newfoundland. According to a reliable source, Mr. Smallwood, the Confederate leader, upon learning of the proposed broadcast, telephoned the Governor from Corner Brook with the result that the playing of the record was forbidden at the last moment for 'diplomatic reasons.'. . . The recording was not made by the Senator himself, Stirling explained to an officer of the Consulate General, as he is a poor speaker, but was made in the Senate Office Building from a reading of a statement prepared by the Senator on the subject."

Infuriated by the ban on their tape, the EUP published the text of the Brooks statement in *The Sunday Herald* for May 30. It was an impressive salvo, coming as it did a mere four days before Newfoundlanders went to the polls. The tone of the senator's remarks stunned the Confederate forces to the same extent that the Hudson memo had devastated the EUP three weeks earlier. At the crucial hour, it now seemed inarguable that the Americans were actively interested in an economic deal that Professor Hudson said couldn't be made:

"At this time when defence and hemispheric solidarity is the main aim in the North American continent, Newfoundland is a key to the future security of the United States and our neighbours. Even this year, the United States is spending $18 million to strengthen American defences in Newfoundland. Because of this and many other reasons, there is nothing to prevent our country and Newfoundland from reaching a satisfactory agreement, providing that that country elects its own responsible government and then sends a delegation to Washington to discuss Economic Union. Many million dollars of American capital might well be invested in Newfoundland should our two countries be able to reach an agreement, and I see no reason why thousands of Newfoundlanders could not enjoy full employment as a result of such American investments. It is possible for a free and independent Newfoundland to arrange economic union with the United States, and there is no one who ought to tell the people of Newfoundland otherwise."

After weeks of emotional debate, Newfoundland was a house bitterly divided on the eve of the referendum. The city was lined up against the country, big business against the working class, newspaper against newspaper, Catholic against Protestant and, all too frequently, family member against family member. Three nights before the vote, there was a riot in front of the Church Lads Brigade Armoury during a Smallwood rally. Smallwood was cut after his glasses were smashed, and Greg Power, punched and bleeding, narrowly escaped after the intervention of a burly policeman who "laid out everyone" in sight. Back at the hotel, a shaken Gordon Bradley, still wearing his Homburg, made his unhappiness known.

"I was a goddamned fool ever to be associated with you," he told Smallwood, who was nursing the gash to his face. "I'm going back to Bonavista tomorrow."

"Go back to Bonavista, you goddamned good-for-nothing, and stay there," Smallwood shot back. Even the people who were trying to manipulate the volatile emotions they had helped to unleash were occasionally overtaken by their handiwork. Everyone breathed a sigh of relief when the furious campaigning was finally over.

On a cool and cloudy June morning in 1948, the moment finally arrived for Newfoundland to pass judgment on the parties that had wooed them for months with competing visions of the island's future. Voter turnout was much heavier than during the election for the National Convention; an astonishing 88 percent of eligible voters marked ballots that day, many of them in voting booths set up just outside American military bases to avoid the charge of American interference in the referendum. Everyone had an opinion about how the vote would go, but the American consul general in St. John's, Wainwright Abbott, hit the bull's-eye with his prediction that Responsible Government would come first, followed by Confederation and Commission of Government, in that order. Abbott doubted that any party would achieve an absolute majority.

Smallwood's right-hand man, Greg Power, remembered the astonishment in the Confederate camp as the results of the vote began to pour in from outport Newfoundland:

"The night of the first referendum, we were listening to the count. The first count came out from Fogo, Responsible Government ahead. We couldn't believe it! Then the count came in from Twillingate proper, Responsible Government ahead. The first time I saw Joe falter, he said, 'Jesus Christ, what's wrong?' Anyway, Charlie Garland was our treasurer and he was drinking a bottle of pop and he was as white as a sheet and he said, 'It's you and Joe are the two fellows I'd pity.' Joe looked over at me and said, 'And don't you forget, there's no place in Newfoundland you can hide from Edward Patrick.' This was Archbishop Roche, Edward Patrick Roche. It was true, you know, you'd have to leave if you lost."

The mood in the EUP camp was even more despondent. All night, Ches had followed the results in Monty Lewin's study in Corner Brook. Like his followers in St. John's, who had stayed up all night drinking coffee in the Crosbie sitting room, Ches could see the writing on the wall in the final numbers: Responsible Government, 69,400; Confederation, 64,066; and Commission of Government, 23,311. The key was the unexpectedly high vote for Commission of Government, a faction that had scarcely campaigned during the referendum. Ches and his brain trust instinctively knew that the Confederates would likely get the majority of those conservative voters who valued the economic security of the British connection above all other considerations. In a buoyant, election night radio interview, Smallwood boasted that he would win a clean sweep of the Commission of Government votes in the runoff referendum to follow. Political bravado to one side, the EUP tacitly accepted his prediction. Don Jamieson said it for the entire Crosbie camp when he wrote, "We had staked everything on an initial decisive outcome and had neither strategy nor stomach for a renewed contest. We had, in short, given all we had. In the post-election dawn as we pored over the results, the reality was inescapable: the movement for economic union with the United States had reached its high-water mark and there was nowhere for us to go but down."

NEWFOUNDLAND'S SECOND AND final referendum was scheduled for July 22, 1948. From the moment the political starting-pistol was fired, Joe Smallwood was off and running while the forces of responsible government spun their wheels in procedural disputes and a doomed attempt at cobbling together a coalition between essentially unsympathetic factions. James Halley, the lawyer who had placed the initial ads announcing the creation of the EUP, mounted a challenge to the legality of the second referendum. He argued that it was illegal to proceed with the runoff vote since Newfoundlanders had already rejected Confederation by a two-thirds majority in the first referendum. With the assistance of American journalist Eugene Griffin of *The Chicago Tribune*, telegrams were sent off to Canada, Britain and the United States, where it was hoped that sympathetic legislators would take up the EUP's cause.

Meanwhile, both the EUP and the Responsible Government League realized that they would have to work more closely together if they were to have any chance of stopping Smallwood. A week after the first referendum, they formed a joint committee that met every Monday and Thursday at 4:30 p.m. in the boardroom of *The Daily News*, the St. John's paper that had long since thrown off the mantle of an objective reporter of events. Various new tactics were discussed, including a family allowance scheme to offset the generous social benefits the Confederates had used so successfully to seduce voters in the first referendum. But it was an uneasy alliance. Ches's youthful supporters were water and the stodgy businessmen and lawyers of the League the thickest of oil; the factions neither mixed nor worked well during the frantic final weeks of the campaign, one of the dirtiest Newfoundland would ever see.

One Sunday morning in June, the city awakened to see crudely lettered signs plastered on Protestant churches reading, "Confederation means British Union with French Canada." It was an underhanded attempt to make the point that Confederation was not the option most in keeping with Newfoundland's long-standing political roots. In fact, the poster writers tried to show that Canada was a far cry from Britain, French-speaking Quebec being the essential difference. As they went to church that Sunday morning, it was hoped that Newfoundland Protestants would ask themselves if they really wanted to join a country where a large number of the citizens spoke French and many, the so-called Zombies, had failed to answer their country's call to arms during the recently ended war. Tellingly, no signs appeared on Catholic churches.

As public outrage spread and the poster campaign backfired, both sides in the referendum fight denied all responsibility in the sordid affair and blamed each other. But the damage was done. For bigots in each camp, the balance of the Confederation debates became an unholy religious crusade initially made possible by the Catholic church's vigorous and public support of responsible government.

According to U.S. government diplomatic despatches, the British governor of Newfoundland, Sir Gordon MacDonald, was horrified by the poor showing of Confederation in the first referendum. After June 3, he intensified his efforts to swing the vote to the Confederation side by paying school teachers fifty dollars a week plus expenses to actively campaign in outport Newfoundland. He also tried to cajole Newfoundlanders on the Commission of Government to declare for Confederation, ultimately persuading two of them to go on radio before the second vote was taken. Concerned that Smallwood himself was a chattering low-life who didn't have enough personal prestige to carry the day, MacDonald leaned on every prominent citizen he knew to lend their respectability to the Confederate campaign. J. B. McEvoy, Leslie Curtis and Leonard Outerbridge were three of the new faces who publicly supported Confederation in the second referendum.

The responsible government side also attracted new blood, including Ches Crosbie's father-in-law, Andrew Carnell, the mayor of St. John's; R. B. Job, an old and highly regarded St. John's merchant; and Calvert Pratt, the president of the Newfoundland Industrial Development Board. And there was another new party worker who had more reason than most to rejoice in his political role that summer. Seventeen-year-old John Crosbie, Ches's oldest son, had just finished grade twelve at St. Andrew's College and was back in Newfoundland for the summer vacation. He had already become deeply immersed in the great political issues confronting Newfoundland, as his poem published in the St. Andrew's College school magazine made clear.

But now are rising men who love their land,
Who soon will try to govern once again,
Their native country, belov'd Newfoundland
Led by these men 'tis hoped to break that chain
Of bondage. Up true Newfoundlanders! Rise!
And fight once more to win proud freedom's prize.

In keeping with his practice of giving his sons tough manual labour, Ches put John to work with a pick and shovel on the construction site of St. Clare's Hospital from seven in the morning to six in the evening. "Geez, I practically killed myself. . . . The first week I could only make it during the morning," Crosbie later recalled.

But more agreeable work was on the way for the shy and sedentary young man who described himself at boarding school as "a quiet, inoffensive little fellow." Ches sent him to his sister Nina's house on Topsail Road, where Geoff Stirling kept an apartment on the ground floor. There, for the next three weeks, he had one of the more interesting assignments his father's party had to offer — eavesdropping on the opposition. "All of the phone calls from here to the mainland were on radio-telephone. Geoff had some kind of apparatus where you could listen to all of the phone calls, so my job was to listen to all phone calls between Newfoundland and the mainland and try to hear what the Confederates were up to, who they were getting their money from."

It was a season of destiny for both Newfoundland and John. That summer there were a number of parties around St. John's where each girl had a card on which the boys had to enter their names if they wanted a dance. Spying the lovely Jane Furneaux at a party given by James Chalker at the Herder family summer place in Topsail, John pencilled himself in on her card for the last dance — a wily strategy that meant that he would get to escort her home that night. As he would later put it, John got a friend to do the driving so "I could get right to work" in the back seat. They took the long way home, arriving at Jane's door at 3:00 a.m. Jane's father, Dr. Furneaux, a veterinarian, was waiting at the door for his daughter and her callow Casanova. "It was the first and only time I ever saw John tongue-tied," Jane recalled. "He left in one helluva hurry." The two fell "madly in love" and exchanged letters every Sunday and Wednesday for the next four years.

Whether eavesdropping on the Confederates in Geoff Stirling's apartment or lost in daydreams of Jane, John was mercifully distant from the low point of the Confederation debates, the infamous "Orange letter," which sparked bitter sectarian battling in the final days of the second referendum. Ches Crosbie had already told his people that he would rather lose the campaign than resort to playing the religious card against his opponents, but Governor MacDonald, a passionate Methodist, felt differently. At a United Church Convention in St. John's, he remarked that one sect had influenced the first referendum and that it was time Protestants pulled together in defence of their interests. Some people took the governor's call for Protestant solidarity in deadly earnest. The Grand Master of the Orange Lodge sent out a letter (written by Smallwood, according to Greg Power) denouncing the pro-Responsible Government position taken by the Roman Catholic Church, particularly in its newspaper, *The Monitor*. It condemned Catholic efforts to "dominate the right of free choice of the individual elector" and urged all order members to neutralize the political machinations of the Roman Catholic Church. The date might have been July 16, 1948, but the cultural clock had been turned back to the nineteenth century; except this time there was no Bishop Mullock to keep the sectarian fires from flaring up all over a suddenly darkened political landscape.

Men were once more expressing their political differences with their fists. Smallwood, who frequently promoted Confederation by raising the spectre of "Rome rule" in the Protestant outports, had taken to carrying a gun, albeit an unloaded one. On one occasion, after he finished a radio show in St. John's, a mob had tried to lynch him. His security guards were armed with brass knuckles, blackjacks, chains and some strategic advice from Irving Fogwill: broken heads make for bad press, while a hearty squeeze of the testicles induces political moderation without a fuss.

Just before the vote, things turned ugly at another Smallwood rally, and he had to be spirited away from the scene in a hidden car. The mob then stormed down Devon Row where Smallwood lived and proceeded to stone the wrong house. With Newfoundland split along religious lines and deeply divided on her political future, it was anyone's guess what would happen on July 22. As the American consul general in St. John's put it, it was "a case really of picking the winner of the Grand National blindfolded, with a pin."

In the run for the political roses, Joe Smallwood crossed the finish line marginally ahead of Ches Crosbie and Peter Cashin. The final vote was 78,323 for Confederation against 71,334 for Responsible Government — a majority of only 7,000, or 52 percent of the vote. Ches Crosbie draped black crêpe over the entrance to 18 Rennies Mill Road and walked out into the morning air with his emotionally exhausted colleagues. Taking a sip of a stale drink as he regarded his dejected workers, he suddenly boomed out, "What the hell's wrong with you? It's not the end of the world. Let's get some breakfast."

Newfoundland had begun the decade in Britain's lap and ended it in the belly of the wolf. But the rocks were still there, and the woods and the wide, blue sea. For Ches Crosbie, the new day dawned over the eternal landscapes of his beautiful and unremitting island and always would.

CHAPTER 10

Skipper Ches

NEWFOUNDLAND OFFICIALLY BECAME Canada's tenth province at the last stroke before midnight on March 31, 1949. No one, it seemed, was anxious for the former colony to begin its historic union with Canada as an April Fool's joke. At exactly 11:00 a.m. on April 1, the bells in Ottawa's Peace Tower played "The Squid Jiggin' Ground" to accompany the gala ceremonies that marked the momentous event. Joe Smallwood was the man of the hour. Sir Albert Walsh had been sworn in as lieutenant governor and he in turn had asked Smallwood to serve as interim premier until a provincial election could be called. When the election was held on May 27, 1949, Smallwood made it official by winning twenty-two of twenty-eight seats for the Liberals in the House of Assembly. With all its flair and fandango, the age of "develop or perish" was about to dawn in Newfoundland, fuelled by Smallwood's heady dreams of industrialization and the diamond-studded schemes of pin-striped hucksters from every corner of the globe. While Ottawa celebrated, Canada's newest citizens began the awkward task of getting comfortable inside their new constitutional clothes.

It was one of those days when everyone would later remember just where they'd been. Confederates and their former political foes gathered in St. John's for drinks and dinner. Someone from the Woods Labour Board proposed a toast, followed by "O Canada." Everyone tried their best, but after a few tentative bars accepted the fact that no one knew the words to their new anthem. James McGrath, a future Canadian cabinet minister but in 1949 a heartbroken supporter of responsible government on his way to a new life in Philadelphia, was stopped by American immigration authorities on the Peace Bridge after showing a Newfoundland passport — proof of citizenship in a country that no longer existed. Lacking a Canadian passport, he spent the next few tense hours as a man without a country. The Americans finally sent him back north.

Gert Crosbie had already had her moment of mortification. After Confederation had been decided but before it was officially implemented, she and a friend had gone to the movies in Corner Brook. The two women "nearly died" when instead of "God Save the King" they played "O Canada." On Confederation Day itself, Gert was profoundly depressed. She was angry at England for allowing Confederation on the ballot, even though a convention of the best and the brightest Newfoundlanders had voted against putting it there. Seven months pregnant with her first child, Gert believed a wake was more in order than a celebration; after all, Newfoundland as she had known it, a place where a cultured oligarchy operated a mutual admiration society complete with dynastic marriages and a code of *noblesse oblige*, was dead.

No one in Newfoundland had more mixed feelings about Newfoundland's new political situation than the man who had fought it to the bitter end, Ches Crosbie. A businessman by nature, he had nevertheless been unable to extricate himself from the ongoing political affairs of his province after the second referendum vote. Two weeks after Newfoundlanders narrowly opted to join Canada, Sir Gordon MacDonald asked Crosbie to serve on the seven-member delegation that would negotiate the Terms of Union with Canada. After conferring with his former supporters, who advised him to "hold out for the moon," Ches accepted, but with the written and public proviso that if he didn't like the final terms he could withdraw from the delegation. In accepting the historic appointment, Ches said, "The most urgent necessity is to overcome the bitterness and antagonism which developed during the campaign, for only by uniting and working together can Newfoundland hope to make real progress."

Ottawa was not impressed with Ches's public call for unity, as a secret memorandum prepared by the secretary to the Cabinet Committee on Newfoundland, J. R. Baldwin, made clear. Pointing out that four of the Newfoundlanders on the negotiating team were sincere about coming to terms with Canada, he added that "one member, Mr. Crosbie, has paid lip service to the idea of co-operation now that the referendum is over, but in reality is stated to be holding back and looking for reasons to claim that his pre-referendum attitude against Confederation was justified. There is real fear that if some reasonable and fairly generous arrangement regarding the financial problem cannot be made, Mr. Crosbie will refuse to sign."

Ches arrived in Ottawa five days late for the final negotiations with a bandage around his head and a story that left his Newfoundland colleagues shaking their heads. He told them that he'd been hunting on the Burin Peninsula and driven off the road in a storm while trying to rush a pregnant woman to hospital. But his late arrival had no bearing on his part in the final negotiations.

On December 11, 1948, Ches made a prophet out of Baldwin when he left Ottawa a few hours before the final deal was struck, refusing to sign the Terms of Union because the financial arrangements offered by Canada were not in Newfoundland's best interests. (One member of the Newfoundland delegation would later maintain that Ches wouldn't sign because he didn't want to disappoint his former supporters who were dead against Confederation.)

Publicly citing the use of Newfoundland's budgetary surplus to cover the cost of giving the new province a modern infrastructure, he correctly predicted a future in which his indebted island would have to rely on Ottawa's largesse to deal with a mountainous deficit. Given what Ottawa was prepared to contribute, he also believed that new and substantial taxes would have to be levied in Newfoundland. Forceful and independent like his father, Sir John, Ches made no apologies for his maverick position: "You can tell the people back home that my conscience is clear. . . . There will be those who will charge me with dividing the country, but the country was divided long before now. I have no wish to see Newfoundland divided but the issues at stake are too great for me to sign terms which I consider unsatisfactory simply for the sake of peace and quietness."

Despite his refusal to sign the Terms of Union, Ches resisted pressure from many of his former supporters who urged him to lead a Newfoundland National Party in the province's first election. Instead, to their shocked disappointment, he supported Joe Smallwood. Ever the pragmatist, Ches astutely guessed that the Liberals under Louis St. Laurent would defeat George Drew and the Conservatives in the June 27 federal election of that year and thought it was essential that Newfoundland have a sister government in place during the first years of Confederation. After Confederation, most of the Crosbie men followed Smallwood for business reasons (both Ches and Bill steadfastly turned down offers to join the cabinet) but there were exceptions that bitterly divided the family. George Crosbie remained an intractable anti-Confederate, as did his mother and most of his sisters; for a year he refused to speak to his older brother over his support of Smallwood. Their once close relationship would never be the same. Even at Devon Place, the emotions released during the Confederation debates exacted a price; Lady Crosbie finally had to declare that politics could not be discussed at her weekly Boys Day luncheons. Newfoundland had been through the wars and every family, including the Crosbies, had the scars to prove it.

Exhausted by his political battles and troubled by the rifts in the family they had caused, Ches turned with relief to the business interests he had put to one side during the last two tempestuous years. Not a few of them provided cold comfort. The company's west coast herring operation, Newfoundland Dehydrating Process Company Ltd., was still losing money, largely because of shortages in raw material. By 1950 the infamous seven-year cycle had struck and the herring had vanished from the waters around Corner Brook. The company struggled along, meeting its obligations, until

October 24, 1952. After that, it sustained heavy losses until it finally closed its doors in 1954. As Lady Crosbie had predicted, Ches's high-tech herring experiment ended in disaster; it accumulated almost $2 million in losses by the time the company decided to abandon the project. The family would still operate a traditional herring business, but it would be for others to capitalize on the innovations Ches had helped pioneer.

Although financially successful, Olsen Whaling and Sealing was short of working capital to modernize its facility at Williamsport, where Ches wanted to process caplin (a small, smelt-like fish then found in profusion in Newfoundland waters), as well as produce whale oil. The Smallwood government assisted with a $375,000 loan guarantee, but a few months later disaster struck when modern science came up with a brand new product that would eventually put Williamsport out of business.

With the introduction of vegetable oils on world markets, fish and whale oil were suddenly obsolete. Overnight, the price of whale oil dropped like a stone, bottoming out at just nine cents a gallon. Instead of making a ten-cent profit per gallon, Olsen Whaling and Sealing was now losing five cents for every gallon of whale oil it produced. Something had to be done very quickly to put the Williamsport plant to an alternate use. Ches decided to make "liquid fish" to be shipped to the company's American partner in Boston, John Ryan. Crosbie and Company already had a similar operation, Liqua Fish, in St. John's, the first of its kind in Newfoundland. Ches had convinced feed mills in the United States to accept liquid fish rather than the traditional fish meal formerly used to enrich their final product. The selling point was cost-cutting; Ches pointed out that liquid fish could be sprayed on their assembly line, instead of resorting to expensive manual labour to open sacks of meal and hand-mix them with the animal feeds.

The plan worked well enough in St. John's, but the conversion at Williamsport turned out to be riddled with problems. First, there were chronic shortages of raw material to keep the plant operating. To assure a steady supply of caplin, Ches sent Bill Crosbie all over the northeast coast to arrange contracts for bulk shipments of caplin to the whaling station. That spring, several vessels loaded to the gunwales began to arrive at Williamsport. But by now there was another hitch. Before the caplin could be put into the digester for processing, it had to be pre-cooked, and the huge cooker Ches had ordered to do the job had not yet arrived from the United States.

Lacking any other practical alternative, Ches and Bill decided to put the raw fish directly into the whaling digester. Normally the fish would be ready to go to the next stage of processing, the evaporators, after four hours, but to be on the safe side, it was left in for eight. Then, with the seven curious captains whose caplin-bulging vessels were tied up to his wharf looking on, Bill opened the digester: "I nearly died because when we opened it up, here were the caplin looking back up at us. I swear to God, some of them were even winking."

The fish were completely untouched, despite the fact that there was 140 pounds of steam pressure from the boilers to force the fish into the digester. The slowly degrading caplin had begun to produce ammonia gas, and its pressure was greater than the pressure from the boilers. Instead of the steam forcing the fish into the digester, the ammonia was driving tons of caplin back towards the boilers. Suddenly, Bill heard screams from the men in the boiler-room and then an explosion; the caplin had completed their deadly journey and tons of raw material were ruined.

The men worked feverishly to correct the problem, but in the meantime, the seven loads of caplin tied up at the dock began to rot. The crews could no longer stay in the fo'c'sles and as the ammonia gas built up, knives and forks turned black, and the paint began to peel off the boats. Eventually the vessels off-loaded their cargoes at the Crosbie plant in Corner Brook. The clock was now running on Olsen Whaling and Sealing. By the end of 1952, the plant shut down, hoping for an upturn in the market that never came. It too would operate on a reduced basis, until 1959, but the days of living off the fat of the sea were over.

As one door closed, Ches, like his father and grandfather, found another — an indispensable talent for anyone doing business in Newfoundland. Fraser, Brace, Terminal Ltd. was a Montreal company under contract to the American government to build a Distant Early Warning (DEW) line of defence for the North American continent in 1952. The president of the firm was an old friend of Ches's and invited him to organize the Arctic shipping required for the project, based on the knowledge and experience the Crosbies had gained from their fishing and sealing operations in northern waters. Ches set up another company, Chimo Shipping, to fulfill the contract that would ultimately see five thousand men put to work in Labrador. The company was run by Percy Crosbie who, though eclipsed by Ches's personality, eventually became a legend in his own right in the world of marine shipping and insurance. A close friend of one of the world's great underwriters, Henry Chester, Percy had a unique status at Lloyd's of London. "At a time when you weren't even allowed to wear a coloured shirt," his nephew recalled, "he was the only man that ever managed to walk through the doors of Lloyd's in a pink seersucker suit and live."

Although work was scheduled to begin in 1952, the outbreak of the Korean War kick-started the project a year early. From August to December 1951, 50,000 tonnes of cargo were shipped to seven remote locations up and down the Labrador coast. The U. S. Army Corps of Engineers supervised the work, which quickly degenerated into an administrative nightmare. For each and every bill of lading, Bill Crosbie was responsible for producing sixty-four copies for his American bosses! When he needed to order supplies, he went through the contractor's Canadian office in New Brunswick, which in turn contacted its New York office. The American contractor would then go to the U.S. army, necessitating further calls to both the navy and the Pentagon. After weeks of delay, a ship would be requisitioned and the cargo would finally be on its way north.

With its forty-foot tides, tricky currents, and awesome winter storms, Cape Chidley was a terrible choice as one of the DEW Line's seven radar sites on the Labrador coast, and if the American military didn't know that the Crosbies did. During the surveying of the site, the 150-ton Crosbie vessel *Linda May* could only bring in the landing party by sending a motorboat ahead to take soundings. The ship that the corps of engineers wanted to bring in to Cape Chidley with the cargo for the main radar site was 14,000 tons! When Crosbie captain Les Winsor appeared in New York, armed with charts to show that the task was impossible, he was greeted with smug disdain by the U.S. Army. "Captain," said one of the engineers, who knew that his outfit had built the Panama Canal, "you don't understand what we can do when we set out to do it." The only concession to Crosbie misgivings about Cape Chidley was an $1,800-a-day tug that the army hired to accompany its huge ship to the construction site.

Assured by the Americans that there was accommodation on board for Canadian stevedores, Chimo Shipping flew men from Saint John, New Brunswick, to Stephenville to meet the ship on its way north. The accommodation turned out to be "third hatch" — the cargo hold. Uncomfortable at the best of times, it was about to be turned into a torture chamber. The ship stood off storm-tossed Cape Chidley for twenty-eight days and nights before the Americans abandoned the site. There were some things that not even the mighty U. S. Army Corps of Engineers could humble; coastal Labrador was one of them.

As the ship steamed back to St. John's, the Crosbies received word that there was trouble on board. For twenty-eight days, the Canadian civilians in the hold of the vessel had been confined to quarters, with water dripping down on their cots. Fearing a confrontation, the American crew dropped food and cigarettes down to the men but wouldn't let them up on deck. Tempers flared, and the ship's captain ordered the cargo hatch locked and posted armed guards to keep the stevedores below. Bill Crosbie gave orders that when the vessel made port in St. John's it was not to be berthed at the dock but anchored instead in the middle of the harbour.

When the ship arrived, Bill went aboard and promised the enraged stevedores twelve hours pay per day from the day they went on board the ship in Stephenville until the day they disembarked in Saint John, New Brunswick. Everyone accepted the terms, and the men were held on board until they could be flown to Saint John. According to the sound insight that a little gold dries up a lot of tears, each man was paid in cash as he walked off the plane. The media scandal the Crosbies had feared had been deftly avoided.

But when the injustices were more apparent than real the Crosbies could be much less accommodating. Simard's, the Quebec firm that had the barge contract for the DEW Line, pulled its men out of Labrador every year when the brutal winter season brought all work to a halt. After Simard's barge captains cabled the Crosbies demanding first-class accommodation back to Quebec and flatly refusing to travel on stevedore ships, Bill sent them a telegram whose cheeriness nevertheless conveyed a message icier than the withering Labrador gales: "Wishing you a Merry Christmas and a Happy New Year at Cartwright, Labrador." The captains came out on the next stevedore boat.

To complement Chimo Shipping, Ches bought control of Newfoundland Engineering and Construction Company Ltd., the small firm he had started in 1937 with Ches Pippy. It was his master business stroke of the 1950s. Through his connection to Joe Smallwood, Ches turned Newfoundland Engineering (NECCO) into a construction powerhouse and a major money-maker. NECCO got the contract to build the seat of government, Confederation Building (Ches used to say that he'd made a million dollars between the basement and the top floor!), most of Memorial University in St. John's, the Technical College and the fourteen-storey nurses' residence on the grounds of the General Hospital. Joe Smallwood would later claim that his government had awarded more than $50 million worth of construction contracts, most without tender, to the Crosbie interests through NECCO.

As Ches cast around for promising ventures, he made another important acquisition in a new and exciting business. In 1949, an ex-RCAF bush pilot, Eric Blackwood, started Newfoundland Airways and approached Ches to become his partner. Ches himself invested and also brought in two of his closest friends and business associates, Charlie Bell and Edgar Hickman. The group worked out individual responsibilities for their collective investments: Ches ran the airline,

Edgar operated the Bavarian Brewery, and Charlie took care of Gaden's Aerated Water Company Ltd., which then had the Coca-Cola franchise in Newfoundland. (After the arrival of Molson's in Newfoundland, the Bavarian Brewery was sold to Labatt's, with Gaden's thrown in as a sweetener.)

Newfoundland Airways grew into a large and profitable bush operation, flying personnel into the DEW Line installations, delivering mail to Newfoundland's largely roadless outports, taking care of emergency medical flights for the provincial government and whisking Ches away on the wilderness fishing trips he loved so much. The company also purchased some of the first Canso water-bombers and leased them back to the government for aerial fire fighting. By the end of the decade, after buying out their partners and acquiring Maritime Central Airways with financial help from the provincial government, the Crosbies would inaugurate a new commercial airline serving Atlantic Canada, Eastern Provincial Airways. The Crosbie business empire was taking flight, but the family itself was heading for a crash landing that would shortly end in divorce, death and a barely suppressed social scandal.

JOAN CROSBIE SHINKLE had always wanted to present Ches with his first grandchild, and on November 5, 1950, she got her wish. Even though it was a Sunday, Ches managed to get a Waterford Bridge Road flower shop to open so that he could present the mother of little Lee Shinkle with a bouquet of roses. The boy was hale and hearty, but Joan had had some difficulty with the birth. To relieve the pain, the hospital had injected anesthetic into Joan's spinal canal. She told her husband that the doctors had hit a nerve with the needle, impairing her balance. She would later attribute her increasingly serious drinking bouts to that loss of balance, which she fancifully or otherwise claimed was improved by alcohol.

As soon as mother and child were able to travel, the family returned to Corner Brook, where they had been living in the Glynmill Inn while Gene managed another Crosbie company, West Coast Building Supplies. Lacking the business training for the position, Gene soon ran into trouble and was called back to St. John's. Gene next spent five months working on the DEW Line before Ches assigned him to help "clean up" his construction company, NECCO, where some managers had been involved in taking payoffs from suppliers. It was a task better suited to the administrative skills Gene had learned in the army, as well as a welcome rest after the rigors of life in the wilds of Labrador. Gene joined his wife and young son in an attractive bungalow on 2 Long Pond Road, just across the street from Bill and Gert Crosbie, and tried his best to resume the role of Prince Charming in a fairy-tale marriage he sensed was headed for the rocks.

To young Lee Shinkle, the world was a sunny day without a cloud in the sky, inhabited by doting parents and his very own friendly giant. Ches Crosbie was a constant visitor in the Shinkle home, making sure that the freezer was always full of Mars bars and the refrigerator "blocked" with Coca-Cola sent around from Gaden's. Every Sunday afternoon, Ches pulled into the driveway in his twelve-cylinder Lincoln to take his grandson for a ride, just as Sir John had once revelled in touring with his first grandchild, June Bennett. Ches would drive to the company premises on the South Side of St. John's Harbour, lifting the loose boards in the wharf to show the marvelling child the cool, sun-dappled ocean below. Lee was given a salt fish for his treat and walked around for the rest of the day picking at it like candy, to his grandfather's delight.

Childhood was an enchanted journey, as magical as the Beaver aircraft that lifted the little boy and the rest of his grandfather's fishing party off Quidi Vidi Lake in St. John's and dropped them for the first time into Kaegudeck, the stunning family wilderness camp south of Gander that his father had helped Ches to build. In looking for a location for their cabin there had been two tests; it had to be the most beautiful spot in the world in certain seasons and it had to pass the test of the three-fly cast. (A three-fly cast is a special trout rig that has three drops on it to which three flies can be tied. The test was to cast that rig into the waters of a prospective site; if it didn't produce three trout, they moved on.) That inaugural night in the camp, the trout were waiting for Lee, his father and grandfather as they cast their flies into a dark pool with the sun sinking behind Kaegudeck's ragged line of spruce, black now in the failing light. Back at the cabin, a huge fire blazing in the floor-to-ceiling fieldstone hearth, the men laughed and told stories, puffing on cigarettes made from tea leaves and toilet paper since they had forgotten to bring in the real thing! Listening drowsily to the reassuring banter of the most important men in his life, the air fragrant with birch smoke and newly cut logs, Lee drifted off to sleep contented and carefree.

The social abyss that Gene Shinkle had feared could not be bridged between himself and Joan Crosbie had widened since his wedding day in 1947. Joan had never been comfortable with the role of housewife, preferring instead to view her relationship with Gene as an extension of the constant and carefree pleasures of courtship. The mundane ledgers of marriage collided head-on with the high fantasy of her fairy-tale upbringing. Cooking and cleaning had always been someone else's responsibility, and she chafed under the unfamiliar restraints of having to live within her young husband's meagre means. Shunning the charitable activities for which the Crosbies were famous, Joan became an incessant shopper with a developing fondness for gin. Since her teenage years, she had drawn thirty dollars a week from Ches's account; after her marriage, she continued to show up at Crosbie and Company on Water Street to collect her allowance. On more than one occasion Gene would forbid her to buy a television or new appliance he couldn't afford only to find it in the house when he got home from work, "sent around by Skipper Ches." The young man realized that he had not married a woman but a family, with whom it was impossible to compete: "If she couldn't get something from me, it was no concern because she always went to Dad and got it. . . . As far as Ches was concerned, the sun rose and set on her ass. . . . She never needed me."

If she got her worldly goods from her parents, Joan turned to another family member for a role model. She settled on Margaret, her beautiful, hard-drinking and ultimately mysterious aunt, who lived like a character out of F. Scott

Fitzgerald's *The Beautiful and the Damned.* Whether driving ambulances during the London blitz or whirling through high society in Montreal or New York, the unmarried Margaret made an indelible impression on everyone she met with her intelligence, wit, stunning Hollywood profile and bohemian spirit. Headed for what looked like the perfect dynastic marriage with Ches's close friend and business partner, Edgar Hickman, she unexpectedly broke their engagement and burned like a comet at wartime parties in St. John's, where she was in high demand. As one admirer put it fifty years later, "She was a girl you'd like to know from a man's point of view, you know what I mean?"

After a star-crossed affair with Sir Roger Hawkey, a British officer stationed in Newfoundland, Margaret was heartbroken. According to the restless and romantic trysts of war, the lovers had been informally engaged. But during what was to have been a vacation in England, Roger, possibly acquiescing to family pressures, married someone else. "I know she [Margaret] was devastated, and I think the family were, too," an old friend remembered.

From 1942 until 1949, Margaret remained at home where she cared for her elderly mother. But by 1949, with Lady Crosbie now seventy-four and Margaret herself approaching her fortieth birthday, she suddenly moved to Montreal, never to return to Newfoundland again. There, at the Ritz Carlton Hotel, Margaret began her descent into a dissipated life, slipping behind the same alcoholic mist that would engulf so many of her brothers and sisters.

Margaret's binges were every bit as spectacular as Ches's. During their 1949 Easter vacation, Andrew Crosbie and his cousin John Perlin were sent to New York where they were to spend the weekend with Ches and Jessie at the Weylin Hotel. John arrived early on a flight from Toronto and the porter, Robert, who knew the family well, sent him up to the Crosbie suite. Ches, fresh from a bender the night before, was not at his best. In a rough Newfoundland term of endearment he asked, "You little fucker, what are you doing here?" John explained himself and Ches invited him in for breakfast. His Aunt Jessie, who had arrived moments before, briefly welcomed fifteen-year-old John, who then cowered on the sofa while Jessie "read Ches the riot act" about his drinking. When Jessie discovered Aunt Margaret passed out on the bed in full evening dress with her fur coat thrown over her, she ordered her out of the apartment.

On her way out, Margaret pointed an aristocratic finger at John and said, "You, come with me." The young teenager was handed two bottles of whisky and the fur coat and told to accompany Margaret to her room on the other side of the hotel. "By this time it's ten o'clock in the morning and in the Weylin if you were on one side of the hotel you had to go down the elevator, cross the lobby and go up the other side. So there I am, trailing after this woman, carrying her fur coat and two bottles of whisky . . . totally psyched out," John Perlin recalled.

When they reached Margaret's room, his aunt announced that she was going to take a bath. With that, she stepped out of her clothes and John, whose knowledge of the fair sex had so far been limited to "skimming" at the girls through holes in the back of the boathouse while they put on their bathing suits, got his New York advanced course in adult female anatomy. After one horrified glance, he remained rooted to the spot, looking out the window. After his aunt finished her ablutions, she dismissed him as summarily as she had summoned him: "Now *you* go back where you came from."

Lady Crosbie was alarmed by the stories of Margaret's excesses and by the steady stream of bank drafts coming through on her account. According to her sister Dolly, Margaret had "inherited the drinking spirit of the Crosbie boys. . . . We were a drinking family. No sense saying one thing and meaning another." Lady Crosbie travelled to Montreal and was appalled at Margaret's condition. But, as one family member put it, "Marg got Grandmother locked up in the hotel room and terrorized her to such an extent and forced her to sign a will leaving everything to her. And then Grandmother had this nervous breakdown."

Lady Crosbie was eventually brought back to Newfoundland by Ches and his sister Vera, the Florence Nightingale of the family. Before leaving Montreal, they had Margaret admitted to a clinic in Verdun where she received treatment for acute alcoholism. When Ches and Vera found the new will, "it was agreed that Mr. [Robert] Leith and a very prominent lawyer who was Grannie's lawyer at the time, Charlie Hunt, they were brought in and they agreed that the new will was under duress and [it] was destroyed and the old will was reinstated. If that hadn't happened," a family member said, "Marg would have gotten everything."

Lady Crosbie never fully recovered from her mental collapse in Montreal. By the end of 1951, Vera Perlin decided to personally nurse the ailing matriarch of the Crosbie clan, making her remaining time as comfortable as she could. A wonderful cook, Vera catered to her mother with special favourites like rhubarb relish made from the Exploits recipe of Mitchie Anne's own mother. To better organize Lady Crosbie's care, the Perlins eventually leased their Water Street West home and moved, *en famille*, to Devon Place.

When they arrived, they found that, at least outwardly, nothing had changed at the Crosbie residence; the establishment was still staffed with a cook, two parlour maids, a laundry woman, a gardener, a chauffeur and an array of other domestics who came and went on a part-time basis. "I used to be sent out in the evenings to see if any of the maids were down in the hammock in the garden with the Yanks," John Perlin recalled.

Lady Crosbie was so ill that she had three nurses attending to her around the clock. As her condition worsened, she underwent electric-shock treatment and, finally, a new medical procedure then in vogue in the United States — lobotomy. Except for the actual surgical procedure, Vera was beside her for the entire ordeal. "Mother was in the room watching all this [the shock treatment], holding on to my grandmother and I think it must have been an absolutely horrendous experience," John Perlin recalled.

Despite the affluence of the later years, Mitchie Anne had carried a heavy burden, raising eleven children, burying two more, and standing beside her husband as they built on the business foundations laid in the previous century by Sir John's father, George Crosbie. Twenty-one years a widow, she had been a prudent steward of her husband's fortune and a good mother. She applauded when her children added to the lustre of the family name and grieved for them when the world proved too much. She had bridged two centuries and watched Newfoundland pass from colony to dominion to province of Canada — this last transformation to her everlasting disapproval. The girl from Exploits had come a long way in seventy-seven years, but on May 22, 1953, the road came to an end. She was buried beside Sir John in the General Protestant Cemetery under the art nouveau headstone she had once worried was too ostentatious.

Under the terms of Lady Crosbie's will, all of her assets were placed in a trust fund administered by Ches, his mother's longtime accountant, Robert Leith, and the Royal Trust company. The family home on Devon Place was to be sold and added to the estate. There were a number of special provisions for Margaret in the will, including an income of $450 a month to be taken from the income of the trust fund — more if necessary to cover future medical or hospital expenses. The trust fund was otherwise to remain intact until Margaret's marriage or death, when it would be divided equally among Lady Crosbie's remaining children, or their children.

In addition to the future capital of her estate, all of her children received specific bequests from their mother — jewellery for the girls and furniture for the boys. Margaret was given a diamond pendant and solitaire diamond ring; Olga, her mother's engagment ring; Dolly, a diamond bracelet; Percy, a poker table and a painting of Winston Churchill; Bill, a nest of mahogany tables and the items he had sent his mother from overseas; and Ches, her personal desk. These inventories of the heart marked an end to an era of family history. For the first time in their lives, the Crosbie children faced the world without either member of the stalwart outport couple that had carved a place for them in the inner sanctum of Newfoundland's business and social elite.

THE OLD ORDER had indeed changed, yielding to the new. In both Newfoundland and the Crosbie business empire things were changing fast. Joe Smallwood was determined to drag his new province into the modern age by creating his own economic miracle. Turning his back on the fishery, which he associated with the feudal regime of rich merchants and indentured fishermen, he set out to make a gazelle out of an elephant. Taking for himself the portfolio of Economic Development, Smallwood tried to impose his vision of what he wanted Newfoundland to become, rather than building on what her bedrock realities made possible; it was to be the signature in red ink across his entire economic development plan. Spouting the same effective rhetoric that had brought him to power, he vowed that Newfoundland would be neither Confederation's "glorified poorhouse" nor "a Canadian stud farm" that educated its citizens to leave for jobs on the mainland. In pursuit of his dreams, Smallwood would squander the healthy budgetary surplus Newfoundland brought into Confederation.

Although Smallwood was all for the industrialization of Newfoundland, he readily acknowledged that he needed an expert to help him realize his dream. He quickly ruled out local businessmen, who he believed were too self-interested for the task at hand. "Most of them were scrambling around like hen hawks eyeing a chicken coop for their share of the millions of family allowances and other cash pouring in from Ottawa," he wrote in his political memoir, *I Chose Canada*. But during a meeting with C. D. Howe he heard the name of a man who seemed tailor-made for the job.

As former Finance minister of Latvia, Alfred A. Valdmanis was a man who came with impressive, if rather ominous, credentials. The brilliant forty-two-year-old had served as an economic planner for Hitler and boasted excellent contacts in a Germany that was then in the process of an amazing rebuilding program under the Marshall Plan. At a personal level, Valdmanis was the man a star-struck Smallwood longed to be: cultured, a superb dancer and linguist, a musician, and more pompous than Charles de Gaulle. Smallwood was so taken by the smooth talking European that he hired him as Newfoundland's first Director General of Economic Development, at a salary that was higher than that of any civil servant in the Government of Canada.

Valdmanis arranged a two-week tour of Germany for Smallwood and two members of his cabinet, Finance Minister Herman Quinton and Health Minister James Chalker. Ches Crosbie went along at his own expense. The group toured every industrial city in West Germany and met with top industrialists, some of whom were still in semi-imprisonment for their role in the Third Reich. Smallwood was overwhelmed by what he saw and longed to see Newfoundland reproduce the miracle of the Ruhr Valley. Ches Crosbie did not share Smallwood's enthusiasm for either the grand plan or Alfred Valdmanis, whom he regarded as a "goddamned crook."

A few years later, Ches's intuition was vindicated. After a string of industrial flops, Valdmanis was summoned back from Montreal and ordered to resign by Smallwood for expense account fraud and demanding "commissions" from German businessmen, ostensibly on behalf of the Liberal Party. Valdmanis was subsequently arrested on the complaint of Smallwood himself and pleaded guilty to defrauding the Newfoundland government of $200,000. A heartbroken Smallwood recorded his bitter disappointment: "I loved him as I loved no brother or sister of my own." On September 19, 1954, Valdmanis was sentenced to four years at hard labour in Her Majesty's penitentiary. He was released on New Year's Eve, 1956; fourteen years later, bankrupt and alone, Valdmanis died in an automobile accident on a lonely stretch of highway in western Canada.

Despite the string of embarrassing ventures Valdmanis enticed Smallwood into supporting, Canadian dollars kept the dynamo of the new regime buzzing. Although many Newfoundland businessmen would go under when faced with competition from large, Canadian firms, the overall effect of Confederation was immediate and tangible. By 1952, family allowance payments alone equalled 25 percent of the total expenditures of the former Commission of Government. In Newfoundland's first ten years as a province, Smallwood would revolutionize the face of the island with four thousand miles of roads, linking formerly isolated outports with the province's mainstream life. The poverty of the thirties was quickly forgotten and in its place Smallwood substituted the false wealth of Confederation — a parlour trick of patronage and transfer payments that created the conviction in Newfoundland's post-1949 generation that the benefits of a welfare state were now and forever an inalienable right.

AS NEWFOUNDLAND UNDERWENT the political renewal of Confederation, new blood was making its way into the Crosbie business empire in the larger-than-life person of Andrew Chesley Crosbie. Unlike his brother John, who preferred politics and the charms of the ivory tower to the hurly-burly of the family business, Andrew had been up to his neck in his father's affairs since he was thirteen. Every summer he gained experience in a new facet of Ches's operations, delivering Coca-Cola for Gaden's, working in the herring and whaling operations on the west coast or punching the clock at the family's South Side fish plant in St. John's.

Both physically and temperamentally, he was his father's son. Already 200 pounds at age fourteen, he loved the outdoors and revelled in physical work, "the dirtier the better." (Andrew nearly drowned in a vat of herring after falling asleep at the fish plant and rolling over in the wrong direction.) Like his father, uncle and older brother, Andrew attended boarding school at St. Andrew's College. In his first year of lower school (grade nine), he spent a lot of time absorbing the exquisite abuse of the senior boys, thanks to his brother John: "John made sure I had a pretty rough time with the prefects there. I always had to wear a conical hat and do all the things you *hate* doing as a new boy."

Over his four years at St. Andrew's, Ches's youngest son passed through the boisterous cycle of crime and punishment common to all boarding schools. For scrapping with a fellow student, he was ordered to clean the bronze statue at the entrance of St. Andrew's with a toothbrush — a task that took a week to complete. For more serious offences, brewing beer in the residence, or slipping away from campus to mingle with the female population of the nearby town of Aurora (even Andrew's prefect, fellow Newfoundlander Frank Moores, was caught climbing down a rope from his residence window, Aurora-bound), Andrew was caned by the headmaster: "You leaned over his desk and he used a bamboo cane on your rump. He never broke the skin, but believe me, it hurt."

Even on those occasions when girls were permitted on campus, school authorities took no chances with the hormonal urgings of their charges. Before the first young ladies from Havergal College, a private school for girls that twinned with St. Andrew's, appeared for the cadet corps dances, careful preparations had been made. "You always knew when the dances were coming," Andrew recalled, "because a week before they would start putting saltpeter into the milk. The night before the dance, it would be so thick with saltpeter you could almost stand a spoon up in it."

After graduating from St. Andrew's in 1952 with the top prize for boxing and marksmanship, Andrew spent an unhappy semester at Boston University. He studied commerce and roomed with seven hundred freshmen in Miles Standish Hall, a former hotel converted to a college residence. Bored by reviewing subjects he had already covered at St. Andrew's, and a little surprised by the number of people getting college credits for "basket-weaving," Andrew decided to quit university. By Christmas of that year he had returned to St. John's for good, rolled up his sleeves and gone to work in the fish business, replacing his Uncle Bill Crosbie at the family herring and whale plant in western Newfoundland. (Although he would now run A. H. Murray and Company, Bill remained a director of Crosbie and Company and a confidant of Ches.) Andrew also developed an early and abiding affection for alcohol, a trait his brother would later attribute to his studied effort to emulate his father. Andrew's first wife, Joan Parsons Parker, traced his affinity for the bottle to a broader influence. "I think it's also environment. If somebody came to your door at six o'clock in the morning at the Crosbie household, they were offered a drink. They weren't offered a cup of coffee." For the next six years, Andrew would spend an average of six months a year managing the Crosbie herring plant in Corner Brook, turning life into a lonely proposition for his young, beautiful and emphatically independent wife.

Grace and Bernard Parsons were a wealthy St. John's family who had made their money in real estate and the stock market. B. D. Parsons Ltd. was the corporate vehicle through which Bernard Parsons financed his various developments, including a golf course, several apartment buildings and a string of movie houses across Newfoundland. In the early 1950s, the Parsons built a summer cabin on Hogan's Pond just outside St. John's, a favoured address of the city's movers and shakers shared by families like the Munns, the Bells and the Crosbies. Their daughter Joan was just fifteen when Andrew Crosbie, whose parents lived across the pond, came into her life. Eighteen-year-old Andrew had dragged himself into the Parsons' cabin in a funk because his girlfriend of the day had thrown him over. Joan, who had already been sent to bed, had been surreptitiously reading a Mickey Spillane novel. As she listened to her parents commiserating with Andrew, whom she found attractive despite the fact that "he was the spitting image of the short guy in Abbott and Costello," she tried to figure out a way to get the young man's attention. Looking down at her detective novel, she impulsively shouted out, "Who killed Madame X?" Andrew was captivated. The two began dating and three years later they were married.

The wedding took place on the last day of August in 1954. The wedding party set out from Virginia Waters, a 640-acre estate on the outskirts of St. John's that had once been the summer residence of Newfoundland's British governors. Bernard Parsons, who now owned the property, gave the newlyweds a large tract of land that became the site of their own sprawling estate, which eventually featured a huge house, tennis court, swimming pool, separate gymnasium and wine cellar and heated garage, where Andrew would keep his racing-green Rolls Royce. The ceremony was performed on a perfect summer night at the Gower Street United Church and was followed by a reception for three hundred people at the Colony Club. "Frank Moores and his bunch from Ontario tried to chase us to Hogan's Pond, where we spent the first night of our honeymoon before we went to Bermuda. They wanted to torment us but they were drunk and went off the road," Joan later recalled.

With the academically accomplished John headed for a career in politics, and Andrew well launched in his new marriage and already acting as the heir apparent of Ches's expanding business empire, an outsider could be forgiven for envying the Crosbies from afar. But just beyond the accolades of academe, the promise of dynastic wedding bells and the seemingly rock-solid base of the Crosbie businesses, human forces were at play that would soon tear the family asunder.

At the centre of the gathering storm was the disintegrating relationship between Ches and Jessie. The slow grind of the years had more sharply etched the profound personality differences between the couple that had once been so in love. To some, it had been an ill-starred match from the very beginning. "I think Nan and Pop's problems started the day that they were on the ship going out of the St. John's harbour to Rio on their honeymoon. And although it may not have been legal rape, Nan's subsequent description of Pop's attack on her for sexual purposes in their cabin was goddamn close to it . . . it goes back to this, Nan Crosbie was never a sexual woman. Pop was highly sexually driven and highly passionate. . . . As Nan said, '. . . I was pregnant before we got out of the harbour,' " Gene Shinkle recalled.

Forced to live so much of her life alone, Jessie had now become grandly aloof, immune to the roguish charm her husband had once used so winningly to break down her disapproval of his rowdyman ways. On one occasion, Ches left on what was to have been a two-day business trip to Montreal; a month later he returned. His itinerary had taken him to New York, California, Toronto and finally back to Montreal, where he caught a flight to St. John's. Gene and Joan Shinkle picked him up at Torbay Airport and drove him to Rennies Mill Road. He found Jessie reading in her chair in the back sitting room by the fireplace. Ches was in good spirits and had favourable news to report from the business trip. Best of all, he hadn't been drinking. With a big smile on his face, he produced a beautifully gift-wrapped box and handed it to his wife. "I got a present for you," he said in his softest growl. It was a mink cape. Jessie looked at it and blandly replied, "Oh, thanks, Ches." Then, without getting up or trying it on, she dropped the fur on the floor beside her chair. Sitting on the chesterfield in the back parlour, her daughter and son-in-law, who had witnessed the encounter, were aghast.

For Ches's part, there were many private dragons to slay, not the least of which was the memory of Sir John. Ches confided to one family member that he was obsessed by an obligation to contribute to Newfoundland's business development because Sir John's accomplishments had already given the Crosbies such a privileged life. Drinking, he claimed, was the only release he had from the constant pressure to put something back. But there was a darker side to his famous father's moral bequest. As a young man, Ches had been driven mercilessly by Sir John, working long hours without a word of praise and often receiving a ferocious tongue-lashing for his trouble. It was his father's way, he said, to make a man out of him and to teach him the business from the ground up. Now, as the distance between Ches and his wife widened into an unbridgeable abyss and the children were no longer at home to provide either a buffer between them or companionship to their mother, Ches's drinking bouts became more frequent and abandoned. And once he started down those alcoholic mean streets, it was woe to anyone who crossed his path. What Sir John had imposed on Ches, Ches would royally inflict on those under his tutelage.

After work one evening, Andrew was at Gene Shinkle's house talking business and sipping their favourite rum, Old Sam, when Ches burst into the living room with Jessie in tow, convulsed in tears. "He took Andrew and I into the den, closed the door and gave us shit for about four hours. I got up to leave and he was sitting in front of the door and he said, 'If you want to get out of here, you got to fight me to do it. Now sit down and listen.' And he just chewed us up one side and down the other. 'This is the way I was treated by my father,' " he added by way of explanation.

Gene Shinkle was shocked and furious at his father-in-law's vicious outburst, but the worst was yet to come. The company was planning an extension to Gaden's and had requested that the supplier of the metal siding send an appraiser down from Montreal to give a price for the materials. But when he arrived in St. John's, NECCO still hadn't prepared the drawings for him to examine. Knowing what the company needed, Gene decided to take the man to the site and informally lay out the building. Suddenly, Skipper Ches appeared on the scene like a black cloud.

"Hey Shinkle," he bawled out, "what are you doing?"

"Well, I don't have the finalized plans for the placement of the building, but the man from Butler's is here and I want to give him some idea of what we want so he can get back to Montreal and start working on it."

By now, Gerry Christmas, the manager of Gaden's, and a few of the foremen had walked over to say hello to Ches. But this night his attention was reserved for his unfortunate son-in-law.

"What the fuck do you know about building?" The crowd of men fell silent.

"Look, Dad," Shinkle replied, stinging from the humiliation in front of the men, "I don't know what's got into you but you can take this fucking job and stuff it up your goddamn ass. And I hope the rest of you fellas heard that."

Gene stormed off the construction site and headed home to make his plans. Later that night, Ches showed up to have his customary drink before joining Jessie for dinner. He seemed befuddled by Shinkle's frosty silence.

"What's wrong with you?" Ches asked, as though nothing had happened.

"Nothing is wrong with me. But I quit. I'm not working for you any more."

"Ah, don't be so goddamned silly," Ches snorted. "If you think that sort of little thing . . . that's nothing. Let me tell you a story about what my father did to me."

"I don't give a shit about what your father did to you. I quit."

The next morning, Shinkle caught a flight to Montreal, where he planned to look for a job. Three weeks later, he still hadn't found one but was having a pretty good time at the company's expense. One night he returned to his room and there was a message tacked to his door asking him to call Ches Crosbie. He crumpled it up and threw it away. Half an hour later his phone rang.

"Why in the Christ didn't you call me?" asked the unmistakable voice on the other end of the line.

"I don't want to talk to you," Shinkle replied.

"Well come on down and have a drink with me. I'm in the Pic." "The Pic" was the Piccadilly Room at the Mount Royal Hotel.

"I don't want to have a drink with you either. We're finished, period and done."

"Ah, Shink, for Christ's sake, don't be like that."

"Dad, I'm not being like anything other than I'm sick and tired of being treated like a total asshole in front of the men that work for us."

"Is that what's bothering you?" Ches asked incredulously.

"Well don't you think that's what's bothering me?"

"Ah, Christ," Ches sighed remorsefully, "I'm sorry. Come on down, I got a couple of good-looking babes."

The ugly side of Ches Crosbie was frightful, but the good side was as beguiling as a summer day. The two men celebrated their reconciliation with a memorable "toot" and caught a plane back to St. John's. But their troubles, to which both men made solid contributions, were just beginning. From this point forward, their unhappy marriages would bind Ches and Gene together like seaweed tangled around the feet of swimmers struggling to make open water before, exhausted, they slip beneath the waves.

IN THE AUTUMN of 1955, Gene Shinkle was pursuing his rocky career as a pseudo-Crosbie, fighting a losing battle for his self-respect within Newfoundland's first family. All that summer, he had been working as an administrative manager for NECCO, which was putting up a new federal building in Grand Bank. Working hand in hand with the construction superintendent, Gene had toiled long and hard all summer and was looking forward to getting back to St. John's to see his wife and child. His departure had been less than ideal. Though her parents did their best to deny it, Joan's drinking problem was now of clinical proportions. Before Gene had left, she told him, "I want to be like my Aunt Marg," who by then was living in an apartment on Côte-des-Neiges in Montreal wrapped in a boozy blanket with an ex-Canadian serviceman known in the family as "Dinky-doo." Hoping that his absence might have rekindled the magic they had once shared, Gene headed back to St. John's not knowing whether it would be his wife Joan or a younger version of her fabled aunt that would be waiting for him.

It was neither. When he got back in the city, Gene found the house at 2 Long Pond Road dark and empty. He called Ches and Jessie, who told him that Lee was with them but that Joan was in Toronto. That night over dinner the Crosbies explained that "Joan had met this fellow and she was head over heels in love with him." Her stunned husband listened as they told him that she had gone off to Toronto to be with the new man in her life. But the relationship lasted only five days, and an uncharacteristically repentant Joan returned to St. John's seeking a reconciliation. More for his young son than his wife, Gene decided to try again. The result was a second child, Matthew Shinkle, who was born April 8, 1957. But by now, the responsibilities of new motherhood were well beyond the Crosbie family's tragic princess. Neither the new child, nor a restorative trip to Bermuda could put her marriage back together again. She continued to look for a knight errant to take her back to the romantic castles of unencumbered youth: handsome, hot-blooded and seven years her junior, John Jenkins was just the man she'd been waiting for. His arrival in Newfoundland just after Christmas in 1958 would touch off the most tumultuous period in the Crosbie family's history.

Ironically, it was Ches's business interests that brought Jenkins to Newfoundland in the first place. Ches had partnered with a man named Jim Hansen in a company called Managers Ltd. to build Memorial University in St. John's. John Jenkins, Sr., worked for Hansen and became friends with both Ches and Gene Shinkle when he came to Newfoundland. When his son, John Jr., was discharged from the air force, he decided to spend Christmas with his father and stepmother in St. John's. Getting into his father's car at the airport, Jenkins caught the pantleg of his uniform on a piece of chrome on the door which drove deeply into his thigh. Explaining that his wife wouldn't know what to do about it, Jenkins Sr. took his son to Joan Crosbie's house for repairs. "Within twenty minutes after I got off the plane, Joan had my pants down and was putting peroxide on a hole in my leg," John Jenkins recalled. "From there, it was all uphill."

Hearts fluttered at the young ex-serviceman's arrival in St. John's, and none more ardently than Joan Shinkle's. According to Gene Shinkle, the relationship began with Joan playing a therapeutic role with Jenkins. Joan was exceptionally good when it came to helping other people with their problems; a former alcoholic in St. John's who met her through Alcoholics Anonymous would later credit her sympathetic gifts with preventing his intended suicide. The dark-haired, square-jawed Jenkins soon became a fixture in the home at 2 Long Pond Road. The long afternoons were filled with sensitive exchanges about life's problems and pitfalls, while the chain-smoking hostess gradually became more and more fascinated with her young companion. When Gene Shinkle came home at night, the two of them were always together.

"And I would say, 'Well have we got any dinner?' And she'd be bombed and he'd be half bombed. And there wouldn't be any meal on. Lee and Matthew hadn't been looked after. And you know, well I just got to the point, I mean, that I would come in and I would tell him to get his ass out and tell Joan, 'This can't go on.' "

The charade of Joan's marriage continued despite the fact that within two months of their meeting, she and Jenkins were having an affair. When her husband was out of town, she would invite Jenkins to serve as bartender and occasionally host at her parties. Jenkins, who was only too happy to accommodate her, noted that Ches and Andrew Crosbie were big drinkers and that Joan wasn't far behind. "At a quarter to twelve, Joan would open the beer, get out the cold pewter mug and put it there and at twelve o'clock she'd pour it and drink it. They owned a brewery and every week they'd come and unload a bunch of beer at her house."

Whether for companionship or revenge, Gene Shinkle himself had begun to have his own dalliances. He spent most of his time at the City Club in St. John's and began to date women during his frequent "business trips" to Montreal, where he met his future wife through an adopted Crosbie "cousin," Freddie Ruggles. One night on the dance floor of the Colony Club where they had once celebrated their wedding, the wartime romance of Joan Crosbie and Gene Shinkle finally crashed and burned. Too drunk to dance, Joan had glumly watched from her table as Gene shared a few waltzes with a mutual friend. When the unhappy couple got home, Joan turned on her husband in a jealous rage, striking him across the face. He responded by knocking her down with the flat of his hand, leaving Joan with "a helluva bruise" on her face. The next day Gene moved out and took up residence in the Churchill Square apartments in St. John's that the Crosbies had built. Shortly afterwards, Ches asked him how Joan had been bruised: "And I said, 'Skipper . . . because I hit her. I'll tell you quite truthfully, I mean I have never hit a woman before in my life. But . . . I give myself total credit . . . for controlling myself to the point that I didn't do more damage than I did.' "

The prospect of the breakup of his daughter's marriage deeply saddened and disappointed Ches Crosbie. Faced with the loss of his own precious relationship with Joan, his prized grandchildren, and the son-in-law who had become an important member of the family (not to mention a nasty social scandal) he did his best to end her affair. The Crosbies first approached Jenkins's father and then his employer to put pressure on the young man to leave. When influence failed, Andrew Crosbie met with Jenkins and bluntly told him to stay away from his sister. "He said that the Crosbie name was at risk and they didn't want any young whippersnapper from the mainland coming in there and stirring it up. I said, 'Well tough. Let's leave it up to your sister.' "

By the late summer of 1959, Joan and Gene were already into divorce proceedings and Ches Crosbie was at his wit's end. He called Jenkins to a meeting at Crosbie and Company above the Woolworth's Store on Water Street and made a final pitch to end the affair that was endangering his family. He told Jenkins that he knew he was seeing his daughter and that, although the family hadn't been able to do much about it, he wanted it to stop. Ches offered Jenkins $10,000 and guaranteed him his commercial pilot training and a flying job at EPA after he graduated. There was only one catch: he had to move to Deer Lake on the other side of the island and remain there for two years. "And I said, 'It's no good talking to me like that. I'll take whatever you give me and go to Joan.' "

Frustrated in every attempt to quietly call off the relationship, Ches confronted his daughter and demanded that she break off the affair with Jenkins. Joan, who vacillated between worshipping Ches and defying him, half-heartedly gave in. She agreed to summon Jenkins to her house and give him the news.

Fearing an outburst from Jenkins, the Crosbies were there in force. Gert and Bill Crosbie, along with their twenty-year-old nephew, John Perlin, watched from behind the curtains in the Crosbie living room, while John and Andrew waited in parked cars on the street. As an extra precaution, Ches had hidden his wharf boss, the hulking Jack Macdonald, in Joan's basement in case of trouble. The tension mounted as everyone waited for Jenkins to arrive. Finally, there he was, standing in Joan's living room, listening with his head cocked to one side as she told him that their affair was over. Heated words were exchanged. A heartbeat later, Jenkins looked behind him and then "hauled off and punched" Joan.

What the posse of Crosbies couldn't see was what had brought on the violence. As the lovers had been arguing, Jenkins heard the basement door open and couldn't believe his eyes when Ches's lumbering stevedore appeared from the cellar like a menacing troll rising from under a bridge with a hammer in his hand. "Well, I hit Joan. All this stuff has been going on and this guy's behind the door and I hit her and I left — in a hurry." With John Perlin and his aunt and uncle "bug-eyed" with what was unfolding in front of them, the chase was on. The wharf boss, John and Andrew were in hot pursuit up Carpasian Road while the man they blamed for bringing grief to the family ran for his life.

He eventually found sanctuary in his father's house. "They came, John and Andrew. Came to the door and told my father they wanted me. And he said, 'Fuck off.' And there was no way I was going to go out to them. They were a lot bigger than I was," Jenkins remembered.

Ches subsequently hired a private detective agency to watch Joan's house to prevent Jenkins from coming back. But by this time, Ches's own marital problems required immediate attention. Ches explained to his nephew, John Perlin, that he had to take Auntie Jessie on a trip, but that he wanted John to stay with Joan in his absence. "Here's the fucking poker," Ches told him when he arrived, "If that son of a bitch comes anywhere near the house . . . hit first and ask questions later!"

True love has a way of outwitting every father's over-zealous protectiveness, and Ches Crosbie, with all his power, was no exception to the rule. Despite her father's vehement prohibitions, Joan kept seeing Jenkins, allowing him to act as a surrogate father to her two young children in Gene's absence. Although Matthew was too young to remember Jenkins, Lee had fond memories of the man so many of the Crosbies, particularly his uncles Andrew and John, held in such contempt. When Lee was sick, Jenkins brought him Hardy Boys mysteries and gave him a "real" hatchet. Once Lee was well again, Jenkins took him fishing at the end of Quidi Vidi gut, where, to the little boy's delighted surprise, they hooked a drowned pig!

The low point in the affair came after the Crosbies tried to hide Joan and the children at 18 Rennies Mill Road in a fruitless attempt to keep Jenkins from seeing her. After Jessie hung up on Jenkins, telling him not to call anymore, he got into the back seat of a Bugden's taxi cab with a bottle of rye and made his way to Ches Crosbie's place. The entire family, including Joan, met the unwanted intruder, who forced his way into their home. The truculent Jenkins told Joan that he would leave for good, but only if *she* told him to, not her father, mother or brothers. "Andrew decided it was time for me to leave. There's Jessie, Ches, John and Andrew in the living room and they were all on at me and told me I was a nothing and a nobody and various other things, which was all true.

But it made me mad enough to hit 'em. So I hit 'em. All of them except Jessie," Jenkins recalled.

Upstairs, Lee Shinkle listened in horrified fascination to the hullabaloo below. Suddenly, Ches appeared at the bottom of the stairs and shouted for his grandson.

"Lee! Call the police and tell them to get over here *now*."

"Yes, Pop, right away." Ten minutes later, the child was back at the top of the stairs.

"Pop?"

"What?"

"How do I do it?"

"Never mind, I'll do it myself."

The constabulary quickly arrived and John Jenkins spent the night in jail but was released the next morning without having to make a court appearance.

Resigned to the fact that his marriage was over, Gene Shinkle resolved to leave Newfoundland and try to rebuild an adult life that had been spent in comfortable bondage to the Crosbies. Ches tried to convince him to stay but understood the broken man's predicament. Jessie was less sympathetic, particularly when Gene let it be known that he believed she and Ches had contributed to the breakup of his marriage by continuing to spoil their daughter once she had become his wife. Although he was always made welcome in Newfoundland, it would be ten years before he saw his sons again.

By late 1959, eight-year-old Lee and his one-and-a-half-year-old brother were spending more time at 18 Rennies Mill Road than they were with their mother. All his life, little Lee had been told every night to "do his teeth and pee." Faced with a world that had turned topsy-turvy, he made a small protest against his unsettling new status; after doing his teeth and pretending to use the toilet, he would urinate on the rug at the end of his bed. As for baby Matthew, he continued to smile up from his crib, but it was now Nan Crosbie, not his mother, who tended to his every need. As Jane Crosbie put it, "The little fellow wasn't even house-broken yet."

On February 4, 1960, John Jenkins left Newfoundland for a job in Panama City, Panama. Three weeks later, Joan followed him, leaving her children in the care of Ches and Jessie, who told her she could have them again when she got settled. At the time, she was three months pregnant with Jenkins's child. On July 19, 1960, the day her divorce from Gene Shinkle went through, Joan married John Jenkins. "It was a great wedding, a Newfoundland-type wedding. Joan was out to here. Nobody spoke English. We didn't have a witness. We had a judge marry us," Jenkins remembered.

Joan finally had her way, but not before being disinherited and damned by the father whose heart she had broken. Neither Ches nor Jessie came to the wedding, although Jessie did come to Panama for the christening of Susan Jenkins that September. Just when her parents needed time to salvage their own marriage, Joan had handed them another family to raise. "The two children moved in on Rennies Mill Road with the grandparents and that was really the straw that broke the camel's back. They were too old for it," John Crosbie's wife, Jane, observed.

JESSIE CROSBIE PUT her heart into raising the two grandchildren she loved so dearly, but as Ches saw it, the boys gave her just one more reason to withdraw from the adult world and ignore his needs. Just before the breakup of Joan's marriage, he had suffered a mild heart attack. Shortly afterwards, on a business trip to Montreal, a blood clot passed through his eye rendering him temporarily blind. Whether it was eternity's tap on the shoulder that spurred him to take one more run at life, or the fact that pressures at home simply made it unbearable to live there, Ches finally took the leap and left the woman he had been married to for more than thirty years. Despite everyone's hope that he would return, Ches escaped the gravitational pull of his past, and the family was never to be the same again.

No longer hanging his hat at Rennies Mill Road, Ches moved in with his sister Vera's family. For a time, with Ches's frenetic comings and goings, it was as if the circus had set up its tents in the Perlin dining room. Even on a normal day, his prodigious drinking habits upset the household regime. Ches would arrive home from Crosbie and Company and Albert from I. F. Perlin & Company and the pair would polish off a bottle of Scotch at five o'clock in the afternoon. Vera, who knew that Albert would then have to sit down and write editorials for *The Daily News*, was having none of it. "Ches Crosbie," she told him, "it doesn't matter how much you drink in my house, but I'm not going to have my husband turned into exactly what you are."

But the affection between sister and brother ran deep. When Ches had to fly up to Port Weller dry dock in Ontario to christen the *Sir John Crosbie*, the latest addition to the fleet of Chimo Shipping, Vera went along as his official escort. The subtle substitution of a sister for a wife was not enough to raise even the most inquisitive set of eyebrows in St. John's, but it became impossible to hide the crack that had opened up down the middle of the family over Ches and Jessie's separation when Ches filed for a Reno divorce and married a beautiful widow, Alice Squires.

The trim brunette's first husband was Harrow-educated Robert Squires, the son of former Newfoundland premier Sir Richard Squires. The couple had two children before Robert died of tuberculosis. Ches discussed the idea of marrying Alice with his own sisters, who knew and liked Alice, and, of course, with John and Andrew. The schism in the family was mirrored in the differing reactions of the two sons: John sided with his mother and was deeply "hurt" by Ches's decision, although in later years he would come to see the situation differently; Andrew stood by his father, and he and his wife Joan were the first to buy Ches a wedding present.

Personally acquainted now with the pain of divorce, Ches paid a surprise visit to his daughter who had returned to Canada with Jenkins in 1961 and was now living at 15 Dublin Road in Halifax. "He came and he was totally different," Jenkins remembered. "He sat down and he talked to *both* of us. He said, 'Finally, I'm beginning to understand some of what you've gone through.' Anyway, Joan told me after he'd left that Ches had put her back in his will."

Back in Newfoundland, before leaving with Alice to get his Reno divorce, he had some final words of advice for his son John at Torbay Airport: "He had a few drinks there and the last thing he said to me was he warned me not to go with Smallwood, he said it was a great mistake for me to go with Smallwood."

On Christmas Day 1962, Ches called Rennies Mill Road from Hawaii and talked to both of his sons. Andrew waited as John and his father exchanged cool pleasantries. When he was handed the phone, an angry Ches complained that it was nobody's business but his own what he was doing with his life. He then told Andrew "to make sure under any circumstances" that he looked after Joan, "because he [Ches] never had a chance to" — a reference to the eleventh-hour reconciliation with his daughter and Jenkins in Halifax. Those were the last words Andrew and his father ever spoke. Two cheques sent by Ches from Hawaii to his sisters Margaret and Dolly were his last communication with the family.

In the early morning hours of Boxing Day 1962, the telephone rang at Virginia Waters and a sleepy Andrew Crosbie made his way past the Christmas tree he had had spray-painted gold that year to answer it. It was his Uncle Percy, and what he said elicited an involuntary scream from the man who was suddenly transformed into a boy again: "Joan, Dad's dead!" Percy came over to pick up Andrew, and as they drove over to John's house he explained that someone had called on behalf of Alice Squires to say that Ches had died on their honeymoon of a heart attack. After John ducked into the car, the grim delegation made its way to 18 Rennies Mill Road to tell Jessie. Regally aloof, she took the news stoically. Before leaving, Andrew went upstairs and awakened twelve-year-old Lee Shinkle, who was asleep in the bedroom next to the one his grandfather and grandmother had shared for most of their married life.

"Lee, wake up," Andrew whispered. "I've got some terrible bad news for you. Skipper Ches is dead."

Lee blinked incredulously as he was pulled out of sleep by the panicked tug of his uncle's words. In an agony of rejecting an adult world that was always deserting him, the boy rolled over and closed his eyes tight, tighter than the knot in his stomach or the small fist he had made under the blankets. Thinking of his lost mother and father and now of the grandfather who had abandoned him, too, he said "I don't care," and then again, fighting back the tears, "I don't care."

When Andrew got home that night, the golden Christmas tree was gone.

CHAPTER 11

The Divided Kingdom

IT WAS AS hard to bury Ches Crosbie as it sometimes was to live with him. Andrew called the president of Canadian Pacific Airlines to have the body flown out of Honolulu to Montreal via Vancouver. His counterpart at Air Canada stepped in to have the remains shipped from Montreal to Newfoundland. Poor weather at Torbay Airport diverted the flight to Gander, where Ches was loaded aboard a train for the trip to St. John's. Once more, Mother Nature intervened. The train derailed in heavy snow outside Clarenville, and the truck dispatched to complete the journey ran off the road twice on the way back to the city with Ches's body. Ten days after he began his transcontinental island hop, "Peck's Bad Boy" arrived back in St. John's. "He came home the way he lived," Andrew Crosbie wryly observed.

Ches's death set off shock waves within the family and beyond. Ever since Confederation, George and his brother Ches had been estranged; now the pitiless hourglass of mortality doomed all hope of reconciliation. "When Uncle Ches died, my father came down the corridor and the tears were streaming over his face, and he said, 'Just remember one thing, don't remain bad friends with people all your life,' " Debbie Powers, George's daughter, recalled.

But if there was remorse, there were also recriminations. When Gene Shinkle telephoned to offer his condolences to

Jessie, he got an unexpected tongue-lashing. "She jumped me, saying it was my fault that Skipper Ches divorced her and that it was my doing that led him to this." Joan Crosbie, now married to John Jenkins, astonished one of her aunts with her self-centred attitude about abandoning her children to the care of their grandparents: "When she came home for her father's funeral, I thought, My God, she must realize what she did to break him, how cruel she was; and Joan just said, 'I really think it was the best thing I did when I left Shink and Daddy had something to do to look after those children.' "

Gert Crosbie had her own theory about the tragedy: "Ches couldn't live with Jessie and he couldn't live without her. I honestly think Ches died of a guilty conscience." (Less staunch Jessie loyalists held an alternate theory of how, on his honeymoon, Ches had entered eternity — a view that added a few smiles to the tears at his funeral.) In typical Carnell fashion, Jessie Crosbie conveyed her own opinion on Ches's fate to her daughter-in-law, Jane Crosbie. "Well, they say you can't change horses in midstream," she quipped — a cutting reference to Alice Squires, whose family home through marriage was Midstream Manor.

Not the least of the Crosbies' immediate problems was the question of protocol at the funeral. Alice Squires had been married to Ches for less than a month, Jessie, for thirty-five years — who was the real grieving widow, and which Mrs. Crosbie should attend at the graveside? Although a few people in St. John's knew about Ches's remarriage, he and Alice had never returned to Newfoundland as man and wife, so word of his divorce had never hit the newspapers. Gracefully, the legal widow bowed to the grieving dowager, discreetly avoiding the funeral to allow Jessie and Ches their next-to-last charade. The final one would take place in August 1982 when Jessie was buried beside her husband in the family plot as if the last month of his life had never taken place. Having virtually annulled the short, happy marriage of Alice Squires, Crosbie pride and power would ultimately jostle the historical record back into its proper place.

Tributes poured in from across the country, and newspapers ran glowing tributes to the man who had made so many friends in Canada and the United States during his business career. Reporters caught up to Joe Smallwood in Montreal as a thousand people were preparing to descend on the Cochrane Street United Church in St. John's to bid Ches farewell. Smallwood was on his way to Japan to drum up investment capital for Wabush Mines with super-promoter John C. Doyle who would later describe Ches as a "likeable drunk." Joey's comments were more in the spirit of the moment and much closer to the truth. He called Ches "a great Newfoundlander and a great friend." In a subsequent tribute in *The Book of Newfoundland*, he wrote, "Ches Crosbie was one of the most generous men I ever knew, imaginative, patriotic, wonderfully energetic, a daring (even gambling) business-entrepreneur, a democratic personality" whose death "was a grievous blow to Newfoundland." (Smallwood was well qualified to pass judgment on Ches's generosity since he regularly contributed $25,000 to the Liberal Party whenever the call went out.)

Having dispensed with his public obligations, the private Joe Smallwood sprang into action. He quickly arranged a meeting with Percy and Andrew Crosbie at the company's headquarters in the Chapel Building on Water Street, where Sir John's car had once thundered over the wooden planks of the Crosbie wharf. Smallwood proposed that they sell the business to Arthur Lundrigan, a prominent west coast Liberal whose family was in the construction business. Just as at Sir John's death his competitors made a bid for his customers thinking Ches was too young to fill his father's shoes, the implication now was that Andrew and Percy couldn't carry on without Ches. Declaring that they would sink or swim on their own, the Crosbies politely told the premier "to go to hell," knowing as they did that to sell to the Lundrigans would be to hand over NECCO, and with it, a lock on the lucrative construction business in Newfoundland.

Under the terms of his will, Ches set up a $250,000 trust fund for Jessie, which was increased to $300,000 under a codicil dated August 7, 1962. (The increased figure may have reflected the fact that shortly before his death Ches received his $1,250,000 share from the sale of Bavarian Breweries and Gaden's Ltd. to Labatt's, a timely windfall reminiscent of the insurance policy that saved Sir John's estate in 1932.) A further codicil dated in Montreal on October 5, 1962, left a $150,000 legacy to Mrs. Alice E. Squires. The shares of Crosbie and Company were placed in his estate, and John and Andrew had the right to purchase the shares as they saw fit, a provision that touched off a game of corporate cat-and-mouse between the two brothers. "John was very clever. He always bought enough shares so I couldn't get control of Crosbie and Company," Andrew chortled.

The balance of Ches's estate, valued at $1,293,049.50, was equally divided among his three children. Joan, John and Andrew were to have the interest from their share, while the capital was to remain invested until Joan's youngest child from the Shinkle marriage, Matthew, reached the age of twenty-one. On the date of division, Joan's share was to be transferred to her sons, Lee and Matthew. But in a codicil to the will dated August 7, 1962, Ches altered the terms of Joan's inheritance. Now, even the income from her share would go towards the maintenance and education of Lee and Matthew. The only way Joan herself could be the direct beneficiary of the income would be if she separated from John Jenkins and required support. Ches might have been gone, but his anger at his wayward daughter smouldered on in the cold declarations of his last will and testament. Given his final telephone conversation with Andrew, and his recent reconciliation with Joan and her second husband, he apparently intended to change it, but time had simply run out.

In keeping with Ches's quiet commitment to charity, he left legacies to five child-care institutions in St. John's, including $500 to the Mount Cashel Orphanage. But that was not the full extent of his generosity. When clearing out his father's desk on a cold January afternoon in 1963, John Crosbie found a sealed envelope with the words, "To my executors, to read as part of my will. Chesley A. Crosbie." It was yet another codicil — the third — handwritten on Ches's private stationery and witnessed by Imelda Davis, a clerk at Crosbie and Company on June 28, 1962. The codicil had purposely been secreted away from his will, but in a place where it would certainly be found after his death.

Ches instructed his executors to transfer all of his shares in Frontier Fishing and Hunting Limited, a wilderness camp in Labrador, to one Phyllis Clibbery. In addition to the shares, there were other benefits to his female partner: "Any monies owed to me by Frontier Fishing-Hunting and any notes endorsed by me unpaid, are to be paid and given to the said Mrs. Phyllis Clibbery free of charge." When the final arithmetic was done, it turned out to be a tidy gift; for reasons unknown, Mrs. Clibbery was given the company free and clear, a legacy that diminished the Crosbie estate by $78,000.

As one of the executors of his father's estate, John Crosbie took the position that this first codicil was revoked by the two subsequent codicils to the will. The courts found otherwise. In finding for the plaintiff, Phyllis Clibbery, Supreme Court Justice Harry Winter observed: "It seems clear that the company was financed entirely by the testator [Ches] . . . it is in effect a legacy to the plaintiff, consisting partly of the forgiveness of debt, amounting to a little over $50,000 . . . and partly of the direction to the executors to pay other debts of the company out of the testator's estate."

Ches Crosbie had spoken for the last time. It was now up to his sons to work out their destinies without him in a Newfoundland run by a man who, in the ten years since he'd defeated Ches Crosbie at the polls, had taken unto himself all the gaudy powers of a tin-pot dictator.

BETWEEN DRAGGING NEWFOUNDLAND into Canada and the death of his old rival, Ches Crosbie, Joe Smallwood had undergone a sea change. He had entered the 1950s as a political visionary determined to transform Newfoundland's rural fishing society into an industrialized province of Canada, but instead it was Smallwood himself who underwent a metamorphosis. By 1960, the political radical who had once attended a meeting with Leon Trotsky and espoused the cause of socialism had been supplanted by an increasingly ruthless demagogue who imposed his vision of Newfoundland on a population that either traded their political support for government patronage or felt the lash of Smallwood's swift reprisals. Vision had begun to blur into megalomania as Joe Smallwood's roller-coaster ride with destiny picked up speed.

From the very beginning, it was obvious that Smallwood's free-spending ways would ultimately leave him dependent on outside capital and an array of smooth-talking foreign developers to advance his economic agenda. His mistrust of the local business establishment ran deep: before Confederation they had opposed him in the National Referendum; afterwards, they never accepted him as a social equal. It was no accident that the site of Confederation Building, handpicked by Smallwood, looked down on the east end business establishments of the Water Street merchants.

By 1951, the provincial government had spent every penny of the $45-million surplus Newfoundland had brought into Confederation. Thirteen million had gone into the fishing industry in the form of loans to various private companies, including some owned by the Crosbies, to assist in establishing fresh fish and fish-meal plants. None of this money was ever repaid, and Newfoundland's fishery continued to lag far behind its competitors. In fact, between Confederation and 1964, Newfoundland's share of the Northwest Atlantic fishery dropped by 100 percent, the shortfall taken up by the large, modern vessels of the Soviet Union, Norway, France, Portugal and Iceland. The only innovation in Newfoundland's most traditional industry was unemployment insurance, a 1957 program that would ever after encourage fishermen to set their nets for unemployment insurance stamps rather than fish. If a fisherman could collect stamps for a mere ten weeks of fishing, he could draw unemployment insurance benefits for the remaining forty-two weeks of the year.

But the bulk of government largesse went into the buzzword of the decade, industrial diversification. After his $30-million spending spree, Smallwood had fifteen "new" industries in the province, including a cement plant, a tannery, a heavy-machinery plant and a gypsum plant. The plan was to establish these new industries and then sell them to private enterprise, using the proceeds to finance more new ventures. At the height of the construction boom associated with Smallwood's industrial strategy, unemployment dropped to 10 percent — an impressive statistic in a place where one out of five Newfoundlanders is chronically out of work.

But a sad pattern was established with the sale of the first project in 1960. Although North Star Cement Ltd. paid $4.3 million for Smallwood's cement plant in Corner Brook, the monies for the purchase were advanced to North Star by the provincial government, defeating the purpose of the program. Making matters worse, many of Smallwood's initial ventures amounted to the economic version of driving square pegs into round holes; millions were lost in ludicrous attempts to establish a light bulb factory, a rubber boot plant, a chocolate factory and even a plant to turn sea water into magnesium.

The consequences of these economic failures went well beyond the financial. To support industrialization, Smallwood introduced a resettlement program that used the lure of jobs in the cities and towns to persuade rural Newfoundlanders to "burn their boats" and abandon a way of life they had known for centuries. Using government grants to pay for their one-way tickets to the modern world, Smallwood erased 115 outport communities between 1954 and 1965, shifting 7,500 people into the island's larger centres. By the time this culturally questionable policy had run its course, 200 outport communities had been obliterated. In depriving thousands of Newfoundlanders of their heritage without giving them a viable economic alternative, Joe Smallwood had created a class of people whose survival now depended on Canada's social welfare programs and his own patronage, rather than on themselves. It was a revolutionary change in a place where rugged individualism had always been the watchword and the ability to survive the proudest virtue.

As Confederation's money tree began to show bare limbs, Newfoundland began to shiver. In 1958, an old political enemy, Prime Minister John Diefenbaker, announced that the transitional grants to Newfoundland agreed to at Confederation would be cut off by 1961. (An outcry in the rest of the country won Newfoundland a reprieve.) With mounting deficits and no new funds in sight, Smallwood turned to larger-than-life figures, some honest, others decidedly shady, to help him with his grand design to impose an industrial revolution on Newfoundland. In some cases they lent him their money; in others, they begged, borrowed and otherwise abused Newfoundland's; but kings or carpetbaggers, Joe needed them now as never before. In his zeal to transform Newfoundland, Smallwood ignored his industrial failures and desperately rolled the dice on progressively bigger and bigger projects, all of which were touted as the way to the promised land. But whether it was a third paper mill in Stephenville or an oil refinery at Come by Chance, the only people who got their hands on the brass ring were the outside developers whose imperial style so completely beguiled Smallwood.

ON THE INTERNATIONAL scene, Smallwood developed an early taste for hobnobbing with the rich and famous. His pet project was the proposed hydro development on the Hamilton River in Labrador, later to become Churchill Falls. In 1952, Smallwood travelled to Britain, where he finally persuaded Prime Minister Winston Churchill to put together the financiers for the mega-project that would take seventeen years to complete. "Churchill listened to Joe, and when he was done, he rang a bell and a girl came in and he said, 'Get me Rothschild on the phone.' He got him and he said, 'Rothschild, come up here on the double.' . . . So Rothschild came up and he was a bit out of breath . . . and he [Churchill] said to Joe, 'Tell him.' So Joe went through it all again . . . 'Must we go to the United States to get the money to develop this great resource? Where is the Elizabethan spirit of adventure? Is it dead? I *refuse* to believe that.' When he finished, Churchill said, 'Rothschild, I want you to put it together,' and that's how it started," Greg Power remembered.

Not all of Smallwood's industrial rainmakers came from the inner circle of European politics and finance. In early 1953, a brilliant stock promoter and developer from Chicago boarded a plane for Newfoundland to collect a debt owed to his company, Javelin Foundries, by United Nail and Foundries of St. John's. By chance, John C. Doyle's seat mate that day was Claude Howse, Newfoundland's then deputy minister of Mines. In casual conversation, Doyle mentioned that it was a pity that the government had given away Labrador to the group of companies that eventually became the Iron Ore Company of Canada (IOC). Howse informed Doyle that there were still vast areas of Labrador open for development and invited the high-rolling American developer to his office to discuss it further.

Two days later, Doyle walked into Howse's office — and a fortune. He was shown an aerial magnetic survey showing mineral deposits taken by the Timmins group of companies. The map included a large tract of land around Wabush Lake that the company had relinquished. The pilot had apparently turned on his magnetometer before he reached the area he had been instructed to scan, and his employers hadn't edited their survey map before handing it over to the government. Judging from the survey readings, Doyle immediately saw that "there was a big potential that was not on the land that they [the Timmins group] controlled." He immediately sent a geologist to Labrador and instructed him to investigate the area around Wabush Lake. The results were astonishing: "All he did was pull the turf off and you could see the speculated hematite [iron ore in the form of coarse sand] under it, and he went all over that area, and the result was that he thought we should take it, grab it as fast as we could." Somehow, the Labrador Mining and Exploration Company had overlooked more than a billion tons of exploitable iron ore!

Before leaving Newfoundland, Doyle wrote a personal cheque for $250,000 to secure the mineral rights to the 2,400 square miles of land involved. That summer, Joe Smallwood himself came to Montreal and put the finishing touches on a deal that would lead to one of the world's largest iron ore developments at Wabush Lake. (The Crosbies quickly capitalized on the projected development with a new company, Wabush Enterprises Ltd., that established the Sir Wilfred Grenfell Hotel and operated a shopping centre and air terminal building in industrial Labrador.)

The premier was swept off his feet by the cultured and brilliant Doyle, who was a linguist, oenophile and musician as well as a financial wizard. Smallwood had found another industrial Rasputin to take the place of the discredited Valdmanis. On July 20, 1964, the day the $235-million Wabush Iron Mine was opened, Doyle was in Hartford, Connecticut, awaiting sentencing on a violation of U.S. securities regulations. A week after being convicted, Doyle jumped bail and returned to Canada rather than serve three months in jail. Despite the legal shadow over his friend, it was a relationship that Smallwood would defend to the end, even after Doyle had become a fugitive from Canadian justice living in Panama — and Newfoundland had lost more than two hundred million dollars on one of his doomed schemes!

In 1961, another dream-merchant rode into Newfoundland on the magic carpet of industrial development. John Shaheen, an American of Lebanese descent, opened a small oil refinery at Holyrood, just outside St. John's. A charismatic maverick in the oil industry, it wasn't long before Shaheen, too, had mesmerized Smallwood with his tales from his days in the OSS (Office of Strategic Services) and his impressive list of friends, which included William Casey and Richard Nixon. Shaheen soon convinced Smallwood to back a huge oil refinery at Come by Chance, which would be opened in 1973 with a million-dollar visit by the luxury liner *Queen Elizabeth II*. Three years later, it would turn into what was then the largest bankruptcy in Canadian history.

Smallwood's penchant for swashbuckling companions coupled with his growing tyrannical streak ultimately alienated the very people who had helped him to win the national referendum. When Harold Horwood, one of Joey's three key lieutenants in the late 1940s, left Smallwood's camp and began criticizing the premier in his column in *The Evening Telegram*, he felt the brunt of his former boss's rage. Using his standard tactic of burying adversaries under a barrage of rhetorical abuse and innuendo, Smallwood denounced Horwood as "a cutthroat, a rat, a dastardly clown, a loathsome scavenger and a literary assassin."

In 1959, it was Greg Power's turn to jump the Smallwood

ship. A stubborn and clever maverick, Power was particularly sickened by the sycophants the premier now recruited for his personal staff. But in Power's case there was more to his decision to leave government than his distaste for the Smallwood style. On January 2, 1959, the terrible conditions in Newfoundland's logging camps had led to a loggers' strike, which Smallwood, the former champion of the working man, set out with a vengeance to crush. When the dust cleared, the RCMP and the Royal Newfoundland Constabulary, sent in by the premier, brought the strikers to their knees. But victory was expensive: a rookie policeman died in the violent confrontation between loggers and police, and the labour movement in Newfoundland would never forgive Smallwood for siding with multinational companies against outport Newfoundlanders. Greg Power was equally appalled.

To maintain his iron grasp on power, Smallwood needed all the influential friends he could get, and that included the two young men who were now trying to pick up where their father, Ches Crosbie, had left off. At first, he would try to win them both with promises of wealth and power; later, he would pit one against the other in a desperate attempt to keep his rotting ship of state afloat.

JOHN AND ANDREW Crosbie had never been particularly close as children; as young men their paths had diverged even more sharply. Except for his brief semester at Boston University, Andrew had come directly out of high school into the family business. When it came to reading, he shared his father's preference for detective novels and comic books. Like his father, he was physically robust, enjoyed the outdoors, loved gardening and made war on the liquor cabinet as only the Crosbies could. His marriage to Joan Parsons, a wealthy woman in her own right, completed the picture of a rising merchant prince whose future seemed bright, although ominously clouded by some of Ches's less healthy bequests. (In 1960, when Joan was in hospital having their son Tim, Andrew admitted to his wife that he had a "serious" drinking problem.) The couple were to have four children, Alexander, Robert, Timothy and Cynthia, who lived as privileged a life as St. John's had to offer on their sprawling Virginia Waters estate.

In sharp contrast, John Crosbie was one of the most brilliant academic minds of his day, with a sedentary, if not ascetic bent and an emphatic lack of interest in the business world. From 1949 to 1953, he studied political science and economics at Queen's University, winning the University medal in politics. For three of his four years at Queen's, and then again at law school, John was president of the Liberal Club, a fitting post for the man who would later become one of Pierre Trudeau's strongest supporters in the 1968 convention to replace Lester Pearson as national Liberal leader.

In 1952, John married Jane Furneaux and demonstrated that there were definite limits to his legendary shyness and no question about his lineage. Their compartment on the train back to Queen's was as steamy as Ches's cabin on his honeymoon voyage to Rio: "We stopped in Montreal to get her a diaphragm, but by the time we got the diaphragm it was too late. Before we hit Queen's she'd somehow gotten herself pregnant."

His next stop was the law school at Dalhousie University, where he covered himself in academic glory, winning six of the school's seven top medals. The Canadian Bar Association recognized the Newfoundlander's brilliance by awarding him the Viscount Bennett Fellowship as the top law student in Canada. He finished off his academic career with a year at the Institute for Advanced Legal Studies in England. In 1957, John Crosbie was admitted to the bar in St. John's. He was now facing the future with his wife, Jane, a growing family that eventually included sons Ches and Michael and daughter Elizabeth, and a new law practice, Lewis, Aylward and Crosbie. Unlike Andrew and Joan, John and Jane lived comfortably but unostentatiously, and no one had any doubt that John would inevitably trade the law for his first love, politics. Everyone also knew that to do so would eventually mean either getting into bed with Joe Smallwood or burying him. Ever the politician, John tried both.

IN THE WAKE of Ches's death, there was a corporate reorganization of the Crosbie business interests, which, according to family insiders, then carried a debt load of $5 million. It was agreed that Percy Crosbie would become the new president of Crosbie and Company Ltd., Chimo Shipping Ltd. and Holdings Corporation Ltd.; Andrew would serve as vice-president of the same companies, as well as of Kaegudeck Cabins Ltd. and Leaseback Projects Ltd. His most important task would be to take over the presidency of Newfoundland Engineering and Construction Company Ltd., one of the family's biggest money-makers. John Crosbie was made president of Leaseback Projects Ltd. and Kaegudeck Cabins Ltd. and secretary-treasurer of NECCO. Through the purchase of Maritime Central Airways, Andrew realized his father's long-held dream of swallowing up his rival, Carl Burke, to become the third-largest commercial carrier in Canada. The new chairman of Eastern Provincial Airways was longtime family friend Edgar Hickman; the new vice-chairman was Andrew Crosbie. Ches Crosbie's then twenty-nine-year-old son was suddenly immersed in a crash business course that would soon leave him astride the peak of one of the largest family business empires in Canada — a happy child sitting on a mountain of ice cream.

It was a job for which he was curiously unprepared. Whatever other talents he possessed, Ches Crosbie was no teacher. Although Andrew had been intimately involved in the family business for ten years, he had served his apprenticeship on the decks of ships, in whaling stations and behind the wheels of trucks rather than in the company's head office. It was all part of Ches's philosophy that his children had to learn the business from the ground up. Now Andrew traded his sweater and dungarees for a briefcase and business suit, initially relying on his Uncle Percy and Edgar Hickman to guide him around the unforgiving circuits of corporate finance and big time entrepreneurship. In more ways than one, Andrew's uncle picked up where his father had left off. "Sure, Ches jumped on Andrew, but no more than Percy did. If anything, Percy jumped on him harder and it used to be more difficult to handle for Andrew," his former wife recalled.

Although more experienced men were temporarily behind the wheel of Crosbie and Company, there was no question that they were there to prepare Andrew for his intended succession to the presidency. He was a keen student. By 1964, Andrew was an executive officer or director of thirty-one companies; by 1968, the number had risen to seventy-seven. In the five years after Ches's death, the Crosbie empire experienced a 100 percent increase in gross sales, largely because of Andrew's drive to diversify the family's interests. The annual corporate payroll was now $10 million for the company's 1,300 employees, and both numbers were rising with every new acquisition.

The centrepiece of the empire was still Crosbie and Company, whose main business was the import and export trade. But the firm was also the agent for underwriters at Lloyd's of London and other insurance companies. NECCO took care of general construction in Newfoundland, which was then booming, thanks to the construction of the Trans-Canada Highway and mega-projects with heavy engineering components like the Churchill Falls hydro development, the Stephenville Linerboard Mill, a phosphorous plant at Long Harbour, and the Come by Chance oil refinery. LeeMatt Traders added the new dimension of a purchasing company. Chimo Shipping's nineteen vessels were now engaged in worldwide trading, operating a coastal service between Montreal and Newfoundland and a tanker service for chemicals and vegetable oils from the Great Lakes to Europe.

The empire's cash flow was staggering; less obvious beneath the surface glitter was the mounting debt equity that made the tremendous expansion both possible and vulnerable. But money was cheap, and the prospect of killer recessions well over the horizon. At the tender age of thirty-three, Andrew became the youngest president in the history of the Newfoundland Board of Trade, exemplifying in his de facto stewardship of the Crosbie companies the board's motto for that year: "Forge ahead."

Not surprisingly, Andrew's real partner in expanding the family business empire was Joe Smallwood, who might have been cash-poor but who still controlled all the lucrative cost-plus contracts that, as a matter of policy, were awarded without tender in Newfoundland. He also possessed Ottawa's golden guarantee to stand behind all provincial borrowing — the only reason Newfoundland had a credit rating. Like every other successful Newfoundland company of the day, the Crosbies would use Smallwood's borrowing power more than once on their climb up the corporate ladder.

Eastern Provincial Airways (EPA) was a case in point. In 1960, the family had begun buying out larger shareholders in Newfoundland Airways with the intention of acquiring Maritime Central Airways from Carl Burke. By 1961, a study was underway to look at the feasibility of transforming the large bush-plane operation Ches had developed into a scheduled airline with regular flights between Newfoundland, Labrador and the Maritimes. By mid-1963, Burke was ready to sell, and it was Smallwood who advanced the money to the Crosbies to make the acquisition. Three years later, when Andrew wanted to acquire 737 jets for his new airline, EPA, it was the provincial government's guarantee that raised the necessary $6 million.

But government patronage never came free, and the bill in Newfoundland was always paid in full to the same man, Joe Smallwood. In the late 1950s, Smallwood began building Russwood Ranch, a sprawling establishment on the Roache's Line an hour's drive outside St. John's. The Crosbies built Joe's swimming pool. The house was a typically grandiose project that had more concrete than class, and Smallwood got a lot of help building it from crews working on the Trans-Canada Highway, as Newfoundland businessman Basil Dobbin remembered.

"I was just a young lad in the mid-fifties when they were building the Trans-Canada Highway just above the access road at Holyrood. There was a camp there, and we sent thousands of tons of material over to Smallwood, who was building the ranch. At the same time, Andrew had sent dozers over. . . . There were pieces of equipment that were on the books that were sitting on Smallwood's farm. And people who didn't go along with that were crushed."

Andrew Crosbie himself clearly understood the nature of obligation in Smallwood's Newfoundland. During a Christmas party at Russwood Ranch, he gave the premier a gift-wrapped present and told him to open it in his downstairs bedroom. "It's only handkerchiefs, but they're the best ones you'll ever get," Andrew told him. The box contained ten handkerchiefs; between each one was a crisp, new, thousand-dollar bill. "When Joey came up from his room he had a big smile on his face and said, 'Andrew, you're right. Those were the best handkerchiefs I've ever received.' "

The gift, of course, was for the Liberal Party of Newfoundland and not its balding godfather. The Crosbies were riding the hog's back, and as long as Joe Smallwood was in power and on side, the future of the empire was secure. No one knew that better than Andrew Crosbie.

BY 1965, JOHN Crosbie had grown restless with the mundane task of handling the legal work for Crosbie and Company. During a round-the-world trip with Jane in August of that year, the restlessness turned into resolve and he made the decision to enter politics. The would-be candidate "mentioned" his political intentions to Joe Smallwood, who thought it was a good idea but offered no encouragement, as if his uncanny political instincts sensed that here was the kind of talented supporter who could very easily turn into a formidable rival.

John first set his sights on municipal politics, deciding to run for St. John's city council in the November 1965 election. His campaign slogan was "You Have a Right to Know." Crosbie's first campaign established a pattern for all his future trips to the polls. The financial records of the campaign were as meticulous as the tiny script in which they were recorded: 100 sandwiches at 40 cents apiece, $250 to the St. John's Boys Club to deliver his 15,000 pamphlets door to door, and a note of a 50 percent discount from Don Jamieson on all advertising at television station CJON.

Several family members were also pressed into the campaign. Cousin John Perlin, who would one day become Newfoundland's culture czar, provided practical political advice. Andrew worked behind the scenes with labour officials and drove John around on polling day as the results came in. Barbara Crosbie, married to John's cousin Roger, worked the telephones. He also got help from Richard Cashin, Fred Rowe, Newfoundland's finance minister of the day, and Geoff Stirling, his father's former ally in the Economic Union Party, who now owned and operated a media empire that included a television station in St. John's. Every worker in the campaign — whether family, friend or ordinary volunteer — would later receive a personal note from the candidate thanking him for his contribution, a tradition John Crosbie would follow for the next twenty-five years.

As voting day approached, the local pundits all agreed that the first Crosbie since Sir John to seek public office would top the polls, and John didn't disappoint them. Despite his painful shyness and difficulty in lifting a speech off the page, his total of 7,419 votes was 1,675 more than the successful candidate for mayor, William Adams. A staunch establishment friend, Noel Goodridge, put the young politician's success in becoming deputy mayor in historical perspective. "I suppose with seven in ten voters voting for you, there must be some primitive fever of appeal. It can't be the Carnell tradition, nor Sir John's appeal to the Pope."

Whatever the attraction, it extended all the way to the eighth floor of Confederation Building. Joe Smallwood was facing a fall election and was determined to wipe out his Conservative opposition. The weakest link in his political machine was St. John's, the bastion of anti-Confederate sentiment in 1949 which, despite all Joey's blandishments, continued to support the political opposition in Newfoundland. As a son of the merchant establishment and a big winner in the recent municipal elections, John Crosbie was a doubly attractive candidate. Gambling that he could keep the young lion's political ambitions in check while he used him for his own purposes, Joe Smallwood offered the political neophyte a cabinet post in July 1966, just six months after Crosbie earned his way into city hall. "I had known

Smallwood for some time because the family was in with him, did business with the government and supported the Liberal Party. He was a fascinating person, voluble, active, bursting with ideas, always talking; he spent all his time on politics and public affairs," John remembered.

The offer was, as it was intended to be, flattering and impossible for the thirty-five-year-old to refuse: the post of minister of Municipal Affairs in a government headed for certain reelection and an imminent leadership convention. Nagged, perhaps, by his father's warning to stay away from Smallwood, John nevertheless made the pilgrimage to his uncle Albert Perlin's den on Water Street West to discuss the matter. Uncle Albert's advice was the same as his father's — steer clear of Joey Smallwood. But ambition's inexorable pull and his sense that Smallwood would soon be resigning proved stronger than the advice of those who had themselves turned down repeated offers from Joey to join the inner circle of government. On July 18, 1966, John Crosbie sent his resignation as a director of Crosbie and Company to his Uncle Percy, wishing the firm now controlled by his brother "continuing success in the future."

It was a voyage across the Rubicon. John knew that a political career meant divesting his interest in the family business, thus turning controlling interest over to Andrew. But he had come to the conclusion that the days were long gone when a politician could mix public and private business, and he was determined to make his mark in public life. He had also grown increasingly uncomfortable with Andrew's conspicuously affluent lifestyle, from the Rolls Royce convertible he drove regally through the streets of St. John's to the annual Christmas party at the Colony Club where each Crosbie company presented "Mr. Andrew" with a gift. (One year in mock deference to Andrew's mania for neatness, his wife Joan arranged to have him presented with a feather duster.) All in all, it was a satisfying arrangement: Andrew was happy to buy his brother out to gain control of the family business, and by selling John was able to pursue an independent career in public life without the hounds of the press baying about conflict of interest. The Crosbie kingdom was now divided. Andrew was ensconced on the business throne and John had his eye firmly fixed on Newfoundland's political crown.

On September 8, 1966, John Crosbie was elected as a Liberal MHA in the district of St. John's West. Smallwood's dream of wiping out the political opposition came dangerously close to being realized; his Liberal Party won thirty-nine of forty-two seats in the House of Assembly, making it Newfoundland's most one-sided election since Confederation. In congratulating Crosbie on his maiden success in provincial politics, Noel Goodridge made an observation that nicely anticipated what was about to happen: "I look forward to great things from you and the government. Joseph Smallwood will have quite a challenge, not only from the future but from the 'young' cabinet minister who, understandably, will be more difficult to subdue than the old guard."

John and Andrew weren't the only Crosbies who were making news in the 1960s. In 1966, their aunt, Vera (Crosbie) Perlin, opened the Vera Perlin School for the mentally and physically handicapped on Pennywell Road in St. John's, the culmination of years of volunteer work in church basements, makeshift classrooms and renovated houses. In 1953, long before the Newfoundland government provided any special facilities or funding for such children, she had persuaded the United Church Conference to sponsor and run an experimental school in the basement of the city's United Church Orphanage. Vera recruited the first teacher, Molly Dingle, and travelled to England where she found and hired a consultant for the school.

Three years later, she walked into her Water Street West home and announced to husband Albert that she had just bought a house at public auction that would be a better facility for her special mission. Until government assumed responsibility for the education of the handicapped in 1971, it fell to people like Albert Perlin and Percy Crosbie to raise the money that Vera needed to run her school from the well-heeled members of the City Club.

In 1967, the National Council of Jewish Women voted Vera Newfoundland's Woman of the Century, and three years later she became an Officer of the Order of Canada and received an honorary doctorate of laws from Memorial University. Like sister Olga, who played Santa Claus at the school's Christmas parties for ten years, Sir John's dutiful daughter helped a lot of people without their ever knowing it.

AS A MINISTER of the Crown, the young John Crosbie quickly demonstrated the scope of his interests and ambition. A self-described liberal in the reform tradition, he showed a deep interest in many social issues outside the scope of his own ministries. He was a strong advocate of a Law Reform Commission similar to commissions set up in the United Kingdom and Ontario. He was particularly keen on reforming family and matrimonial law in Newfoundland, which was still based on the Ecclesiastical Courts of England as they existed in 1832. He was highly critical of the federal law that permitted divorce on the basis of adultery, but not for desertion, mental cruelty, lengthy incarceration or insanity. (In Newfoundland, even a petition for divorce on the grounds of adultery had to be referred to the Canadian Senate.) The law, Crosbie argued, was a century behind reality: "The commission of an act of adultery may be just a momentary or temporary lapse by one partner but desertion and the other grounds suggested here are permanent in their nature and reflect the fact that the marriage in question is ended in any event."

Crosbie also advocated a government-sponsored legal-aid program, consumer protection legislation and compensation for the victims of crime, an issue he would revisit in the famous Donald Marshall case from both sides of the House of Commons in the 1980s.

Crosbie's zeal for social reform was whetted by the distance he knew Newfoundland still had to travel in order to achieve the standards of living that were taken for granted on the mainland. As minister of Municipal Affairs, he was inundated with letters from poor constituents, who often included informal proof of membership in the Liberal Party in the same envelope as their request for help. The housing conditions complained of were grotesque: no plumbing, sewage seeping in under houses, six children billeted in a windowless, six-by-ten room, fire hazards and mould that grew to tropical luxuriance in permanently damp living quarters. In each and every case, Crosbie meticulously responded to individual complaints and developed new policies to deal with those problems he saw as generic. While in the Housing portfolio, he established the Newfoundland and Labrador Housing Corporation, which, for the first time, enforced minimum standards in the subsidized housing industry.

Sixteen months after joining the cabinet, Crosbie was shifted to the Health portfolio, where he prepared the legislation that brought Newfoundland into medicare, including the Medical Care Insurance Act. (After Crosbie's resignation from cabinet, a reporter asked Smallwood what would become of medicare. "Joe was good enough to say that if I'd never been born, we would still have medicare," John recalled.) John quickly gained a reputation as an excellent legislator and, in winning the cooperation of the Newfoundland Medical Association, an able and respected negotiator.

On more than one occasion during his career in provincial politics, John Crosbie was brought face to face with a monster created by Smallwood's promise of universal social welfare during the Confederation debates. The taxi-medicare scam was one of the clearest examples of how the promises of Confederation had run amok in the outports. Doctors in cottage hospitals in rural Newfoundland, where 70 percent of the population was on welfare, were having a serious problem with patients who insisted on being classified as unable to work, even though there was nothing wrong with them. As one government report put it, "Some doctors have been threatened with violence to their families and themselves," for refusing to sign the necessary testimonial slips. According to government reports, what the "welfare patients" really wanted was free cab fare from their outport community to go on a shopping junket in the nearest town.

"The main reason for the abuse of doctors' time is that the Welfare patient needs a slip from the doctor in order to have taxi fare paid. It seems to be a most profitable item for both the taxi drivers and the people. If six people come from say Round Harbour to Baie Verte, the taxi fee is perhaps fifteen dollars. The six people get six slips for which the taxi driver gets $90 and splits it with the passengers. The people get their trip to town plus some spending money, but to do this they must get the slip from the doctor. Because the people are lying it usually takes the doctor a longer time with the person because he is trying to diagnose an illness for which he can find no symptoms."

In the rural area around the small town of Baie Verte, the annual fraudulent taxi bill to government was a staggering $100,000. Monday was the only day when the so-called welfare patients didn't crowd into doctors' offices — the day the stores were closed. Not only was the public purse being plundered, rural Newfoundland was also losing a priceless resource. Appalled by the bellicose demands of healthy patients to be certified as unfit to work, many doctors preferred to leave the province rather than participate in the fraud or suffer intimidation.

Alarmed by the situation, Crosbie refused to let a single doctor leave the outports without first trying to put right the working conditions that were often behind their resignations. He also brought recommendations to his colleagues to have the welfare patients taken to town in school buses on down time in order to eliminate the necessity of taxi fares. He could not have helped but remember his father's warning during the national referendum that Canada's social programs would be the ruin of Newfoundlanders when he read the concluding paragraphs of a report on the taxi-medicare scandal: "Suddenly in 1949 Welfare payments of all kinds appear and more money is paid into the household from government than was able to be earned from the hard work and long hours they put in in the fishing boats, on the flakes and in the woods. Since then incomes have increased but not in proportion to Welfare payments and all its side benefits. It is literally more profitable to be on Welfare than to work."

Despite the discouraging evidence of what Confederation had become in many parts of rural Newfoundland, Crosbie remained progressive, compassionate and hardworking. He even dealt promptly and respectfully with the outlandish wish lists of voters who had been trained by Smallwood to expect goodies from politicians in exchange for their votes; one man wrote demanding help in selling his silver mine, a second to get a refund on an unused EPA plane ticket, another for an electric pump for his well, and yet another who believed his vote was worth a set of false teeth from his MHA.

Despite the dogged good cheer he put into his ministerial work, Crosbie was growing deeply pessimistic about whether anyone's best efforts could overcome Newfoundland's enormous problems as long as public life was a one-man circus in which the acts were getting more and more bizarre and the price of admission increasingly outrageous. There was no better place to demonstrate what was wrong with the province's public life than the cabinet room where the aging ringmaster of Confederation ruled with an iron hand and an indefatigable tongue. "The cabinet meetings consisted of Joe coming in and talking, you know, hour and a half, two hours, everybody else listening, nodding their heads. He was completely dominant, there was no debate or discussion or dialogue at cabinet meetings. . . . You would have to agree to things that you thought were stupid. . . . I knew it was only going to be a question of time. I couldn't stand it," Crosbie recalled.

For new cabinet ministers who did not necessarily understand Joe's fondness for unanimity, there was a quick lesson in cabinet protocol. Myles Murray spent his first cabinet meeting revelling in the cut and thrust of debate, posing thoughtful questions and drawing the premier out on some of his more arcane points. When the cabinet meeting was over, Joe put his arm around Myles and asked him what he thought of his first cabinet session.

"Oh, wonderful, Premier, wonderful, wonderful."

"Oh, that's swell," Smallwood replied, "I thought you hadn't enjoyed it at all."

The new minister took the hint and in future cabinet

meetings absorbed the premier's monologues in respectful silence until it came time to vote for whatever it was Smallwood wanted.

John was also appalled by Smallwood's dictatorial dismissiveness of the official Opposition. On one occasion in the House of Assembly, Gerry Ottenheimer, Tom Hickey and Ank Murphy — the entire Loyal Opposition — called for a recorded vote on a matter under debate. Knowing that the Opposition needed four members to force a vote, Smallwood smugly refused. John Crosbie decided to take the bull by the horns.

"It was a terrible piece of bullying. I was sitting behind Joe in the second row and they stood up to try and force a vote . . . and unbeknownst to Joe, I stood as well from the Liberal ranks so that they had to have a recorded vote . . . I just couldn't take this goddamn, you know, dictatorship. . . . And then the clerk called for the vote and he turned around and he saw me. Well, you should have seen his face . . . that was the last proof that I was out to get him. . . . I voted with the government, you know, when we had the vote, but everybody in the chamber figured I was a dead man."

Joe quickly realized that Crosbie would never be one of the palace eunuchs that passed for cabinet ministers in the era of development at any cost. In exchange for assuming his collective responsibility for cabinet policy, the young minister demanded more financial information on megaprojects like the Churchill Falls hydro development. Crosbie openly defied the premier over his cherished "third mill," an abortive effort by John Shaheen to add another pulp-and-paper operation to Newfoundland's industrial map. He also opposed an outlandish enterprise promoted by John C. Doyle in which trees harvested in Labrador would be shipped to Stephenville for manufacture into linerboard. Despite Doyle's glowing predictions for the $150-million enterprise, Crosbie knew that there were no favourable feasibility studies and believed that the whole concept was "insanity." After repeated confrontations with Smallwood over escalating costs on the linerboard project, the premier agreed to have John Crosbie, Clyde Wells and Alex Hickman negotiate with Doyle on behalf of the government. But it was mere tokenism aimed at appeasing his young lions. Whenever Doyle ran into a roadblock on the project, he simply did an end run around Smallwood's talented negotiating team and got what he wanted directly from the premier.

To John Crosbie, it was part of a grossly irresponsible, seat-of-the-pants fiscal policy that was fast bringing Newfoundland to ruin. A recent royal commission on economic prospects had laid out several reasonable recommendations, all of which were ignored by Smallwood. Crosbie had written memos to the premier criticizing the decision to sell power to the Bowaters paper-mill and the Electric Reduction Company of Canada (ERCO) for only two and a half mills per kilowatt hour — well below the cost to the province's hard-pressed Power Commission. The question Crosbie kept raising and Smallwood refused to answer was whether the benefits of subsidizing particular industries would outweigh the long-term costs. The provincial debt was pushing a billion dollars, and Crosbie was alarmed at the cost of borrowing ever-increasing amounts of money on the open bond market for highly dubious projects. Echoing his grandfather's grave concerns about Newfoundland's financial condition, voiced in his budget speech of 1924, John pressed Smallwood to adopt a tough austerity policy, "so that we can avoid a situation where the government might not be able to meet its obligations."

To Joe Smallwood, a man who walked with kings and spent like one, the invitation to live within his means was like forbidding him to wear bow ties or horn-rimmed glasses. In May 1968, Joe came to cabinet seeking another $5 million in interim financing (government had already guaranteed $10 million) for his friend John Shaheen, who was running into problems with his $200-million oil refinery at Come by Chance. It was part of a classic pattern. Smallwood would announce a mega-project before a deal was negotiated, and the developers would then raise the price, knowing that the premier was publicly committed to the project. It was the last straw for John Crosbie and his two young colleagues, Clyde Wells and Alex Hickman. (Hickman, now Newfoundland's Chief Justice, soon dropped out of the troika of discontent, prompting Crosbie to snort, "Hickman fluffed out. No guts, you know.") They informed Smallwood on the morning of Tuesday, May 8, that if he used a lieutenant governor's warrant to get the money for Shaheen they would collectively resign. "It was either you made a stand then on it or it was just as well to get out . . . you know, there was no point in staying if you had no influence," Crosbie recalled.

The crafty politician played for time. Pierre Trudeau had recently called an election, and Smallwood said he would deal with the crisis when he returned from Ottawa, where he had work to do on the federal campaign. That night, he paced the premier's office, "fuming" over the palace revolution in the company of his parliamentary assistant, Ed Roberts. When he returned from Ottawa, Smallwood met with Crosbie while Clyde Wells was left waiting in an outer office cooling his heels. When he emerged from the meeting, Crosbie was somewhat mollified. Smallwood had promised not to permit Shaheen to actually implement the letter pledging another $5 million in government support for Come by Chance, and had also invited John to oversee the implementation of the recommendations of the recent royal commission on the economy.

For a few uncomfortable hours, Clyde Wells was the only minister who stood firm in his opposition to Smallwood. He telephoned his wife, Eleanor, and warned her to expect the worst from the man whose vindictiveness and absolute power he had seen firsthand. Meanwhile, Crosbie consulted with senior family members, who argued that Smallwood couldn't be trusted and urged their nephew to follow through on his original plan to resign. John agreed. Once more, he and Clyde Wells stood shoulder to shoulder against Smallwood. Crosbie drafted his letter of resignation, in which he carefully stated both the reasons for his decision to leave cabinet and his regret that the government's legislative agenda had forced his hand on the eve of a federal election.

"I have now served 21 months in your administration. . . . I have found it is very difficult to express an opinion that is contrary to a course of action which you wish to adopt. I have found that in many instances the Cabinet is just expected to ratify decisions already taken by you. . . . I have found that in your administration there is one master and that anyone who does not accept the opinions and decisions of the master is suspect. . . . I cannot accept collective responsibility for decisions made for me by someone else. . . . I regret very much that the legislation which forced my resignation has come along at the commencement of a Federal election campaign but the issues about which I am concerned are Provincial issues and not Federal. It is my intention to support the Federal Liberal candidate in this province and to vote for Mr. Joseph O'Keefe in St. John's East.

Yours Faithfully, John Crosbie."

On the morning of May 14, 1968, Crosbie and Wells were summoned to the premier's office for the final time. The night before, Smallwood had called in his private secretary, Betty Duff, who was famous in the building for her ability to take letter-perfect dictation at the rate of 300 words a minute. With Ed Roberts listening at the door, Smallwood taxed her abilities to the full as he reeled off a letter dated May 13, 1968, dismissing John Crosbie. With Crosbie and Wells standing in front of him, Joe asked if they had changed their minds about resigning. They began to explain that that was what they were there to do when Smallwood peremptorily cut them off.

"You can't, you're fired," he said, handing Crosbie the letter he had dictated the night before.

"Like fuck I am," Crosbie replied, slapping his letter of resignation, dated May 14, on the premier's desk. "I quit."

Smallwood accepted Clyde Wells's resignation.

The gauntlet had been well and truly flung down, and it didn't take long for the rebellious ministers to get a taste of what they were up against. Smallwood hurried to the cabinet room, where he had already scheduled a press conference to announce the cabinet departures. True to form, the premier tried to bury John Crosbie in a variety of allegations, including abuse of his public trust and violations of his oath of cabinet secrecy. He accused Crosbie family members of trying to extort government business from John Shaheen, and John himself of demanding government contracts for the Crosbie construction interests.

"I was disturbed, a short time after you entered the Cabinet, when you came to my office and virtually demanded that your family's construction company be given the contract to erect the new Elizabeth Towers apartment building," the premier wrote. "I reminded you sharply that you were supposed not to have any interest in your family's companies. I said that we had better have a clear understanding that you were not in the Cabinet to represent your family or your family's companies or business interests."

Andrew Crosbie vehemently denied Smallwood's allegations that John had sought government business for the Crosbies: "There was nothing further from the truth. John is not the type of person to ever *think* of it. If you asked him, he would probably punch you in the mouth." Nevertheless, it was an allegation that would be backed up years later by Ed Roberts, who, in his capacity as the premier's parliamentary assistant, was present when Crosbie approached Smallwood for government business on behalf of his family's companies.

"Now I was there!" Newfoundland's current Justice minister said. "I heard John and I can see him now standing in front of the premier's desk with his eyes cast down. . . . I heard every word of the exchange. 'What do you mean, John? You want it without tender?' 'Well, yes, premier, things are slow. We need the business.' . . . Not necessarily improper, just politically dubious. . . . I can tell you his father had asked for these things many times, as had hundreds of others. There was certainly nothing illegal about it — it was the way the game was being played. And I guess he was a little embarrassed and sheepish because it wasn't John's normal way."

By noon, the two former cabinet ministers found themselves scrambling to organize a press conference to give their side of the story. With thirty-year-old Clyde Wells at his side, a visibly shaken John Crosbie announced his resignation in a tremulous voice to a press corps that had already been told he'd been fired. While they tried to steer a judicious course between disagreeing with the premier over policy and vilifying him and the party he led, Smallwood was engaging in another pre-emptive strike in the legislature that would reinforce the impression that theirs was an act of disloyalty rather than dissidence. Although both Crosbie and Wells had made it clear that they were still Liberals, Smallwood rearranged the House of Assembly to make a powerful symbolic statement about their new political status.

"We never said we were leaving the caucus and we had just resigned from the cabinet, but when we went upstairs, our desks had been moved across. . . . Clyde's seat and mine were across on the other side of the House of Assembly screwed into the floor, you couldn't move them, so we had to go over there and sit down," John recalled. The message was loud and clear: either you were for Joe Smallwood or you were against him, and if you were against him, you could forget about calling yourself a Liberal.

When the House convened for the day's business, Smallwood initiated a passionate debate that raged on until 2:15 a.m. Accusations and counter-accusations were hurled across the legislature by the premier and John Crosbie. In his fury, Smallwood attacked individual family members by name, including Bill Crosbie, whom he subsequently accused, outside the legislature, of improper business practises. (Years later, Bill Crosbie would describe Smallwood as "an amoral brute who seized on innocent people by the throat.") The family reacted with typical solidarity, "herding like elephants" behind their defamed relatives, in particular John Crosbie. The air was thick with threats as Bill and Percy vowed to vindicate themselves in court, allegedly with the help of some homemade tapes of telephone conversations with Joe Smallwood.

The exception was Andrew Crosbie. Watching the débâcle from the sidelines, he quickly realized that a public slanging match between the government and the Crosbies was in no one's interests. After consulting with his two closest associates, Grant Chalker and Barron MacDonald, Andrew called a few members of the cabinet and made his views known. The next afternoon he received a call from the Premier's Office: "I went up to see Smallwood. . . . He and I had a private session for about an hour and then he called in the Honourable Jim Chalker and the Honourable Les Curtis, who was the attorney general, and we drafted up a statement which Joe said he would release, which was a retraction of what he had said about John and the others."

Andrew took the statement down to Bill Crosbie's house and key family members assembled to consider their next move. The prevailing opinion was that Smallwood would never issue so abject an apology and that he was playing for time. But the next day, Joe Smallwood rose in the legislature and ate his first and only meal of political crow, withdrawing his allegations of improprieties against John Crosbie and other family members. It was a remarkable spectacle that made the front pages of newspapers all across the country. Quoted in a story in the Montreal *Star*, John Crosbie appeared to put an end to the matter when he said, "This takes a lot of doing for a public man. It is very handsome of him."

Whether as a result of Andrew's diplomacy or his Uncle Bill's threat of a lawsuit, the sixty-seven-year-old premier appeared to be making his peace with the Crosbies, and the Crosbies seemed to have reached a detente with Smallwood. In reality, both sides had merely postponed the day of reckoning. Power was still the prize: one man was reluctant to give it up, the other impatient to wrest it away. The situation was so clear that even a child writing a school composition could see what was happening.

"My daddy was in the City Council and was at many meetings because he was the Minister of Health but he got into a fight with Premier Smallwood and resigned. My daddy's name is Mr. John Crosbie. I hardly ever see him. Yesterday daddy went away . . . when he comes back he is going to run for premier and if he makes it I'll be happy." Eight-year-old Beth Crosbie would have to do without her father for many a night as he prepared to avenge his own father's political defeat at the hands of Joe Smallwood, the only man between him and the premier's office.

JOE SMALLWOOD'S POLITICAL instincts were too finely tuned not to sense his increasingly precarious hold on power as the decade wound down. He knew that the showdown with Crosbie and Wells was no more than a temporary setback to their political careers. If he was to remain in charge of the Liberal Party he had guided to an astonishing six electoral victories, Smallwood knew he would have to steal their reform fire. The provincial Conservatives had pulled off a stunning by-election victory in Gander in the fall of 1967 when Harold Collins upset the Liberal candidate, but the federal election of June 1968 was a far more troubling development for the provincial government. While the rest of the country was being swept by Trudeaumania, the federal Tories won six of seven seats in Newfoundland. There was no mystery to the outcome. Preferring to pass on Trudeau in order to send a message to Smallwood, the Newfoundland electorate made clear that it was time for a new political era and a new leader.

A few weeks after the federal election, Smallwood wrote to Senator William J. Petten, the Secretary of the Liberal Party Association of Newfoundland, ordering a massive reform of the Liberal Party. Smallwood pledged that the Young Liberals would be reorganized to become "a powerful political influence"; women would be forged into "a province-wide body of active Liberal women"; and university Liberals "could become the most influential part of the Liberal Party." It was a blatant attempt to usurp the natural constituency of his youthful rivals. It was also a strategic recognition of the fact that whoever controlled the party apparatus would surely win the upcoming leadership convention.

The sharpest arrow in Smallwood's reform quiver was his announcement that he would not lead the party in another election, a declaration he had made on several occasions after his party's 1966 landslide victory. After nearly twenty years of one-man rule, Newfoundland would get a new leader who would be democratically elected by his reorganized Liberal Party, or so Smallwood promised. Emancipation Day was hazily set for somewhere before the end of 1969.

John Crosbie was one of many people encouraged by Smallwood's apparent recognition that his political day was done. But he soon learned that Joe was a political leopard who would never change his spots. Admission to the September 28, 1968, meeting in Grand Falls to kick off the reform process was by invitation only; John Crosbie was not invited. After a public skirmish with the premier, Crosbie finally got his invitation, but it came with an application form that every prospective member of the party had to sign, pledging loyalty to the Liberal Party, its leader and the government. (Smallwood's one concession to the twentieth century was that it didn't have to be signed in blood.) Stinging from the premier's personal attacks over their policy disagreements, Crosbie refused: "I cannot affirm loyalty or faithful allegiance to the present Leader of the Party. I do not see how, in the circumstances, such an affirmation of loyalty can be expected but, in any event, such a pledge I will not give."

Crosbie did, however, formally reapply to enter the Liberal caucus. But when John began making speeches at reform meetings around Newfoundland, Smallwood had the party change the rules so that only the leader could address these new gatherings of certified Liberals. Defiant and determined, Crosbie continued to travel the province gathering support. In the fall of 1968, he met the secretary of the Green Bay District Liberal Association, Brian Peckford. Peckford, too, felt that it was time for Joe to retire. He joined a growing list of young Crosbie organizers, including west coast campaign manager Clyde Wells, who were tired of the politics of grovelling and graft that characterized the later Smallwood years. (Ironically, both Peckford and Wells would one day capture the office that eluded the man they worked for and who wanted it so badly.) Crosbie's natural supporters were young teachers, lawyers and university students living in the cities who were tired of life under Smallwood's regime.

Jon W. Kieran, a public relations consultant from Toronto, directed John's overall campaign, although there was also help from well-known political rainmaker Bill Lee, who provided a thirty-five-page outline of how a political campaign ought to be run. From the very beginning, Lee was candid about Crosbie's prospects: "We have been doing some sounding out on the prospects in Newfoundland, as they look from here. Your estimate that you have a formidable task ahead of you is most definitely borne out by these discussions. However, this does not mean you should not try."

The early political book on Crosbie's possible opponents in the leadership came down to five people, only one of whom finally ran: Don Jamieson, Alex Hickman, Richard Cashin, Fred Rowe and Ed Roberts. In an unsigned campaign memo, the handicapping was blunt and occasionally brutal. Jamieson was "extremely personable" but "gutless" according to Crosbie. Jamieson's financial backing would come from millionaire Geoff Stirling, who also provided him with a power base at television station CJON, which he owned. Hickman was "widely known and respected" but insiders considered him "lazy" and "nervous on television." According to the document, Hickman could count on money from Lewis Ayre (husband of John's aunt, Olga Crosbie), Henry Collingwood and Gordon Winter. Richard Cashin, president of the Liberal Party, was "little known" through much of the island but "reasonably well regarded." Although his financial support was unknown, he did have another valuable asset — "an intelligent and very attractive wife with her own women's public affairs show." Fred Rowe, whose son Bill was also in the Smallwood cabinet, had "long visibility" in the public eye but was a "poor speaker." As for his handsome son, "Rowe Jr. will not be a factor in this campaign . . . on paper is beautiful, in person is both stupid and immature." (The stupid, immature young lawyer would later become Liberal leader, a successful broadcaster, and an accomplished novelist.) Finally, Ed Roberts was "the brightest member of the cabinet and a top notch behind-the-scenes politician," but "like other members of his family has a well-deserved reputation for being abrupt, sarcastic and patronizing to people of lesser ability and incorrect opinions." The strategists concluded that the twenty-eight-year-old rising star of the Liberal Party, who used television "better than any other politician in the province," would likely be "inextricably tied in to Joey for the balance of the campaign."

John's report card as a candidate had its own share of political Ds. According to documents prepared by his political handlers, he had shortcomings not unlike the ones candidate Ches Crosbie presented to Don Jamieson during the Confederation debates. "There are three basic weaknesses in the candidate as speaker and/or writer — He is unnecessarily verbose. . . . He is boring. . . . His thinking appears to be disorganized and his proposals non-specific." In charge of a candidate with virtues only Polonius could love, Kieran arranged for Crosbie to take a closed-circuit TV training program in which the candidate would undergo interviews and then watch videotapes of his own performance. These sessions were reinforced by weekly meetings with close friends who coached John in Dale Carnegie methods to make him a more effective public speaker. As a political candidate, John Crosbie wasn't the man on the top of the wedding cake, but he went to work on his weaknesses with a vengeance. As Clyde Wells frequently observed during the campaign, whatever Crosbie's cosmetic inadequacies as a candidate, he had two things going for him: he was honest, and he knew how to work.

Crosbie set up his unofficial campaign headquarters in an office above a dry-cleaning store at 179 New Gower Street in St. John's. Sonia Dawe, Frank Ryan, Janet and Peter Gardiner and several other young professionals ignored the risk to their own business interests by openly working for John against Smallwood. Not everyone was as courageous in a campaign that humorist Ray Guy compared to "a particularly dirty ice-hockey game." John Crosbie was on the receiving end of most of the butt-ends, elbows and high sticks. On one occasion he paid a visit to an executive member of the Placentia West Liberal Association in Marystown seeking his support. The man respected Crosbie but he also had a provincial government license to sell beer and was anxious to keep it.

"When I went into his store he turned pale, you know, and started to shake. . . . I knew there was something wrong with the poor devil because he'd been quite receptive when I'd been there earlier." The man had received a call from Confederation Building telling him that if he spoke to

Crosbie again, he could kiss goodbye his license as a brewer's agent. The man's Marystown customers continued to have their Black Horse ale and the Smallwood forces had scared up another delegate.

BY THE SPRING of 1969, the only person to have publicly declared his candidacy was old-time Smallwood cabinet minister Fred Rowe. But behind the scenes, the Crosbie forces were feverishly at work, awaiting word from Smallwood as to when they would get the chance to do battle for his mantle. On July 3, the premier went on province-wide television to set the date on which Liberals would be voting for a new leader — Hallowe'en Night, 1969. Still Crosbie waited. Only after the decision was made to establish Liberal associations in each of Newfoundland's forty-two electoral districts, which would in turn be sending delegates to the upcoming leadership convention, did he officially throw his hat into the ring. "You know," he told *Evening Telegram* reporter Ron Crocker, "whatever I've been involved in I've wanted to get to the top of it. Whether in law, business, Kinsmen, university clubs or politics I've wanted the top job because that's where things get accomplished."

At long last, the prize seemed to be within reach. In a one-on-one fight with Fred Rowe, John Crosbie was almost certain to emerge the victor. Even after Alex Hickman belatedly entered the race, the Crosbie forces never felt the result was in doubt. But just when he could see himself in the premier's chair, where Joe had had him photographed when he entered the cabinet as a green city councillor, a political earthquake struck Newfoundland politics. While campaigning on the Burin Peninsula, Crosbie received a tip that Smallwood was about to postpone the Liberal leadership convention he had already announced and to cancel his plans to retire. Crosbie raced back to St. John's to denounce the premier for this spectacular breach of faith. But whether Smallwood had cold feet or not, there was no stopping the promised leadership convention. Liberal associations had already been formed in over two-thirds of the electoral districts, and their officers "raised hell" at the prospect of a delay.

The stage was now set for the biggest shock of all. Realizing that he couldn't block the convention and that Crosbie would coast to victory over his chosen candidate, Smallwood forced Fred Rowe to withdraw from the race and announced his own candidacy — a course of action he had decided on at the Peninsula Hotel in Hong Kong during a recent round-the-world tour. Declaring that he would not be "dictated to by any man who could actually taste ambition," the most successful political warhorse in the country defiantly drew the line in the sand: "No man is going to boot me out." In the twilight of the emperor, the last absurdity was about to unfold; Joe Smallwood was now running to replace himself.

From the moment Smallwood entered the leadership race, it was all over but the jeering. In each district, there were six executive members of the Liberal association and an elected slate of thirty-four delegates. Since Smallwood had handpicked most of the people who served on the Liberal executive during the period when he was "reorganizing" the party, it was a relatively easy matter to get his slates elected. Long before the 1,750 delegates, alternates and party members poured into St. John's Memorial Stadium, the matter had been decided in the bulging troughs of constituency politicking. The Smallwood forces, backed by Shaheen and Doyle, would spend an estimated $1.5 million in their bid to hold on to power. "By that time I was beyond being reasoned with, and I also didn't realize what this was going to cost us in money as well as time and effort, so I continued on in the race," John remembered.

ON A COOL, blustery day, with sleet falling from a leaden October sky, the civil war within the Liberal Party moved onto its final battlefield — Memorial Stadium in the city of St. John's. The police were expecting the worst; all 209 members of the Newfoundland Constabulary were placed on standby duty for the weekend convention and plainclothes RCMP officers circulated among the rambunctious crowds. Hotels were overflowing with delegates so the *William Carson,* a ferry then in dry dock in the CNR shipyard in St. John's, was used to put up 212 people. Since liquor was flowing like the Labrador current, the vessel was ringed by ten train cars to prevent tipsy delegates from falling into the twenty-seven-foot-deep dry dock. Seventeen cars from the legendary "Newfie Bullet" were pressed into service to accommodate a further 304 delegates, including Joe Smallwood. The wily politician had purposely chosen to be billeted with the outport voters he knew would be the key to keeping him in power. "I'm still a bayman," he had crowed over and over again as he toured the outports with his trusty bullhorn in hand.

Smallwood, Crosbie and Hickman all had their hospitality suites at the Holiday Inn, where the Crosbie camp, wearing their famous "red badges of courage" with the red Crosbie "C" emblazoned on a field of white, whooped it up on Friday night with Harry Hibbs and the Caribou Showband. At one point, John himself mounted the stage to sing the Crosbie campaign song, "John was every inch a Liberal." A fight broke out on the fourth floor between an irritated Smallwood worker and a man wearing an "Alex" button on his lapel who kept shouting, "I'm for Joey, King of Welfare." It was Hallowe'en, it was a political convention in Newfoundland, and the bedlam was *de rigueur.*

On his way into Memorial Stadium on voting day, Crosbie was met by a Hickman campaign worker who fastened a yellow Hickman button to his lapel. Later, when Crosbie workers clapped nearly as enthusiastically for Hickman as they did for their own candidate, rumours began to fly of an eleventh-hour alliance to stop Smallwood. John spent the day meeting with small groups of delegates, most of them from the Smallwood camp, in a last-ditch attempt to switch their allegiance. But in his heart of hearts, Crosbie could read the writing on the wall. A few days earlier, in acknowledging a donation to his campaign, he had written: "The odds appear to be against us but we still have a good fighting chance and there may be some surprises in store. No matter whether we are successful or not, I certainly do not intend to cease the struggle."

When it came time for the speeches, Newfoundland's version of the David and Goliath story unfolded in the tropical zones of Memorial Stadium, where the temperature got so steamy that several delegates succumbed to heat prostration. Cast in the role of David was John Crosbie, who, at six foot one and 210 pounds, towered over tiny Joe Smallwood, Newfoundland's undisputed political Goliath. Their followers were as different as their physical statures: John's supporters, young and vibrant, included the so-called Crosbie Girls decked out in their snappy red-and-white custom outfits; Smallwood's workers were dull but confident, a solid phalanx of grey immune to every blandishment from the other side. When Crosbie spoke of reform and renewal, they remained in a loyal trance, dead to any message that Joe was anything but a messiah. After Smallwood led them back through the comfortable halls of memory and refought the battles of Confederation, they did what they had always done — gave him their votes. The final result was announced at 6:00 p.m., a mere hour after the first-ballot votes had been cast: Smallwood, 1,070; Crosbie 440; Hickman, 187. No sooner had the vote been announced than a pre-installed neon sign outside Memorial Stadium flashed the news to passersby — "Joey Wins." For the second time in his remarkable career, Smallwood had vanquished a member of Newfoundland's most powerful family, to the frustration of any ghosts or goblins of elections past that might have been flitting through Memorial Stadium.

For a moment, all was as it should have been — the successful candidate, with tears streaming down his cheeks, accepting the adulation of the surging crowd that surrounded the speaker's platform, chanting his name. But then hundreds of delegates began to sing the Crosbie campaign song and to shout, "We want John." As Smallwood tried to wait them out, another group of Crosbie supporters, led by Trevor Bennett, shocked the delegates by holding up their right arms and screaming, "*Sieg Heil*" at the platform as they marched around the stadium, keenly aware that the Smallwood campaign colours were red, white and black. One of the fringe candidates, university student Randy Joyce, stood in his box and made the thumbs-down sign towards the stage before publicly burning his Liberal Party membership card. Finally, as Smallwood tried to deliver what would be an uncharacteristically brief victory speech, another Crosbie supporter, Dr. Ted Monaghan from Corner Brook began bawling out, "Fuck the Bunk! Fuck the Bunk!"

Amid the ugly pandemonium, Alex Hickman pushed his way to the stage and offered his congratulations to the hard-pressed winner. "Mr. Hickman has given me his congratulations, now I wonder about Mr. Crosbie. Will Mr. Crosbie come up and make it unanimous?" Smallwood cried, insisting on his pound of flesh. In fact, John was comforting his tearful nine-year-old daughter, Beth, who hadn't been told that her father had virtually no chance of unseating the premier. Finally, Crosbie and Wells fought their way through the crowd to perform one of the emptier gestures in the history of Newfoundland politics — congratulating a man who had used every underhanded trick in the book to engineer a result that did not reflect the mood of the people. The associate editor of the *Evening Telegram* faithfully recorded the moment:

"Mr. Smallwood's victory was resounding enough but it had a hollow ring. . . . It was more the triumph of an aged and tottering regime kept in power by a highly skilled and ruthlessly efficient political machine than it was a sweeping success by a vibrant and forceful leader whose personality and charm took all along with him. . . . He [Smallwood] now has a bare two years to find the pot of gold at the end of the rainbow that he couldn't find in twenty years of searching. He seems likely to continue to drop the substance while grasping for the shadow; more speculators with wonderful plans but no money, except ours. . . ."

Crosbie was inundated with messages of congratulation and condolence, none funnier than a telegram he received from his sister Joan, who clearly knew how much the campaign had cost John and Andrew. "Will join you on welfare for next two years. Congratulations, marvellous performance, how exhausted you must be. Love to both — Sis."

On the first Monday morning after the convention,

Smallwood was gracious enough to kick everyone out of cabinet who had not supported him at the convention. Alex Hickman, along with former Smallwood Finance minister Val Earle, didn't stop rolling until they had travelled all the way to the Conservative Party. Four dissident Liberals, including John Crosbie, whom Smallwood boasted he had "buried ten feet deep," formed the Liberal Reform group, dedicated to the early assassination and burial of Joseph R. Smallwood.

But the aging autocrat had one more surprise in store for the Crosbie who would be king.

CHAPTER 12

Prince John and the Godfather

JUST THREE DAYS after his defeat at the convention, John Crosbie was back in the lists tilting against his old rival, encouraged by the fact that unless Joe Smallwood suspended the constitution, he would have to call a provincial election within two years. Crosbie's audience was a clapping, chanting, foot-stomping collection of Memorial University students, who crammed the Little Theatre on campus to hear their hero talk about "round two" of the fight to democratize the Liberal Party. Many of the students in the audience that day had marched around Memorial Stadium directing *Sieg Heils* at the triumphant but wounded figure on centre stage, and later joined the president of their student council, Randy Joyce, in a public burning of their Liberal membership cards.

Dismissing Smallwood's boast that he had buried his upstart former cabinet minister, Crosbie bellowed, "Smallwood nor no one else is ever going to bury me. There is room for rebels in the Liberal Party. They will take over the party." Applause punctuated his emotional address, and the students waved Crosbie banners they had saved from the convention. When John rhetorically asked if they wanted him to continue the fight against Smallwood, they gave him a standing ovation. (It was a far cry from the treatment Smallwood would get when he subsequently visited the College of

Trades and Technology. After rhetorically asking the students there if they thought he was a liar, Joe was drowned out by their resounding "yes," prompting him to storm out in a huff.) When Crosbie had finished, a student shouted, "Why don't you lead the PC Party?" It was a question John would face many times during the coming year. "Because I'm still a Liberal," came his terse reply, though beneath the partisan exterior beat the heart of a political pragmatist.

Evidence quickly mounted that Smallwood's convention triumph had been very much a Pyrrhic victory. Smallwood biographer Richard Gwyn elegized in *Saturday Night* magazine that Joe had won a convention and lost a political mandate; one of John's supporters wrote to him complaining of a Liberal Party that was "thriving on lies, deceit, and intimidation"; finally, a survey of Liberals after the convention showed that 65 percent of respondents wanted John to take over the party by attracting new members and capturing the district executives — the very thing he had failed to do at the recent convention. Virtually no one wanted him to sit as an Independent Liberal or to found a new political party. Reading the political tea leaves as best he could, and drawing comfort from the fact that 38 percent of the delegates to the convention had voted against Smallwood, Crosbie continued to sit in the House of Assembly as a member of the new Liberal Reform group, ready to pick up the crown when Smallwood finally stepped down as he'd promised to do before the next election.

John was bitter about the staggering cost of his unsuccessful leadership campaign. On January 22, 1970, he received a dunning letter from his own campaign manager, Jon Kieran, complaining that he had had to suspend payments to his Newfoundland creditors because the Crosbie camp hadn't paid its bills: "I am uncomfortable about this. . . . Barron [MacDonald] and Andrew [Crosbie] have assured our office that these accounts would be paid promptly . . . but that goes back to November. . . . I would be very grateful if you could expedite payment of both accounts so that we can do the same for those to whom we owe money. . . . Meanwhile, warm regards to Jane and good luck with That Old Bastard when the House opens."

Eleven days later, a disgruntled and disillusioned John Crosbie replied that the bill would be paid in full if Kieran insisted. But he also expressed his displeasure with the way campaign finances had been managed, primarily because total costs had ballooned from an estimated $250,000 to actual expenditures of $460,000. "Certainly if I had known at any stage that there might be an expenditure involved of that kind of money," Crosbie wrote, "I would have either ceased the campaign or changed drastically the way in which the campaign was being run and money spent. The expenditure of this vast sum of money on such a campaign as this indicates certainly poor management and loose control to say the least. . . . The information I have given you on the cost of my campaign is, of course, confidential as I would never want that to get out."

Crosbie nursed his private wounds and worked out a deal with brother Andrew that featured the exchange of more stock in Crosbie and Company for the retirement of his political debt, a transaction Andrew would later say cost him $500,000. John had learned an important lesson. Four-legged pretenders to one side, politics was the real sport of kings and the consequences of losing could quickly empty the most extravagantly endowed royal treasury; never again in his lengthy political career would John Crosbie personally pick up the tab for any of his campaigns (or many lunches for that matter, to the amusement of some of his closest friends).

With his financial lumps behind him, he spent the next eighteen months treating his convention loss as a temporary setback on the road to ousting Smallwood as Liberal leader and premier. Joe would later describe John as "the most pig-headed, determined, self-willed, self-opinionated, prodigious worker" he had ever met. Together with three Liberal Reform colleagues, five Conservatives and one New Labrador party member, Crosbie took part in the daily Opposition muggings of the premier over an economic program that had become a national joke. A cool hundred million dollars in government bonds were about to come due and Smallwood's approach to redeeming them was to "roll them over," a breezy euphemism for more borrowings.

Denis Groom, Smallwood's highly respected financial adviser, resigned his position in 1970 just four years into a lucrative ten-year contract because of the premier's refusal to follow sound advice. When Crosbie asked Smallwood to establish a select committee of the legislature to investigate the financially troubled Come by Chance oil refinery project, the premier rushed to the defence of its promoter, John Shaheen, who he said had "the unquenchable courage of a John Doyle." He also lashed out at Clyde Wells for his "indefensible slander" of Shaheen. "He sees him as virtually a criminal — well, the president of the United States doesn't," Smallwood crowed. The president of the day, Shaheen's former lawyer, was one Richard Milhous Nixon.

By March 1970, the Toronto *Telegram* was reporting that some critics were advocating that Newfoundland be placed under federal trusteeship as its provincial debt edged toward the billion-dollar mark. The province had come a long way since the days of its $45-million surplus — all of it fiscally downhill. No one understood better what would happen if Confederation ended in a latter-day form of Commission of Government than Newfoundland's seventy-year-old premier, but no one was less able to call off the economic circus than its chief ringmaster. After just three weeks of facing the unfriendly fire of a rejuvenated Opposition — one that now boasted several ex-cabinet colleagues, including his former minister of Finance who liked to remind the premier that he had kept a careful diary of his years in cabinet — Smallwood adjourned the legislature. With four cabinet ministers and John Shaheen in tow, he flew off to London to sign the final financial agreements for the ill-fated Come by Chance oil refinery. After years of fiscal delinquency, Smallwood was finally off the financial ledge without a parachute.

The premier was getting to be an embarrassingly easy target for his sanguine opponents. Joe seemed to believe that patronage, like charity, began at home. He set up the Newfoundland Farm Products Corporation, a government-sponsored co-op in which the Smallwood family's Russwood Poultry Ltd. was the largest member. The co-op moved into a government-owned building for the nominal fee of one dollar, and the province paid for all renovations and the heating bill, which amounted to $700,000 per year. The province also paid a grant of $210,000 to the Newfoundland Farm Products Corp. to defray operating costs, and another $22,000 to cover direct expenses, which had the effect of underwriting some of the losses and the costs of the Smallwood poultry business. When Smallwood was confronted with this spectacular conflict of interest, he replied that he had sold off his shares in the operation. But his divestiture offered cold comfort: the new owners were his son, Ramsey, and his son-in-law, Ed Russell. "Because my son is in eggs and I used to be his partner, should that make everybody in Newfoundland believe I am a dirty, rotten grafter?" he asked.

The answer to that question became easier for the Opposition when, despite the premier's frequent lectures on the grandeur of cabinet secrecy as the cornerstone of the British parliamentary system, former Smallwood Finance minister Val Earle finally opened his diary and began reading to the legislature about Smallwood's bizarre intervention in the affairs of the Stephenville Atlantic Brewing Co. Ltd. During the period that Atlantic Brewing was operating, the company had not only been exempted from paying provincial tax, it was also permitted to keep the $2.70 per case that all breweries paid by law to the Newfoundland Liquor Commission. The special dispensation had come directly from Smallwood in the form of a signed directive on the premier's letterhead. In defending himself in the House, the premier claimed he had signed the letter without reading it; then he made what the newspapers called "a heady appeal to the fallibility of man" to excuse his negligence. The same argument would be trotted out when Joe ordered a feasibility study two years *after* he used public money to build the doomed Newfoundland Steel Mill with $8.5 million of taxpayers' money, or when he added $3 million in civil service and teachers' pension deductions to the government's current account revenues instead of placing it in a trust fund! It was Alice in Wonderland economics, but Newfoundland's new generation of politicians led by John Crosbie was finally wiping the grin off the face of the Cheshire Cat in horn-rimmed glasses.

They savaged him daily for the blatant patronage

practices that favoured longtime Smallwood associates. There was no shortage of examples. Lundrigan's Ltd., owned by personal friend Arthur Lundrigan, was given a $3-million contract without tender to build an apartment complex for employees of the Janeway Children's Hospital in St. John's on the feeble basis that the company already had equipment on site doing repairs to the hospital. There was no reply when critics of this juicy government plum pointed out that the cost per square foot of the complex was more than double what it should have been.

Smallwood cronies such as Arthur Noseworthy and Joseph Ashley also received large government contracts without tender, a practice Smallwood baldly defended on the basis of their partisan support: "Art Noseworthy is one of the finest electricians in the whole province; he is a very ardent campaigner. . . . In every election since Confederation, Joe Ashley takes six weeks off to campaign — he has failed lamentably to endear himself to the Tories."

The Opposition found a boondoggle under every construction project. The provincial government invested $5 million in an apartment complex in St. John's called Elizabeth Towers, even though there was a dubious market for luxury accommodation in a province where the unemployment rate was double the national average. After a year, only 40 of its 102 suites were rented. But that didn't include one of the building's two sumptuous penthouses, which was occupied by O. L. Vardy, Smallwood's deputy minister of Economic Development and chairman of the St. John's Housing Corporation.

Beyond Smallwood's brazen abuse of public contracts, there were also some mysterious operations in which the Opposition suspected Smallwood's hand without being able to prove it. The most intriguing one involved a company called Investment Developers Ltd., which leased retail space to the Newfoundland Liquor Commission for seven of its retail operations at unusually high rates. Although many observers sensed skulduggery, the identity of the company's owners could never be determined. When they were, it would blow up into one of the most serious scandals the Liberals, by then in opposition, ever faced.

With the legislature adjourned, John Crosbie kept up the offensive against the premier's follies in a series of public meetings, including the Independent Liberal Conference held in Gander in the spring of 1970. In a speech that hammered Smallwood for his inept economic policies (the provincial Department of Economic Development headed by Smallwood himself did not have a single economist on the payroll), Crosbie zeroed in on the ruinous Come by Chance refinery project to symbolize the extent of the government's mismanagement. He depicted John Shaheen as a man who had been handed the keys to the Newfoundland treasury in every aspect of the mega-project — free land, subsidized electric power and an estimated profit of $300 million for the developer over thirteen years with no requirement to reinvest any portion of it in Newfoundland. Adding insult to injury, Shaheen would own the refinery lock, stock and barrel after fifteen years for the princely sum of $2,000. If for any reason the project should falter before that, the entire $155-million capital investment was guaranteed by the credit of the Newfoundland government, such as it was.

Every political development in Newfoundland now became an occasion for Crosbie and Smallwood to lock horns. When a by-election was forced in the district of St. John's East after the resignation of the sitting Conservative member (he was caught in a police raid of a Montreal brothel), the premier decided to let the seat go uncontested, believing that Crosbie and the Liberal Reformers had also agreed not to run a candidate. But Crosbie subsequently attended the nominating meeting of John Murphy, a Liberal Reform candidate who went on to run in St. John's East. Smallwood exploded in the House of Assembly, railing against what he portrayed as Crosbie's bad faith, touching off a bitter exchange between the two rivals.

Crosbie's attendance at the meeting made him a "filthy liar," Smallwood told the legislature. When Crosbie denied that any such promise of non-attendance had been given, the premier upped the ante. "That's a lie . . . the honourable gentleman is a foul liar, a contemptible liar, an utter liar . . . that's a contemptuous, a downright lie." Not to be outdone, Crosbie replied, "And anyone who says that is a lie is a foul liar and a complete liar and an utter liar and a 100 percent liar."

As the Speaker tried in vain to get between the two barons of bombast, Smallwood named the two people Crosbie had allegedly lied to: "Number one, Mr. Derek Lewis . . . you lied to him . . . number two, Andrew Crosbie . . . you lied to him . . . that's the two you lied to." Vexed that his brother still maintained a relationship with Smallwood, Crosbie doggedly kept up the defence: "There's not a word of truth in it." Smiling wickedly at John across the House, Smallwood persisted: "It's a filthy lie!" Red-faced, Crosbie shot back, "You dirty scoundrel." Unperturbed as he wriggled more deeply under his victim's skin, Smallwood adjusted his bow tie and matter-of-factly repeated his charge: "A filthy liar." Turning to face his colleagues in the house, with his hands still extended palms up in Crosbie's direction, Smallwood declared, "You can't deal with a liar."

The day after the exchange, Derek Lewis, Crosbie's law partner and the treasurer of the Liberal Party, sent a sharp note to 16 Circular Road backing up the premier's allegation: "I would like to remind you of our telephone conversation of about 2:15 p.m. on May 31, when I spoke to you requesting on behalf of the Provincial Liberal Association assurance as to whether or not it was your intention of attending the Nominating Meeting that night. . . . I clearly understood you to say that you would not be attending the meeting. . . . I cannot believe there could be or was any misunderstanding of our conversation. . . . I feel if the *Evening Telegram* has incorrectly reported your position in this matter [Crosbie's statement in the house denying he had promised not to attend] that you will so inform the paper."

Although maintaining his denial, John's reply showed that Smallwood's arrow had come perilously close to finding its mark. "It may be that I misunderstood the conversation or am confused about it because I can assure you that at that time on Sunday I had had my belly-full of politics and argument about the situation and was in quite a dejected mood. If I misled you, I certainly apologize. I can only assure you that I did not knowingly violate any agreement with you, nor would I have done so. Looking back, I can also see that it would be quite possible for you to have been misled by our conversation. . . . Apart from yourself, I can certainly assure you that I had no conversations with any other person, including Andrew Crosbie, wherein I gave any promise not to attend that meeting."

With Newfoundland adrift in an economic never-never land, the House of Assembly turned into an Evelyn Waugh novel come to life. After William Marshall, a Conservative Opposition member, mentioned Clara Smallwood during a discourse on slum landlords, the premier's son, Bill, the MHA from Green Bay, streaked across the floor of the legislature and punched the future Supreme Court justice in the face. When Bill was thrown out of the House by the Speaker, the premier's reaction betrayed how disdainful he had become of any authority that conflicted with his own interests. "How does a young man sit there and listen to his mother being slandered?" he "innocently" asked. Smallwood was immediately charged with breach of privilege by the Opposition, who boycotted the House. While they were absent, the Liberals raided the provincial treasury, as *The Globe and Mail* scornfully noted in an editorial excoriating Smallwood and his kangaroo legislature: "One might have supposed that nothing could really make the situation worse than it was — but this is to underestimate the Liberals. This, they decided, was the moment for brisk business — so they shoved through $74 million worth of it in less than 25 minutes, unimpeded by Opposition arguments or the slightest concern that the machinery of democratic government was badly out of order."

The question was — how to set it right? Ever since his convention loss, John Crosbie had based his future ambitions on badgering Smallwood out of the party leadership and then leading a reformed Liberal Party into the next election. But it was becoming increasingly clear that Smallwood would never step down, and that, despite repeated batterings in the House, he would be difficult to dislodge on the hustings. Time was running out for Crosbie to declare his own political future. His colleague, Clyde Wells, had already announced that he was returning to private life. It was either lead a dissident rump deprived of one of its stars, create a new party, change political stripe or bow out altogether. Brian Peckford, one of John's most trusted political organizers, warned him of the approaching political dilemma: "It is my contention that continued silence as to a positive course of action will gradually decrease the logic of even considering the alternative of a third party. You will become boxed in. You will have pushed yourself into either joining the P.C.s outright or staying out of the political situation altogether."

The Progressive Conservatives in Newfoundland had long been Joe Smallwood's whipping boys and he relished reminding them of their political impotence. But with the emergence of a new Tory leader, all that changed. Frank Duff Moores came equipped with "balls as big as church bells," according to his jubilant supporters. Before capturing the leadership of the provincial Conservatives, Moores had been a federal member of parliament and the president of the national Progressive Conservative Party. During Moores's 1968 federal campaign, in which the PCs stunned the Liberals by capturing six of seven seats, Smallwood had worked very hard for Frank's defeat, calling him "the wealthy young man who bled the fishermen," a reference to the fortune Frank had made from the sale of the family fish business. Nevertheless, he romped to victory, winning the poll in which Smallwood himself voted by a 2 to 1 margin.

Worn down by his wars with Smallwood but more obsessed than ever with driving him out of office, John Crosbie sensed a powerful ally and a political winner in the charmer from Harbour Grace. But could he ever abandon his Liberal roots? Wife Jane presented another option: "John thought he was born a Liberal and he had to die one, and he agonized a long time, and I said, 'Well, get the hell out of politics anyway, why stay in?' " The two-word answer was Joe Smallwood. On June 3, 1971, John Crosbie joined the Progressive Conservative Party. "When he called to let me know what he was doing, I told him I had already joined the PCs a week before," former Crosbie campaign worker Brian Peckford recalled. Crosbie was spared the trouble of having to cross the floor thanks to the premier, who had already moved his desk in 1968. "I decided," he recalled, "that there was no way, you know, no other way of stopping Smallwood."

UNBEKNOWNST TO JOHN, five months before he officially changed his political spots, he had come tantalizingly close to ending Smallwood's stranglehold on power all on his own. Stung by the vitriolic reaction he had inspired in the youth wing of the party and driven to distraction by Crosbie's relentless attack on his crumbling administration, Smallwood had decided to resign. But his exit from politics was based on a plan as bizarre as his most wild-eyed industrial daydream: Joe would leave Confederation Building, but not before handing the premier's job to the one person his arch-enemy, John Crosbie, could never vilify — his own brother, Andrew.

In both 1969 and 1970, articles appeared in *The Daily News* (purchased by the Crosbies in October 1967), suggesting that Andrew might succeed Smallwood as Liberal leader. It was an interesting speculation. Half a dozen other names continually cropped up in the press as possible successors to Joe, usually revealing more about their current standing with the premier than any real possibility of succeeding him. But on the night of January 12, 1971, Andrew was elevated into a different category from the Don Jamiesons, Bill Rowes or Richard Cashins of the party. He received a telephone call from Smallwood's right-hand man, O. L. "Al" Vardy, who asked Andrew to attend a mysterious meeting in Montreal: "He said he wanted to meet me on behalf of Joe, and he couldn't see me in St. John's, it had to be out of the province, and he wanted it quickly, like the next day."

Andrew was cautious but curious. He knew that Vardy was quite capable of using the premier's name to advance his own projects, but he also knew that Smallwood was in difficulty. He suspected that this time the invitation was bona fide and the agenda would turn out to be political — possibly an invitation to shore up sagging Liberal fortunes by running in a by-election. Andrew called Vardy back and agreed to the Montreal meeting, which took place at John C. Doyle's suite in the Port Cartier apartment buildings on the corner of Sherbrooke and Peel.

The men met at seven o'clock. The florid and fleshy Doyle puffed on a La Primadora cigar as he poured fine burgundy into crystal wine glasses and regaled his youthful guest with the same beguiling monologues that had so mesmerized Joe Smallwood. Vardy, his round face an inscrutable mask, restlessly shifted his stout body in his chair and said little. After an hour of social chatting, Vardy got up to leave and asked Andrew to accompany him. There was no mention of where they were going.

The two men put on their coats. Vardy turned up his collar and pulled his fedora low over his forehead, leaving him "looking like a fella from the C.I.A." Outside, they hailed a cab and drove to the top of Mount Royal. Vardy then dismissed the taxi. With the city glittering coldly below them and their breath making white plumes that rose and vanished on the frosty air, Joe's emissary finally revealed the purpose of the meeting.

"We were on top of the mountain. I don't know what's behind a tree or what's coming down off the mountain — it's a way out feeling," he recalled. "I don't know if I found it all comical or nerve-wracking. We started to walk along and Al asked me — on behalf of Joe — if I would consider being the premier, taking over from Joe." The gold fillings in Andrew's teeth had been aching in the cold, but the pain was suddenly gone. History had unexpectedly come calling, and, numb with surprise, he listened carefully to the rest of what Vardy had to say.

Over the next two days in Montreal, Andrew considered Vardy's proposition from every angle. Without making up his mind, he headed back to Newfoundland, half concluding that the whole affair had been a whim of Al Vardy's. But the day after his return to St. John's, he received another telephone call from Vardy asking him to come to his penthouse suite in Elizabeth Towers for a meeting with Smallwood himself. Andrew was told not to drive his signature Rolls Royce and to come around to the back of the building where Vardy would be waiting for him. Curious, and always ready to meet the premier, Andrew borrowed a relative's car and met Vardy at the basement door of Elizabeth Towers.

Andrew walked into the penthouse apartment to find Joe already waiting impatiently to shepherd him into Vardy's den. No sooner had Vardy left the room than Joe turned on a radio and began talking. Andrew was having trouble hearing him and asked why the radio was being played so loudly. Smallwood explained that the apartment might be bugged and that he wanted their conversation to remain private. To Andrew's astonishment, Joe took him through the same proposition that had already been put to him in Montreal, but in more detail; Vardy had extended the plum, now Joe was presenting the bill. He wanted Andrew to immediately assume the premiership on the condition that he protect Shaheen and Doyle from the inquisitional powers of the government that John Crosbie wanted brought to bear: "He really wanted an undertaking that they would not be pursued or driven out, that they would be allowed to complete whatever they were doing on a normal, ordinary basis . . . he didn't want a royal commission to go uncovering what they had done up to that stage."

For an hour and a half Smallwood laid out the deal, continually glancing at his watch. Suddenly, as if time were literally running out, he forced the issue.

"It got to be a quarter past eleven, thereabouts, and Joe said, 'Fine, you've got to make your mind up, you've got ten minutes to make your mind up.' I said to Joe, 'What's the rush? I've got a lot of things to think about, business and the other things you want, and all sorts of things.' He said, 'The lieutenant-governor is standing by,' and I said, 'Standing by for what?' 'To swear you in and swear me out.' I said, 'What about your cabinet?' He said, 'Piss on them.' He said, 'I *have* the resignations of all my cabinet ministers. I *always* have them.' He said, 'They either accept you or they get fired.' I said, 'I'm not elected.' He said, 'You can be premier, you can run the province, you don't have to sit in the House. You can have somebody else sit in the House until you're ready to have an election.' "

The young businessman sucked in a long breath as he weighed the dizzying offer, fully aware of the irony of the moment; the very thing John had laboured so feverishly to obtain was now being dropped in his lap. But whether it was the 1,200 employees who counted on him, or the thought of his older brother's face glowering at him across the floor of the legislature, he declined Smallwood's cloak-and-dagger power play. "I literally came within ten minutes of being premier," he later remembered.

UPSET AS HE was at Andrew's refusal, Smallwood was determined to have this Crosbie in his camp. In June 1971, he invited Andrew to his office to seek his opinion on Newfoundland's immediate political future. The deadly courting dance had begun. Smallwood had just issued cabinet directive C-72 '71, which set aside $8.6 million for "special projects" — convenient code for a provincial election. The paving machines were already revving up in construction yards all around Newfoundland. Smallwood had always believed he would have to wait at least a year after the divisive convention before going to the polls; Andrew disagreed. He believed that the longer Joe let Frank Moores and his brother depict him as an aging dictator clinging to power at all costs, the worse the political situation would get. He advised the premier to arrest the drop in his popularity by going to the polls sooner rather than later, arguing that there was even a chance the election could still be stolen before his young adversaries had a chance to organize.

History told Joe otherwise. He had always believed that the main reason the Confederation vote had been so close was that the final referendum had been held in July, when a lot of his support was away fishing and couldn't be turned out. It was a lesson he never forgot. The ideal time to hold an election was autumn, after a good season of fishing and undisturbed enjoyment by Newfoundlanders of the brief spell of fine weather.

In the summer of 1971, however, no amount of sunshine could improve the electorate's mood. The discontent with the government was broad and deep. A confidential Goldfarb poll secretly commissioned by Smallwood himself predicted that the election would be close. Fearing the worst, Smallwood uncharacteristically put off pulling the plug on what all signs were telling him could very easily be his last administration. By the time Newfoundlanders finally voted, it would be more than five years since the last election.

Notwithstanding the gathering political gloom, Joe was still looking for ways to spite his longtime adversary John Crosbie and in September 1971, he finally found one. Smallwood was a strategic master of flattery. Knowing of the rivalry between Andrew and John, he now exploited it for his own purposes. "He said to me, 'I hate John.' . . . He used to say that John never had the ability I had . . . John never had that political charm to be a politician," Andrew recalled. Smallwood was ready to spring the trap. He offered Andrew the post of campaign manager in the imminent but still uncalled election. Without consulting John, Andrew Crosbie shocked Newfoundland and the family by accepting. While John was gambling his entire political career on putting Smallwood out by switching parties, his own brother was now on the opposite side of the fence trying to get Joe reelected. Andrew was well aware of the rift his decision would cause in the family, but he also had strong feelings about how Newfoundland's father of Confederation ought to bow out: "John felt it was a slap in the face to him. And he felt I was foolish to be out supporting Smallwood because Smallwood should be out. I felt the best way for Joe Smallwood to retire was to be elected and then retire. I didn't think Smallwood should have been tossed out after twenty-three years."

Unaffected by such gentle considerations, John was furious at what he regarded as Andrew's fraternal treason. "He was in a rage," friend and advisor Frank Ryan remembered. "I remember him saying, 'If I had a gun and I had him here, I'd shoot the bastard.' . . . That's what he said, 'I'd shoot the bastard.' " Although most of the family backed John in the continuing fight with Smallwood, Andrew's wife, Joan, had a different definition of loyalty more in line with the family's traditional support of the Liberal Party: "Just because John became a turncoat, he expected everyone else in the family to follow him."

In September, a float-plane carrying Andrew Crosbie, Grant Chalker and Joe Smallwood settled noisily on Kaegudeck Lake, sending a shiver over the surface of the black water that matched the premature autumn chill in the air. For the next three days, the men, who were joined by Ed Roberts, John Nolan, John Mahoney and Eric Dawe, worked out campaign strategy over fresh trout and fine wine. Banking on Newfoundlanders feeling the same emotional debt to Smallwood that he did, Andrew laid out a campaign strategy based on giving Joe one last victory in exchange for an ironclad promise to retire within a year. He had shared his theory with ordinary Newfoundlanders and political pros like Bill Lee; all agreed it was the only chance Smallwood had of holding back the tide of youth ranged against him. Reluctantly, Smallwood gave Andrew his agreement in writing that if he won the 1971 election, he would retire within a year. Despite Joe's unshakeable conviction that he could always count on thirty-four of Newfoundland's forty-two seats no matter how rough the political water, Crosbie and Chalker knew he would be lucky to get twenty-five. On the afternoon of October 6, Joe finally broke his silence and called an election for October 28. When John Nolan heard the date of the election, he called Ed Roberts and reminded him that October 28 was St. Jude's Day — the patron saint of lost causes.

Smallwood's campaign literature was designed around a single objective — to wring gratitude from a population that had seen its collective life dramatically altered by Smallwood's great political achievement, Confederation. It depicted Smallwood as Newfoundland's departing hero, who was introducing the new Liberal team before he headed into the political sunset. Joe also appeared in a film produced by Andrew, *The End of the Beginning*, in which he spoke about Newfoundland's great men as he strode from seat to empty seat in the Colonial Building, seat of Newfoundland's first legislature. After delivering a moving eulogy to the very first men who served with him, Smallwood majestically left the House, closing its massive doors behind him with a resoundingly final clang — heavy-handed symbolism for his imminent resignation. The only thing missing were the angels descending to carry Joe off to that great legislature in the sky — a touch Andrew Crosbie would no doubt have added if he'd thought it would have helped to get his candidate elected.

It was a typical Smallwood campaign — twenty-one days of Christmas in which votes were purchased for a variety of useful things only government could provide. Every morning, Andrew had his eyes opened a little wider about the true nature of the electorate when he read the fresh batches of telegrams that arrived overnight in Joe's office requesting paving in exchange for the community's support on October 28. In their haste to complete the jobs before election day, government crews often laid down asphalt over unprepared cart tracks, guaranteeing that the "roads" would heave and crack the following spring. Obligingly, Smallwood would supply community leaders with copies of his telegrams ordering the Department of Public Works to do the job. Asphalt machines became a hazard to public safety. As Andrew observed, "If you stood still in the road, you would be paved over."

During the first week of the campaign, things were going as well as could be expected for a party that had no reason to expect victory. Andrew's strategy of inviting Newfoundlanders to send Joe an early Valentine's card seemed to be working. Crosbie had even assigned Senator Bill Petten to travel with Joe to make sure that he didn't respond to provocation from the PCs, who were basing their campaign on an equally successful attack on Smallwood's political style. All was going as planned until a Liberal candidates' meeting in Clarenville. Tired after the all-day event and anxious to spend the night at Russwood Ranch, Joe somehow shook loose of Senator Petten and decided to drive back to the Roache's Line. Unfortunately for his organizers, his car was equipped with both a radio and a telephone — a fatal combination, as things were to turn out.

As Smallwood headed down the highway for the one-hour drive to the ranch, he turned on the radio, only to hear his nemesis, John Crosbie, making disparaging comments about the candidates' meeting Joe had just attended. Not for nothing had John suffered Joe's outrageous slings and arrows since his resignation from cabinet in 1968. Having learned a few tricks from the master, he now turned the tables, needling the premier by describing him as a political Charlie McCarthy to Andrew Crosbie's Edgar Bergen. In a blind fury, Smallwood sent the gravel flying as he pulled over to the side of the road and called the radio station. He raved that he would not only win the election, but that he would stay in office for the next five years and no one, including Andrew Crosbie, would push him out.

Joe's megalomania was irrevocably declared, and the effect on the Smallwood campaign was devastating. As Andrew Crosbie put it, "We could tell from the next day on, we could see that the polls were falling apart. Joe just couldn't be dispassionate. In his own mind he had to win, and he couldn't understand why people would put him out of office."

Two days before the election, four thousand people jammed into Humber Gardens in Corner Brook to hear Frank Moores announce Newfoundland's New Jerusalem. The highlight of the evening was a takeoff on Smallwood by local actor Jim Butt, complete with Joe's intonations and gestures and razzle-dazzle promises to build four new paper mills in Corner Brook and a new park that would employ, "not 20,000, not 40,000, but 68,000 people!" After assuring the delirious audience that he wasn't making political hay, Butt asked, "Am I a liar?" When the crowd roared back in the affirmative, the actor stalked off the stage in a deadly imitation of Smallwood walking out on the students at the College of Trades and Technology. Old age is a station of life measured in many ways, some having to do with occupation; as Smallwood found out, staying in office long enough to become a caricature of your former self is surely the cruellest.

Joe Smallwood must have felt very old on election night driving around St. John's with his son Bill and a few relatives, listening to the returns. When the big picture emerged, it was clear that Newfoundland had arrived at a political watershed, but only just; the PCs had won twenty-one seats, the Liberals twenty, and there was a New Labrador Party MHA elected in Labrador.

What was to have been the Liberal victory party at the Holiday Inn in St. John's turned into a boozy wake. A drunken woman cried hysterically in a corner of the room festooned with pictures of Smallwood. One young man wailed inconsolably, "Everything is going to be cut." No one could convince him that the baby bonus, the old age pension, welfare cheques and unemployment insurance would keep on arriving from Ottawa as they always had since 1949. A fight broke out and arrests were made. In a room full of broken bottles and shattered dreams, the only symbol of defeat that was missing was the candidate himself.

At 3:00 a.m., Gary Callahan of the *Evening Telegram* caught up with the premier at Russwood Ranch. Joe was looking for scapegoats and he wasn't long in finding one. He called the CBC a journalistic "house of prostitution" for its relentless criticism of his policies. Recovering himself, Smallwood then claimed that only his leadership and Andrew Crosbie's organizational prowess had saved the party from defeat. But the facts were otherwise. The PCs had not only won more seats than the Liberals, they had captured 8 percent more of the popular vote — 52 to 44 percent. If the electoral districts had not been so hopelessly gerrymandered, that would have translated into a healthy majority for Frank Moores, John Crosbie and company. Instead, the next two months turned into a gaudy, political meat market where each side tried to bribe the other's members to bolster their standing in the legislature, and every opportunist on the scene attempted to flog his support to the highest bidder.

On election night, a triumphant John Crosbie made his way from campaign headquarters, where he accepted the congratulations of his Liberal opponent, Alma Badcock, a Smallwood loyalist for more than twenty years, to the television studios of CJON. The station had arranged for Crosbie to speak directly to the man of the hour, Tom Burgess, an Irishman from County Wicklow who, as the New Labrador Party MHA from Labrador, was suddenly the unlikely kingmaker of Newfoundland politics. Andrew Crosbie was one of the viewers looking in as his brother made very clear what the Conservatives planned to do next: "He was talking to Burgess and he was raising his eyebrows and winking at him as if to say, 'Well Tom, you're in a good place, wait till we get to you.' You could see the overture that was going to be made."

A desperate Joe Smallwood played for time. In a special hour-long interview with his former opponent in the national referendum, Geoff Stirling, aired at nine o'clock on the night after the election, Joe refused to resign until a number of judicial recounts were conducted. That posed an immediate problem since in St. Barbe's South, at Sally's Cove, the deputy returning officer had burned the ballots after counting them the first time and narrowly awarding the election to the Conservative candidate, Ed Maynard. The matter ended up in court and Smallwood clung to power, hoping against hope that the Supreme Court would decide to either call a by-election or award the seat to the Liberals. The Tories complained that regardless of the outcome of the Sally's Cove incident, the Liberals would still fall short of a working majority in the House and should therefore resign immediately. With Smallwood flouting the will of the people, John Crosbie wrote a blistering memo to Frank Moores laying out the message the PCs should take to the public: "Why are they so desperate to retain power? Is it . . . the facts of the ownership of the liquor stores, of the facts concerning the present financial position of the province, of the facts concerning the additional millions of dollars spent since August of 1971 in attempting to win the election, is it because it may take several more months for Mr. Smallwood, Mr. Vardy and others to carry away all damaging documents and files from the Confederation Building? . . . The only reason for these desperate acts in defiance of the will of the majority of the people of Newfoundland must be because the affairs of government cannot stand the light of day."

While the Tories fumed, Smallwood and company went shopping for MHAs, with Tom Burgess topping their list. As soon as the consequences of the electoral dead heat were clear, John C. Doyle arranged to meet Burgess in Labrador. According to Burgess's comments in the press of the day, Doyle's suitcase contained more than his toothbrush and jammies. Burgess would later claim that he had been offered $100,000 in cash and "a cool million" after he was "squared away," in return for supporting Smallwood. Although Doyle himself would later deny offering Burgess money, asking reporters if they thought he was "crazy," Smallwood's campaign manager, Andrew Crosbie, had a different recollection. "I know that Burgess was visited by John Doyle on Joe's behalf at the Sir Wilfred Grenfell Hotel which I owned at the time, suite #129, and Doyle did offer Burgess money. I know he had $100,000 cash in his briefcase."

After his meeting with Burgess, Doyle hired a jet from the Bank of Montreal and flew the hottest political property in Newfoundland back to St. John's. All day Saturday, Burgess revelled in his star billing, boasting to the press that "Tom Burgess could not be bought." But could he be rented? That was the question that both Moores and Smallwood tried to answer on Sunday morning when they huddled with the maverick politician from the wilds of Labrador. Both leaders offered him a cabinet post, and Joe even promised to support Burgess as his replacement at the next Liberal leadership convention — a promise that was getting nearly as shopworn as Smallwood himself. Burgess danced a noncommittal political jig, relishing the blandishments and enticements heaped on him from both sides. "I'm the guy who's auctioning the whole thing off . . . I'm the guy who calls the shots . . . I'm the one who asks for specific things and I haven't seen a refusal from either party yet," Burgess boasted to the press.

Burgess's shopping list for his vote was long and ludicrous. He wanted a cabinet post but without resigning his position as leader of the New Labrador Party; a promise that any party he supported would not oppose his party in the next provincial election; a doubling of Labrador's representation in the House from three to six members; the abolition of the gasoline tax in Labrador; free school bus service for all Labrador children; and a water and sewage system for fifty communities in coastal Labrador. Despite the fact that the Sultan of Brunei could not have financed the Irishman's wish list, both political parties described Burgess's demands as "reasonable." Such was the state of the realm in Newfoundland's political Land of Oz.

Adding to the confusion was a developing storm inside the Conservative party. Two weeks after the election, the *Daily News* reported that Frank Moores had withdrawn

$200,000 of his own money from Malone Lynch Securities the day before it went bankrupt and was delisted from the Toronto Stock Exchange. With the clouds of scandal swirling around their new leader, the Tory caucus was doubly shocked when they learned that while Frank was away enjoying a post-election holiday with his secretary and soon-to-be-wife, Janice Johnson, in St. Lucia, his wife Dorothy had filed for divorce on the grounds of adultery and mental cruelty.

During a full caucus meeting held Sunday, January 9, 1972, ten of twenty members demanded Moores's resignation and only four members supported the leader. The leaders of the passion putsch were John Crosbie and John Carter. When Frank arrived back in town, red-faced under his suntan, he quickly put things back in order. Dorothy Moores issued a terse press statement saying that she was not divorcing her husband (she was and she did), and Tom Burgess once again became the main preoccupation of the Tories.

In the end, Burgess dithered away his strategic position. On Tuesday, January 11, the Newfoundland Supreme Court ruled that the ballots at Sally's Cove had been inadvertently burned and upheld Ed Maynard's election for the Conservatives. The Smallwood era was over. On January 13, Joe read a thousand-word statement to the press in which he submitted his official resignation as premier. He also called a leadership convention for February 5. On January 18, 1972, Frank Duff Moores was sworn in as Newfoundland's second premier since Confederation.

Stranded by an air-traffic controllers' strike, John Crosbie was an hour late for his own swearing-in. When he finally arrived at Torbay Airport in a small private plane, he crossed paths with Joe Smallwood, who was departing on a chartered flight that would take him to Clearwater, Florida, for a vacation. Smallwood had left the keys to the premier's office, the private elevator and the front door of Confederation Building with his office staff to be passed over to the new premier. Without speaking, the two men passed each other, one to ostensibly begin a writing career, the other to define the politics of the future. But Newfoundland's new day dawned in a political fog so thick that constitutional experts couldn't figure out who in the name of Eugene Forsey was on first.

At the time of Moores's swearing-in, the count in the House was twenty-one Conservatives, nineteen Liberals, and the capricious member for Labrador West whose ongoing game of political hopscotch would shortly place him back in the Liberal camp, depriving the Tories of their majority once they appointed a Speaker. But a few days after naming his cabinet, Moores had more to worry about than what side of the political bed Tom Burgess happened to wake up on. "Hughie" Shea, a disgruntled grocer who was passed over for a cabinet position, bolted the new PC government and decided to sit as an Independent en route to the Liberal caucus along with the mercurial Tom Burgess. The PCs now had twenty members to the Liberals' twenty-one, which meant that the new government would fall after the first non-confidence vote.

Moores responded by convincing Liberal MHA and former judge Augustus Oldford to resign in exchange for resuming his seat on the bench, which looked like a more secure place to be now that the cabinet post he had been given by Smallwood appeared to be lost. As a result of this rampant political body-snatching, the count in the legislature fluctuated like the Newfoundland weather. (The Tories actually posted sentries outside the hotel room doors of MHAs they feared might wrestle with their consciences and lose if Smallwood got to them with his well-stocked loot bag.) Moores knew that to meet the House could prove fatal; not only would his government likely be defeated, but, depending on how many PC flies could be attracted by Liberal honey, the lieutentant-governor might also ask the Liberals to form a government of their own without another trip to the polls. Ed Roberts, who had won a landslide victory at the Liberal leadership convention over Tom Burgess, had already written the lieutenant-governor offering his party as an alternative government.

Although Moores had originally intended to meet the House, he now desperately pressed Lieutenant-Governor "Jack" Harnum to give him a dissolution, confident that he could crush the Liberals in a runoff election just as national leader John Diefenbaker had in 1958. But after consulting with constitutional expert Eugene Forsey, Harnum refused, insisting that Frank had to call the House of Assembly together and elect a Speaker. Knowing that the Liberals would have the numbers to defeat him in the legislature if he tried to govern, Moores asked Harnum if he would grant a dissolution in the event of a tie in the House. Acknowledging that such a turn of events would bring the apparatus of government to a halt, Harnum said he would. That night, as he drove down the winding lane of the lieutenant-governor's residence in the east end of St. John's, with its stately trees and manicured gardens, Frank Moores knew what he had to do. By hook or by crook, he had to secure the resignation of an elected Liberal member.

On February 28, Premier Moores announced that he would meet the legislature on March 1. Forty members were sworn in that morning, twenty PCs and twenty Liberals. Another Liberal member, Bill Saunders, was elected but didn't take his seat due to illness. After the election of Conservative MHA Jim Russell to the Speaker's job, Ed Roberts and his nineteen attending Liberals found themselves looking across the legislature at a mere nineteen government members. It looked like the Tory victory was going to be short-lived.

Despite Saunders's personal assurances before the House convened, Roberts soon began to hear rumours that Frank Moores might have the Liberal MHA in his pocket. When he passed that word to Smallwood, Joe scoffed. "He said, 'Look, you know Bill has been my man for thirty years. He was Confederate and he would walk on broken glass for me,'" Roberts recalled. But Smallwood called anyway, and Saunders assured him that he would be taking his seat. As Premier Moores moved to adjourn the House until the following Monday after presenting a brief Speech from the Throne, Ed Roberts was already composing the non-confidence motion he believed would very shortly be making him premier.

But Frank Moores had no intention of meeting the House only to be defeated by a numerically superior Opposition.

On February 28, the same night that he announced he would meet the House, Moores had obtained a signed and dated resignation from Bill Saunders that he now carried around in his coat pocket. Remarkably, the veteran Liberal never returned to the House. If Saunders had taken his seat and then resigned, he would have been paid his $10,000 sessional pay as well as a full government pension as a thrice-elected MHA. Instead, he broke faith with both his old leader and his new one and walked away from a large sum of money. In the process, he enabled the party he had run against to achieve parity with the official Opposition in the legislature and therefore bring about dissolution and the new election Frank Moores so badly wanted. The question was, why?

Informed sources on both sides of the political fence, including Andrew Crosbie, would later say such unexpected consideration had been worth $100,000. John Crosbie, who confirmed a financial transaction, believed that whatever it had cost the PCs, the price was worth paying:

"I don't care what Frank Moores arranged to have paid to Bill Saunders, it was justified. There wasn't any other way that we could end this and shake the province free from the clutches of Smallwood and these tawdry types that he was associated with. So if you didn't use their tactics to defeat them . . . then you were finished, you were never going to get a change of government in the province. So, whether he paid them $100,000 or what he paid, to me he was fully justified in doing it. There was a transaction, but what it was, I don't know. Because Bill Saunders, had he turned up and been sworn in, would have been entitled to a pension. Now, you're not going to give that up for nothing."

After the House adjourned, Crosbie and his colleagues retired to "drink her up," and Moores took the Saunders resignation to the lieutenant-governor. The House was dissolved and a new election was called for March 24. This time there was no doubt about the result. The Liberals were routed; the Conservatives swept into power with thirty-three seats compared to just nine for the party that had run Newfoundland and Labrador for the previous twenty-three years. Two of the men who had held such personal power during the zany days of the tie election — Tom Burgess and Hughie Shea — were both defeated in their second bid for office, doubtless because the electorate was exhausted at the mere prospect of following their political gyrations over a full five-year term! A jubilant John Crosbie, who would soon be Finance minister and minister for Economic Development, announced that Newfoundland would be abandoning Smallwood's industrial ultimatum to develop or perish and returning to its traditional economy based on fishing, forestry, tourism and mining. As Crosbie worker, friend and confidant Frank Ryan celebrated John's sweet moment of victory, he couldn't help thinking about the brother who had backed the wrong side. "Poor Andrew," he later recalled, "he jumped back on the ship that was sinking."

FOR MOST OF the 1970s, it would have been hard to find anyone in Newfoundland with much pity for Andrew Crosbie. He might not have been having lunch with the premier every day, and for a period of time after the election things were "awkward" whenever he and John found themselves together, but he was still the czar of Newfoundland's biggest business empire and very much the godfather of the Crosbie family. In a personal sense, his wealth had never been more obvious. In addition to his Virginia Waters estate, Kaegudeck and a summer cabin close to St. John's, he had added a luxury home in E. P. Taylor's exclusive development in Lyford Cay, in the Bahamas. After the 1974 death of her parents, his wife Joan became a wealthy woman in her own right, with an annual income from her inheritance valued at $250,000, according to Andrew, who was the trustee of the estate. When a local television interviewer jokingly referred to Andrew as Newfoundland's Aristotle Onassis, Crosbie proceeded to answer his question seriously; when you're sitting on a mountain of ice cream wearing a watch worth more than most people's houses (it had been to the moon on the wrist of the first American astronaut), the warm glow of success is just a hop and a skip away from delusions of grandeur. After all, who else in Newfoundland could say he had donated a giraffe to a zoo in Montreal, or that wine (Chateau Le Fournas Bernadotte, *propriétaire* Andrew Crosbie) had just arrived from his very own French vineyard?

By 1967, Andrew had moved the corporate headquarters of the family business from the original offices on Water Street established by his grandfather to the Sir John Crosbie Building in a city suburb, out of sight of the harbour. The move was symbolic of the company getting out of the fish business to concentrate on diversified activities in construction, manufacturing, transportation, shipping, communications, insurance, foreign exchange and real estate development. Like a lot of Newfoundland companies, the Crosbie empire tended to be asset-rich and capital-starved, but it was definitely in the big leagues. In his 1975 book, *The Canadian Establishment*, Peter C. Newman estimated the net worth of the Crosbie empire to be $50 million. Under Andrew's aggressive expansion of the family business (twenty-four companies in Newfoundland and another eight in Toronto and Montreal), that number would become $100 million by 1976. At the peak of his empire, Andrew Crosbie was signing the cheques of an astonishing 2,400 Newfoundlanders.

Always on the lookout for new opportunities, Andrew began considering a new hotel development in downtown St. John's. The old Hotel Newfoundland was on its last legs, and someone might be able to make a very good profit by putting up a new facility, provided they didn't have to compete with the existing hotel's owners, Canadian National. Andrew hired consultants to do a feasibility study. They reported that a large retail and office complex could be profitable, but only if it were part of a new hotel development downtown. Andrew came up with the concept of Atlantic Place, a twenty-storey complex that would be built on land fronting on Water Street and looking back over St. John's Harbour — a kind of one-bird Canary Wharf.

The best way to ensure that he wouldn't be competing with CN was to get them involved. Andrew proceeded to negotiate a contract to put a 300-room CN hotel above his three storeys of retail and office space; it would make Atlantic Place the tallest building in Newfoundland and the largest commercial development in the history of the city, with a price tag of $20 million. Under the terms of the deal, Crosbie also had the right to buy ten acres of prime city land adjacent to the St. John's dockyard (owned by CN) which he intended to use for further industrial development. Atlantic Place sparked a heated debate with heritage-conscious citizens who thought a twenty-storey building would ruin the waterfront (Gert Crosbie would later describe it as "the ugliest building that God ever made, absolutely awful"). When Crosbie's plan was approved he had to sneak into city hall to sign the final deal to avoid angry protesters. Nevertheless, things just kept rolling along.

Public honours followed business success, and the two, as if by magic, became one. In April 1974, the City of St. John's appointed Andrew Crosbie chairman of the 1977 Canada Summer Games, and Andrew became the first Newfoundlander to win a gold medal without the inconvenience of having to compete. Ten million dollars in public funds was set aside to pay for the games, including $3 million from the provincial government, in which his brother John was the Finance minister. The provincial contribution would more than double before the project was completed. Whispers of conflict of interest became roars when Andrew's own construction company, NECCO, was awarded the $4.5-million contract to build the swimming pool and track-and-field facilities. Crosbie and St. John's mayor Dorothy Wyatt assured everyone that the contract was "above board" and had been awarded by tender to the lowest bidder.

In fact, the project had never gone to tender. Instead, the seventeen-member board of directors of the Summer Games, which was appointed by Andrew and included three of his own employees, had itself unanimously voted to award the large contract to NECCO. City hall not only approved of the arrangement, it authorized it. In April 1974, shortly after Crosbie had been appointed chairman, the city had written him an obsequious letter giving him the green light for his companies to participate in the project and exonerating him in advance of any conflict of interest. Adrienne Clarkson of the CBC's "the 5th estate" thought that was a story and came to town to get it. Andrew would later tell guests how the glamorous journalist had interviewed him wearing a see-through blouse in an attempt to distract him. But the only really transparent element of the story was the obvious conflict of interest. A chagrined Andrew Crosbie complained to *The Evening Telegram*, "It would be easy to rake off money from the games. But I'd be pretty damn foolish to do it. My reputation's at stake." Andrew eventually admitted that the contract had never gone to tender, protesting a little sheepishly that there hadn't been time to follow normal tendering procedures. Joe Smallwood would have smiled. Old habits, it seemed, died hard.

By 1975, Andrew found himself alone at the top of the Crosbie empire. In April of that year, the chairman of Crosbie and Company, Percy Crosbie, died on his annual trek to Puerto Rico, where for years he'd been a familiar sight at the blackjack tables. His funeral at the Cochrane Street United Church drew three hundred mourners, including Premier Moores and Liberal leader Ed Roberts. An official tribute in the legislature called Percy "a tower of strength" in Newfoundland's business community. Premier Moores, whose father, Silas, had known Percy well, spoke for everyone when he said, "Newfoundland is a better place today because Percy Crosbie lived amongst us." A person was never quite so popular in Newfoundland as when he died.

The personal loss to one Crosbie in particular, Andrew, was best put by his aunt, Dolly: "If Percy had lived, Andrew would never have gotten into the mess he got into. Then he was left in charge of everything, and Andrew got too big for his boots."

The new chairman of Crosbie and Company could be forgiven if his worldly success turned his head. Apart from sex in high places, there is nothing that gets the press drooling faster than the appearance of great wealth. Andrew found himself the subject of fawning articles in national magazines that depicted him as an infallible captain of industry who steered his corporate ship from success to success while his slack-jawed crew looked on in wondering adoration. "He fairly glows with confidence, the knowledge of his own correct decisions, and the buoyancy of his charm," one profile gushed.

It was the same story in his companies. Crosbie's success turned many of his senior employees into toadies rather than sober business advisers. Meetings were often conducted in Andrew's private office, where he sat behind his imposing desk on a raised dais and held court. Colleagues became drinking partners, and Andrew was often unreasonably generous with senior managers, who were given major equity in the companies they ran and were rarely fired, even when they failed to perform. Loyalty to "Skipper Andrew" meant a job for life. Andrew's wife Joan grew bitterly critical of the hangers-on she believed were taking advantage of her good-natured and curiously innocent husband: "He surrounded himself with weaklings and sycophants, but never recognized them for what they were. There were a lot of those, sleeveens, bastards, I call them. However, I wouldn't call them that because then they went higher up in his estimation. Andrew had to be the godfather."

But not even Andrew could control events in the wider world, where a crippling recession was shutting down the economy and driving interest rates up to dangerous levels. The government of Newfoundland itself, which was responsible for 75 percent of construction in the province, pulled back on the throttle and private developers quickly followed suit. The first sign of trouble was Atlantic Place. When John MacDougall was replaced as president by Robert Bandeen, CN began to rethink its commitment to building a hotel in the development. Since CN had to approve plans for the hotel, they had the whip hand. Faced with delay after delay from his partner, Crosbie couldn't go out for tender and had to watch helplessly as inflation drove his costs higher and higher. Finally, he had to go back to CN to increase his rental rates to cover his losses. It was only then that he learned CN wanted out of the deal.

With the very expensive mechanical plant for the hotel already installed in the lower levels of Atlantic Place, it was a catastrophe in the making. CN eventually paid $750,000 to break the deal but, saddled with a partially constructed complex he could not rent, Andrew felt the first shudder go through his extensive empire: "My total loss in the project, my own money, was about $9 million. And that's really what happened. I got myself so in debt over Atlantic Place that when I needed funds for something else, I had no funds, which I needed to prop up my other businesses."

Faced with heavy losses in the shipping business because of CN's artificially lower freight rates, and unable to complete other large construction projects like the Village Mall in St. John's without more working capital, Andrew turned to the banks and their 22 percent money to get him through. With close to $60 million in loans already out to the Crosbie companies, the four banks involved insisted that Andrew liquidate some of his assets to improve his cash position — demands that led to Crosbie's corporate restructuring in 1978. The days of securing multi-million-dollar loans from bankers who weren't allowed to see the company books were gone. So was the financial shell game that left the impression with the public at large that the Crosbie empire was a healthy, happy and endlessly profitable enterprise.

Business wasn't Andrew's only worry in the grindingly unhappy days of 1979. At the same time as the banks were squeezing her husband's companies, Joan Crosbie decided to leave Andrew for a man she'd met on a cruise. The sad fact was that for most of their life together, the marriage had been one of appearance only. With Andrew away for six months of every year, initially at the herring plant and later in Montreal, Joan, like Jessie before her, had raised her four children as a single parent. She had had her fill of loneliness by the time Andrew began to drink prodigiously, earning himself the nickname "the workaholic alcoholic." It was the last straw: "When he started drinking again, I think I lost all hope."

ONCE IN OFFICE, the Moores government was forced to deal with the past before it faced the future. The chaos in the economy was the immediate priority. In the dying days of the Liberal regime, Smallwood had slipped through an improper order-in-council that allowed Doyle to borrow $30 million on European money markets on the guarantee of the provincial government. No one else in cabinet knew about the transaction until Newfoundland's deputy minister of Finance, Dirk Peper, received a tip from a friend in the European financial community and told Liberal cabinet minister Ed Roberts. When Roberts directed Peper to contact the Banque Nationale in Paris, he learned to his horror that the entire $30 million was in a private account under Doyle's control. The transit instructions on the account were to move the money to the Union Bank in Panama. Doyle and Smallwood were immediately contacted by Roberts and his colleague, Bill Rowe, who both threatened to resign if the money was not immediately transferred to an account controlled by the province. When the Conservatives took office in January 1972, Crosbie could only gasp at the monstrous indiscretion and ensure that the money was now in an escrow account.

The war with John Christopher Doyle had just begun. As minister of Economic Development, John Crosbie set to work drafting Bill 55, the legislation that would wrest control of the Stephenville Linerboard Mill from Javelin and John C. Doyle. By early May, Doyle was forced to accept $6.6 million for his interest in the mill, which by now faced a $50-million cost overrun. After years of hammering Smallwood over the Stephenville mill, the government was suddenly in the linerboard business for a short and very expensive lesson in cutting its losses.

Finance Minister Crosbie was appalled at the government's financial situation and brought in an austerity program to control government spending. "It is very obvious that our financial position is indeed a very serious one, that we are heading for substantial current account deficits and possible bankruptcy unless very strict and stern measures are taken," he wrote to the premier.

If John had mentioned salmon flies or dancing girls, he might have communicated better with his hedonistic leader; but "strict" and "stern" were words that made Frank's eyes glaze over. A month after receiving the confidential memo from the parsimonious Mr. Crosbie, Moores asked John to give up the Economic Development portfolio. He had great respect for his bulky associate, but John was an administrative Clydesdale who had a habit of flattening the toes of those closest to him. As one of the premier's friends would later observe, "Frank was here for a good time, not a long time, and in those days John could be a real pain. Next to 'Witch Hunt Willy' [Bill Marshall], no one in cabinet made the premier more uncomfortable than Crosbie."

As for John, although he acknowledged Frank's charisma and political acumen, he was not overwhelmed by the premier's capacity to work: "I used to go over to see him sometimes around eleven in the morning and Frank might be just getting up. He had his own sort of hours, and so on, so he was very much an uncertain quantity." The indefatigable Crosbie was always ready to fill a vacuum in any organization, particularly if it was at the top. In the early years of the PC government, he was the de facto premier, championing a variety of progressive legislation, from wage parity for women to a modern tendering system — a reminder of Crosbie's essential liberal bent. Everyone was impressed with him, except his wife Jane, who thought he was "crazy" for doing the premier's work while Frank thinned Newfoundland's fish and game stocks and pursued his personal version of the sport of kings. But as John single-handedly tried to drag Newfoundland into the modern political age, the legacy of the Smallwood years kept drawing the government away from its own legislative agenda.

One major piece of unfinished business from the previous administration was to find out who owned Investment Developers Ltd., the mysterious company with the sweetheart leasing arrangements with the Newfoundland Liquor Corporation. The Conservatives appointed former lieutenant-governor Fabian O'Dea to inquire into the matter, and on July 5, 1972, he submitted his report. Even John Crosbie, who expected the worst, was appalled by the commissioner's findings.

It turned out that Investment Developers Ltd., incorporated in the 1960s to rent space to the Liquor Commission, was equally owned by Arthur Lundrigan, O. L. Vardy and Joe Smallwood. The company was set up to supplement Smallwood's income after he retired. The partners had then used their shares in the company to secure a $1.6-million loan from the government's banker of the day, the Bank of

Montreal. The purpose of the loan was to purchase shares in the British Newfoundland Corporation (Brinco), the syndicate of financial giants put together by the Rothschilds to develop Churchill Falls. The stock purchase came at the same time that Brinco was seeking concessions from the Smallwood government in its negotiations to build the mammoth hydro project! When O'Dea's findings became public, Smallwood denied he had any involvement in the scheme and painted the report as "an attempt to get me, to destroy my name."

The rhetoric was wearing pitifully thin. Sitting in the government's file was a confidential letter from the Bank of Montreal to Premier Moores setting out the plain and painful truth. "It is a fact that in the spring of 1965 Messrs. Smallwood, Lundrigan and Vardy were granted . . . loans secured by pledge of marketable shares. . . . I spoke with Mr. Smallwood and Mr. Lundrigan and informed them of the basis on which we would accommodate them, with the understanding that advances would be repaid as soon as possible, to which they agreed," the bank's president wrote.

When the Brinco shares went down in value instead of appreciating, the Bank of Montreal forgave hundreds of thousands of dollars in interest payments on the loan to then-Premier Smallwood, his deputy minister, Al Vardy, and his longtime business associate and Bank of Montreal director Arthur Lundrigan. In the letter to Moores confirming the write-downs, the bank observed, "It is difficult for this or any other bank to sit in judgment on the degree of propriety of financial transactions of persons in political life."

No mention was made of the propriety of the bank's own director, Arthur Lundrigan, being involved in the transaction, and only passing reference to the fact that one of the conditions on which the monies were advanced was that Smallwood and company make all future borrowings through the Bank of Montreal. As far as John Crosbie was concerned, there were more than a few unsightly wrinkles in Pontius Pilate's pin-striped suit. When the Bank of Montreal subsequently invited Newfoundland's new Finance minister to lunch, he curtly refused. His sense that the bank had acted improperly was vindicated when the Bank of Montreal's

Newfoundland director, Arthur Lundrigan, resigned from the board in the wake of the scandal over the Brinco loans. Lundrigan's replacement was Andrew Crosbie.

In making public O'Dea's investigation, Premier Moores said, "We must have honesty in our society, and that applies even more so to the leaders of society. In the case of the persons who will be named today, while many people including myself feel genuinely sorry, one can only say they have reaped what they have sown." It would have been more accurate to say that the individuals involved were about to have their reaping privileges withdrawn rather than face justice; despite the stupendous breach of public trust, no charges were ever laid in connection with the liquor leases and the Brinco affair. A week after the premier's announcement, the provincial government merely cancelled all business with the three partners of Investment Developers Ltd., and the matter was closed.

Although Premier Moores quickly lost his zeal for pursuing the peccadilloes of his predecessor, partly because the Newfoundland public exhibited little interest in a witch-hunt, the RCMP did not. While Joe Smallwood was vacationing in Florida, eight officers, backed up by two more in a helicopter, swooped down on Russwood Ranch with a search warrant to seize records pertaining to the former administration's financial dealings. At the same time, investigators raided the homes of both Al Vardy and John Doyle looking for incriminating documents.

The visit to Doyle's Montreal apartment turned up some interesting information. From Doyle's suitcase, the Mounties seized a copy of a bank application for a numbered bank account at Banque Romande in Geneva, Switzerland. The undated application was signed by Joe Smallwood. They also found a document indicating that $2 million of the proceeds from the sale of Labrador timber rights to a mysterious Liechtenstein corporation, Société Transshipping S.A., were to be divided among six people. The document, dated January 30, 1968, showed $375,000 earmarked for Joe Smallwood and a like amount for his former Justice minister and at that time president of the executive council, Les Curtis. The number 31–323 was listed beside Smallwood's name, the same number that appeared on his signed but undated application for the Swiss bank account. There was no clear evidence that Smallwood ever received any money. Interestingly, the March 3, 1965 letter granting the timber concession to Société Transshipping appeared to be "a fabrication." At least that was the opinion of Pierre Bourque, a lawyer who looked into the deal as part of an investigation into Canadian Javelin Ltd. by the Restrictive Trade Practices Commission (RTPC) of the federal Department of Consumer and Corporate Affairs. The letter granting the rights was written on the premier's letterhead and signed by Smallwood, but there was no order-in-council approving the letter. Despite a thorough search of government records, the original land grant was never found.

Pierre-Raymond Lafleur, a former employee and confidant of Doyle's, testified at RTPC hearings into Canadian Javelin that some of the proceeds from the timber concession sale were destined for Doyle's friends in Newfoundland, Curtis and Smallwood. Smallwood declined to testify at the 1982 hearings, justifying his refusal to obey a federal subpoena on the basis of his oath of cabinet secrecy. Doyle and Vardy were subsequently charged with fraud after lengthy RCMP investigations into other matters, but both eventually fled the country and never stood trial. Smallwood was untouched. As John Crosbie would tell a reporter, the immense political popularity of Smallwood, "the only living Father of Confederation," was the deciding factor.

FOR A GRAND moment, on October 10, 1973, thanks to Smallwood's dogged industrial vision, it looked like Newfoundland's ship had at last come in. In fact, it quite literally had, in the form of the *Queen Elizabeth II*, rented by John Shaheen for $97,000 a day to bring his one thousand guests to the gala opening of the controversial Come by Chance oil refinery. Before the opening, Shaheen had put up his guests at the Waldorf Astoria in New York, where they made merry for four days before boarding the luxury liner for the trip to Newfoundland.

Andrew Crosbie and his wife, Joan, were friends of Shaheen's, having been his guests at both the U.S. Republican national convention and the launch of Apollo 17 in 1972. (Brother John had turned down a seat on Shaheen's private jet to attend the same space launch.) They now joined his Come by Chance party in the United States, though instead of "living off Shaheen," as hundreds of others did, they stayed in their own suite at the Pierre Hotel. The striking Joan went all out, determined that she wouldn't be lost in a blaze of high fashion displayed by the bevy of American beauties who attended Shaheen's $1-million party with the elite of the Republican political and business establishment: "I had to walk around the deck about three times a day just to use all the jackets. My God, I wouldn't put Newfoundland to shame!"

The tricks of history were as bizarre as the greeting the *Queen Elizabeth II* received as she steamed into Placentia Bay. A sailboat approached the luxury liner with flags flying the message in naval code "Fuck off," a salutation from local fishermen who were afraid that the presence of supertankers in Placentia Bay would ruin the fishery. Then, just as the official opening was about to take place, Spiro Agnew resigned in disgrace and the Watergate scandal came to a rapid boil, threatening the Nixon presidency. As discomfited as he was by the trouble that had come to his Republican friends, Shaheen was far more worried by the empty staterooms on the *Queen Elizabeth II*. Two hundred of his invited guests had been unable to come because of the outbreak of the Yom Kippur War five days earlier, an event Shaheen rightly feared would have disastrous consequences for his new refinery.

With the temperature hovering above freezing and 80-kilometre-per-hour winds buffeting the blue-and-white tents that bulged with a huge supply of lobster and tropical fruit, the official ceremonies proceeded. Joe Smallwood left in a tiff when he discovered that his name wasn't on the program and that Frank Moores would be conducting the official opening. John Crosbie, who had resigned from the Smallwood government over Come by Chance, gambled quietly in the casino along with a number of other

Newfoundland politicians — to the consternation of Joan Crosbie: "I was a bit disgusted because the Newfoundland politicians weren't doing what I thought they had a great opportunity to do — meet these big guys with the bucks instead of sitting around the bars and playing the slot-machines."

For the moment, Shaheen's gamble at Come by Chance appeared to have paid off, and the man John Crosbie had tried so hard to drive out of Newfoundland was now back on the inside track with the provincial government. As impressed with Shaheen's entrepreneurial showmanship as he was unmoved by John Crosbie's appeals for prudent fiscal management, Frank Moores agreed to the building of a second refinery at Come by Chance.

The return of the former Smallwood crony touched off a new round of cynicism in a press corps that was still reeling over the revelations of corruption in the previous government. Moores didn't help the cause with his spotty attendance record in the House and obvious lack of interest in the day-to-day work of governing. But despite his own lackadaisical approach to the drudgeries of public life, Frank was no fan of concentrating power in the hands of powerful personalities like John Crosbie, who marched to a different drummer.

In the cabinet shuffle of 1974, John was relegated to the post of Fisheries minister, a portfolio with little power and endless problems. Although he was still deputy premier and minister of Intergovernmental Affairs, he ended up even further from the purse-strings — and the power — of government by losing his place on Treasury Board. The new economic power in cabinet was the premier's confidant and drinking buddy, Bill Doody, who took over Industrial Development and Treasury Board. The more obedient Val Earle became the new Finance minister, and Crosbie was left to testily dispute his widely perceived demotion with a mocking press. "Of course John Crosbie was dumped," wrote *Evening Telegram* columnist Wick Collins. "Demoted. Pushed down to a job where he can no longer be a thorn in the side of the happy trio who run the province: Frank Moores, Bill Doody, and Tom Farrell. To call it anything else is a lot of hogwash."

Although he continued to attend to his ministerial duties as meticulously as ever, Crosbie was becoming increasingly disillusioned with the electorate's demands, which often amounted to Smallwood-induced fantasies. Shortly after he was sworn in as Fisheries minister, Crosbie received a list of modest proposals from the 550 souls of Port Hope Simpson in coastal Labrador, a typical request for what were called "local improvements." The list included: a multi-purpose fish plant complete with cookers, freezers, a smoker and cannery; water and sewage facilities; a re-routing of the Trans-Labrador Highway through their hamlet; fire-fighting equipment; improved telephone service; an airstrip; a bank; and a recreation centre, which "would be an asset during the winter when our weather is most severe, and we cannot play all that much outdoors."

Crosbie remained patient through it all. When a fisherman applied for the post of deputy minister, the minister personally thanked him for his interest and raised only incidentally the nettlesome issue of qualifications. Crosbie must have smiled when many of the requests for personal help arrived with Conservative Party membership cards, as they had once crossed his desk with Liberal credentials. From the voters' perspective at least, the political revolution of 1972 was skin-deep. Joe Smallwood had created a monster, and it would be the job of many a future government to go on feeding it.

John Crosbie did so only grudgingly and under protest. In 1974, the federal and provincial governments offered a $3-million program to fully finance the replacement of gear fishermen had lost that year in unusually heavy ice conditions. A total of 6,500 claims were submitted to government, many of them fraudulent. In the end, the gear replacement program ended up costing $7.5 million, more than double the amount that had been allocated. Crosbie was philosophical in his disgust with the wanton abuse of the public purse: "If a person was prepared to cheat, there was an excellent chance to do so." It was a far cry from his days in Finance, when a citizen sent him a $200 cheque accompanied by a two-word note: "conscience money." With each passing week, the game of politics played outside the inner circle of cabinet grew more onerous and less satisfying. Not the least of the reasons for Crosbie's growing unhappiness was the province's desperate and deteriorating financial situation.

As the Moores administration floundered in a mid-term vacuum of policy and leadership, all that glittered from the former Smallwood administration suddenly turned to fool's gold. The worldwide recession sparked by the 1973 energy crisis turned the massive Upper Churchill power development into a financial disaster of unprecedented proportions. Under the ruinous contract with Hydro-Québec signed in the heady days of cheap oil, Newfoundland was obliged to sell power to Quebec for the equivalent of a dollar a barrel until well into the next century. And although the province had borrowed a record $160 million to buy Brinco, and with it the rights to develop hydro power on the Lower Churchill, rampant inflation doubled the costs involved to a staggering $2.3 billion, bringing all work on the project to a halt. The Come by Chance oil refinery, locked into long-term contracts to supply Kennedy Airport with jet fuel at pre-1973 prices, was in the throes of problems that would turn it into a spectacular $600-million bankruptcy just three years after John Shaheen's Hollywood opening — a failure that would cost the Crosbie business empire $450,000. (Thanks to John Crosbie's renegotiations for the second Shaheen refinery, the province's previous exposure was transferred to private investors and the Japanese would bear the brunt of the bankruptcy.) Finally, the Stephenville Linerboard Mill was hopelessly uncompetitive and would eventually be closed down, with the loss of another $200 million of public money.

Despite his growing restlessness, Crosbie retained his seat in the provincial election of 1975, which was more than five of his cabinet colleagues could say. Adding a little spice to the proceedings was the political resurrection of Joe Smallwood. Having failed at a 1974 leadership convention to succeed his successor, Ed Roberts, he returned to the House at the head of the Liberal Reform Party, which won four seats. Despite the addition of nine new electoral districts, the Tories won three fewer seats than they had in 1972, a measure of the public's growing displeasure with the country club politics of Premier Moores. Crosbie was appointed minister of Mines and Energy with the responsibility for negotiating offshore resource ownership with Ottawa — a subject that would soon vault from the theoretical to the practical with the discovery of oil on the Grand Banks. Diligent in his ministerial responsibilities, Crosbie was much less visible in the political forum. When he was absent for the budget speech in 1975, the press began to openly speculate about a rift between Crosbie and some of his Conservative colleagues. Whether they were right or wrong, he had run his last campaign as a provincial politician.

By late 1975 and into early 1976, the political situation in Newfoundland had been further soured by a series of bitter labour disputes. The RCMP had to be called in to restore order during a strike at Churchill Falls, where enraged workers attacked a company executive's car and then went on a rampage of the town. Local 1093 of the Canadian Paperworkers Union went on a 103-day strike at the troubled Stephenville Linerboard Mill. Although Premier Moores left the impression with all he met of being the horn of plenty (which to many of his female supporters he was), it was left to John Crosbie to acquaint the strikers with financial reality. Following his grandfather's practice of looking trouble straight in the eye, Crosbie gave a speech to the strikers in which he pointed out that not only had the recession reduced the demand for their product, but the wood being used as the raw material in their plant was costing fifty dollars more per cord than wood in the United States. The double-barrelled truth was that not only would there be no pay increase, there was a real possibility the mill would have to close. The strikers returned to work.

John Crosbie was finding it harder and harder to return to the cabinet table. Shut out of the premier's inner council, depressed by the economy and worn down by doing the work of several ministers, he began to look for greener fields. In 1976, he worked for Flora MacDonald in the national Tory leadership convention, turning to Joe Clark when his candidate dropped from the ballot. Encouraged by Clark's statements that he favoured confirming provincial ownership of offshore resources, Crosbie suddenly saw another political arena in which he could advance the interests of Newfoundland — and himself. When he resigned to run in a federal by-election in St. John's West, Frank Moores offered his public blessing. But he expressed his private feelings to his old St. Andrew's schoolmate in a poem that makes clear that Frank Moores was a man fully in touch with Crosbie's strengths and his own weaknesses.

> John, I just got your letter and got such a fright
> I couldn't close my eyes for the rest of the night.
> You just can't leave me, you know you can't go
> What would I do, what do *I* know?
> I know I act foolish and not very wise
> But if you leave me now I'll be up to my eyes
> Who'll make the decisions, who'll carry the weight
> Who'll take all the flak if I lose my first mate?
> Please John do not leave, I'll give you your letter
> And promise in the future to try to do better.
>
> Yours Sincerely,
> "Frankie" (Alias Chicken Shit)

Immune to the fatal Moores charm, even in the form of poetic *mea culpa*s, the first mate jumped ship into a wider political sea. He was elected as the federal member for St. John's West on October 18, 1976 — an ominous birthday present for the prime minister of Canada, a man whose leadership he had so avidly supported in 1968. But in the long run, it would be Joe Clark, not Pierre Trudeau, who would have the most to fear from John Carnell Crosbie. As Joe Smallwood or Frank Moores could have told him, the Crosbies weren't built to follow.

AS ONE CROSBIE prepared to leave Newfoundland for a new career in Ottawa, another had just come back. Joan Crosbie, the tragic princess who had left everything to run off with the handsome John Jenkins in 1958, had finally exhausted the days of wine and roses. The romance that had burned so rapturously in Panama burned out in a red-brick farmhouse in Ancaster, Ontario, seventeen years after she walked out on her first husband, their children and the Crosbie family.

The couple, who now had three children, Susan, Glynis and John, had travelled a rocky road since leaving Newfoundland. During their stay in Panama, Joan was inadvertently introduced to hard liquor when Jenkins unluckily gave her a case of Bacardi rum for Christmas. She quickly developed a frightening capacity for Cuba Libres that alarmed her young husband, who up until then had known Joan as a heavy beer drinker. By 1966, she was hiding alcohol in bleach bottles under the sink in their Hubbards, Nova Scotia, home, which the Crosbies helped them to buy.

Appalled by Joan's condition, Jenkins took his wife to the Addiction Research Foundation in Halifax but to no avail. "The Foundation's offices were right above the Victory Lounge, beside the Lord Nelson Hotel. She would go down into the Victory Lounge straight from the Addiction Research Foundation, and then zigzag home," her second husband recalled.

Hating to go home at night, Jenkins began seeing another woman. The fights with Joan were now physical and increasingly violent. He was on his way to work one morning after a particularly nasty battle when he was picked up by the police: "She got in touch with John [Crosbie] and got some kind of court order thing that I'd beaten her up. They threw me in the clink." The court placed Jenkins under a bond to stay away from his wife. Concerned about the children, he nevertheless placed regular calls to Joan, becoming more and more convinced that she wasn't fit to look after Susan, Glynis and John. After one telephone conversation, in which his wife was totally incoherent, he sent the RCMP and Child Welfare authorities to check on the children: "Joan told them to fuck off, you know. She tried to close the door, and that's when the cop comes up. He says, 'No, they're [the child welfare authorities] coming in.' She punched him. She kicked him. By the time I was called in, Joan was crawling around in the living room, you know, just completely out of it."

A few days later, Joan and the children moved to the Windjammer Motel in Bridgewater with money provided by

Andrew Crosbie. The thirty-five-year-old Jenkins then sold the furniture in their house and ran off to Montreal with the seventeen-year-old daughter of a neighbour: "I had a Chevelle convertible. Put the top down. Loaded the Chevelle up. Betty in the passenger side, me in the driver's side. We drove all through Hubbards, waving goodbye to everybody. If Joan didn't want me, then anybody could have me. Boom! On our way to Montreal we went!"

Joan divorced Jenkins in early 1969. But their passion stubbornly smouldered on. Every weekend, Jenkins would fly from Montreal to Halifax, hitchhike to Queensland, and trek two miles through the woods to the rural house where Joan and the children were living. Buoyed by the happiness of these visits, the family joined Jenkins in his Montreal apartment that year for Christmas. After he left his job at Canadair in Montreal to work in Ancaster, Ontario, Jenkins invited Joan up to spend a weekend. While she was there, he proposed to her and she accepted. A year after their divorce, the couple remarried.

But the explosive mixture of Joan's alcoholism and Jenkins' temper and philandering overtook them again. After five happy and alcohol-free years together, Joan fell off the wagon and the marriage reverted to the terrible pattern of the past — wild drinking bouts, brutal fights, and a string of affairs by Jenkins that finally brought the relationship to a close. It was not that love was dead; it had just become impossible to sustain.

The final straw came when Joan discovered a typewritten note in which Jenkins outlined his plan to leave her for another woman. Choking back her pride, she called her brother Andrew and asked him to bring her home. In one way, her call was a godsend. Jessie was in poor health, and Andrew knew that the only way his mother could remain at home during her illness was if she had a live-in companion. He and Joan agreed that she would come back to Newfoundland to look after Jessie, and to raise her children far from the upsetting influence of John Jenkins.

Andrew dispatched Lee Shinkle, Joan's son from her first marriage, to the Ancaster farmhouse. Having been raised on stories of Jenkins's alleged brutality to both his wife and children by his Uncle Andrew, Lee was so frightened he wanted to take a gun along. He arrived at the farm in a green station wagon borrowed from his in-laws in Ontario to collect his mother and his half brother and sisters. A pick-up truck driven by an employee of one of Andrew's companies was loaded with their belongings. Anything but menacing in his white shirt, a drink held casually in his hand, Jenkins stood back and watched as his family's belongings were loaded aboard the Crosbie truck. Even though fifteen-year-old Susan had recently taken pictures of the note outlining her father's plans to run off with a woman named Mary, thinking her mother would need them in any future divorce proceeding, she still loved her father. It was a day of pain for everyone.

"Mom and Dad sat us down and told us. They sat us on their knee and we bawled and screamed and we're splitting up and all of us are going to Newfoundland and Dad's staying here and this and that. John screeched his head off. And Sue flipped right out. I can remember Dad standing at the bottom of the driveway. He gave us all our kiss, right? And that was it. I was hanging out of the back of the station wagon just screaming my head off," Glynis Jenkins, twelve years old at the time, recalled.

On the way to the airport, the station wagon broke down in the pouring rain on Highway 401 and the whole family squeezed into the pick-up truck, leaving their luggage behind. Joan took charge and they arrived on time for their flight. When they touched down in St. John's around midnight, Andrew Crosbie was waiting to take them to the house where he and Joan had grown up. It was an emotional reunion. Joan cried as her brother hugged and kissed her. The night was uncharacteristically hot, and the children enjoyed the ride in Andrew's convertible Rolls Royce, playing with the power windows until the headlights caught the wrought-iron fence of 18 Rennies Mill Road.

The frail and white-haired Jessie Crosbie was seriously ill with cancer, but the welcome she extended to what would become her third family was warm and considerate. She gave the children the run of the place, which they explored like otters. They were fascinated by the "big, airy and beautiful" old house whose rooms were filled with mysterious antiques like the brass fireplace curtain that caught young John's eye. But when they stumbled into the hired man, the elfin and partially blind Mr. Hobbs, who lived with his wife on the third floor, the children were terrified. They ran downstairs and tumbled into Jessie's bedroom. Though beautifully appointed, the room was curiously evacuated, "like there wasn't any emotion in it," as one of them put it. Exhausted after the day's upheavals, they finally went to bed. John slept in the room used by Matthew, who was away at St. Andrew's College and would in a few weeks be moving out to marry his childhood sweetheart, leaving the graceful and cavernous house to its newest residents.

In the early autumn of 1975, John Jenkins made his last attempt at getting his family back. His brief fling with his former babysitter now over (he made good on his agreement with the girl's parents to pay her way back to Nova Scotia if things didn't work), Jenkins packed everything he owned into his car and drove non-stop to St. John's. Joan agreed to see him, and she and the children went driving with Jenkins "around the Bay."

Calamity continued to preside over their affairs. Glynis had to be hospitalized after suffering an epileptic seizure on the beach. During a trip to the hospital to visit their daughter, Jenkins and Joan got into their last fight: "We got into a hassle and I kicked her. I kicked her in the goddamn leg. I did. I guess I'd lost it." Despite the scene, the couple continued to work out the terms of their separation. Joan informed her husband that their son, John, wanted to live with his father, and that Jenkins could pick him up at Rennies Mill Road that night. But when he braked to a halt in front of the Crosbie residence, a welcoming committee was ready and waiting. "Sue comes running out," Jenkins recalled. " 'Don't get out of the car, Dad. They're going to beat you up.' Here's these guys, these off-duty policemen, up and down Rennies Mill Road. I just climbed in the car and drove away and that's the last time I ever saw Joan."

In the beginning, things worked out well enough for Ches Crosbie's repatriated daughter. Jessie was in and out of the hospital, and Joan attended to her during her stays at home. There were the normal stresses and strains of an unusual living arrangement. A forty-seven-year-old woman would not easily take to being told how to prepare supper, just as a seventy-year-old matriarch dying of cancer would not quickly adjust to three rambunctious youngsters she barely knew suddenly dropping into her household. "Nan" criticized her daughter for her permissiveness with the children; Joan chafed under the incessant carping of a woman she could never please. But for the time being, at least, there was no acrimony. For nearly three years, the prodigal daughter and her dying mother co-existed in a barren relationship of convenience.

Joan and her children received a cool reception from the rest of the family. "We were the black sheep," Glynis recalled. "We weren't considered Crosbies but we kids didn't want to be. But you could tell that it would bother Mom sometimes when someone like Uncle John would be impersonal with her." But there were warm and loving exceptions. Aunts Olga Ayre and Gert Crosbie were as "good as gold," always making sure that the Jenkins children were part of family gatherings.

Although Joan returned to many a charred bridge in Newfoundland, she remained a charming and compassionate friend to the few who entered her lonely life. The severe alcoholism that had been partially responsible for the chaos in her marriages to Jenkins was temporarily behind her. She joined Alcoholics Anonymous and, together with Elliot Leyton, soon to be an internationally acclaimed sociologist and author, did radio spots warning of the dangers of drinking and drug addiction. She also tried to mend the relationship with her son Matthew, who saw her for the first time at thirteen when he was away at boarding school. Although she had sent birthday and Christmas presents to her Shinkle sons throughout her marriages to Jenkins, there were just too many lost years to make up for; Joan and Matthew now visited twice a week, and if she could not pretend to be his mother she at least tried to become his friend.

When eighteen-year-old Matthew decided to marry his sixteen-year-old girlfriend, Joan gave the couple her blessing, even though she was sceptical that such a youthful match could last. She arranged to have Andrew give the young couple a basement apartment in the former house of Bernard Parsons, Andrew's father-in-law, who had died within a week of his wife in 1974. To both of Joan's families, Andrew Crosbie was a pinch-hit father with a heart of gold. "You could always call Andrew night or day, weekdays or weekends and he was there for you," one of Joan's children said. By comparison, John Crosbie was viewed as a gruff authoritarian whom the children rarely saw and never missed. "Every time Uncle John came he'd say, 'You guys aren't allowed to smoke. What are you doing lighting that cigarette?' Overstepping her [Joan's] authority with her own children when he didn't even live in the same house, let alone visit very often," Glynis said.

By 1979, very few members of the Crosbie clan were dropping in at 18 Rennies Mill Road. Jessie's slowly advancing illness had robbed her of the natural grace that had earned her the nickname "the Duchess." The frightening changes in her body were matched by the incomprehensible chaos that had invaded her house. The Jenkins children started "hanging around with the harder crowd," and two of them started smoking marijuana. Heavy-metal rock music pounded out of the living room where Jessie had once enjoyed Agatha Christie novels. Then, towards the end of 1979, with her mother dying of cancer and her children on drugs, the third component of the afflicted household, Joan Jenkins, fell apart. Shattered by the sudden death of her forty-six-year-old cousin, Dr. Jack Crosbie, and the surprise remarriage of the love of her life, John Jenkins, Joan jumped into the fire with her personal demons and began to drink. Unable to cope with the deteriorating situation at home, Glynis returned to Ontario for a brief reunion with her father. In a letter to her former husband, Joan made clear how bad things had become: "If you talk to Glynis long enough, you will know that Mother nearly drives us all around the bend. However, I am a survivor, and hope to get out of here . . . after Xmas. These children will never have me as a liability."

Loving as he was, Andrew wouldn't be riding in at the head

of the cavalry to save his older sister. Locked in a battle with his own alcoholism that had already cost him his marriage, he was desperately trying to keep his balance on ground that was suddenly shifting under the foundations of the seemingly invulnerable Crosbie business empire. The hour that every public family dreads was creeping ever closer.

WITH OMINOUS CLOUDS gathering over the family fortunes, the one bright spot seemed to be John Crosbie's meteoric rise in national politics. From the moment he arrived in Ottawa in 1976, the droll Newfoundlander was an instant hit with politicians and the press alike. (Some observers would attribute fellow Newfoundland MP Jim McGrath's greenish tinge to his worry that Crosbie would usurp his cabinet seat in any future Clark government.) As an Opposition gadfly, Crosbie often stole the headlines with his memorable one-liners and carefully crafted outrageous suggestions.

When the French prohibited the sale of seal skins because they considered Newfoundland's seal hunt to be barbarous, Crosbie proposed a ban on imports of *pâté de foie gras* to put an end to cruelty to French geese. Referring to Ed Broadbent and Pierre Trudeau as "Tweedledum and Tweedledumber," he had the press gallery, and the people of Canada, laughing. Beneath the froth of his buffoonery was a strategic lesson gleaned from the Confederation debates and the battle with Joe Smallwood: the first step in disposing of a political opponent was often no more complex than making him appear ridiculous.

As the Conservatives moved into 1979 priming for the May 22 election, their prospects of ending sixteen years of Liberal domination of the federal government appeared excellent, with one crucial exception — the stubborn conviction in the Canadian public that Joe Clark just didn't have the royal jelly to assume the country's top job. Never had a man paid so heavy a price for the lack of a chin. As John Crosbie quipped, "If Joe looked like Clark Gable, he'd take 250 seats in the coming election."

Once again, fate had placed Crosbie in a political constellation where there was the tantalizing possibility of becoming the brightest star. Although no one dared predict what would happen on May 22, there was a widespread sense that, with Crosbie as leader, the Conservatives could rout the exhausted Liberals and their aging rock star, Pierre Trudeau, whose political guitar had gotten so badly out of tune. Everywhere Crosbie went, he was surprised by the number of people who said he should be leader of the party. When asked about that possibility by the Vancouver *Sun*, it was his vaunting ambition that answered: "That's a very difficult question when you already have a leader. . . . Sure I would like to be leader — but there are very few who get the opportunity."

On May 22, 1979, the Conservatives won 136 seats, 6 short of a majority government. In keeping with his lame-duck image, Joe Clark now found himself at the head of a hobbled government. A month later, former Crosbie worker Brian Peckford, who had replaced Frank Moores as provincial Conservative leader, became premier of Newfoundland. With a major oil strike about to be announced off Newfoundland's shores and a former protégé occupying the eighth floor of Confederation Building, Crosbie had hoped that Clark would make him minister of Mines and Energy. But he was not to get the chance to work with Peckford to reproduce Alberta's oil miracle on the east coast. At a time when the country was battered by runaway inflation, high unemployment, an exploding federal deficit and a precarious energy situation, John Crosbie was named Canada's thirty-first minister of Finance. He keenly appreciated that history's slow curveball might finally and forever strike him out. "I've already been minister of Finance once, and barely survived. I don't expect to survive long this time," he prophetically told *Maclean's* magazine.

Having made the fatal decision to run the country as if he had a majority government, Joe Clark was anxious that all Conservative election promises — including a $2-billion personal tax cut, incentives for small business and a generous mortgage deductibility plan — be included in his government's first budget. Crosbie firmly disagreed, refusing to increase the country's $12-billion deficit. Although the mortgage deductibility program would stand, the man who had already tried to force austerity measures on two Newfoundland premiers now imposed his will on Clark. If there was one thing John Crosbie knew how to do, it was how to get his way with a guy named Joe. He prepared a budget that promised "short-term pain for long-term gain," substituting new taxes instead of the promised Tory tax cuts. Betting that he could excite the country with a promise to halve the deficit in four years, "the millionaire in mukluks" walked into the House of Commons on December 11, 1979, and delivered his first and only federal budget. Watching proudly from the gallery were Frank Ryan, Andrew Crosbie and John's favourite relative, Uncle Bill Crosbie.

The horseshoe Crosbie's chauffeur had given him for good luck held no magic. By a vote of 139 to 133, the government immediately fell after a non-confidence motion by Bob Rae of the New Democratic Party. It was the signal for pandemonium from coast to coast. Crosbie found himself lionized by the financial community, who would make him Man of the Year, and reviled in editorial cartoons as "'the Newf' who stole Christmas." Faced with a choice between Joe Clark's chin and Pierre Trudeau's middle finger, Canadians headed into what *The Globe and Mail* called the most unnecessary election in Canadian history.

"The plump Kiwanian figure," as one Toronto magazine described John, became the star of the 1980 Tory team. Laid low in the early stages of the campaign with medical problems, he displayed a large kidney stone at his first press conference and said it was either Liberal or NDP. If the Liberals made a false step, it was Crosbie who pilloried them with his lumbering but effective wit. He called them "vampires" and "drug addicts" who couldn't survive for even six months out of power. When Pierre Trudeau skipped a party policy convention in Vancouver to go dancing in New York, Crosbie quickly dubbed the Liberals and their leader "Disco Daddy and the Has-Beens." Dalton Camp astutely noted that Crosbie's predominance in the Tory ad campaign made clear who was supplying the real horsepower in their run for the roses and who the party brass really blamed for the fall of the government. "What might appear as confusing to you is, in fact, strategy to the Conservatives. The television commercials are designed to remind you of Trudeau and, as well, to accommodate the popular suspicion that if Crosbie were the Tory leader, rather than Clark, the election would be a romp for the Conservatives."

The political reality was much less subtle; John Crosbie had set the government the impossible task of running for reelection on the promise of additional taxation. On February 18, 1980, Pierre Trudeau won 146 seats and a majority government without even working up a campaign sweat. Rubbing salt into the Tory wounds, he quickly raised the tax on gasoline to the point where Crosbie's eighteen cent increase looked like a rebate. The Conservatives had fumbled the ball horribly, and the party brass were out for blood. National PC president Robert Coates blamed the Crosbie budget and Joe Clark's image for the election debacle and promised a speedy PC convention in which a review of Clark's leadership would figure prominently.

The magic words had been spoken and visions of 24 Sussex Drive danced in Crosbie's ever ambitious head.

CHAPTER 13

Flood Tide, Neap Tide

JUST AFTER ELEVEN o'clock on the morning of March 15, 1981, a Lincoln pulled up in front of the large house at 16 Circular Road in the heart of old St. John's. Frank Ryan and Basil Dobbin, business partners and two of the city's most influential Conservatives, could be forgiven if they didn't stop to admire the three-storey behemoths that lined the street facing the expansive grounds of the lieutenant-governor's mansion. Both men had been born and raised in St. John's, and Ryan, the son of the province's longtime fire commissioner, had once lived on Circular Road, so the impression made by the stately row of Victorian homes was muted by sheer familiarity. Pulling up their collars against the icy wind gusting in off the North Atlantic, they hurried to the door, anxious to get down to the business that had brought them to John Crosbie's house.

But John Laschinger, the only non-Newfoundlander in the group, paused in the chilly March air to watch the sunlight sparkle in the leaded-glass windows along what had once been the city's most exclusive street. With the brass door-knocker at number 16 breaking the morning silence, Laschinger turned towards the harbour half a mile below, cut off from view by the bright facades of the east end's famous wooden houses. One thing about Newfoundland, he thought, breathing in the tart salt air — there was never any mistaking where you were. Bemused that fate had once again drawn him into the very centre of Newfoundland politics (he had worked on Brian Peckford's successful leadership campaign in 1979), the newly appointed Ontario deputy minister joined his associates at the door, wondering what "the meet" would bring.

If there was uncertainty about the outcome of the next few hours, there was no mystery about why they were all there. The national Conservative Party was in crisis. Having finally recovered from the stunning election defeat of 1980, the party now stood squarely in front of the issue that many Tories believed had cost them the government after a mere nine months in office and doomed any chance the PCs had of regaining power in the foreseeable future: the bunglesome leadership of Joe Clark.

At the annual party meeting in February 1981, John Crosbie was still vigorously supporting his disgraced leader and denying any interest in the party leadership. But in the bitterly reflective summer of 1980, the consensus had begun to build, at another party meeting in P.E.I., that Clark had lost an election he should have won. John Crosbie, who liked Clark personally, now strongly believed that the leader had to go. Although flattered to be named to the powerful Finance portfolio in the short-lived Clark cabinet, he had always thought that his leader's resolve to govern as if the Tories had a majority was "the stupidest thing" the prime minister could have done.

Never one to mince words, Crosbie was "pissed off" that Clark's political clumsiness had led to the defeat of his first budget in the House of Commons, and thence to the government's crushing defeat by the Liberals in the February 1980 general election. It was a defeat that had almost convinced Crosbie to retire from politics, an option that was rejected after a long and restorative trip to China with his wife, Jane. From that point on, he viewed Clark as an earnest schoolboy who had parlayed a lifetime of playing at politics into the top job: "I'd certainly come to the conclusion that we couldn't win an election with Joe Clark leading us," he recalled. "In the TV age, Joe Clark just wasn't going to make it." The question was, where was the Conservative who could?

Crosbie was publicly supporting Clark, but privately he was intrigued by the possibility of succeeding Joe if the party itself should decide to hold a leadership review, an option supported by one-third of the delegates to the party's 1981 annual convention. But it was the kind of undertaking that no politician could pull off alone. Crosbie needed sound and discreet advice, and the three men he had invited to his house were the people whose political judgment he valued most. As his vivacious wife passed out the "noggin" that morning — a ritual familiar to all visitors to the Crosbie home — he wondered if the men who had helped him so many times before would encourage him now to go after the biggest political prize of his life.

It was a talented group with clear and long-standing connections to Newfoundland's favourite political son. Laschinger had first met John Crosbie five years earlier. As national director of the Conservative Party, he had accompanied Joe Clark to Newfoundland to meet potential candidates for the 1976 federal by-election in St. John's West. Laschinger thought two of the prospects were frivolous, but the other two, John Crosbie and Leo Barry, impressed him.

Barry was a brilliant, Yale-trained lawyer from rural Newfoundland who had served as Energy minister under former Conservative premier Frank Moores before suffering a surprise personal defeat in the 1975 provincial election. Crosbie had an even more stellar academic record in the law and a much longer political career, including a previous leadership bid as a Liberal when he had taken on Joe Smallwood. Since neither Crosbie nor Barry would fight one another for the nomination, Joe Clark had to choose between the two men. Anxious to consolidate his newly won leadership, Clark turned to Laschinger for advice. Laschinger suggested a meeting with Premier Moores to settle the question of who should contest the seat of former Conservative MP Walter Carter, who had decided to forsake Ottawa for provincial politics.

They picked John Crosbie. His name was much brighter on the marquee of Newfoundland politics than Leo Barry's, and there would be plenty of time for his youthful colleague to run in future elections. Besides, Frank Moores had reasons of his own for wanting Crosbie out of his cabinet, Newfoundland, and his prematurely thinning hair.

Laschinger spent a lot of time in Newfoundland during the 1976 by-election, largely because the party didn't want its candidate to run afoul of the new Election Expenses Act that had been passed in 1974. He needn't have worried. John Crosbie would never forget the financial disaster of his earlier leadership campaign against Smallwood, and his parsimony was now legendary. "If he walked across a nickel, his arse would snap at it," his younger brother Andrew liked to joke. Besides, the fifty-year-old politician didn't need to spend money to be successful on his home turf. Despite a much-remarked-upon awkwardness in dealing with people one-on-one (Norm Atkins would later express concern about Crosbie's inability to look him in the eye when he was sizing him up as a potential leadership candidate), the panda bear Newfoundlander with the engaging brogue somehow transformed his gruff, and at times condescending, personal style into political gold. He won a seat in the House of Commons on October 18, 1976 — the same day that another Laschinger protégée, Jean Pigott, brought John Turner's Ottawa–Carleton seat into the Tory camp. The double-barrelled victory had turned Laschinger into the political marksman of the hour and one of the most sought-after campaign organizers in the country.

Frank Ryan, a dashing promoter with a hint of actor Michael Caine about him, had been an ardent Crosbie supporter ever since the brutal battles of the Smallwood era. As a young commerce student in the 1960s, he was among the first of the university elite to abandon the Liberal Party in revulsion against the corruption of the Smallwood government. A member of the St. John's establishment through his early business career at Chester Dawe Ltd., a building supplies operation (he would subsequently marry one of the owner's daughters), Ryan had been part of a small group, which included John Crosbie, that used to meet secretly at the home of a St. John's friend to discuss politics and to plot Joe Smallwood's demise. Faced with Smallwood's frightening personal power, the dissidents had used Reginald

Good's basement on Winter Place in the same way the early Christians used the catacombs. In the end, Ryan had been one of the handful of people who persuaded Crosbie to abandon his idea of reforming the Liberal Party from within and join the Tories.

The third man in the room was formidable in less obvious ways than either his flamboyant business partner or the gifted backroom boy from Ontario. Basil Dobbin, a soft-spoken engineer who had parlayed boundless energy and a knack for making deals into a successful construction company (and a personal fortune), was arguably the best fund-raiser in Newfoundland. Like a lot of other Newfoundland entrepreneurs, he had passed through the powerful Crosbie business empire before striking out on his own. Unlike Ryan's, Dobbin's affiliation with John Crosbie had been preceded by a short and profitable stint with John's younger brother, Andrew.

At the age of twenty-seven, Basil Dobbin had climbed the stairs of the Crosbie head office above Woolworth's on Water Street and signed on as an engineer. It was 1966 and the era of "cost-plus" in the construction business, a golden age when the government of Newfoundland paid contractors whatever it cost to put up a building plus 10 percent. The principle underlying this system was simple: the greater the cost, the greater the plus. Dobbin shared in the prosperity; at thirty, he was making $400,000 a year for Andrew Crosbie, owner of Viking Construction and czar of the Crosbie family's rapidly expanding business interests.

But despite his rising star at Viking, Dobbin was uncomfortable in the Crosbie empire, which he believed was run along the lines of a southern plantation. He disliked the paternalism of the corporate set-up that seemed to place a higher value on loyalty to "Mr. Andrew" than on productivity. To a profit-driven young turk like Dobbin, the consequences were often frustrating. "To give you an idea of how fat they were," Dobbin recalled, "any time I requested a mechanic for the backhoes and bulldozers, they couldn't be disturbed because they were washing Mr. Andrew's car, they were washing the Rolls Royce so the job shut down."

More concerned with how many feet of pipe he could get

in the ground or how many cubic yards of earth he could move than currying favour at corporate court, Dobbin decided to strike out on his own. In 1970, he walked into Andrew Crosbie's new office in the Crosbie building, sat down in the boss's elevated chair and, with "Mr. Andrew" seated several inches below him, made an offer to buy Viking Construction. "That's where we negotiated from because I wouldn't sit there in a low chair. I did it in joking fashion and he took it as a joke," Dobbin said. But from where both men sat, it must have seemed like a good deal. Andrew accepted, and one of the dozen men he would later take pride in making millionaires was well launched.

Dobbin maintained his link to the Crosbie business empire through a partnership with Andrew, but in the early seventies John Crosbie became a much more important person in his life. There were several reasons for the new association. As his company grew, Dobbin needed more and more legal advice and turned to Crosbie to get it. He admired the young lawyer for his intelligence and integrity. He also found him refreshingly free of what he took to be his brother's imperial airs. But the real bond between them was forged by the politics of the day and the deadly battle with Smallwood. Like Frank Ryan, Dobbin disapproved of the graft, favouritism and reprisals that dominated public life under Smallwood, conditions he had witnessed first-hand in the patronage war zones of the construction trade. The "dictatorship" had to be brought low, and Basil Dobbin fell in behind the person he considered to be the best Newfoundlander for the job — John Crosbie.

The movement to dump Joe Clark, however, was a far more sophisticated call to arms. No one was anxious to openly subvert the only Conservative leader who had been prime minister since John Diefenbaker, especially before a leadership convention was called.

After the pleasantries were out of the way, Crosbie and his advisers vacated the Victorian living room and climbed the broad staircase to his second-floor study. For the next three hours, the four men examined the proposition of a Crosbie candidacy from every angle. Dobbin and Ryan, who had been consulted in 1976 when Crosbie resigned from the Moores government to seek a federal seat, were enthusiastic. They had never had any problem raising money for Crosbie in the past and gladly took on that task. Neither man had any way of knowing that it would take just under $2 million — more than three times the amount of money they talked about needing that day — to make Crosbie a serious contender. But they would have been behind their man at any price, as Frank Ryan made clear. “As a national candidate, I thought he had the intellect, the confidence, the decisiveness and the honesty to be a terrific prime minister. I'd do anything for the man.”

John Laschinger made a more critical appraisal. He knew that national politics was a house of mirrors in which perception gave way only grudgingly to reality. It would be very difficult to present Crosbie as a man of ideas and intellectual accomplishment, which he undoubtedly was, when his national reputation was built on stand-up comedy; as Allan Fotheringham quipped, John Crosbie was the only Canadian Finance minister to have graduated from “Laugh In.” He also wondered if it would be possible to take a man with a political base of only seven seats and turn him into a national candidate — a problem that had plagued another east-coaster, Robert Stanfield, who never did rise above the stature of a fine regional politician in the eyes of the Canadian electorate.

The biggest problem of all was Crosbie's inability to speak to Quebeckers in their own language. How could he expect to win the party leadership, let alone a federal election, without French? “At that point, my feeling was that there would be some difficulty in getting him elected as leader,” Laschinger remembered. “He can draw a lot of people to see him give a funny, an entertaining speech, but there is a big difference in being a leader. We knew Crosbie had substance, but the rest of the country saw him as a stand-up comic. To have any chance at all, we had to change that.”

Finally, there was the issue of Crosbie's health, a not-insignificant factor in a family whose men rarely saw sixty. At five o'clock one frosty January morning in 1979, John awakened to discover that his left arm was paralyzed.

Dr. Robert Young rushed to Circular Road and informed Crosbie that he had suffered a pre-stroke warning caused by a nagging weight problem, high cholesterol and his weakness for "noggin" and fatty foods. On his release from hospital, Crosbie jokingly told the press, "I had a brain scan that showed I had a brain."

Misgivings to one side, Laschinger decided that if Crosbie wanted to run for the leadership of the Progressive Conservatives, then he would be his strategist. The deal was cemented by Basil Dobbin's guarantee of $50,000 to Laschinger for masterminding his friend's candidacy. He knew that Crosbie was very popular in the party. He also suspected that any anger over the Clark government's untimely demise was directed more at the prime minister for his bungling in the House of Commons than at John Crosbie for bringing down his ill-starred budget — an intuition that subsequent polling would bear out. The Crosbie forces had time on their side: two or three years might pass before a leadership convention was called, which meant that there was time for their man to learn French, hone his speaking skills, identify possible supporters and develop winning policies. The secret was to organize quietly and then to lie out in the weeds until Joe Clark, unwittingly or otherwise, declared open season on the Conservative leadership.

By the time that happened, a great deal of sophisticated work would be accomplished on behalf of John Crosbie by the three men who left his house that Sunday afternoon. Watching them drive away in the gathering dusk, Crosbie was entitled to his optimism. After all, if the same people could make a teacher from Green Bay premier of Newfoundland, could it be so difficult to make a national Conservative leader, and perhaps even prime minister, of a man whose family had been in training for the top job through four generations?

It was a tantalizing thought. But just a month later, John Crosbie would have more to worry about than his place in history. In the course of one terrible year, 1981, it was as if the ancient family curse had come crashing down on their dreaming, durable heads.

Despite the cold April rain, it felt good to be outside, where the fragrance of last year's leaves and the spongy earth announced another spring. After a terrible day at his grandmother's house, John Jenkins, Jr., and his girlfriend, Irene Tucker, were enjoying the tranquillity of early nightfall in Bannerman Park. Glynis and her boyfriend, Ronnie Martin, had gone to the Fountain Spray store for cigarettes, returning fifteen minutes later to join the other couple. Life had truly become a soap opera. Their awkward attempts at frivolity were as sodden as their dripping clothes. There was no place to go except back to the house, but for the moment that didn't seem like such a good idea. Watching a rummy shuffling through the park, his black overcoat glistening in the rain, they smoked, and talked, and considered what to do next.

The morning of April 21, 1981, had started out reasonably well. The previous night Irene had slept over, and even though Joan Jenkins disliked her daughter's friend she had been cordial enough that morning when the two teenage girls, wrapped in their housecoats, joined her in the parlour where she was curled up with a magazine. It was obvious that John Jenkins was very much on the lonely woman's mind. A photograph of a ferryboat in one of the articles she was reading launched Joan on a lively reminiscence of the days when she and Jenkins loved to travel by boat. But "the silly, good mood" would soon be drowned in prodigious amounts of vodka, unleashing what the children called "the evil" in their mother.

Although Joan was adept at concealing the effects of alcohol (towards the end of her lengthy stint as a secretary in brother Andrew's office, she sipped straight vodka from an ever-present can of Coke), her daughter knew that she had already begun the mind-numbing binge that now saw her drinking "up to two forty-ouncers a day." Since the fall of 1979, for every hidden bottle of liquor the children had found and destroyed, another quickly took its place. Money was not a problem; Joan had her salary from her part-time job with Andrew, the interest from her share of her father's estate, and she held power of attorney over her mother's funds. As Joan's typical drinking day wore on, hugs had a way of turning into harangues. Glynis's stomach knotted. She knew that her mother's good cheer would soon become the hot, alcoholic pursuit of a relief that flitted and danced in the bottom of her glass like a shadow she could never quite embrace.

In the year and a half since Joan had become an all-day drinker, everyone else in the house had been forced to seek their own form of refuge. Jessie Crosbie found it by becoming a living relic in a house of dreams, holed up in her room with the slow boll weevil of a cancer that had gnawed at her for years. Glynis and John went deeper into delinquency and the darker dealings of the street, trying to blot out "the total madness" that reigned at home — drinking, drugs and arguments that clashed and rolled like thunder across the abyss of three generations crazily compressed under a single roof. "We'd sit in the den and just smoke our brains out," Glynis recalled. "It was more like an escape for me and John."

As the eldest child, Susan Jenkins had seen it all before. Her mother had polished off a bottle of Governor General rum most days until Susan turned seven. In those days, she and her father made a game of looking for Joan's hidden liquor supplies. But ferocious arguments followed whenever Joan discovered that they had poured her rum down the sink. When, after a ten-year dry spell, Joan started drinking again, Susan immediately called Alcoholics Anonymous. Sadly, help never arrived for the woman who had done so much for other problem drinkers. Instead, Susan began to get hectoring, irrational phone calls from her mother at the printing company where she worked as a secretary. Afraid that Joan was going to kill someone in the company car Andrew had given her, Susan called the police and reported her. Somehow, Joan avoided them but ripped the bumper off her car when she hit the wrought-iron railing in front of 18 Rennies Mill Road. By the summer of 1980, the twenty-year-old Good Samaritan couldn't take it anymore; she moved to her own apartment, far from her alcoholic mother, furiously senile grandmother and increasingly wild seventeen-year-old sister and fifteen-year-old brother. Susan Jenkins was running for her life.

Day-to-day responsibility for their mother's well-being now fell to Glynis and John. With Joan's drinking beginning to accelerate, the frightened teenagers called their half brother, Matthew Shinkle, for help. At first he believed his mother when she told him that her slurred speech was just a side effect of some medication she was taking. But when he was called to the house a week later with Joan suffering the same suspicious symptoms, he called the family doctor to check her story. He was told that nothing the doctor was giving her would produce those effects. Joan finally admitted that she was back on the bottle and there was nothing Matthew could do to stop her.

During the six months leading up to her mother's death, Glynis repeatedly turned to John Crosbie, the patriarch of the family now that her Uncle Andrew, "the only human being out of the lot of them," was himself fighting a losing battle with the bottle and the banks. "If we called Uncle John and would say, 'Look here, we need some help in this household,' he'd say, 'Tomorrow, tomorrow, next week, next week.' I would have called Uncle John six times in the six months before she died because I was getting more and more worried. He wouldn't believe she was drinking. Nobody was there at all. Nobody was there for her, let alone us."

If John Crosbie didn't come to the rescue, it might have been because Joan was a textbook "covering" alcoholic, a drinker who attempts to mask the ravages of alcohol by attributing them to other causes; in Joan's case, she blamed her deteriorating physical condition on the behaviour of her "bad ass" children. Several family members would later be shocked when they discovered the true extent of her affliction, never having seen through Joan's artful disguise — or preferring not to. "What Mom did was went around and said, 'My children are druggies. And the next thing you know they are going to be murdering people.' So everybody thought we were just terrible, shameless kids, and we were doing everything terrible," Glynis remembered.

John Crosbie carried on with the hurly-burly of his own life, believing that teenagers, whom he thought of as "nothing but problems and trouble and pimples and sex," were at the root of Joan's unhappiness. In reality, the sister who had returned to Newfoundland as *persona non grata* in the family was about to go down for the third time, dragged under by forces the Crosbies either couldn't see or refused to acknowledge until it was too late.

THE TROUBLE HAD started when the two girls "decided to screw the boyfriends up and become blondes." They got several packets of dye and retreated to an upstairs bathroom. To their consternation, they only succeeded in lightening their naturally red hair by a few shades. When they decided to get more dye, Joan tried to put her foot down. With help from brother John who restrained their mother, Glynis managed to get her friend back into the bathroom until the girls could finish the job.

Thwarted and miserable, Joan spent the last afternoon of her life locked in an unbearable present, longing for a past that was irretrievably lost. Although she forbade Irene to stay for supper, the children proceeded to grill their steaks and spitefully exclude their mother from the meal. It was an empty punishment; by that time, Joan had lost all interest in food and was down to a bowl of pea soup a week.

The increasingly caustic bickering continued into the evening. Joan "called Irene right down to the dirt" and the teenagers decided to leave the house until things settled down. Joan intercepted them at the door, where she continued to berate her hard-pressed daughter. When Glynis told her mother to "shut up," Joan shrieked even louder. At the end of her rope, Glynis shouted, "Look, will you just fuck off!" They were the last words she ever spoke to her mother. With Joan standing dumbfounded in front of her, the teenager slammed the front door and left with her friends.

Glynis's sister, Susan, happened to stop by the house to see how her mother was doing. Appalled by Joan's condition, she told her as they parted at the door, "Mom, you're only hurting yourself." After she'd gone, Joan turned to the one person on earth who could give her comfort — John Jenkins. But when the phone rang in the living room of his

Hamilton apartment, it was the new Mrs. Jenkins who answered. Sandra Jenkins covered the receiver and told her husband, who was on his way to a meeting at the Hamilton Library, that it was Joan. All too familiar with the boozy conversations that moved in melancholic circles and loops towards nowhere, he shook his head and quietly closed the door behind him on his way out.

By eight o'clock, Bannerman Park lay in soothing, total darkness. While the others continued to talk, Glynis stood off by herself in the wet grass and looked uneasily towards the house, regretting her abusive words to her mother. She couldn't help thinking of the other Joan, the funny, generous woman who had once shared a toke with them and at times seemed younger than they were. Or the lioness who had protected them from their father's rages when they were little — the compassionate friend, the irresistible personality. Unpleasant as the day had been, Glynis was overcome by a powerful desire to return home. At first the others refused, but a little after eight o'clock they headed home.

Moving gingerly up the walk to the front door, it was anyone's guess what kind of reception awaited them. Glynis noticed that the basement lights were on and concluded that her mother had gone downstairs to hide her liquor. Always looking for an advantage in the grim game of hide-and-seek they had played with their alcoholic mother since childhood, Glynis was the first through the door. Once in the house, she hurried through the kitchen to the top of the cellar stairs, intending to find Joan's vodka and pour it down the sink.

John, who followed his sister into the house, was surprised to see his grandmother, bedridden at that time, slowly walking up the stairs towards her room. He heard Jessie mumbling that something was wrong with Joan and that she was going to call her son John. Back in the kitchen, meanwhile, Glynis was momentarily blocking out what her eyes finally forced her to see at the bottom of the first landing of the L-shaped cellar stairs. There, framed between two full, green garbage bags, was her mother's pale face, her neck dreadfully askew. The teenager let out a hellish scream. When he heard it, Glynis's boyfriend fled the house with a chill running up and down his spine, knowing that something truly terrible must have happened.

John raced to the kitchen, where he found Glynis jumping up and down and screaming uncontrollably. He pushed past her and raced down the stairs. For ten desperate minutes he tried to breathe life back into his mother's motionless body. For a moment he thought he had brought her around, but then her flesh grew colder and colder to his touch. He raced back upstairs and called 911. Ten minutes later, there was still no sign of help so he called again. This time he got a different operator, who tried to make John repeat his story. "Just go fuck yourself," the exasperated teenager shouted before slamming down the receiver. Glynis meanwhile had gone to the bottom of the stairs and tried to pick up her mother and make her walk — just as she always did when Joan passed out. But this time, the limp, lifeless body slumped in her arms like a rag doll: "I don't believe what happened to the two of us that night. It was like we lost the last thing we had."

The old house began to fill with an assortment of relatives and total strangers that reinforced the impression of unreality. Dr. Gordon Higgins, son of Judy Carnell, Jessie's sister, arrived in his capacity as family doctor to pronounce Joan dead. Her neck was broken, and later tests would show very high blood-alcohol levels. The police, a nurse and several ambulance attendants also appeared.

Unaware of the gravity of the situation, John Crosbie had calmly finished his dinner after receiving his mother's by now routine call complaining of trouble at the house. "That's the two of them at it again," he and his wife thought. But when he pulled into the driveway, he caught the unmistakable scent of tragedy in the air. On learning of his sister's death, John tried to comfort the Jenkins children, offering tea to a hopelessly distraught Glynis who angrily blamed him for failing to come to their mother's aid despite several desperate calls for help. More than a few relatives would later wonder why Joan was never given professional care for her acute alcoholism, when so many other Crosbies, including her businessman brother, had been. One of her sons, Lee Shinkle, had an answer: "They didn't commit Mother because they couldn't figure out what to do with Nan if they committed Mother. . . . Basically what you had was two women who had to be dealt with."

Lee Shinkle had been at a Dale Carnegie session at the Holiday Inn when he got an urgent message from his wife, Martha, that his mother was dead. He was stunned. A few months earlier, he had driven Joan to the top of Signal Hill for a "heart-to-heart." Better than most people, Lee knew how serious her drinking had become and what lay behind it: "She wanted Jenkins, really wanted him. She was lonely and he was her man." The thought that she was now dead was incomprehensible.

All the way over to Rennies Mill Road, Lee kept thinking that his wife must have meant "dead drunk." Memories came flooding in of recent events at the Crosbie offices, where on two occasions his Uncle Andrew had instructed him to take Joan home: "He'd get pissed, and Mother'd get pissed, and he'd call me in and I'd take Mother home. It was great trying to do a big business deal and Andrew'd call you up pissed as a rat and say take Mother home." Still, *dead.* It just couldn't be.

When Lee arrived on the scene, Dr. Higgins gravely confirmed that Joan was gone, words that only took on their full meaning when he walked over to the top of the basement stairs and looked down. There on the landing was Glynis, cradling their mother's head in her lap and repeating over and over again like a deranged Ophelia in blue jeans, "She's not dead, she's not dead." For the second time in his life, Lee's mother had left him.

In the unhinged emotions of the moment, dreadful theories formed and vanished like steam rising from a cauldron. After learning from his grandmother that the two women hadn't fought that night, Lee Shinkle wondered if the children had had anything to do with their mother's death. He knew that there had already been violent incidents in the house, and that Glynis had written her mother some abusive and threatening letters after earlier arguments, letters that Andrew Crosbie now kept in his safe. Lee took Glynis and John into the pantry, "to push them to find out just what in the Christ happened."

The Jenkins children resented what they took to be Lee's sly intimations, the more so because they had their own notion of what might have happened to their mother that night. They could not believe that their bedridden grandmother had come down from her second-floor room to see what had happened after allegedly hearing a crash in the basement. And if, as she claimed, she had been on her way upstairs to call John after finding Joan's body, why hadn't she used the downstairs phone, which was closer? From personal experience, Glynis knew that her grandmother, frail as she was, was capable of raising her hand in anger. Jessie had struck Glynis on more than one occasion, and to her surprise it had hurt. Again and again they reenacted the terrible event and half convinced themselves that their mother's death had been no accident. But as the misfits of the family, they weren't surprised at their treatment that night. "They're never going to believe us if we say we're at the store. . . . So of course they are going to blame us. All they did was interrogate us black sheep."

As the house gradually emptied, Jessie Crosbie gave her verdict on the night's dread events before the sedatives the doctor gave her took effect: "At least she's better off than I am."

JOAN CROSBIE WAS buried just behind her father, Ches, in the General Protestant Cemetery in St. John's. She was fifty-four. John Jenkins, Sr., was there to bid a tearful farewell to the woman he had once burned with in the glory of young love. "Dead, twenty minutes after she tried to phone me. And I said no. I didn't feel good," Jenkins recalled. Gene Shinkle stayed away. Bill St. Croix, a reformed alcoholic Joan had saved from the fate that overtook her, steadied Glynis from behind as her mother's casket slowly descended to its final resting place. To those curious enough to ask, the official word was that Joan had died of a heart attack. The insurance company paid double indemnity on her policy and her death was ruled accidental by the authorities of the day — a drunken woman who had fallen down the stairs and broken her neck while trying to put the garbage out. There was no mention made of Joan's alcoholism in the press, and John Crosbie dissuaded Susan Jenkins from soliciting donations to A.A. in her mother's memory. The woman who had made such waves inside the Crosbie family for more than twenty years passed under the still waters of eternity with scarcely a ripple.

A few days after Joan's death, a family council was held in Jessie's dining room. Seated around the table were John and Andrew Crosbie, Lee and Matthew Shinkle, John Jenkins, Sr., his wife Sandra, and his three children, Susan, Glynis and John Jr. For Lee Shinkle, it felt like *déjà vu*. He and his brother Matthew had been the subject of a similar meeting when their mother had run off with Jenkins in 1960. Now it was the turn of her second family to learn their fate within the Crosbie clan.

The first decision made that day was that seventy-six-year-old Jessie Crosbie would have to leave the house where she had raised three families over forty years. Although Lee and Martha Shinkle wanted to take Jessie in — an unusually selfless offer considering that they had four young children at home — both John and Andrew Crosbie felt that their mother needed professional care. After one more attempt at a new housekeeper, Bridie McGrath, the Crosbies would eventually move Jessie to the Salvation Army Home at the corner of Torbay Road and Elizabeth Avenue, where she would die a little over a year later.

The more difficult problem was what to do with Joan's children, who had lived in their grandmother's house since their mother's return to Newfoundland in 1975. From a Crosbie perspective, Rennies Mill Road was no longer an option. But what could be done? For years, the pair had run wild in a dysfunctional family; they were now used to the freedoms of the adult world without its responsibilities. Life within a traditional family would be difficult if not impossible for all concerned. Education, too, posed its problems. At ages seventeen and fifteen, and with poor academic records, it was doubtful if Glynis and John could avail themselves of the private-school treatment that Lee and Matthew had been given at a much younger age.

The difficulties with a Jenkins-driven solution to the problem were equally formidable. Although John Jenkins, Sr., was willing to take his children back to Ontario, too much water had passed under the bridge since they had last lived together, some of it decidedly murky. John Jr. didn't respect Jenkins for having left his mother for another woman. He hadn't even seen him in six years, and both John and Glynis had by now sunk roots in St. John's. Twenty-year-old Susan was already out on her own and had no desire to pull up stakes yet again to become a part of her father's new life. There were no easy answers on either side of the dining-room table.

Although Lee and Matthew offered to take the teenagers in, it was a duty-inspired proposal that met with little enthusiasm. It was ultimately decided that, like it or not, John Jr. would return to Ontario with his father. Glynis would move in with sister Susan and Uncle Andrew would get her a job in one of his companies. But the pull of the past was too strong. Within months of agreeing to the new living arrangements, John left Ontario, despite his father's best efforts to win him over and blatant attempts by the Crosbies to discourage him from returning to Newfoundland. He and Glynis then picked up their life in the city's underground, imposing themselves on their older sister for the basic necessities. "Me and Glynis went the wrong way," John later recalled, long after he and his sister had put their lives in order. "We hung around with the wrong people. And eventually I would have to say we forced Sue to move out of her apartment. Sue used to come home from work and we used to have our friends over and it was really rotten."

By October, with winter fast approaching, John and Glynis were finally evicted from the apartment they had virtually commandeered from their sister. They went to the welfare office but were turned down for assistance. " 'Oh, ask your Crosbie uncles for money.' That's all they said to us. 'Get out, you're not getting any money,' " Glynis recalled.

Glynis temporarily moved in with her boyfriend, but John still had nowhere to go. He began sneaking back to his grandmother's house, now vacant and for sale, where he climbed the fire escape and broke into his old bedroom to sleep on the floor. After nearly getting caught by a neighbour, he took to the streets. Destitute and homeless, John relied on his sister, who helped him to survive any way she could: "We would go up to the Dominion store and rob the ham and the cheese and the bread. And we'd go down to my place and have a chomp, chomp, chomp. And then we just branched out from there, got odd jobs here and there. And we were mostly dopeheads, that's all. And not so much doing it, but making the money from selling it. If it wasn't for that, we'd be dead. John would be frostbitten in a snowbank. And I'd be starved to death, a skeleton and nothing more."

Reflecting on the pitiful plight of his half brother and half sister, brought on, in part, by themselves, Lee Shinkle would later reduce their dilemma to the bald reality of a world where human compassion and moral resources had their limits — even inside a family like the Crosbies: "Nobody wanted to take them in, nobody knew what to do with them, nobody knew how to handle it."

ANDREW CROSBIE MIGHT have wanted to succour his motherless nieces and nephews, but by the spring of 1981 he was too much in need of a lifeline himself. Just as his sister Joan was careening towards tragedy, Newfoundland's most powerful businessman was headed for the biggest fall of his life. With the fiasco of Atlantic Place still unresolved and his corporate debt now topping $75 million (virtually all of it secured by his personal notes), the Bank of Montreal rejected Andrew's optimistic cash projections for the Crosbie companies. A management team was imposed by the bank, and after they reported, Andrew received a visit from head-office officials. They asked him to sign a letter agreeing to take direction from the accounting firm of Clarkson Gordon — a none-too-subtle precursor of receivership.

Knowing what was coming next, Andrew balked. John Crosbie then made one of his rare approaches to his younger brother, who normally neither sought nor followed John's advice, jealously guarding the business world as his exclusive preserve. But with the banks closing in, Andrew, who was going through a forty-ouncer of Scotch a day before lunch, was in no position to stand on his pride. "Some of the people who were working with him and advising him got me to persuade him to sign what the bank wanted signed, which I was able to do. But he was in pretty bad shape," John Crosbie remembered.

Like a child seeking solace in a favourite toy, Andrew went to ground in Kaegudeck, accompanied by longtime friends Grant Chalker and Edsel Bonnell. He no longer owned the camp established by his father, having sold it along with Eastern Provincial Airlines in 1978 to get badly needed cash to pay down his ballooning bank loans. But the airline's new owner, Harry Steele, who paid $5.56 million for EPA, was only too happy to give the tottering legend of Newfoundland business a temporary sanctuary. There, in the same woods he had often ranged through, with Sylvester's Brook running like clear amber under a cloudless sky, Andrew first tried to blot out and then faced the inevitable: "I guess after I signed that letter I went to Kaegudeck and got drunk for two weeks. And I guess when I was in there, I said to myself, 'Look, it's going to happen and you got to make the best of a bad situation.' "

The end came with stunning swiftness. Local bank managers who had once decided who should live or die commercially based on more than a particular day's bottom line, now took their instructions from distant executives in other provinces, who neither knew nor cared about the Crosbies' unique history or amazing commercial resiliency. In June 1981, just a month after Joan's death, Avalon Lounge Ltd., a bar, became the first Crosbie company to go bankrupt. Clouding his personal situation even further was the sudden death in Toronto of his beloved Uncle Bill Crosbie, who died of a heart attack after addressing the fortieth reunion of the University of Toronto's class of '41. In July, Domac Enterprises, Crosbie's heavy-equipment company, went into voluntary liquidation. A few days later, he "sold" his biggest corporate headache, Atlantic Place, to the Canadian Imperial Bank of Commerce, reducing his indebtedness from $75 million to $30 million. In August, Chimo Shipping went bankrupt with a bitter twist; the action was precipitated after the vessel that carried his name, the *A. C. Crosbie*, was arrested and held under marine lien for non-payment of shipyard debts and an outstanding fuel bill with Imperial Oil of $175,000. Versatile Vickers of Montreal also claimed $1.5 million for a 1980 refit of the ship, tearing a few more strips from the Crosbie corporate carcass.

Two months later, Andrew's tabloid, *The Daily News*, was sold to senior management. In November, it was the turn of once-mighty NECCO, the construction company that had built much of modern-day St. John's, including Confederation Building and the Arts and Culture Centre, in the heady days of political connections and cost-plus. Ironically, the bankruptcy occurred while NECCO was putting up the Toronto-Dominion Bank Building in downtown St. John's. Everything folded into the companies was liquidated, including Crosbie's luxury home on Lyford Cay, which Andrew personally closed up and sold. By July 1982, Crosbie Enterprises was officially in receivership and a total of twenty-four companies under its umbrella had either been sold or taken over by the banks. The Crosbie who had once been lionized as the youngest director in the history of the Bank of Montreal was now forced to resign his place on the board. By the time the carnage in his empire was over, Andrew Crosbie had personally lost the princely sum of $12 million. The mountain of ice cream was gone.

A remarkable feature of the bankruptcy was how Crosbie's 2,800 employees and numerous creditors were left relatively unscathed by the largest corporate bonfire in Newfoundland history, an outcome guaranteed by Andrew's generosity and unfailing sense of loyalty to his people. Most of his executives received a year's salary, and all creditors were paid at least a portion of what they were owed. "I was the only fellow that ended up without a pay cheque," Andrew chortled with a wink. "Me and the banks."

While others dined out on his misfortunes, Andrew took a measure of comfort from the fact that he had at least been able to protect some of his personal fortune, including the family home, Virginia Waters. In the early 1960s, he had placed most of his personal assets in the Andrew Crosbie Lifetime Trust, whose beneficiaries were his four children.

Although the banks circled, they weren't able to descend on any more Crosbie assets, however irksome they might have found the spectacle of a corporate bankrupt living on a sprawling estate and driving a Rolls-Royce cabriolet. Outwardly, at least, not much would change in his day-to-day life. But on the inside, Andrew Crosbie was a human shipwreck, aground on the rocks of a recession that could not have come along at a worse time: "One day you are busy and successful and the next day you are being hounded to death by rumours and speculation and bankers and newspaper stories. And the so-called friends who are not what you thought they were are nowhere to be found."

Battered as he was, family history offered some solace. "This was a repeat of Sir John and a repeat of my father," Andrew philosophically observed. "Unfortunately, it was happening to me. I spent six months selling what I had spent twenty years building." Happily, the family guardian angel appeared in the midst of his gloom. Just as his grandfather had left an insurance policy, and his father the proceeds from the sale of Bavarian Breweries and Gaden's Ltd., Andrew was the recipient of a final windfall. Fittingly, it emerged from the sea that had always nurtured the family fortunes. From the middle seventies onward, Andrew had established an informal division within the Crosbie group of companies looking into business prospects in the offshore oil industry. Crosbie executive Stuart Peters was put in charge of determining the best activities for the company to pursue. He reported back to Andrew that there were few better opportunities than operating supply boats, the sturdy vessels put on long-term charter to oil companies to ferry personnel and supplies to and from their enormous offshore rigs. It was a lucrative business with large profits and little capital investment for any businessman with an oil field on his doorstep and the right connections. Andrew Crosbie had both.

As more and more drill ships appeared in Newfoundland waters, the provincial government, then spearheaded by John Crosbie and Leo Barry, had been developing oil and gas regulations in expectation of a major oil strike. After years of searching, Chevron Canada Ltd. finally found the pot of oil at the end of the rainbow. In November 1979, a jubilant Brian Peckford announced the discovery of the Hibernia oil field, an "elephant" by offshore standards, with reserves of light, sweet crude initially estimated at two billion barrels. The same month the discovery was announced, Crosbie and Richard Spellacy incorporated a new company, Crosbie Offshore Services Ltd. (COSL). As chairman of the new enterprise, Andrew held 51 percent, while Spellacy, as president and chief executive officer, took 49 percent.

The rough-and-tumble Spellacy, whose raspy voice could take the skin off a shark, was the perfect partner for the venture. British-born but raised in Australia, he had already worked in Newfoundland in 1974 as port captain in charge of a fleet of supply boats. As a longtime supply boat captain himself, he had sailed on every ocean of the world: few people were more knowledgeable or better connected in the freebooting, old boys' club of the international oil industry than swashbuckling Richard Spellacy.

The industry grapevine was buzzing with rumours about Hibernia, and Spellacy liked what he heard. At Stuart Peters's suggestion, Spellacy made a trip to St. John's, where he and Andrew hit it off famously. He pulled up stakes in Houston, where he'd been working as a marine surveyor, and moved to Newfoundland, settling into the first car of the Hibernia roller coaster for the wildest ride of his riotous life.

Newfoundland had never seen anyone quite like Richard Spellacy. He blew into St. John's like a tropical typhoon, taking the city, and Andrew Crosbie, by storm. A little over a year after arriving, he met twenty-one-year-old Charmaine Ingerman, a former Miss Newfoundland, at one of the many parties to celebrate the dizzying promise of Hibernia. Just before Christmas of 1980, he married the tall blonde who was barely half his age. (A few weeks later, Andrew Crosbie, who had been his best man, would marry her older sister, Carolyn, a secretary in his insurance company.) Spellacy drove around town in a $90,000 Maserati and settled his young wife into a large house on Cowan Avenue. The striking couple lived lavishly and threw a string of epic parties, to the delight of the city's fusty business establishment, for whom Spellacy was the exotic embodiment of the new business energy generated by oil.

At Dick Spellacy's house, the prospects always seemed limitless. When an associate marvelled at the $8,800 bill Dick received after importing some Australian wine, he was shocked to learn that it represented only the *duty* on the wine. Select visitors to his house were treated to a peek at Spellacy's treasure trove of Australian opals. More than a few St. John's matrons began sporting opal rings on their fingers, and Crosbie Offshore Ltd. itself purchased $192,500 worth of the stones. What everyone was really buying was a piece of the towering optimism swirling around the word lingering reverentially on everyone's lips — Hibernia. In the inner circles of St. John's society, Dick Spellacy's opals became a kind of talisman of Newfoundland's coming Golden Age.

Working "like a whore with two beds," as one associate put it, Spellacy quickly proved to be an invaluable acquisition. A month before the Hibernia discovery was formally announced, he returned from Germany with a contract with Vereinigte Tanklagger und Transpittal (VTG), a huge European company that owned ninety-seven supply boats worldwide. VTG wanted in on the Hibernia play, and by partnering with COSL, which was 51 percent-owned by a Canadian, Andrew Crosbie, the company was able to get around restrictions on foreign participation set by the Foreign Investment Review Agency. Andrew, in turn, got access to supply vessels with no capital outlay. Crosbie and the Germans set up a third company, Crosbie Offshore Supply Association (COSA), on whose behalf Spellacy approached Mobil Canada, offering to furnish supply boats and catering to its offshore rigs in Newfoundland. Knowing Spellacy, and having worked with the Crosbies on an earlier project off Sable Island, Mobil entered into three long-term leases with COSA, which made everyone happy — VTG, because it got a piece of the Hibernia action; Mobil, because Ottawa smiled on oil companies who "bought Canadian"; and, most of all, Andrew Crosbie, because an accident of history and geology had put him in a position to make a fortune.

For simply leasing vessels from VTG and then sub-leasing them to Mobil through COSA, the Newfoundland company made a net profit of $10,000 a week without investing a nickel. And that was on top of Spellacy's $18,000-a-month salary and Andrew's monthly stipend of $10,000.

It was the stuff of which comebacks are made, and Andrew Crosbie knew it. To protect his one cash cow from the bank action he feared was pending, he spun off COSL from the other companies of Crosbie Enterprises before it went bankrupt. But by 1985, what should have been the base for his business recovery turned into an anteroom of corporate and personal hell.

ALTHOUGH JOHN CROSBIE was deeply troubled by the tragedies working themselves out in his wider family, there hadn't been much time to devote to matters over which he had little control; he had a date with destiny and the lady had served notice early that she would be a demanding mistress. Just a month after the meeting on Circular Road, during which his candidacy for the Conservative leadership had been sealed, Crosbie had an eleven-person national campaign organization in place. During the summer of 1981, he lined up an extensive national speaking schedule that would take him to a different Canadian city or town once a week for a year. The locations were carefully restricted to those federal ridings where potential Tory delegates might be recruited. These were party events designed to let people know that here was a man who was no mere regional MP. John Laschinger's busy computers also had a master list of 12,200 names of influential grass-roots Conservatives, gleaned from previous leadership conventions, who received Crosbie's sophisticated mail-outs with their customized messages. By Christmas of 1981, the Crosbie camp had a detailed blueprint of their entire campaign strategy. All that remained was for a reluctant Joe Clark to put his neck into the noose of a leadership review and let his would-be successors spring the trapdoor he had been standing on since the party's 1980 election defeat.

Although John Crosbie and many other senior Conservatives publicly paid homage to their leader, it was a different story behind closed doors. On January 26, 1982, Crosbie was called to a secret meeting in the East Block office of Conservative House Leader Erik Nielsen. When he arrived at 11:00 a.m., a group of his colleagues were already there, including Jake Epp, Don Mazankowski, Pat Nowlan, Sinclair Stevens, Jim McGrath, John Fraser and Michael Wilson. David Crombie had been invited but missed his plane, and Walter Baker had not been able to attend.

There was only one item on the agenda: Joe Clark's floundering leadership. Even though the Liberals were listless and unpopular, many Canadians just couldn't seem to hold their noses and vote for a man they considered to be the political equivalent of Mr. Magoo. Regular and embarrassing leaks were coming out of a disgruntled Tory caucus, which only reinforced Clark's image as a man too weak to govern the country. Nielsen wanted to know what it would take to silence Clark's high-profile caucus critics so that the Conservatives could get on with their main Opposition task — defeating what John Crosbie privately described as the "lickspittles, brothel-creepers and upwardly mobile types" who had shamelessly usurped the government from the Tories in the 1980 election.

Don Mazankowski instantly cut to the heart of the matter: Joe Clark had to agree to a leadership review or a leadership convention before the next election if he expected the continuing support of caucus. Michael Wilson supported that view and, fearing that Clark would put his own career before the party's best interests, recommended that the leader form a committee of caucus members to "advise" him on the leadership question. Taking a leadership review for granted, Jake Epp drew a finer bead on the dilemma: if Clark didn't achieve a considerable improvement on his tepid vote of confidence from the 1981 annual meeting, where only two-thirds of the delegates had supported him, there would have to be an immediate leadership convention.

Carefully waiting for a consensus to emerge before he spoke, Crosbie sided with the dissidents. Brushing aside criticism from some Tories that the caucus was causing

Joe's problems, he said that the public and many party members just didn't see Joe as a winner. Working from the premise that the Conservatives had to win the next election, Crosbie argued that it was impossible to avoid the issue of a leadership review. Clark would have to make a clear commitment to calling one before the next election, and possibly earlier if the Liberals tried to upstage the Tories by calling a leadership convention of their own. With Pierre Trudeau on his way to the political glue factory, the last thing Crosbie wanted to see was a new Liberal thoroughbred breaking from the electoral starting gate while the Tories languished under the swaybacked leadership of Joe Clark.

Nodding his head as Crosbie spoke, Sinclair Stevens suggested that Joe be invited to meet with the dissidents following their Opposition Day motion at ten o'clock that evening. Erik Nielsen relayed the invitation to Clark, and then informed the group after the daily Question Period that the leader had agreed to meet them.

The blunt message discussed in Nielsen's office was delivered to Joe Clark in person, reinforced by the added support of David Crombie and Walter Baker, who were now in attendance. Clark told his caucus colleagues that there would be no postponement of the January 1983 annual meeting, and that a leadership review vote would be held at that time. Crosbie thought that the leader needed to go one step farther. Since the Liberals were holding an annual meeting of their own in November 1982, he wanted a commitment from Clark that if the Grits called a snap leadership convention, Clark would be prepared to follow suit. Joe demurred, arguing that the party's national executive was the only body that could make that decision.

The venue then switched to the full Tory caucus, which met for four gruelling hours the next day between 10:00 a.m. and 2:00 p.m. Clark spoke first, giving the full caucus the same assurances he had already given to the dissident group — that the annual meeting would go forward and it would feature a review of his leadership. But he refused to say what he would accept as a vote of confidence. The farthest he would go was to assure them that he would put the interests of the party ahead of his own interests — something Walter Baker told him he had not done in the past.

Although Marcel Lambert expressed his anger at certain unnamed troublemakers in caucus, there was almost unanimous agreement that Clark had to deal with the leadership problem in a clear and decisive way. Elmer MacKay made the same point that Jake Epp had made at the previous meeting with Erik Nielsen — that the leader of the Conservative party should require more support than Clark had garnered in 1981 in Ottawa. In other words, if one-third of the delegates to the 1983 annual meeting again voted for a leadership convention, then Clark should immediately call one.

When Crosbie rose to speak, the more perceptive among them might have noticed that the MP from St. John's West was dressing more tastefully these days. There were no more second-hand suits from brother Andrew and he had lost weight — all part of his careful preparations for a run at the leadership. He told his colleagues that Joe Clark had been a good leader but that a lot of Canadians and party members didn't see it that way. He was also careful to point out that, under the circumstances, the caucus had behaved well — a pat on their collective back that reinforced his popularity with his peers. The issue before them was simple, Crosbie lectured. There had to be a leadership review that would either reaffirm or replace Clark before the next election. Even at that, he warned, it would be difficult to win a majority government since he didn't think the party would pick up many seats in Quebec. The elusive majority the Tories were seeking would have to be found in English Canada. If Clark would agree to a leadership review in early 1983, then Crosbie believed caucus could put the "disunity crisis" behind them for the balance of 1982.

After listening patiently to his colleagues, Joe Clark reiterated that he wouldn't put his own interests ahead of the party's, but he wouldn't agree to a leadership convention before the next election, or commit himself on the moot point of what percentage of dissident votes at the 1983 annual meeting would be enough to trigger one. All he would say was that his level of support would have to be higher than it had been in February 1981 if a leadership convention were to be avoided. Although John Crosbie believed that Clark had missed an opportunity to resolve firmly the party's leadership dilemma, the caucus was sufficiently mollified to get through 1982 without an open split in the Opposition ranks.

A year later, Joe Clark found out just how cold Winnipeg can be in January. Once again, one-third of the delegates to the party's annual meeting voted in favour of a leadership review. After an intense moment of personal and political angst, Clark gave his detractors their wish, announcing a June convention in Ottawa and his own candidacy at the same time. Crosbie, who had kept as low a profile as it was possible for a man to keep who had already spent $100,000 on his leadership drive and spoken in 125 federal ridings over the past year and a half, could now safely come out of the campaign closet. On March 21, 1983, the same day that political neophyte Brian Mulroney threw his hat into the ring, Crosbie formally announced his candidacy in a speech to the Canadian Club in Toronto. In 1945, Dr. Raymond Gushue, then chairman of the Newfoundland Fisheries Board and a close friend of Ches's, had addressed the same group on the possibility of Newfoundland entering Confederation: "If she does come in, since the wise men come from the east, your problems as to future prime ministers will naturally be solved." John Crosbie now stood before them looking for the job.

As national chairman of Crosbie's finance committee, the quietly efficient Basil Dobbin made sure that John Crosbie had the money to run a first-class, professional campaign. He put together a country-wide financial network, including a diligent twelve-man team headquartered in St. John's. Out of a total of $1.35 million raised for Crosbie, "Dobbin's Dozen" came up with $750,000 in Canada's poorest province. (A measure of how far Andrew Crosbie had fallen was his personal collection for John — a mere $3,000.) Later, when the campaign discovered that it had overspent, Dobbin and Robert Foster of Capital Canada Corp. in Toronto came up with another $500,000 to protect Crosbie from the sizeable personal debts he had faced after his 1969 leadership bid. "We paid for John's clothes, John's hairdressing, Jane's clothes, Jane's hairdressing, limousines, transportation, everything, on a daily basis. We raised almost 1.9 million after-tax dollars, out of Newfoundland. And we had so much fun with it!" Dobbin recalled.

Crosbie was as well organized as he was financed. Thanks to John Laschinger, the Crosbie campaign was the fastest off the mark and the best prepared, boasting a space-age computer command centre in Ottawa and a team of seasoned and efficient workers, including Jim Good, Jean Piggott, Bob Wenman and Chester Burtt. It would be hard to imagine a better political wife than Jane Crosbie. She was beautiful, earthy, and totally devoted to her husband, but not to the point of being steamrollered by his cranky wilfulness. Despite the buffoon image his handlers were so worried about, Crosbie quickly showed his true intellectual colours. He was the first major candidate who had reasoned his way through the big issues facing the country and worked out a coherent policy platform. The centrepiece was a policy that would soon dominate Canadian politics — freer trade with the United States. Having borrowed the central plank of Ches Crosbie's economic union movement during the Confederation debates, he proceeded to name his campaign bus the *Jessie and Ches*. If it was political plagiarism, at least John Crosbie had come by it honestly.

During the early stages of the campaign, Crosbie projected a moderate and right-of-centre image, concentrating on a market-driven approach to the problems of the economy, which he believed were of paramount interest to the voters. He developed his own policy positions looking out over Hogan's Pond from the small den where he worked. He argued persuasively that the next federal government had to prepare Canadians for the transition from an industrial-based economy to the information age. His twenty-seven-page "Agenda for Action" was mailed to all three thousand delegates to the Ottawa convention, who Crosbie hoped would not be offended by his appeal for foreign capital to develop Canada or his aversion to economic nationalism — the touchstone of Liberal popularity for many years. It somehow seemed appropriate that his campaign song was "The Gambler" by Kenny Rogers.

Crosbie and his brain trust did their best to improve the odds at the convention by a creative approach to delegate selection. Under party rules, every federal riding association was eligible to send four senior and two youth delegates to Ottawa. In Newfoundland, with seven federal seats, that amounted to a grand total of forty-two delegates, not counting alternates and *ex officios*. But college campuses were also allowed to send delegates; for the purposes of the Tory convention, a number of organizations in Newfoundland briefly became degree-granting institutions, including beauty schools, flying schools and driving academies! When Crosbie's contingent arrived in Ottawa, it was 170 strong. Crosbie jokingly told his youthful contingent to seek out boys and girls from other delegations, particularly from Quebec, and seduce them to his side.

By the second week in May, a little less than a month before the convention, John Laschinger had every reason to feel pleased with himself. A Southam poll showed that his candidate was the clear second choice of the party, an excellent position to be in with the front-runners, Joe Clark and Brian Mulroney, drawing each other's fire. The long months of preparation had obviously paid off. Crosbie's key policies of freer trade and fiscal restraint were popular with the banking and business communities. Best of all, John had proved to be a major hit with the press, luring them with his quotable zingers and then converting them with his first-class mind and command of the issues. No one was running harder than candidate Crosbie. Up at 5:00 a.m. and plugging away until 1:00 a.m., he lived up to the description of fellow Newfoundlander and writer Bill Rowe, who called Crosbie "a living Protestant work ethic."

Crosbie's suspect health held up admirably, despite the hectic pace. John Laschinger's only scare of the campaign came when he received a midnight telephone call from Ross Reid in Edmonton informing him that the candidate was being attended to by a doctor: "I said, 'My God, what's wrong?' All I had visions of was heart attacks and strokes and I thought, 'I killed the poor bugger,' because we rolled him pretty hard that last little while." When Reid replied that Crosbie was suffering from the same complaint that prevented Napoleon from sitting his horse at the Battle of Waterloo, Laschinger, giddy with relief, went into "hoots and stitches" of laughter: "He [Crosbie] came back two days later. Tough, tough son of a bitch. He walked with a Kotex between the cheeks of his ass for about a week afterwards, but he did not miss a single event."

The high-water mark of the campaign was reached on May 23, 1983, when *Maclean's* magazine put John Crosbie on the cover as "The Tory to Watch." It was exactly the kind of national media endorsement that Laschinger believed would help attract support from the 3,000 delegates whose loyalties were constantly shifting as the convention approached. Joe Clark clearly perceived the danger over his other shoulder and began attacking Crosbie as a right-winger who had ignored minorities in Canada and had made no attempt to learn French. (Clark's barb was essentially accurate, although Crosbie had, in fact, taken a ten-day French immersion holiday in St. Jean, Quebec, in a futile attempt to get some basic French.) Crosbie stoutly countered that French was an asset, not a requirement, for any political leader in Canada and that the public was more interested in a candidate's honesty than his bilingualism. "They're going to care whether he is honest and sincere in the one language he speaks or whether he's a twister and a trimmer in both languages," Crosbie told *The Globe and Mail.*

The fatal stumble that all campaign managers have nightmares about overtook Crosbie at Longueuil, Quebec, in the lobby of the Holiday Inn. Tired and irritable from the rigours of the campaign (John was the oldest candidate in the leadership race) and exasperated by relentless media questions about his lack of French, Crosbie blew his regal stack. Behind his tantrum was the excruciating frustration of trying to campaign in Quebec through an interpreter: "It was just extremely awkward. You know, nobody likes to feel like a goddamned dummy, that you can't talk somebody's language." When English-language reporters began pestering him on the language issue, he snapped that unilingualism was no crime. The questions kept coming. Crosbie shot back that 3.7 million bilingual Canadians shouldn't think of themselves as "some kind of aristocracy" from which the country's leaders must always be drawn.

The assembled reporters looked at one another, sensing a major *faux pas* in the making. Press secretary Diana Crosbie, who had set up the impromptu scrum, was wishing she had never let the candidate out of the elevator. Then came the deadly utterance: "I cannot talk to the Chinese people in their own language either . . . I can't talk to the German people in their own language. Does that mean there should be no relationships between China and Canada or Canada and Germany or whatever?"

Crosbie might have more aptly reminded the assembled press that fellow Newfoundlander Frank Moores had not been impaired by his lack of French when he organized Brian Mulroney's Quebec delegates to the Winnipeg convention, but that was now water under the bridge. In the struggle to convince Quebeckers to give the Tories a chance, John Crosbie's inadvertent implication that their province was like a foreign country within Canada was blown up into a Joe Clark-sized blunder. For John Laschinger, the damage was more immediate; like a man in a braking elevator, he felt the Crosbie campaign's momentum come to a stomach-turning halt. His candidate had just kissed goodbye six hundred francophone delegates from the province of Quebec, and with them, any chance of being close enough on the first ballot to catch the front-runners. Longueuil was the Boot Hill of the Crosbie leadership campaign.

In the gloom of the next few days, Crosbie tried to repair the damage, admitting it had been a mistake to compare his lack of French to not knowing German or Chinese and coating his remorse with the sugary if transparent promise to move part of the PMO to Quebec if he became prime minister. But the damage was done. On the eve of the convention, Southam published a poll showing that Crosbie had slipped badly in delegate support, dropping 250 votes behind Mulroney on the first ballot and slipping a full six percentage points as the convention's second leadership choice. Since his entire campaign strategy was built on being close enough after the first ballot to attract strong second-ballot support, they were devastating numbers.

The only thing between Crosbie and the instant oblivion of a political also-ran was his convention speech. He had wanted to deliver an off-the-cuff address, but Laschinger insisted on a written speech carefully rehearsed by Crosbie. For days, the candidate practised in front of a video camera and under the critical eye of Newfoundland politicians like Brian Peckford. Crosbie turned out to be a very coachable star. On Friday, June 10, he delivered the best speech of the convention, a barn-burner that even included an anecdote in French about a young francophone whose problem wasn't language but his lack of a job. One of the many people pulling for John that night back in Newfoundland was his heartbroken Uncle George Crosbie; his wife, Audrey, had died the day the convention opened, but the family television was nevertheless tuned in to watch his famous nephew make his run for the roses. Crosbie pride was a mighty force.

The 3,000 delegates applauded John's speech enthusiastically, but on the first ballot only 639 of them voted for him. With his candidate trailing second-place Brian Mulroney by 235 votes, John Laschinger immediately saw the writing on the wall. In the end, he would say that Crosbie could have "won the whole thing" with a mere 75 more delegates on the first vote. "We were dead after the first ballot," Laschinger said. "We were too far back."

For the second time in his life, John Crosbie found himself sitting in a crowded arena praying for a political miracle. Michael Wilson and Peter Pocklington immediately went to Mulroney, robbing the Crosbie camp of critical momentum. Laschinger hurriedly met with two senior Tories in the middle of the packed floor and tried to build an alliance for his candidate. "I met up with Mazankowski and McKnight after the first ballot. They said, 'If Clark doesn't go [up] after this first ballot we'll come with you. We'll meet here after the second ballot.' " When the second-ballot results were announced, still showing Clark in first place but clearly stalled and Brian Mulroney now 240 votes ahead of Crosbie, Laschinger shouldered through the tightly packed crowd towards the meeting he thought would bring badly needed western delegates to Crosbie. It was not to be: "They said, 'You're too far behind. We can't go. We're going to have to split them [the delegates] up.' " For Basil Dobbin, the irony was staggering: "The three western provinces are the ones who defeated John Crosbie and put a Quebecker in there. We got nothing out of Manitoba, Saskatchewan or Alberta. And it was all because they believed if you weren't from Quebec, then you couldn't win a federal election."

The demanding and complex preparations of the last two years suddenly boiled down to a single, unenviable task. Joe Clark would have to be persuaded that it was better to lose to John Crosbie than to Brian Mulroney. If Clark could not be moved, then candidate Crosbie would be history after the third ballot. After meetings between Lowell Murray and John Laschinger, it became clear that Joe Clark didn't consider it much of a treat to choose between one of two political swords that were poised to run him through. Laschinger's pleas were met by a counter offer that would have seen Crosbie supporting Clark on the third ballot. After all, if the real issue was stopping Brian Mulroney, as Laschinger pleaded, why shouldn't the candidate in third place defer to the man who had led the party since 1976 and was leading the pack?

Arguing that if Crosbie dropped off the ballot he couldn't deliver his delegates, Laschinger rejected a reverse deal with the Clark forces and threw his last political weapon into the fray — the premier of Newfoundland, Brian Peckford. With millions of people watching on national television, Peckford gamely tried to convince Clark to stop Brian Mulroney from capturing the Conservative Party by coming to Crosbie. Joe had done a lot of fiddling while other Romes burned, and this, Peckford told him, was his last chance to balance the record with one, decisive act that would change the history of the country. The huge television audience saw Clark bite his lower lip and shake his head in the negative. But they couldn't hear the blunt phrase with which Maureen McTeer poleaxed the Crosbie camp's last hope of victory. Looking Premier Peckford straight in the eye, and remembering, perhaps, that it had been her husband who had agreed to give Newfoundland control of offshore resources, a furious McTeer hissed, "Fuck off, you nerd."

Crosbie collected 858 votes on the third ballot and, as low man behind a stagnant but stubborn Clark and a surging Mulroney, was forced to throw in the towel. It was only his second political defeat in eighteen years, both of them in leadership contests. All day long the candidate had been sipping Scotch out of a flask that Ross Reid had been charged with refilling. He rose a little unsteadily on his feet and began to move towards one of the exits. The only thing left to do in the cauldron of Ottawa's Civic Centre was to meet with his sweat-drenched troops a final time and decide where to take his support. Retreating to a locker room under the stadium with a large tumbler of Scotch in his hand, looking "like a big bear" as he settled into his chair, Crosbie asked the thirty or so people present what they wanted to do. It had been a completely open campaign from beginning to end, and Crosbie wanted to keep it that way.

The general consensus was that Brian Mulroney was headed for victory and that there was a lot to be gained by supporting him. A tipsy young Ches Crosbie, bitter about his father's loss and carried away by the acrimony of the moment, shouted "Fuck Mulroney." His angry father told him to be quiet. After everyone had said their piece, it was John's turn to tell his assembled supporters what he planned to do. Longtime friend and key adviser Frank Ryan was not surprised by Crosbie's final decision: "He said, 'When Joe Clark was elected prime minister of Canada, he did me the honour of making me Finance minister. Now there's no question that Brian Mulroney is going to win. But I'm not going to go out and put the last knife in Joe Clark's back for my own personal advancement. I'm going to go back to our own box and we'll let the delegates go and vote as they wish.'" In keeping with his conviction that the party could never win with Joe Clark, Crosbie stoically voted for Brian Mulroney on the convention's fourth and final ballot.

When Crosbie returned to his box in the sweltering Civic Centre, pungent now with the spent ambition of several of the country's largest egos, the 100-degree heat, the Scotch, the 37,000 miles of campaign travel, the 122 breakfasts, lunches and dinners, and now the loss were all showing on his flushed, fifty-two year-old face. Earlier in the campaign, Crosbie had jokingly said, "If I win, I win. If I lose, I spare myself untold agony." Clearly, he would have preferred the agony.

Jane Crosbie, who had suffered through all the exhilaration as well as the indignities large and small of seeking high political office, had had enough of politics. As she and her husband watched Brian Mulroney, the untried outsider with the silver bilingual tongue, assume the leader's mantle, her bitter disappointment was tempered by a single thought: now, and finally, John Crosbie would be getting out of public life.

Judging from her husband's caustic remarks to the press in the wake of Mulroney's victory, it looked like she was right. Asked to account for his convention defeat, Crosbie snapped, "We didn't count on the ardent stupidity of Joe Clark." More inured to adversity, Joe Clark gracefully let his irritable colleague off the hook of his patrician petulance: "We're all tired, and I think Jane should take John away on a holiday." Later that night, the Crosbie camp barred Barbara Frum, and all other media, from his hotel room while he and Jane enjoyed a quiet dinner. Only a few close friends and political colleagues, like New Brunswick Premier Richard Hatfield, were allowed in to congratulate the game but defeated candidate. For a man who had been born the citizen of another country and who had once worked alongside his father to keep Newfoundland from entering Canada, John Carnell Crosbie had come a long, long way.

A few days later, the Crosbies were back in St. John's to attend a party for the Prince and Princess of Wales aboard the Royal Yacht *Britannia*. Twenty thousand Newfoundlanders jammed the waterfront that night for a glimpse of the royal couple. As John and Jane Crosbie mounted the gangplank, a spontaneous cheer went up, solid and respectful at first, but quickly building into an adulatory roar of Newfoundland pride and respect and pure, healing love. It was a far cry from the boos and hisses that greeted Jim McGrath, a public scourging for his decision to support Joe Clark over Newfoundland's favourite political son. Jane

Crosbie's disillusionment with public life lifted like a cloud. She turned to Frank and Barbara Ryan and said, "There's more than one prince on this yacht tonight."

Buoyed by his royal reception, John Crosbie's love affair with Newfoundland, politics and the pursuit of power surged back stronger than ever. There were still Liberal dragons to slay and miles to go before he slept.

DURING THE YEARS when John Crosbie was establishing his national political reputation, his brother Andrew was valiantly struggling to put his shattered business life back into some semblance of order. After the bankruptcy of his companies in 1981 and 1982, he settled on the strategy of lying low while quietly rebuilding his career. His new wife and the four children from his first marriage rallied around him as he faced and conquered his number-one problem — the debilitating alcoholism that had been one of the main factors in his business demise.

By 1985, there was no resemblance between the trim and fit-looking businessman and the swollen drinker whose enlarged liver had bulged visibly under his clothing in the dark days of 1981. After taking treatment at the same Verdun clinic where his Aunt Margaret had been a patient, he never touched alcohol again, taking to heart his doctor's warning that to do so would mean certain death. Filled with a zeal to live and enthusiastic about the business plans that he hoped would allow him to live well, Andrew Crosbie rolled up his sleeves and tried to get back to work.

Although he had serious plans for a huge, offshore supply base at Freshwater Bay, just over the South Side Hills from St. John's, the entanglements of the past refused to let him go. Since 1981, the Bank of Montreal had been trying to force the sale of his 51 percent interest in Crosbie Offshore Services Ltd. to satisfy outstanding debts from his corporate bankruptcy. The debt the bank was most anxious to have satisfied was the $4.9 million owed by Ambassador Manufacturing Company Ltd. of St. Lambert, Quebec, one of Andrew's out-of-province businesses, which had gone bankrupt.

COSL was a very profitable company and, according to Richard Spellacy, Andrew had persuaded him in late 1980 to roll Ambassador's debt into the company they jointly owned. Even though Spellacy was warned against the move by financial advisers from Clarkson Gordon, he proceeded out of respect for Andrew, signing the legal documents against the church wall where he'd just been married on December 19, 1980.

When Spellacy returned from his honeymoon, he was shocked to find that "COSL was being raped" by the Bank of Montreal, who had been given access to the company's chequing account. The bank was removing payments for Ambassador's debt faster than the company was making money. By May 31, 1981 the bank had withdrawn $866,000 in interest payments accrued from Ambassador's loans. Instead of showing a modest profit of $157,000, COSL recorded a loss of $729,000. Confronted by his angry partner, Andrew Crosbie promised to rectify the situation by selling his 51 percent share in COSL and using the proceeds to pay down his debt to the bank. But by July 1981, the matter was taken out of Andrew's hands when the Bank of Montreal seized his shares in COSL.

Spellacy then negotiated with the bank to bring Ambassador's loan down from $4.9 million to $2 million. But the bank wanted $500,000 up front to consummate the deal. Andrew Crosbie then lent Spellacy Associates Newfoundland Ltd. (SANL), Spellacy's personal company, the money from the Andrew Crosbie Lifetime Trust. SANL then paid the half million dollars to the bank, which in turn reduced Ambassador's debt, which COSL had agreed to pay, to $1.5 million. COSL now had monthly loan repayments of $36,000 plus interest — $11,000 to the Andrew Crosbie Lifetime Trust and $25,000 to the Bank of Montreal. On a yearly basis, those loan repayments equalled three-quarters of the company's yearly profit. The complex arrangement got the bank off Andrew's back, but the once-profitable venture was now placed under an enormous financial burden that was exacerbated by salaries, dividends and corporate perks that pushed its fixed expenses to nearly $1.5 million a year.

Knowing that the arrangement was likely to collapse because of the onerous repayment schedule, the bank urged Spellacy to look for a buyer for Andrew's former 51 percent interest in COSL. By December 1981, he appeared to have found one in the person of Peter Bawden, a Conservative MP and caucus colleague of John Crosbie's, who considered paying $4.5 million to acquire Andrew's former shares in COSL. But the deal fell through when VTG came back to Spellacy wanting out of their existing contract with COSL. Faced with the spectre of a tough renegotiation with the Germans, Bawden backed out of the deal, which was to have closed at the end of May 1982. Although Harry Steele's Newfoundland Capital Corporation showed interest in acquiring COSL, the tough businessman would not agree to retain either Crosbie or Spellacy beyond a six-month transition period. Faced with an offer of only $2.3 million to retire some of the debts of the company and $1 to take it over, Spellacy balked, realizing that he would have to pay $400,000 into the deal if the sale were to proceed. The crusty mariner who had gone to sea at age fifteen for $36 a month was not about to walk away from COSL empty-handed. For the second time, a potential sale fell through.

Despite the crushing depression that set in after a hundred-foot wave sent the oil rig *Ocean Ranger* to the bottom of the Grand Banks with all eighty-four hands on February 15, 1982, Newfoundlanders were still riding the euphoria of oil's promise. On April 6, 1982, they gave a messianic Brian Peckford forty-four of fifty-two seats in a provincial election to back him up in his David and Goliath showdown with Pierre Trudeau over ownership of offshore resources. So feverish was the interest in seizing control of a resource people believed would transform their lives, it was scarcely noticed when Canada's new constitution — with Quebec dissenting — was proclaimed in 1982. In fact, the talk at many society parties around St. John's was that Newfoundland should separate from Canada if Ottawa deprived her of offshore ownership of her fabulous oil fields.

Against the backdrop of the province's patriotic enthusiasms over Hibernia, COSL still looked like a rollicking success to the outside world, exactly the kind of business to own in the new Newfoundland. But in mid-1983, far from the public eye, a deadly confrontation began between Andrew Crosbie and Dick Spellacy and their rich, powerful and very angry German partners, VTG. It all started when VTG's Canadian-based representative, Frank Euler, accidentally discovered that COSL was billing Mobil Oil a month in advance for the charter of COSA's supply boats, a practice that was contrary to the partnership agreement between VTG and COSL. Nearly a million dollars was being deposited for thirty days each month in COSL's account before being paid into COSA. The Germans didn't appreciate the deception, or the fact that their Canadian partners were pocketing approximately $10,000 a month in accrued interest on the advance payments from Mobil.

In the summer of 1983, Heinrich Sikora, the president of VTG, met Andrew Crosbie in St. John's and demanded the money he believed his company was owed. But in the financial shell game COSL was by then playing, the money wasn't there to put back into COSA's account. Crosbie agreed that the money was owed and asked for time to repay his partner; anxious not to embarrass his Canadian partner, or lose his foothold in the Hibernia project, Sikora agreed. In the meantime, COSL continued to pay large salaries and substantial perquisites to both Crosbie and Spellacy, as well as hefty loan repayments to the Andrew Crosbie Lifetime Trust and the Bank of Montreal.

For a year nothing happened. Then, in July 1984, Sikora decided to apply some pressure. Although VTG still paid COSL to deal with the bills of COSA, it no longer remitted any additional fees to the company. Previously, COSL had received a cheque equal to 15 percent of the cost of crewing the supply vessels as one of its many lucrative management fees. When those payments stopped, it touched off a fatal cash-flow crisis: the end for COSL was now in sight.

It came in November 1984, just eight months after the Supreme Court of Canada ruled that Ottawa owned the huge oil reserves in offshore Newfoundland, and two months after the federal Conservatives crushed John Turner and company in a federal election and John Crosbie became Canada's Justice minister. A Nova Scotia shipyard,

Mulgrave Machine Works Ltd., seized one of VTG's vessels for an unpaid repair bill of $129,000. As Andrew Crosbie put it, "Unfortunately, there were funds that the company [COSA] was earning that were not being kept in the company for company use . . . so when the time came that the company required cash to meet its obligations . . . people couldn't get paid."

Having run out of patience with its Newfoundland partners, VTG quickly purchased the debt and began bankruptcy proceedings against COSL. By now, the company owed a total of $3.4 million, including $750,000 to the Bank of Montreal, $375,000 to the family trust and $322,400 to Revenue Canada for taxes collected from employees but not forwarded to the federal treasury.

In its suit against COSL, VTG alleged that the company was bankrupt and owed the Germans $1.5 million, as well as the interest from payments not properly credited to COSA's account, amounting to another $500,000. In the second day of hearings into the dispute, VTG lawyer Ed Roberts alleged that COSL had used COSA revenues to pay the Bank of Montreal monies owing from Andrew Crosbie's former debts on Ambassador, which COSL had agreed to assume in 1980. Crosbie's counter suits alleging interference in deals for the sale of COSL that would have discharged the company's debt in full were quickly dismissed. On January 24, 1985, Mr. Justice Noel Goodridge declared COSL bankrupt. The judge also found that COSL had indeed taken money owed to VTG and observed in passing that its corporate activities "smacked of fraud" and a form of theft known as "conversion."

Taking in the high-profile civil case from the courtroom's gallery were members of the commercial crime squad of the RCMP. Soon after winning its civil action, VTG instructed Ed Roberts to lodge a criminal complaint with the Newfoundland Justice Department. In mid-February 1985, the RCMP seized COSL's books and commenced a long, complex and expensive investigation into the conduct of COSL's senior corporate officers, including Andrew Crosbie.

Meanwhile, the trophies and trinkets of Crosbie Offshore Services Ltd. were hawked around St. John's like baubles in a gypsy bazaar. Expensive Swiss watches, paintings, a builder's model of a German warship that eventually found its way into the private collection of Conrad Black and even Dick Spellacy's opals and Maserati were put on the block. There were no more grand parties at the house on Cowan Avenue or ruinously expensive bottles of wine over gourmet lunches at the Hotel Newfoundland. Andrew retreated to the lonely splendour of Virginia Waters, accusing Dick Spellacy of mismanaging Crosbie Offshore. Spellacy pulled up stakes to begin a printing business in Toronto, ruing the day he had allowed Andrew to roll the debts of Ambassador into their once-profitable company. With each partner blaming the other, a befuddled public watched and waited.

A little more than three years later, on October 12, 1989 Andrew Crosbie, Richard Spellacy and accountant Wayne Sooley were charged with multiple counts of fraud, theft and possession of property obtained by crime. Spellacy, who was arrested in Toronto and brought to Newfoundland in handcuffs aboard an Air Canada flight, was eventually released on a $25,000 cash bond and a $10,000 surety after his passport was seized. Crosbie and Sooley were released on their own recognizance. (In 1991, Sooley entered a guilty plea and was handed a 90-day jail term, to be served on weekends.) After a brief court appearance, Andrew Crosbie was escorted through the back door of the building to avoid having to run the gauntlet of the waiting media.

From the corporate quietude of the Crosbie Building, once a beehive of activity, seated behind the same elevated desk from which he had directed much of the province's private business for nearly twenty years, Andrew Crosbie composed a press release denying any criminal guilt in the matter of COSA and VTG and vowing to defend his reputation to the end. He claimed that he had not received any personal benefit from COSL, and that he expected to be exonerated on all charges. But his date with the criminal courts would cast a shadow over his affairs much deeper than the inspired gloom of the David Blackwood prints that covered the panelled walls of his office. The man who had been ridiculed in business circles for having lost a fortune would now be gossiped about for having stolen one.

As in Voltaire's France, so too in Crosbie's Newfoundland; though a throng might come to see a man honoured, twice as many would gather to watch his execution.

ON THE EVENING of September 4, 1984, just thirteen minutes after the polls closed, John Crosbie became the first Progressive Conservative to be elected in Brian Mulroney's national thrashing of John Turner and his exhausted band of Liberals. He crushed his closest opponent, Liberal Walter Carter, by 25,000 votes and captured 74.6 percent of all ballots cast — his best performance in eleven electoral victories. A jubilant Crosbie attributed Tory success in Newfoundland, where the party picked up two Liberal ridings as well as their traditional seats in St. John's East and West, to the offshore agreement reached on June 14, 1984, between Premier Brian Peckford and Prime Minister-in-waiting Brian Mulroney.

On September 17, Crosbie was sworn in as Justice minister in the first Mulroney cabinet. He was one of twelve senior ministers to be named to the powerful Planning and Priorities Committee of Cabinet and would also sit on the Security and Intelligence and Social Policy committees. Crosbie was given the additional role of acting Fisheries minister whenever Vancouver South MP John Fraser, who had been named to the portfolio that was so important to Newfoundland, was not available. It was a cornucopia of political power for the titan of Newfoundland politics compared to the stone soup served up to fellow Newfoundlander Jim McGrath. As the senior MP from Newfoundland, McGrath justifiably had call on a major role in the Mulroney administration; instead, he was left out of the cabinet altogether — the payoff, insiders claimed, for his principled refusal to do Mulroney's dirty work at the Winnipeg convention where Joe Clark was manoeuvred into calling a leadership convention. Crosbie regretted his colleague's fate but didn't go into mourning.

Private blessings added to his public successes. The day after Crosbie was sworn in, he and Jane became grandparents with the birth of "Baby Jane," the daughter of their son

Michael and wife Lynn. Two weeks later, "Baby Charlotte", the daughter of Ches Crosbie and wife Lois Hoegg, came along. That New Year's Eve, the Crosbies would forgo the merriment of publicly ringing in the New Year to take on their first baby-sitting assignment at Hogan's Pond: "It's a night to howl for most," the proud grandparents wrote to longtime friend Bobbie Robertson, "but I'm sure Baby Jane and Sweet Charlotte will be angels." By spring, all three of John's children would have produced a daughter, with the arrival of "Baby Megan" on May 10, 1985, to daughter Elizabeth and her husband, Brian Alexander.

Crosbie took hold of his new portfolio with characteristic vigour. With wife Jane ensconced in a small office in the Justice Department, where she toiled without pay five days a week, he set to work on a legislative record that, by the time he left the post in June 1986, would be truly impressive. He reformed the Divorce Act, brought in tough new laws against impaired drivers and designed better controls on prostitution, which he said could never be stamped out but ought to be dealt with "as humanely and reasonably as possible." Despite strong opposition from his own caucus, he announced plans to liberalize the treatment of homosexuals within the Armed Forces and the RCMP. There was more to John Crosbie than fiscal responsibility; behind the tight-fisted exterior was a man who was deeply interested in social justice — a trait he learned from some of the strong Crosbie women in his life, aunts Vera, Olga, Gert and grandmother Mitchie Anne.

It was not John Crosbie's legislative role that caught the media's eye in 1985, but his part in a string of scandals and improprieties that hijacked the agenda of the young Mulroney government and very nearly brought it down. One of the first involved New Brunswick Premier Richard Hatfield, the man who had offered Crosbie his congratulations after John's bitter loss at the 1983 leadership convention. Marijuana was found in Hatfield's luggage during a 1984 royal visit to New Brunswick, and there was a long delay before a decision was made to lay a charge. In the interim, the solicitor-general of Canada, Elmer MacKay, met with Premier Hatfield in an Ottawa hotel room to discuss his case while the police investigation into the matter was ongoing. After the premier was acquitted, the Opposition demanded a public inquiry into the handling of the Hatfield case, accusing the government of giving favourable treatment to a political cousin.

Crosbie, who got into trouble by expressing his pleasure when Hatfield was eventually acquitted, angrily told the Commons that there had been no special treatment in the case and that he would charge his own mother if it were warranted. He added that while he knew Solicitor-General Elmer MacKay had not interfered in the case, "the political wisdom of meeting Mr. Hatfield is another question."

By June of that year, the barbs of the Opposition and the press struck a lot closer to home. While Crosbie was giving a speech to the Canadian Bar Association in Halifax, *The Globe and Mail* reported in a June 1 piece that he had appointed his two sons, both of whom were lawyers, to be legal agents for the federal government in Newfoundland. The Opposition raised the hue and cry of conflict of interest against the minister, which Crosbie angrily dismissed as a "cowardly, despicable and dastardly attack" on his family.

After sparring with Liberal Justice critic Bob Kaplan over the alleged impropriety of the appointments, Crosbie shouted to a heckling Sheila Copps, "Quiet down, baby." Copps later exacted an apology, but it was the first of a series of confrontations between the two MPs that would go a long way towards winning Crosbie his ill-deserved reputation as a sexist bully. In fact, it was John Crosbie who pressed his colleagues to appoint more female judges, to federally enforce maintenance and custody orders, to stop discriminating against women in the armed forces and to put an end to the sexual exploitation of women and children in pornography. But when it came to a choice between his legislation or his limericks, the press ran with his off-colour humour every time.

John, with a fondness for bawdy humour, was often his own worst enemy; on one occasion while speaking to an audience of ophthalmologists, he turned to the huge replica of a human eye hanging behind him on the podium and said,

"It's a good thing I'm not talking to the gynaecologists." But his detractors didn't know what his friends did: that Crosbie's jokes were frequently at his own expense and designed to entertain rather than sting. When he and Jane made a trip to India together, Dr. Jim Roberts wrote some doggerel, which John liked so much he put it to memory and frequently repeated it:

> Are you doing your thing in the far Eastern climes,
> If so, how often, how many times?
> Do strange foreign beds detract from the game,
> Or do they incite you to more of the same?
> To put it quite bluntly, to make it quite plain,
> Is sex by the Ganges attractive to Jane?

It wasn't Shakespeare, but it wasn't Lenny Bruce either.

Sensing that they had Crosbie on the ropes, the Liberal rat pack bore in. Pointing out that Andrew Crosbie owed $322,400 to Revenue Canada, Don Boudria sarcastically wondered if either Michael or Chesley Crosbie would be prosecuting their uncle if the matter came to court. Shaking and red-faced, John Crosbie later told reporters outside the House of Commons that he hadn't been as outraged over a political low blow since he left the provincial cabinet of that Nolan Ryan of mud-slinging, Newfoundland Premier Joe Smallwood.

After the daily Question Period, he tried to rise in the Commons on a point of personal privilege to defend himself against "shabby aspersions on myself, my sons, and false allegations against my brother which are being repeated on the radio in St. John's and are interfering with his business dealings with other people." The Speaker, John Bosley, who by then had called for ministerial statements, finally turned off Crosbie's microphone and asked him if he was speaking in his capacity as Canada's Justice minister or as Andrew Crosbie's brother. Crosbie snapped that he was only trying to set the record straight. When he was later asked point-blank if his brother owed Revenue Canada the $322,400 in question, Crosbie replied, "The poor devil doesn't owe them a cent."

Technically speaking, he was right; the monies were owed by the now defunct Crosbie Offshore Services Ltd. As a former officer of the company, Andrew Crosbie was personally liable for the money, but John Crosbie wasn't about to sell family loyalty down the river on a technicality. Four days after the affair erupted, the Opposition finally settled for the resignation as federal legal agents of the law firms that employed his sons. Crosbie also promised that he would not discuss his brother's tax case with Revenue minister, Perrin Beatty.

Crosbie's ill-considered outbursts were not always restricted to political matters. When a Radio-Canada reporter, Bertrand de la Grange, was arrested after he carried a starter's pistol and a simulated bomb made of fake sticks of dynamite aboard a People Express jet to show the lack of security at Dorval and Mirabel airports, Canada's Justice minister declared that he was guilty of mischief, a conclusion he reached without troubling to wait for the alleged miscreant's trial. Judge Michel Paquin subsequently stayed proceedings against Mr. de la Grange and his cameraman, Michel Kinkead, after finding that Crosbie's remarks had compromised the rights of the accused to a fair trial.

Brian Mulroney was not amused by the string of embarrassments his ministers, including John Crosbie, were causing him. His support for Crosbie during his nepotism tribulations in the Commons had been less than overwhelming; rather than defending his Justice minister, he preferred to talk about the need to tighten up existing conflict-of-interest guidelines. The press were now openly speculating on how long the two former leadership contenders could share the same cabinet room.

The betting was not long. During a break in a Vancouver television interview, Crosbie complained that the country was headed towards a presidential system of governing without any checks and balances — a clear shot at Brian Mulroney's Ottawa. Columnist Stewart MacLeod reported that Crosbie was thinking of a career change and would not likely be running in the next federal election. Unbeknownst to MacLeod when he expressed those opinions, Brian

Mulroney's sour and saucy Justice minister was about to take another step closer to the cabinet door.

By the fall of 1985, scandal had become the official aftershave of the Mulroney government. In trying to distance himself from the stench of the rancid tuna affair, in which the federal government had permitted the sale of rotten tinned fish to an unsuspecting public, John Crosbie made some disparaging remarks about staffers in the Prime Minister's Office during a radio interview in St. John's. Crosbie said that the prime minister's political staff, who knew about the scandal two months before Fisheries minister John Fraser released the product for sale, should have taken swift action to have the tainted fish taken off the shelves of Canadian supermarkets. When asked if the PMO was staffed by "dolts," Crosbie replied: "I wouldn't say it's staffed by dolts, but perhaps you could say they aren't as astute politically or as politically intuitive as they should be."

The way his mild reproof was received in the exalted zones of the Langevin Block exposed how thin Brian Mulroney's political skin was getting. When Crosbie got back to Ottawa he was immediately clotheslined by a fuming PMO. He defended himself initially by denying the report, but the Canadian Press had by then obtained a copy of the program tape from radio station VOCM that confirmed the offending comment, word for word. Liberal leader John Turner said Crosbie's duplicity called into question his ability to command public respect in the administration of justice.

Brian Mulroney had been broadsided one too many times by his opinionated colleague. In front of the entire inner cabinet, a furious Mulroney gave Crosbie a tongue-lashing for his unsolicited critique of his staff — an encounter that was later reported in the press. NDP MP Lorne Nystrom extended mock sympathy to his friend in the government front benches: "I rise in defence of our poor, bedevilled, beleaguered, befuddled minister of Justice. The prime minister read him the riot act and chewed him out. . . . He emerged befuddled, confused and red-faced and put his tongue in reverse."

Whether that was true or not, Crosbie ducked out of the Commons by a back door, preventing reporters from getting more details about his run-in with the prime minister. A few days later, a repentant John Crosbie became the fourth senior Tory to revise his statements about the fishy scandal that cost John Fraser his place in cabinet. In reply to a tuna taunt on CTV's "Question Period," Crosbie replied that *he* was not "as politically astute as I should be" for criticizing the PM's staff. In fact, he continued to believe that incompetent personal staff was the driving force behind the prime minister's image problem and a major impediment to good communications between Mulroney and his ministers. "They get more time with the PM in a day than even the minister of Finance would get in a month," he complained. But now he no longer did his complaining on the radio.

When the prime minister shuffled his cabinet, his verdict on the member for St. John's West was to terminate his days in Justice. On June 30, 1986 Crosbie became Minister of Transport, and quickly showed that the diplomatic skills first displayed at Longueuil, Quebec, had not diminished during his two years as a federal cabinet minister. Irritated by persistent questions about what he was going to do for the "have-not" provinces in Atlantic Canada, Crosbie said, "It isn't 'have not' if you compare it to Bangladesh. It's not 'have not' if you compare it to Haiti, and it's certainly not 'have not' if you compare it to Jamaica. . . . It's very healthy occasionally to look at Haiti or Sri Lanka and then we're very 'have' when we do that." The merits of his observation to one side, it was not the best of messages to be bringing to a conference on regional economic development in a part of the country where unemployment was often double the national average.

Crosbie's words quickly came back to haunt him when he was roundly booed by 1,000 blue-collar workers, 432 of whom stood to lose their jobs when CN Rail's repair shops in Moncton were sold to General Electric. Many of the workers wore signs saying "Moncton Boat People," a reference to the 155 Tamils who had recently arrived on Newfoundland's shores in two lifeboats. Another sign proclaimed, "If things are so good in Atlantic Canada, why did the Sri Lankans go to Montreal?"

A politician might change his ministry but not his spots. Allegations of patronage abuse followed the ill-starred Newfoundlander from Justice to Transportation. The Canadian Press reported that Crosbie and his two sons went on a fishing trip in Labrador with executives of two airlines that dealt directly with the minister's department. Crosbie claimed that he didn't discuss business with either Don Carty, then president of Canadian Pacific Airlines, or Craig Dobbin, president of Air Atlantic. Crosbie also pointed out that he and his sons had paid their own expenses for the trip — a claim he couldn't make when Liberal MP Robert Kaplan later criticized Crosbie for sending his wife, Jane, and their daughter Elizabeth on a trip to Thailand paid for by Thai International Airlines. Initially, Crosbie called the trip a "gift," but as the controversy escalated he revised his story and said that his wife was representing Canada in a "semi-official" capacity.

Although Don Mazankowski said that Crosbie was within the conflict-of-interest guidelines, "technically speaking," he emphasized that tougher regulations were on the way that would deal more clearly with spouses enjoying benefits because of their public status. The clear implication was that although Crosbie had got away with it this time, it would be a different matter once the regulations were changed. Yet again, Crosbie was on thin ice. In the wake of high-level resignations from the likes of Robert Coates, Sinclair Stevens, André Bissonnette, Marcel Masse and John Fraser, the prime minister was becoming obsessed with his government's image problem. But if anyone thought that Crosbie was about to kowtow to Brian Mulroney to save his job, they were sadly mistaken.

In early 1987, Ottawa signed a deal with France that allowed French trawlers from St. Pierre and Miquelon to harvest cod in Canadian waters off Newfoundland's south coast. Despite severe economic hardships in places like Grand Bank and Fortune caused by depleted fish stocks, the federal government concluded the deal to give "surplus cod" to the French without even informing the government of Newfoundland, private fishing companies like Fishery Products International or influential bodies like the Fishermen, Food and Allied Workers union. More importantly, they didn't inform John Crosbie, who made a practice of guarding his political turf like a junkyard dog.

When news of the deal became public, the political explosion in St. John's could be heard all the way to Ottawa. Despite the prime minister's denial of Opposition charges that Ottawa's high-handedness had touched off a crisis in federal-provincial relations, a livid John Crosbie demanded that the Mulroney government apologize to his home province for its monstrous failure to consult with provincial officials before giving Newfoundland fish to the French. Crosbie hinted to reporters that the secret agreement between Canada and France had been worked out behind the back of the federal Fisheries Department. In fact, Fred Doucet had ordered the Canada–France deal to smooth the prime minister's way at the upcoming Francophone Summit. Doucet had been helped in his plan by mandarins in the Department of External Affairs who were annoyed that "little Newfs" were getting involved in the delicate Canada–France boundary negotiation around St. Pierre and Miquelon. "Never having eaten a cod fish in their lives," Crosbie privately fumed, "they just didn't understand there is no such thing as a 'surplus cod' to Newfoundland."

Although it never became public, Crosbie was ready to resign if the prime minister couldn't give him the assurance that never again would things affecting Newfoundland be done without his knowledge. Crosbie was already having enough trouble with a truculent Brian Peckford over Hibernia and a proposed "roads for rail" deal that would see CN pulling out of Newfoundland, without having his own government weakening his hand. The prime minister gave Crosbie the assurance that "not even a nickel" would be spent in Newfoundland without Crosbie's say-so on projects such as Hibernia, an inshore fisheries agreement and the Labrador power question. This time Crosbie had the whip hand and his widely perceived declining influence in the Mulroney cabinet was once again set to soar. But before that happened, the embattled quipster would find himself embroiled again in allegations of callous sexism.

Once more, the object of his unwanted attentions was outspoken Liberal MP Sheila Copps. Responding to the government's campaign to popularize North American free trade, which was being headed up by John Crosbie, Ms. Copps said that any such deal would enable American lawyers to seek Canadian surrogate mothers who would be cheaper to contract because of Canada's national medicare plan. In a speech to the Board of Trade, Crosbie cracked, "All Canadian womanhood are going to have to go creeping around with their legs crossed because the Americans are going to be up here trying to make them become surrogate mothers." Copps called Crosbie a "disgrace" and said that he shouldn't be allowed to represent the government of Canada on the free-trade issue.

Although Crosbie was chastised, he would return to his favourite target a few years later when she was running for the leadership of the Liberal Party. He told a PC fund-raiser in Vancouver that Copps's candidacy reminded him of an old song: "Pass the tequila, Sheila, and lie down and love me again." Canada's new minister for the Status of Women was in the audience, but Mary Collins laughed along with her colleagues at the amusing Mr. Crosbie. Once more Copps was appalled, as was Brian Mulroney, who called Crosbie's remarks "clearly inappropriate." But the prime minister was satisfied by Crosbie's by now standard apology and refused to ask for his resignation. "If you got rid of all the politicians who put their feet in their mouths from time to time," said the master of mis-speak, "there wouldn't be any left in the House of Commons."

On March 31, 1988, Crosbie was promoted to the post of International Trade minister, the most important portfolio in the Mulroney government, which was pinning its hopes of reelection on selling the Canadian public on the historic free trade agreement that Brian Mulroney had signed with U.S. President Ronald Reagan on January 2, 1988. Basking in the success of his constitutional initiatives at Meech Lake, Mulroney turned to John Crosbie to explain the Conservatives' grand economic design to the people, a task many Tories believed the abrasive Pat Carney had been unable to handle. Crosbie was the perfect choice. Witty and talented, he not only had a good grasp of economic issues, it had been the Crosbie leadership campaign that had first introduced the policy of freer trade to the Conservative Party. But the real credit was due to John's father, who had said in 1948 that all countries would eventually come together economically, and that if Newfoundland were to prosper she needed free trade with the United States. "It is only a matter of time before Canada herself will have to seek such an alliance," Ches Crosbie once observed. That time had come, and, fittingly, his son John was the man of the hour.

The rest of 1988 unfolded like a political fairy tale for John Crosbie and the Conservative Party. From his maiden speech as International Trade minister, where he called the opponents of free trade "CBC-type snivellers, the Toronto literati, the alarm-spreaders, and the encyclopedia-peddlers," to his controversial national award and $10,000 prize from the National Citizens' Coalition for promoting the values of economic and political freedom, John Crosbie was on a roll. He slugged it out with opponents of the free trade deal like Ontario Premier David Peterson and won. In his role as national door-to-door salesman for free trade, he once again reached back into his family history to make his pitch. When critics attacked the deal as the "Sale of Canada," Crosbie countered with, "For a Brighter Tomorrow," precisely the same slogan Ches Crosbie had used in 1948 to promote economic union with the United States.

In July, Ottawa, Newfoundland and four private companies signed an agreement in principle to proceed with the mammoth Hibernia oil development 150 miles southeast of St. John's. In August, Bill C-130, the 152-clause free trade bill, received its third and final reading. With a constitutional deal apparently in their pocket, a daring legislative package to offer the Canadian people and the scandals that had marred the early years of the Mulroney government a faded memory, the Tories headed confidently into the 1988 election. On November 21, Brian Mulroney won his second straight majority government and ended John Turner's valiant attempt at a political comeback. But when the dust settled, the taste of political victory was, at best, bittersweet.

Although John Crosbie easily won his own riding, Atlantic Canada emphatically rejected the Mulroney Conservatives, giving only twelve of thirty-two seats to the Tories, an indication of what the region believed it stood to lose in social programs if free trade became a reality. Despite the fact that he retained his high-profile portfolio as International Trade minister, Crosbie knew that his political hand had weakened considerably in the wake of the 1988 election. It would now be much more difficult to push through the $5.2-billion Hibernia project with other regions of the country that were Tory blue vying for the same federal funds. But much worse news was on the way.

After ten years of running on adrenalin, an exhausted Brian Peckford decided to leave politics, having failed to achieve any of the three great goals he had set himself in 1979: offshore ownership, a revamped Labrador hydro power contract with Quebec and control of the fishery. His often-spectacular decade in power had exacted a heavy personal toll, including the destruction of his first marriage. His once-unimpeachable credibility was in tatters over the $22-million Sprung greenhouse fiasco. The premier had disregarded all scientific advice to bankroll a foolhardy scheme to corner the world market on hydroponically grown English cucumbers in a province that had the country's lowest level of sunshine. A subsequent royal commission concluded that the miracle Sprung fabric that formed the shell of the seven-acre greenhouse actually blocked the passage of light. But in March 1989, long before that report came in, Peckford informed the party that he would be leaving office.

Whenever a vacancy occurred at the top of the Conservative Party in Newfoundland, everyone always thought of John Crosbie and this time was no exception. The prospect of Crosbie returning to Newfoundland set up some fascinating possibilities. Clyde Wells was now leading the Liberal Party, and a provincial battle between the former colleagues from the Smallwood cabinet would have all the drama of a mediaeval joust. But Crosbie quickly ended the speculation by emphatically denying that he was interested in returning to provincial politics. Hibernia and the Lower

Churchill were still on the drawing board and Crosbie told reporters that he preferred to stay in Ottawa to see these historic pieces of unfinished business put to rest.

If that became more difficult after the results of the 1988 federal election, it was about to become well-nigh impossible after political developments in his native province. In May 1989, Clyde Kirby Wells became the first Liberal premier since Joe Smallwood, breaking seventeen years of Tory rule in Newfoundland. One of his first public pronouncements was his vow to either negotiate changes to the Meech Lake Accord, which all ten provinces, including Quebec, had agreed to in principle in April 1987, or scuttle the deal. Some observers put Wells's declaration down to simple horse-trading; to realize Newfoundland's desire to get Hibernia financing or greater control over the fishery, he would have to demonstrate to the prime minister that Newfoundland had something the federal government badly needed — the new Liberal government's support of the Meech Lake Accord. Nothing could have been further from the truth. As former Trudeau aide Michael Kirby was fond of saying, "Give me anything in a political negotiation but a man of principle." Better than most people, John Crosbie knew that was exactly what Brian Mulroney had on his hands.

The core of the Wells position was his unshakeable belief that no province of Canada should end up with greater legal powers than any other under a renewed constitution. Quebec had already used the notwithstanding clause in December 1988 to strike down a Supreme Court decision that found it was unconstitutional to ban English-language signs in Quebec. The premier also resented the way Ottawa approached the debate; one should sign, the federal government argued, because of the consequences of not signing, rather than out of a genuine approval of what Meech Lake actually proposed.

Unable to generate a debate on the issues, Wells was unwilling to endorse the accord under duress. After seven days of high-pressure, secret negotiations, the best Brian Mulroney could wring out of the passionate federalist was his token signature on a joint communiqué from all ten premiers, signifying no more than his promise to put the Meech

Lake Accord to a vote of the Newfoundland legislature or a public referendum. Clyde Wells would not use his personal power to change history, but he refused to exclude Newfoundlanders from that awesome process. On the same day that Premier Wells brought that message to the country on national television, the Hibernia financing bills received second reading in the House of Commons. Given the unknown outcome of the Meech Lake Accord, it was anyone's guess when, or even if, they would get third reading.

Although Prime Minister Brian Mulroney flew to Newfoundland to address the legislature before it decided on his constitutional deal, the free vote was never held. With a vote stalled in the Manitoba legislature because of the filibuster of a single member, the June 23, 1990, deadline for ratification of the deal came and went. Elijah Harper might have driven the stake into the Meech Lake Accord, but it would be Clyde Wells and Newfoundland that a bitter Brian Mulroney would hold responsible for depriving him of the grand constitutional triumph that would have made him successful where Pierre Trudeau had failed.

No one knows what went on in the stormy Tory caucus meeting of Tuesday, June 26, 1990, but in the wake of the meeting the Mulroney government's Hibernia financing legislation was mysteriously "put on hold." The people who knew John Crosbie best said that the days immediately following the demise of the Meech Lake Accord were the most turbulent in his long political life. It was widely rumoured that the prime minister and his Quebec caucus wanted to punish Newfoundland because of the stand Clyde Wells had taken on the constitution by shelving the giant oil project. CTV's Mike Duffy reported on national television that reliable sources said Crosbie flatly refused to go along with any punitive action against Newfoundland and threatened to resign from the cabinet if Hibernia didn't proceed. Looking visibly depressed and exhausted at a St. John's press conference, Crosbie refused to comment on what had happened in the June 26 caucus meeting, except to reconfirm his determination to see the mega-project proceed: "Before I'm finished in politics, I want to see the Hibernia project underway. That is my great ambition."

The summer of 1990 was the season of John Crosbie's discontent. Since his election in 1988, he had had to deal with a disaster in the Atlantic fishery, the failure of the Meech Lake Accord and threats to the Hibernia project from inside his own caucus. Worn out with fighting his region's battles with a downsized Atlantic caucus and depressed by the economic hardship the failed fishery had visited on various parts of his own federal riding, Crosbie once more became the subject of resignation rumours. While pundits speculated about the imminent political demise of the fifty-nine-year-old cabinet minister, he spent the summer doing constituency work in hard-hit places like Trepassey and Fermeuse, rural fishing communities that faced extinction if the cod, as many experts were saying, were really gone. But a day never went by without Crosbie hammering away at the forces within his own party that would deprive Newfoundland of Hibernia. Only when he convinced cabinet that the mega-project would bring work to Quebec as well as Newfoundland did Crosbie prevail.

On Friday, September 14, 1990, Newfoundland's eleven-year wait for Hibernia, the biggest project in the history of the province, came to an end, thanks to John Carnell Crosbie. The delay had gone on too long to produce euphoria. The sense of relief, however, in the thousand people who attended the reception where the announcement was made, and who had survived on dreams of an oil bonanza for the last decade, was palpable. The ceremony was attended by five Newfoundland premiers, including an old and frail Joe Smallwood, who, in 1964, had sent a team of divers to the floor of the Grand Banks near the Virgin Rocks to lay a bronze plaque asserting Newfoundland's ownership of offshore resources. The actual signing was done by Clyde Wells and John Crosbie, ostensibly because the prime minister was so furious over Meech Lake that he didn't want to be in the same room with Newfoundland's premier. In fact, Brian Mulroney was in the final stages of putting through an order-in-council that would send three Canadian warships to the Persian Gulf to help in the fight to dislodge Saddam Hussein from

Kuwait. *The Evening Telegram* summed up the mood in the province at the long-awaited deal on Hibernia. "More than anyone, it must be said that this is Mr. Crosbie's day."

ANDREW CROSBIE COULD be excused if he watched his brother's moment of glory with mixed feelings. On the one hand, he was elated for the man he knew had battled tremendous odds to make this day happen. On the other, he smiled at fate's ironies. The deal he had been waiting for since 1972 to realize his dreams of an offshore supply base at Freshwater Bay had been announced seven months after he had been diagnosed with terminal cancer in his brain, liver and lungs. On the day the Hibernia deal was signed, no one knew that Andrew Crosbie had exactly three months and twenty-five days to live. His son Alex was in the hospital room when the doctor told him that his condition was beyond hope. Like a good poker player, Andrew accepted the cards that were dealt him and played them as best he could. For weeks after his chemotherapy began, he retained his hallmark head of dark, wavy hair. When he began to lose it, he vowed it would grow back. "They won't have Andrew in a breadbox for Christmas," he joked with friends.

There was a new serenity and an old courage in the Crosbie who had spent a lifetime trying to live up to his father's mythic image. He was not happy about dying but did it well. There was no bitterness towards the many people who had abused his good nature and profited from it. There was no anger at the society that accused him of crimes that were committed in a company he believed he no longer controlled. In dying, as in business, Andrew Crosbie believed in people, and he believed in Newfoundland.

With the end in sight, he gave his love unselfconsciously to his wife Carolyn and his four children from his first marriage. On his last night on earth, his family gathered around him, a human barrier between the man they loved and eternity. But the pain became a too private burden and he needed to be alone. That night, when his doctor came in on his rounds and said he would see him in the morning,

Andrew smiled and said, "No, you won't."

Sometime during the night, he paid his last bill. *The Globe and Mail* reported his death in one of those cold juxtapositions of facts in which the man is somehow lost. "Businessman Andrew Carnell [sic] Crosbie, brother of federal Trade Minister John Crosbie, died yesterday, one day before he was to face charges on 38 counts of fraud and theft. He was 57."

John Crosbie was in Vietnam on government business when he received word of his brother's death. He and Jane waked Andrew with caviar and vodka before beginning the long journey home from Ho Chi Minh City. On January 9, 1991, the George Street United Church was filled with family and old friends who had come to say goodbye. Joe Smallwood, who would be dead himself in less than a year, wept openly in his pew. He had once told a reporter, "If you want to know how much I like Andrew Crosbie, I like him as much as I *don't* like John Crosbie." Suffering from malaria, John Crosbie gamely delivered the eulogy. He spoke of Andrew's love of his mother and sister, and his "support for his brother John in his sometimes unconventional political career, no matter the costs sometimes entailed for himself."

The most stoic member of a family not known for its public displays of emotion was finally overcome when he described his brother with his favourite lines from *Julius Caesar*:

> His life was gentle, and the elements
> So mix'd in him that Nature might stand up
> And say to all the world, "This was a man!"

When John Crosbie left the church that day, he stepped out into a new emptiness and a world that, despite his fever, had grown forever colder.

Epilogue

ON A STORMY December night in 1991, eight hundred friends and admirers gathered in St. John's to pay tribute to the man Brian Mulroney once called a national treasure. At $500 a plate, the dinner to celebrate John Crosbie's twenty-fifth anniversary in politics (the *first* twenty-five years, as he called it) was decidedly upscale. A band of less fortunate people held a protest dinner (soup at 50 cents a bowl) outside the hotel. Ignoring them, Crosbie's well-heeled guests tried to disembark from their cars and enter the chic lobby of the Radisson Plaza Hotel without stepping in the slush. Protesters from the Coalition for Equality, warming their hands over a fire in a fifty-gallon drum, shouted "Shame, shame!" and "Enough is enough!"

Crosbie would later claim to be in such a good mood that night that he generously chose not to call this "motley crew" exactly what he thought they were: ". . . hypocrites, poseurs, skimmers, carrion birds, buzzards of the boulevards, boobirds and twisters of the truth." Instead, he settled a little uneasily into his chair and listened to a torrent of praise from the assembled potentates of his political past and present, including the prime minister of Canada. By the time they were finished, he felt more than a little like Tom Sawyer hovering over his own funeral. "This is really a fund-raising occasion," he pleaded. "I didn't expect to hear my obituary."

His friends needn't have bothered; his political obituary, it seemed, was already being written. On April 21, 1991, Crosbie had been called back to a family tradition as deep as the rolling North Atlantic. Just when the region's oldest industry was collapsing under the weight of ferocious overfishing on every front, Brian Mulroney had been kind enough to make John Crosbie Canada's minister of Fisheries and Oceans. Times had certainly changed since John Cabot's voyage of discovery in the fifteenth century, when cod were taken in profusion simply by lowering a weighted basket over the side of his wooden ship and pulling it up on a rope. Now the silver mine of the North Atlantic was played out and while no one was prepared to own up to their own role in the pillage, all were quick to wag an accusing finger at a host of other villains. The Canadians blamed the foreigners; the foreigners blamed the Canadians; the domestic inshore and offshore fleets blamed each other and everyone blamed the federal government — Atlantic Canada's old, sad song.

Crosbie knew that, in the end, he would have to weave a web of appeasement that would offend everyone. Stopping overfishing on the high seas would not prove as simple as putting an end to smoking on commercial jetliners, which he'd done as Transportation minister. Negotiations would be seen as dithering, and strategic trades as spineless concessions. When the European Community asked for more scientific evidence before agreeing to conservation measures beyond the two-hundred-mile limit, Newfoundlanders fumed. Their empty nets were all the science they needed to tell them that an eco-disaster was brewing off their once teeming shores. "The question is," Crosbie observed after a *tête à tête* between EC president Jacques Delors and Prime Minister Brian Mulroney, "whether they lynch me before we get something resolved."

The mounting frustration over Ottawa's ultra-conservative stand on the fisheries crisis focused sharply on the beleaguered member for St. John's West. Signs appeared on local inshore fishing vessels urging Crosbie to kick the Russians out of Canadian waters. Instead, he ordered navy frigates to arrest Newfoundland vessels that were illegally fishing in areas where they had no quota. Without raw materials to supply their shore operations, companies like Fishery Products International and National Sea were forced to close fish plants in one-industry towns, which then turned to Crosbie for help he could no longer deliver.

On Thursday, July 2, 1992, Newfoundland's miseries bottomed out with the stunning announcement that Ottawa was imposing a two-year moratorium on the northeast coast cod fishery. With the spawning stock of the once mighty schools of northern cod reduced by 75 percent through severe overfishing, there was no alternative. As John Crosbie made the announcement to the media in a barricaded salon at the Radisson Hotel, angry fishermen milled around, demanding to be let in. Their attempt to batter down the locked doors ended only when the police arrived in force. Responding to the ruckus, a visibly shaken John Crosbie said, "They don't need to go berserk trying to batter on doors to frighten me. In the first place, I don't frighten. I'm not going to be bullied."

Just a year earlier, Crosbie had discounted scientific evidence that the stocks were in serious trouble and refused to make dramatic cuts in the quotas. Now, he was back to announce the largest layoff in the history of Canada — 19,000 Newfoundlanders whose families had made their living from the cod fishery for hundreds of years. Although the government eventually announced a billion dollar aid package, there was no buffering Newfoundlanders from the unthinkable consequences of Ottawa's mismanagement of the cod stocks. Dr. Leslie Harris, who tried two years earlier to get the federal government to make drastic cuts in fish quotas, told the Canadian Press, "This news is so bad that we might never recover from it. We have no guarantee the stocks are going to rebound. If they don't, the East Coast is essentially dead as a place to live."

The catastrophe in the Newfoundland fishery became a lightning rod for other disenchantments with the member for St. John's West. His critics now remembered that it had been John Crosbie who let CN dig up the tracks of the railway he had once insisted Canada had a constitutional obligation to operate in Newfoundland, regardless of its losses, which, when the end came, had reached $50 million a year.

The Atlantic Canada Opportunities Agency (ACOA), with Crosbie at the helm, had become a new vehicle for distributing political patronage under the guise of yet another regional development program — especially in the eyes of those who failed to qualify for grants. As for his great political achievement, rumours abounded that Hibernia was in trouble. They were confirmed when Gulf Canada announced that it was divesting its 25 percent interest in the giant offshore development because of low world oil and gas prices. Once more, Newfoundland's ship had come in; once more, she had failed to drop anchor. Showing the wear of twenty-five years of high-flying, John Crosbie's durable political engines sputtered, gasped and finally seemed to be in danger of stalling altogether.

Perhaps there was consolation in the knowledge that, as it was in his grandfather's and father's time, Newfoundland was always on the brink of disaster or prosperity, depending on the old benchmarks of the economy: fish catches, the price of cod, the foreign exchange rate and whatever wealth lay undiscovered beneath or just beyond the granite treasure house of their island home. He had scratched a career out of making the best of many a bad situation. There were the long years in Opposition, when he had been able to convince Canada's most needy constituents that there was more to a good MP than someone who could shell out government patronage. Then there had been his two terms on the other side of the House of Commons, when the task had been to temper the bottomless demands of citizens who believed that a vote for the Conservatives was a blank cheque made out to them awaiting the signature of John Crosbie.

In the end, Crosbie's conclusions about public life revealed more about the people who kept electing him than about the man himself. Obsessed with its own self-interest, and dripping with cynicism on most other occasions, the electorate that Crosbie had come to know was a harsh and hypocritical taskmaster. "The public want to look down on politicians," he said. "If they can't, they want to look at them and say 'These are bloody rogues.'. . . The public doesn't want to be fooled, but it doesn't want to hear the truth. They can't have it both ways."

Having surrendered at last to the artful dodging that permits a politician to achieve and hold power in this country, John Crosbie had mastered the techniques of expediency and compromise: the man who had started out as an idealist had ended as a Canadian.

Whether the cards hold one last election victory for John Crosbie, or the bum's rush on the coattails of Brian Mulroney, or even a season of corporate grazing in the lush pastures of Boardroom Canada, the time is approaching when a retreat from the hurly-burly of his very public life is unavoidable. Much of the world that had once sustained him is gone or changed terribly. The General Protestant Cemetery now holds his father, mother, brother and sister. As for the former Crosbie business presence in Newfoundland, it is as if the ancient family curse uttered on the battlefield at Bannockburn had come to pass. Although most of Andrew Crosbie's businesses have reemerged from bankruptcy, new owners are now their beneficiaries: Devon Place, where Sir John raised his large family in style, has become a no-star hotel; Clovelly Farm, purchased by his great-grandfather is someone else's riding academy; even Kaegudeck, the fabled family retreat, is now a corporate hideaway for an out-of-province company. An old cycle has nearly ended, and a new one is yet to begin.

John's most important constituents these days are his grandchildren. With his own political career winding down, his sons, Chesley and Michael, are too busy trying to establish their private careers to give much thought to the public obligations of their famous name. But at least one of them could end up following in his father's footsteps. "My number-one priority is making a living for my wife and children, but there's a good possibility that if the opportunity arises, I would enter public life," thirty-six-year-old Michael Crosbie shyly admits.

With the family's political future in the hands of John's sons, its business prospects rest with Andrew Crosbie's four children, Alex, Robert, Timothy and Cynthia. From the very beginning, the road has been rocky. Their first lesson at the helm was that banks observe no official period of mourning; at word of Andrew's death, they swooped down and tied up his estate until they had removed their share of his worldly goods. But adversity has forged a new bond between these Crosbies, a family compact to finish some of the projects Andrew started during his quiet push to rebuild after the demoralizing reversals of the 1980s.

Alex Crosbie's house still looks across Virginia Waters to the expansive spread where his stepmother lives, but he now has more company on the once-private family lake. King William Estates, a luxury development that Andrew started after his corporate bankruptcy, boasts some of the city's most spectacular homes. The effort to see it through has been a family affair. Alex's brother, Robert, a former investment broker, looks after the financial planning and banking for the Crosbie business activities; brother Tim runs Proco, their new property management division; and Alex, the eldest, operates Crosbie Industrial Services and Newfoundland Scaffolding. Although the company has gone from 150 employees down to just 12 as the provincial economy continues to stagnate, Alex is poised for the day when Newfoundland finally turns the economic corner. "Resurgam," it seems, is a motto that has held true down the centuries.

Shimmering just ahead of them, like an oasis in the endless sands of recession, lies Freshwater Bay, a huge tract of land purchased by their maternal grandfather, Bernard Parsons, as an investment in the future; Andrew Crosbie had it earmarked as Hibernia's main supply base. Subject to zoning battles with city hall, maddening delays in offshore development and the demands of Swedish partners, Freshwater Bay is still the Crosbies' best hope of restoring their former commercial glory. "It might not be in my generation," Alex says. "Maybe it's the next generation."

If they do pull off an economic comeback, it won't be because of the "good old system" that Sir John and, to a degree, Ches lived by. That was dying from the moment Newfoundland joined Confederation — an intricate system of obligation that did business on a handshake, never left a friend in the lurch and drew class lines as stark as chalk marks on a blackboard in the feudal society it supported. There are no more Joe Smallwoods to transform a company with the magic wand of government patronage, no more family friends who compete fiercely in business but sit across your bridge table at night, no more trading on the family name. Ironically, the commercial ascendancy of the Crosbies has been one of the most spectacular casualties of Confederation — just as Ches Crosbie probably knew it would be. People like Gert Crosbie, who lived in the golden age of obligation, feel that modern Newfoundland has made them strangers in a strange land. "We don't really know our way around the new world that we're living in."

CANADA, WITH ALL its great institutions and estimable endowments, casts a cold shadow over a place that once operated along the lines of a rollicking village shaped by a succession of flamboyant head men. There is more prosperity now but less personality, wider experience but deeper alienation. The covenant with the land and the sea has been undermined by a bargain with bureaucrats. Heart and soul have been traded for mind and body.

Some things, though, have remained constant. The fishery has continued in its cycle of boom and bust, as it always has — though in 1992, a dread watershed may have been reached. There are still more people without jobs here than in any other part of Canada — an astonishing 30 percent in the wake of the cod moratorium. Working Newfoundlanders have the lowest per capita incomes, a mere 60 percent of the national average. And just as Newfoundland's debt as an independent dominion once ballooned to $110 million, its public sector debt as a province of Canada has skyrocketed to $5.2 billion in the early 1990s. Without a wealthy patron, Newfoundland is as vulnerable today as it was in the 1890s when its banks crashed, or when Canada and Britain saved it from bankruptcy during the Great Depression.

The dancing partner has changed, but the tune is still the same. The fishery can no longer sustain the ever-growing number of people who depend on it, and all attempts to diversify the economy have failed. Although the island has other natural resources, it lacks the wealth to finance their development, which puts a construction project rather than a pot of gold under every rainbow. Now, and perhaps forever, real wealth here is an outbound ship with a foreign captain at the helm.

Pipe dreams and political partners to one side, Newfoundland will always be a place where the inglorious projects of survival prevail, a bald rock surrounded by a cold, sustaining sea. Few people in history have called it home; for most, it has been a way station on the road to someplace better. But for those who cleave to it, there is no place on earth quite like it. It is not because the hundreds of villages huddled around its rugged inlets and bays are pastoral havens against the evils of a post-industrial and polluted world; the struggle with nature is too unremitting to produce any rural Camelots. Whether it is E. J. Pratt's "tides of the heart," or long-ingrained hardship, this much is true: like wind soughing through a flake-house, the place insinuates itself into the soul, holding its children with a loving but iron hand.

LITTLE JOHN CROSBIE walks to class each day, but young Joey Smallwood arrives at the Brigus schoolhouse by bus from his home on the Roache's Line. Joey Smallwood III is the son of Judy and Joe Smallwood and the great-grandson of Newfoundland's most famous premier. John Crosbie IV is the son of Jean and Dr. Douglas Crosbie, the first cousin of the Conservative cabinet minister. The sloping meadows overlooking the harbour where George Graham Crosbie once supplied the sealing ships from his dry-goods business often ring with playful taunts inspired by young John's famous relative. "We saw you on television last night," his classmates tease. His mother, Jean Crosbie, feels the gentle weight of history: "The first day I took John to school, I was having a chat with Judy Smallwood and I said, 'Judy, here it is . . . this is history repeating itself.' "

In a fertile cleft above the empty harbour, the buds of an ancient apple tree unfurl in the late-June sun, and children's voices rise deliriously above the ocean's thunder before blowing out to sea like sparrows caught in a sudden gust of wind.

Bibliography

Manuscript Sources

Official papers

A. C. Hunter Library, Arts and Culture Centre, St. John's. Various collections.

Charles Granger Collection, Moving Image and Sound Archives, National Archives of Canada, Ottawa. Previously unaccessed taped interviews with participants in the Confederation debate, including: Jack W. Pickersgill, Charles H. Ballam, Joseph R. Smallwood, Joseph Patrick Fowler, C. Max Lane, A. H. "Bill" Crosbie, Gregory Joseph Power, A. B. "Bert" Butt, Mrs. A. H. Crosbie, Wickford Collins, Burnham Gill, Chief Justice R. S. Furlong, Melvin Rowe, Captain John White, P. J. Lewis.

Charles Granger Collection, National Archives of Canada. MG 32 C-48, volumes 1 and 2, material pertaining to the Economic Union Movement.

Dumfries Archives Centre, Dumfries, Scotland. Various collections.

Ewart Library, Dumfries, Scotland. Various collections.

John Carnell Crosbie Collection, Centre for Newfoundland Studies Archives, Queen Elizabeth II Library, Memorial University, St. John's.

J. R. Smallwood Collection, Centre for Newfoundland Studies Archives, Queen Elizabeth II Library, Memorial University, St. John's.

National Archives, Washington, D.C. Record Group 84: Foreign Service Posts of the Department of State; Ottawa Embassy, Security Segregated Records 1936–49 pertaining to Newfoundland union with Canada; St. John's (Newfoundland) Consulate, general records, 1936–49, pertaining to Newfoundland union with Canada, political reports and correspondence.

Proceedings of the House of Assembly, St. John's, 1908–1928, 1966–1968. Newfoundland House of Assembly Verbatim Report, 1969–1976.

Provincial Archives of New Brunswick, Fredericton. Census material, land grants, school records, 1840–61.

Public Archives of Newfoundland and Labrador, St. John's. Various government documents including: Department of Economic Development, Fisheries Department, Department of Justice, Department of Natural Resources, Brigus Court records and genealogical material.

United Church of Canada, Newfoundland and Labrador Conference Archives, St. John's. Brigus Parish Register.

Private papers

Correspondence of Lady Crosbie and A. H. "Bill" Crosbie, 1934–45, held by Mrs. A. H. Crosbie.

John Laschinger, private papers regarding 1983 Conservative leadership campaign.

A. B. Perlin Collection, including correspondence of Sir John Crosbie, private papers held by John Crosbie Perlin, C.V.O., A. de C.

Newspapers and Periodicals

Canadian Business
Chatham *Gleaner*, Chatham, New Brunswick
The Daily News, St. John's, Newfoundland
The Evening Telegram, St. John's, Newfoundland
The Financial Post, Toronto, Ontario
The Globe and Mail, Toronto, Ontario
Maclean's, Toronto, Ontario
The Morning Post, St. John's, Newfoundland
Newfoundland Herald, St. John's, Newfoundland

Original Interviews

In the course of research for this book, the following original interviews were conducted:

Fred Adams, Andrew Ayre, Mrs. Lewis (Crosbie) Ayre, Randy Bell, June Bennett, Mrs. Ella Maud ("Dolly" Crosbie) Carleton, The Honourable James Chalker, Margaret (Butt) Chalker, Roberta (Crosbie) Cook, Alexander Crosbie, Andrew Crosbie, Mrs. A. H. "Gert" Crosbie, Jane Crosbie, The Honourable John Crosbie, Michael Crosbie, William Crosbie, Basil Dobbin, Thomas Dormady, John Christopher Doyle, F. Burnham Gill, Charles Granger, Janet (Crosbie) Guzzwell, Edgar Hickman, Susan Jenkins, Glynis Jenkins, John Jenkins, Sr., John Jenkins, Jr., John Laschinger, John Leamon, Joan (Parsons Crosbie) Parker, John Crosbie Perlin, Gregory Power, Deborah (Crosbie) Powers, Doyle Roberts, The Honourable Edward Roberts, Dr. Harry Roberts, Frank Ryan, Gene Shinkle, Lee Shinkle, Martha Shinkle, Matthew Shinkle, Geoffrey Stirling, The Honourable Clyde Wells, The Honourable Gordon Winter.

Secondary Sources

Bridle, P., ed. *Document on Relations Between Canada and Newfoundland* 1940–49. Ottawa: Department of External Affairs, Canada, 1984.

Cardoulis, J. A. *Friendly Invasion: The American Military in Newfoundland.* St. John's: Breakwater, 1990.

Cashin, P. *My Life and Times 1890–1919.* St. John's: Breakwater, 1976.

Crosbie, John. "Local Government in Newfoundland." *Canadian Journal of Economics and Political Science*, 1956, pp. 332–46.

Cuff, R. H., ed. *A Coaker Anthology.* St. John's: Creative Publishers, 1986.

Cuff, R. H., ed. *Dictionary of Newfoundland and Labrador Biography.* St. John's: Harry Cuff Publications Ltd., 1990.

Eggleston, W. *Newfoundland: The Road to Confederation.* Ottawa: Government of Canada, 1974.

Gwyn, R. *Smallwood: The Unlikely Revolutionary.* Toronto: McClelland and Stewart Ltd., 1968.

Hiller, J., and P. Neary, eds. *Newfoundland in the Nineteenth and Twentieth Centuries: Essays in Interpretation.* Toronto: University of Toronto Press, 1980.

Horwood, A. *Newfoundland Ships and Men.* St. John's: The Marine Researchers, 1971.

Horwood, H. *Joey: The Life and Political Times of Joey Smallwood.* Toronto: Stoddart Publishing, 1989.

Innis, H. *The Cod Fisheries: The History of an International Economy.* Toronto: University of Toronto Press, 1978.

Jamieson, D. *No Place for Fools: The Political Memoirs of Don Jamieson*, volume 1. St. John's: Breakwater Books, 1989.

Lench, C. A. *Souvenir: Brigus Methodist Jubilee 1875–1925.*

Lockwood, D. *Dumfries Story.* Dumfries: T. C. Farries & Co., 1988.

MacKenzie, D. *Inside the Atlantic Triangle.* Toronto: University of Toronto Press, 1986.

McDowall, W. *History of Dumfries,* 4th edition. Dumfries: T. C. Farries & Co., 1986.

Martin, P., A. Gregg and G. Perlin. *Contenders: The Tory Quest for Power.* Scarborough: Prentice-Hall, 1983.

Neary, P. *Newfoundland in the North Atlantic World 1929–1949.* Kingston and Montreal: McGill-Queen's University Press, 1988.

Neary, P., ed. *The Political Economy of Newfoundland 1929–1972.* Toronto: Copp Clark, 1973.

Neary, P., and P. O'Flaherty. *Part of the Main: An Illustrated History of Newfoundland and Labrador.* St. John's. Breakwater, 1983.

Newman, Peter C., *The Canadian Establishment,* volume 1. Toronto: McClelland and Stewart Ltd., 1975.

Noel, S. J. R. *Politics in Newfoundland.* Toronto: University of Toronto Press, 1971.

O'Neill, P. *The Oldest City: The Story of St. John's, Newfoundland*, vols. 1 and 2. Erin, Ontario: Press Porcépic, 1975, 1976.

Pottle, H. *Newfoundland, Dawn Without Light: Politics, Power and the People in the Smallwood Era*. St. John's: Breakwater, 1979.

Prowse, D. A. *History of Newfoundland from the English, Colonial, and Foreign Records*. London: Macmillan and Co., 1895.

Pumphrey, R. *The Crosbies and the Herring: A Study in Tenacity*. Printed privately, commissioned by Andrew Crosbie, 1967.

Reid, R. C., ed. *Edgar's History of Dumfries*. Dumfries: J. Maxwell & Sons, 1915.

Roberts, H. *Sailing Ships of Newfoundland: The Newfoundland "Fish Boxes."* St. John's: Breakwater, 1986.

Rowe, F. *A History of Newfoundland and Labrador*. Toronto: McGraw-Hill Ryerson Ltd., 1980.

Ryan, S. *Fish Out of Water: The Newfoundland Saltfish Trade 1814–1914*. St. John's: Breakwater, 1986.

Ryan. S. *Seals and Sealers: A Pictorial History of the Newfoundland Seal Fishery*. St. John's: Breakwater, 1987.

Smallwood, J. *The Book of Newfoundland*, vols. 3 and 4. St. John's: Newfoundland Book Publishers (1967) Ltd., 1967.

Smallwood, J. *I Chose Canada: The Memoirs of the Honourable Joseph R. "Joey" Smallwood*. Toronto: Macmillan, 1973.

Stevens, P., and J. Saywell. Lord Minto's Canadian Papers, vols. 1 and 2. Toronto: The Champlain Society, 1981.

Walsh, B. *More Than a Poor Majority: The Story of Newfoundland's Confederation with Canada*. St. John's: Breakwater, 1985.

Wynn, G. *Timber Colony: A Historical Geography of Early Nineteenth Century New Brunswick*. Toronto: University of Toronto Press, 1981.

Index

Printed in Canada